Eye on
Science Fiction

"No, Mr. Weaver, I'm *really* not interested in submitting to an interview.
And, by the way, how did you get my number?"

Eye on Science Fiction

20 Interviews with Classic SF and Horror Filmmakers

by Tom Weaver

McFarland & Company, Inc., Publishers
Jefferson, North Carolina, and London

The present work is a reprint of the illustrated casebound edition of Eye on Science Fiction: 20 Interviews with Classic SF and Horror Filmmakers, *first published in 2003 by McFarland.*

OTHER BOOKS BY TOM WEAVER AND FROM MCFARLAND

Earth vs. the Sci-Fi Filmmakers (2005)

It Came from Horrorwood (2004)

Science Fiction and Fantasy Film Flashbacks (2004)

Double Feature Creature Attack (2003)
(A combined edition of the two earlier Weaver titles
Attack of the Monster Movie Makers and
They Fought in the Creature Features)

Science Fiction Confidential (2002)

I Was a Monster Movie Maker (2001)

Return of the B Science Fiction and Horror Heroes (2000)
(A combined edition of the two earlier Weaver titles
*Interviews with B Science Fiction and Horror Movie
Makers* and *Science Fiction Stars and Horror Heroes*)

Poverty Row HORRORS! (1993; softcover 1999)

John Carradine (1999)

Universal Horrors (and Michael Brunas and
John Brunas; 2d ed., 2007)

Frontispiece: **Paul Blaisdell contends with a crank caller in** *The She-Creature* **(1956).**

LIBRARY OF CONGRESS CATALOGUING-IN-PUBLICATION DATA

Weaver, Tom, 1958–
Eye on science fiction : 20 interviews with classic SF and horror
filmmakers / by Tom Weaver.
p. cm.
Includes index.

ISBN-13: 978-0-7864-3028-4
(softcover : 50# alkaline paper) ∞

1. Science fiction films—United States—History and criticism.
2. Horror films—United States—History and criticism.
3. Motion picture actors and actresses—United States—Interviews.
4. Motion picture producers and directors—United States—Interviews.   I. Title.
PN1995.9.S26E9   2007   791.43′615—dc22   2003021839

British Library cataloguing data are available

©2003 Tom Weaver. All rights reserved

*No part of this book may be reproduced or transmitted in any form
or by any means, electronic or mechanical, including photocopying
or recording, or by any information storage and retrieval system,
without permission in writing from the publisher.*

Front cover (design by Martin Baumann): Cyclopean occupant in *The Atomic Submarine* (1959)

Manufactured in the United States of America

*McFarland & Company, Inc., Publishers / Box 611, Jefferson, North Carolina 28640
www.mcfarlandpub.com*

Dedicated to
John Agar
Samuel Z. Arkoff
Herman Cohen
Anthony Eisley
Anne Gwynne
Louis M. Heyward
Kim Hunter
Paul Landres
Jacques Marquette
Walter Reed
Randy Stuart
Kenneth Tobey
William Witney
William Reed Woodfield

Acknowledgments

Tracking down these 20 new interviewees, locating copies of all their pertinent movies, preparing the questions, fact-checking the resultant transcripts and finding appropriate illustrations—this is *not* a one-person job. And so, once again, I got fabulous support from a galaxy of true-blue friends and new acquaintances, most notably Marty Baumann (*The Astounding B Monster*), Radley Metzger, Liane Curtis, Mark Clark, Paul Picerni, Boyd Magers, Joe Lozowsky, Bob Burns, Kathryn Indiek, Richard Heft, Mark Phillips, Don G. Smith, Greg Krieger, Michael F. Blake, Glenn Damato, Scooter McCrae, Michael Fitzgerald, Bob Tinnell, Linda Harrison, Tyler McVey, Mary Runser, Richard Gordon; Eurosin, Taraco, Gamm3000, GaryP11111, Chesterbelloc and all the other great guys on AOL's Classic Horror Film Board (the best in cyberspace!); Gary Rhodes, Arianné Ulmer, Tim Lucas, Nancy Parke-Taylor, John Morgan, Bob Skotak, Wade Williams, Dave Baumuller, Richard Bojarski, Joe Indusi, Joe Kane (*VideoScope*), John Antosiewicz, Robert Clarke, Buddy Barnett (*Cult Movies*), Dave McDonnell (*Starlog*), Tigger, Rufus and Erin Ray Pascaretti, The Little Prince, the phriendly pholks at Photofest, Steve and Mike Kronenberg, Ted Bohus (*SPFX*), Oconee and Jeanne Provost, Jim Nemeth, Bob Madison, Bill Littman, John E. Parnum, Scott MacQueen, John Cocchi, Jack Dukesbery, David Bailey, Barry Murphy, Ray Nielsen, Greg Mank, Kevin Clement (*Chiller Theatre*), Diane Norman, Rich Scrivani, Tony Timpone and Mike Gingold (*Fangoria*) and the Lincoln Center Performing Arts Library crew (Louis Paul, Christine Karatnytsky, Dan Patri, Christopher Frith and the late Brian O'Connell).

Mark Martucci, owner of the world's primo video collection, was always there when needed, as were research associates Mike and John Brunas.

Abridged versions of the interviews featured in this book originally appeared in the following 'zines:

HERMAN COHEN: "Cohen My Way—A Tribute to Herman," *The Astounding B Monster* webzine, July 2002
MIKE CONNORS: "Touch of Action," *Starlog* #309, April 2003
SUSAN DOUGLAS: "Among the Final Five," *Starlog* #290, September 2001
ARNOLD DRAKE: "*Flesh Eaters* and Fantasy," *Fangoria* #219, January 2003
ROBERT M. FRESCO: "Horror al Fresco," *Fangoria* #214, July 2002

ALEX GORDON: "*The Atomic Submarine*: Producer Alex Gordon Recalls His 1959 Submariners-vs.-Space Alien Epic," *Chiller Theatre* #16, 2002
BRETT HALSEY: "Many Horror Returns," *Fangoria* #215, August 2002, and "The Italian Jobs," *Fangoria* #216, September 2002
JOHN HART: "Getting to the John Hart of the Matter," *Western Clippings* #35, May-June 2000, and "The Other Lone Gunman," *Starlog* #285, April 2001
DAVID HEDISON: "Taking a Dive," *Starlog* #303, October 2002
RUSS JONES: "*Dr. Terror's Gallery of Horrors*," *Horror Biz* #7, 2002
RICHARD KIEL: "Eegah to Please: The Richard Kiel Interview," *Video Watchdog* #97, July 2003
KAY LINAKER: "Kay Linaker—At War with Tod Browning & James Whale," *Video Watchdog* #90, December 2002
TEALA LORING: "Working in the B's," *Classic Images* #327, September 2002
ROBERT NICHOLS: "And Another Thing," *Starlog* #302, September 2002
WILLIAM SELF: "Self Analysis," *Starlog* #290, September 2001, and "Self Appraisal," *Starlog* #299, June 2002
NATALIE TRUNDY: "The Day of the Apes," *Starlog* #290, September 2001
MARTIN VARNO: "*Night of the Blood Beast*," *Chiller Theatre* #17, 2002
BEVERLY WASHBURN: "*Thriller, Science Fiction Theater, Superman, Star Trek*—and *Spider Baby*: The Amazing Genre Career of Beverly Washburn," *Chiller Theatre* #16, 2002
WILLIAM WELLMAN, JR.: "Down with *Macumba Love*," *Fangoria* #225, August 2003

Contents

Acknowledgments vii

Herman Cohen on Lon Chaney, Jr. 1
Mike Connors 16
Susan Douglas on *Five* 36
Arnold Drake on *The Flesh Eaters* 51
Robert M. Fresco 73
Alex Gordon on *The Atomic Submarine* 94
Brett Halsey 114
John Hart 140
David Hedison on *Voyage to the Bottom of the Sea* 156
Russ Jones on *Dr. Terror's Gallery of Horrors* 175
Richard Kiel on *Eegah* 192
Kay Linaker on Tod Browning and James Whale 215
Teala Loring 234
Robert Nichols 243
Ted Post on Bela Lugosi 258
William Self 269
Natalie Trundy 302
Martin Varno on *Night of the Blood Beast* 318
Beverly Washburn 332
William Wellman, Jr. 347

Index 365

Herman Cohen on Lon Chaney, Jr.

> *Lon was unhappy because of his career—his career went no place outside of [his Universal horror films] and a couple others. He was a damn good actor, but nobody gave him the credit. So he wasn't a very happy man.*

The early 1950s found Lon Chaney, Jr., in a state of transition: The trim, physically imposing star of the classic *Of Mice and Men* (1939) and Universal horror favorites like *Man Made Monster* and *The Wolf Man* (1941) was now freelancing, now coping with middle age, now playing supporting roles for movie companies both major and minor. And, as always, the actor always seemed at his best in horror and Westerns—exactly the genres in which he was cast by neophyte producer Herman Cohen, who signed Lon to appear in three of his early Realart productions. Chaney played a jungle police commissioner in Cohen's *Bride of the Gorilla* (1951), a south-of-the-border chiller written and directed by *The Wolf Man*'s Curt Siodmak; an aged, wheelchair-bound landgrabber in the post–Civil War Western *The Bushwhackers* (1952); and, most memorably, the title role of the noble Indian leader in *Battles of Chief Pontiac* (1952), a (loosely) fact-based Colonial American tale shot on location in South Dakota.

In this interview, Cohen talks about these productions (and, in the process, the beginnings of his own motion picture career) and his memories of his professional association with Lon Chaney, Jr.

How did you get your job with Jack Broder's Realart Pictures?

After I got out of the Marine Corps in 1949, I was working for Columbia, in their publicity department. What was I making? Fifty bucks a week? Anyway, Jack Broder and his family owned theaters in Detroit. I'm also from Detroit. But I had never met the man. And I talked to a couple of people who said, "Oh, Jack Broder's looking for an executive assistant." At that time, Jack was president of Realart Films—did you ever hear of Realart?

They were re-releasing Universal's old monster pictures at the time.

Not just the monster pictures. Jack Broder had put up a tremendous amount of money, millions, for all of Universal's old pictures. But what a mistake he made: He bought 'em for theatrical only, not knowing at that time about TV, video, DVD, you name it. Oh, God, the millions more he would have made! Universal at that time was in trouble financially, so they sold him the reissue rights to all their Abbott and Costellos, *all* their pictures. And now that Jack was making a lot of money with this, everybody started asking him, "Why don't *you* make films? Why don't you go into production and make second features?" At that time, there were still double features in the drive-ins and what have you. "You could make money with second features if the price was right." So Jack Broder decided to put together a unit called Jack Broder Productions to make some second features.

And that's when you came into the picture.

That's right. I was interviewed by him—I think I had a *couple* of interviews with him. I had to meet his wife Beatrice and his kids, too, for *them* to say yes or no. (They had six kids.) Anyway, he hired me. And that's how I started working for Jack Broder.

He hired you because he was about to start making pictures, and he was looking for a...

He needed a schlepper—he needed somebody to stick the broom up their ass and clean his office [*laughs*].

What prompted Broder to make a horror picture, Bride of the Gorilla? *Was it the fact that the Universals had done well for him?*

That's right. Siodmak ... which Siodmak was it? Curt? Yes, *Curt* Siodmak had this story, *Bride of the Gorilla*—well, it wasn't called *Bride of the Gorilla* at first. But anyway, he had a horror story which needed a lot of work. So we *all* worked on it. And we hired [as director] Curt, who had been in this country a long time but, if you talked to him, you'd think he arrived yesterday! And that's when we did *Bride of the Gorilla*. We had a pretty good cast, because I was able to sign Lon Chaney ... Raymond Burr, who was tremendous. I used him, even when I went in production myself.

You hired Lon Chaney based on the fact that he was popular from the Universal horror pictures.

Right.

Whose idea was it to get Barbara Payton?

Jack Broder. He played cards with Jack Warner at the Friars, at the Hollywood Athletic Club on Sunset Boulevard and what have you. They would play for money. Jack Warner mentioned that he had this cunt under contract, doing nothing, sitting on her ass, and Jack Broder said, "Gee, I need a young, sexy girl for this film I'm gonna do." And Jack Warner said, "*Take* her! You can *have* her." They didn't like her [at Warner Brothers]—she was fucking everybody on the lot. I think we paid hardly nothing to borrow her from Warners, Jack Warner said, "I gotta get rid of that cunt." So … it was a very cheap deal for Jack Broder to borrow her from Warners. This was *after* she did a big picture with James Cagney, *Kiss Tomorrow Goodbye* [1950].

And what was her attitude about being loaned out like that?
　　She was very unhappy about being loaned to do *Bride of the Gorilla*. Here she thought she was gonna be another Joan Crawford or Bette Davis, and she ends up doing *Bride of the Gorilla*! We rented space at the Sam Goldwyn Studios, which was the old United Artists Studios, and that's where we made *Bride of the Gorilla*. The entire picture was shot on the set. The jungle, everything, we built the whole thing on the set. I think we shot it in ten days.

When I interviewed Curt Siodmak, he said his title for the movie was The Face in the Water. *Does that ring a bell?*
　　Now that you mention it, I think that *was* his title. 'Cause at one point in the movie, when Raymond Burr turns into a gorilla, he looks in the water and he sees his reflection. But I changed the title. Jack wanted an exploitation title, and I came up with *Bride of the Gorilla*.

Did anyone notice, or care, that Siodmak's screenplay was very much like Lon Chaney's The Wolf Man, *which he also wrote? It's South America and a gorilla instead of Britain and a werewolf.*
　　Nobody [at Realart] ever saw *The Wolf Man*, including me. Well, you look at the horror pictures, they all stole from each other. But I never saw *The Wolf Man*.

Lon Chaney—depending on the movie, and depending on who I'm talking to, he could be either a wild man or a pussycat. Which one did you wind up with?
　　For some reason, maybe because I was so young at that time (I was in my early twenties*), he got to like me. He was my responsibility. And he was a pussycat. He didn't like the other actors, though, and he didn't like Siodmak—he couldn't understand him! Lon would come to me and say, "What the hell's this man *talking* about?" [*Laughs*] So I would have to interpret! I was the only one who could understand Curt Siodmak's English, so they all came to *me*: "What did he say? What did Curt say?"

Did he like Barbara Payton at least?
　　Ummm … not really. No. When he was through shooting, he walked off and he went into his dressing room and started drinking—he was drinking in those days. He just did his job. I don't think he was too happy *doing* it because everyone would compare him to his father. But … he needed the money, and he did the job. And *we* wanted his name.

**After Cohen's death, it was discovered that, throughout his many interviews, he had consistently lied about his age. In 1951, when he first worked with Chaney Jr., Cohen was about to turn 26.*

And even with him taking his nips in the dressing room, he was still always ready for the cameras when needed?

He never held us up. He was very professional in front of the camera.

You also had a very professional guy behind the camera, Charles Van Enger.

Oh, he was wonderful, that oldtimer, he was great. We used him on a lot of pictures at that time. Charley Van Enger did a lot of big pictures years before, and he taught me a great deal also. See, I was *learning*—that's why I took the job with Jack Broder. 'Cause I'd be doing *everything*. And instead of giving me money, Jack would give me titles—he made me a vice-president of Realart, a vice-president of Jack Broder Productions and what have you.

You made Bride of the Gorilla *at the time when Barbara Payton was romantically linked with both Franchot Tone and Tom Neal.*

Franchot Tone was a very wealthy man and he had been quite a star at one time. In fact, he had been married to Joan Crawford—did you remember that? So he was dating Barbara. And Barbara was *also* swinging with this ex-cop half-assed actor from Republic Pictures named Tom Neal. We told the captain at the Goldwyn gate that, if Tom Neal was coming, call the stage immediately, and *especially* if Franchot was there—she had to get rid of him!

Tone and Tom Neal didn't know about each other?

They could have known about each other, *that* I don't know, but they never met at the studio. They came close, but they didn't meet. The big fistfight they had was after our picture was made.

So both visited the set individually?

Oh, yeah.

Did you like Barbara Payton?

Yes, I liked her. Look, like all whores that I've ever met, she had a heart of gold. She was just a fun person. She liked to laugh ... and she was a little crazy. I think she was doing drugs ... she certainly was drinking. But not on the set. And as much as she was pissed off at Warners, 'cause she *knew* they were gonna dump her, and that therefore *Bride of the Gorilla* was on her way to being dumped, she never let it interfere with her work. I've got some pictures ... very intimate pictures of her with me.... I was a young guy, she was a beautiful girl at that time. Barbara Payton was a lovely person. She was a whore who got lucky. And deep down, she was a lovely person, she was very sweet. It was horrible how she died, downtown, as a whore, selling herself for five, ten bucks. That just made me ill when I heard about that. I actually liked her.

Despite your youth, did Jack Broder have a lot of confidence in you once a picture got rolling?

I doubt it [*laughs*]! But Jack Broder didn't *know* anything about production. And I was *learning*. I always hired the top production supervisors and assistant directors, people who really knew their stuff. And when things would come up in a

According to producer Herman Cohen, "there were no friends among the actors" in *Bride of the Gorilla*. **Lon Chaney, Jr., and Steve Calvert furnish photographic proof. (Photofest)**

meeting and they'd ask me to make a decision (I was making the decisions on the film), I'd say, "We'll discuss it tomorrow morning." And that night, I would dash to UCLA, to the Cinema Library, to read up on what the fuck they were *talking* about [*laughs*]! That's a true story! I'd read up, *or* I'd call up a couple friends, a couple film editors I knew from Columbia, and ask *them*. The next morning, suddenly I became *very* bright!

These early Realart pictures—was Broder on the set a lot, or did he leave everything to you guys?

He would only go there to take pictures with his kids. And watch a few important scenes. He was more interested in the schedule, if we were behind. He was always threatening, "Herman! If you're late, I pool the switch! I pool the switch!"

On Bride of the Gorilla, *you were the "Assistant to the Producer"—*

But I was actually running the show for Jack.

Broder took the producer credit; and the associate producer is somebody I never heard of, Edward Leven.

Oh [*laughs*]—oh, God. What a thief! He wasn't the associate producer, he was *nothing* on it. He *talked* his way into it—he was a great talker! Edward Leven was somebody that Jack met at the Friars Club, he was the son of a very wealthy friend of Jack's. All of a sudden one day, Jack brought in this guy to the studio and he said, "Herman, Edward Leven needs credits. He has to get into the business." So he made him associate producer of *Bride of the Gorilla*. Jack instructed me, "I want you to tell him what he has to know"—and here *I* am, learning myself! *And*, Jack added, "*Don't let him make any decisions!*" [*Laughs*] That's how Edward Leven got involved. Then one day, our prop man told Jack that *all* the furniture that we rented at the prop house, Leven had had delivered to his home—he stole it all [*laughs*]. Leven had the prop man ship all the furniture that he picked out at the prop house to his home—just as we were building the sets and what have you. He was furnishing his house on Jack Broder!

How in the world did he think he was going to get away with that? Didn't he think that people would eventually notice that there was no furniture on the sets?

No, no, no, no, no! We had our furniture too—it was a double order! He picked out what he wanted for his home. Our prop man told Jack Broder, who threw Leven off the Sam Goldwyn lot. I wonder if he's still alive.... I've never seen him since he was fired.

Seven months after Bride of the Gorilla *was shot, Leven filed a breach of contract suit against Broder claiming, for one thing, that he'd never been paid. He had the nerve to do what he did and then sue Broder?*

Yeah, because he didn't know that we *knew* everything. He wasn't paid and he was thrown off the Goldwyn lot. He thought he was Sam Goldwyn [*laughs*]! But he was kind of a likable guy. I mean, *I* got along with him—he didn't want to get *me* pissed off at him, because he didn't even know where to park his *car* when he came on the lot. So that's Edward Leven...!

Curt Siodmak told me that one guy that Chaney reeeally didn't get along with was Raymond Burr. Do you have any memory of that?

[*Scoffing*] We didn't have the *time* for them not to get along with each other. We made the whole picture in ten days and we came in under budget. So there was no time to fight, not at all. But, on this picture, there were no friends among the actors.

But you got along with everybody.
I learned very young that you have to be a diplomat. Therefore I was kissing *every*body's ass. 'Cause I knew that if I kiss their butts, they're gonna be on the stage, they'll know their lines. I was even reading lines with Barbara and reading lines with Lon. With Raymond I didn't *have* to, 'cause Raymond knew *all* his lines. Oh, he was so professional. And a wonderful guy.

And you used him in at least one other picture...
I used in *several* pictures—I used him again in *The Brass Legend* [1956] and in *Crime of Passion* [1957]. His agent was a nice guy, too, Lester Salkow, I remember him well. Once they got their deal to do *Perry Mason*, it was wonderful, because Raymond became a millionaire. Raymond was a hell of an actor. Great actor, great voice, and I *knew* he was gonna become something. God, when I gave him the part of the inspector of the LAPD in *Crime of Passion*, he was terrific. And he was terrific in *Bride of the Gorilla*. It wasn't a bad picture if I remember, *Bride of the Gorilla*, considering we did it in ten days.

I thought Chaney was excellent in The Bushwhackers, *playing an elderly, arthritic villain—and looking rather like the old sheriff he played in* High Noon *[1952].*
That was our best picture [the best Broder-Cohen picture], I think. What did you think of the cast I put together for that? Names like Lawrence Tierney, Wayne Morris (he'd just left Warner Brothers), Dorothy Malone, John Ireland ... for a cheap picture, it had a hell of a cast. And we signed a young guy who had never directed before, named Rod Amateau. A hell of a talent. Rod and a buddy of his [Tom Gries], a guy he was rooming with, wrote the script. They were very close friends at that time. For *The Bushwhackers*, we rented the Western Street from Warners, and we also used the Western Street at Columbia a couple days. We shot in and around town, we didn't go on location any further than the Western Streets.

Why did Broder want to get into Westerns? Because it was just "the thing to do" at that time?
That's right. The first picture we did was *Two Dollar Bettor* [a 1951 movie about a compulsive racetrack gambler], and the only reason for that is that Jack Broder loved to go to the races [*laughs*], that's why we did it. We did *Bride of the Gorilla* because we thought, "Hey, let's do a horror picture. They always make money." At that time, Westerns also all made money. That's when these two young guys Rod Amateau and Tom Gries brought in their [*Bushwhackers*] script, and Jack liked the script. Jack's ten-year-old son Bobby used to read it to him! Bobby Broder's a top agent now, by the way.

And he's in The Bushwhackers, *according to the credits.*
I think a *couple* of Jack's kids were put in *The Bushwhackers*. Bobby was the oldest son. Jack would come in some mornings, when there was something that he had to make a decision about, and say to me, "Bobby told me last night that..." blah blah

Heavily made up, Chaney (then in his mid-40s) played an aging, arthritic baddie in Cohen's *The Bushwhackers*. (Photograph courtesy JC Archives)

blah, "and here's what I've decided." Well, I had already *called* little Bobby the day before and said to him, "Look, tell your dad..."

Oh, that's brilliant!

I used to take Bobby for ice cream sundaes and stuff, to get him on our side! I knew that he would tell his dad what to do, and his dad would do it. He was 11 or 12, maybe, at that time.

How was Chaney on The Bushwhackers *and* Battles of Chief Pontiac? *Did he seem to like those pictures better?*

He liked Rod Amateau on *The Bushwhackers*, he had a lot of respect for him, and he liked the cast. However, Lon never spent time with any of the cast. When he finished his work, he went his own way. He was never close to John Ireland. Of course, John Ireland was hot, trying to "make" Dorothy Malone all the time.

On Battles of Chief Pontiac, *who made the decision to shoot in South Dakota?*

While we were trying to determine where to shoot, we found out from talking to location people that MGM had just built a fort outside of Rapid City, South Dakota, for a movie. I called the Chamber of Commerce and found out that the fort was still standing. It needed some work but it was still there, right by the lake. I went there several times to check the locations before I made the deals.

On this picture, you were the associate producer, and the producer was Irving Starr.

Irving Starr was a card-playing buddy of Jack Broder, they used to go to the track together and what have you. And Irving Starr was down on his luck—he'd been a producer at Columbia until he had a fight with Harry Cohn and he was thrown out of Columbia. That just killed him. He was out of a job, needed money—and Jack Broder was always helping his friends. So he hired Irving Starr to produce *Battles of Chief Pontiac*, and Irving Starr had nothing to *do* with it. In fact, he never even came to the location. But he was a nice guy, I have nothing bad to say about Irving Starr. He said, "Herman ... *you* make the picture."

I flew up to South Dakota, oh, three or four times, to check the locations, to talk to the head of the Office of Indian Affairs—we also needed Indians for the picture, right? I met a couple of the chiefs, chiefs of the different segments of the Sioux tribe, because I had to make a deal with them. That was quite fascinating for *me*. (There wasn't a picture I made that I didn't *learn* something—my entire life in this business has been a learning process.) To make the deal, I had to go to a peace meeting, and I had to smoke a peace pipe, me and my assistant director Richard Dixon— oh, he was a wonderful guy, I used him on half a dozen pictures. What a sweetie he was. Anyway, here we are in this huge teepee, the chief's teepee, sitting on fur pelts and what have you, talking about how many young braves we needed, and who could ride horses, and this and that and what have you. And they passed the peace pipe along. Then the chief said, "Me want $5000 a day." Well, *Battles of Chief Pontiac* was a cheap budget picture! MGM had *ruined* these guys by paying 'em a lot of money. So I got pissed off. I got up, and I wiped my lips from the pipe, and I said, "For $5000 a day, *I'll* be the chief!" [*Laughs*] I turned to Dick and I said, "Dickie. Come on. Let's get the hell out of here." And we started walking away. Well, as we walked away, the tribal council came out of the teepee, running after us, bowing to me: "If you don't make a deal, we get a new chief!" They all wanted to be in the film!

I walked away. Got in my car and left. (I thought I was gonna get an arrow in my back as I was leaving!) Next morning, oh God, it's like six-thirty, seven o'clock, I hear, "*Woo* woo woo woo, *woo* woo woo woo, *woo* woo woo woo," tom-toms going and what have you, outside of the Alex Johnson Hotel. The phone rings and it's Dickie, my assistant, and he says, "Herm, look out the window, look out the window." I say, "What? What?" He says, "The chief and his tribe are here to make peace with you!" See, the Sioux tribe had all kinds of different tribes-within-the-tribe, and these guys I had met with didn't want me to go some place else, they wanted to make peace with me. They came up to the hotel and they brought me a magnificent pair of cowboy boots—I don't know where they stole 'em or how they got my size, I never did find out. And I did make peace with 'em. I can't remember what I paid the chief who I put in charge—I think it was five *hundred* a day, not five *thousand* a day.

And the chief who asked for the $5000 a day—was he "out" at that point?
No, no—he was the main dancer in front of the hotel! We kept him as the chief, and he got 500 a day or something like that. He was like the wrangler, he was the one who got the [Indians] we needed. Each day Dick Dixon would tell him, "Tomorrow we need 12 braves" or "We need six women" or "We need five kids"—and he would get 'em.

For the Indian village in the movie, we got the land, and then the Indians all came with their teepees—they brought their teepees and everything from where they *were*. They put the village together, and that's where they *lived*. In the morning, food had to be delivered to them. We made a deal with a bakery in Rapid City and they each got a loaf of white bread ... they got a hunk of buffalo meat ... and a quart of milk. That was their breakfast. However, one morning, I got a call that the Indians were packing their teepees, they were leaving. "*Leaving*?" "Yes. The bread truck didn't show up!" So I woke up Dick Dixon and we dashed to the bakery—they were late in baking the white bread, and they didn't have a driver for the truck. So I ended up driving the bread out to the location, in the truck, with Dick, to stop them from leaving!

And Lex Barker, the star of Chief Pontiac?

Lex was quite a ladies' man, and a nice guy. He just came off doing Tarzan, so he was used to cheap films. This was one of his first films with clothes, playing this scout. Lex was a nice guy and he knew exactly what he had to do. But he was a lousy actor [*laughs*]! The leading lady, Helen Westcott, was a very good actress.

And where did you get the actors and extras who played all the English soldiers, and the German Hessians?

I went up there scouting locations and they had an Air Force base, Rapid City Air Force Base. I knew I needed extras—we couldn't bring 'em from Hollywood, this was a budget picture! So I called the commanding officer, who was Brigadier General Richard Ellsworth, and went to meet him. We became instant friends. General Ellsworth said, "You can have whatever you want." For instance, water was at a premium, so he sent out the Air Force water trucks for my whole company. And, of course, that's where I got the army for the Brits as well as the Hessians. Ellsworth and his wonderful wife and two daughters, we all became good friends and we'd have dinner in their home on the base. He told me not to touch his daughters—and not to let Lex Barker get *near* 'em [*laughs*]! Then there's something I shouldn't tell you but I will: On weekends, if I had to get to L.A., he'd have an Air Force jet take me back! With Dick Dixon, and with Ellsworth's wife, who wanted to go shopping in Beverly Hills, and Lex Barker—whoever wanted to get back to L.A. for the weekend. This could never be done by a president, but if you were the commanding general of a base, you were the king. You didn't requisition anything, you just did what you wanted to do [*laughs*]! Especially if you were in a base like in Rapid City, South Dakota! He was so happy that I would hire his people, 'cause they were so *bored*—there was *nothing* fuckin' to do there. And we hired several hundred of his people. To determine which of his guys we were going to give speaking parts to, we had interviews at the Service Club on the base. I remember this one Saturday morning, I was going there with my staff to interview whoever would show up. Since it was the weekend, we doubted that anyone would be there. Well, as we drove close to the Service Club, there were guys standing around the *block*! They all wanted to get in the film. After all, Rapid City, South Dakota, there was nothing to do there, except go to Mount Rushmore. And how many times can you see it?

A short time later [March 1953], General Ellsworth was on board a plane that hit a mountain in the Azores, and that's when he was killed. They renamed the base after *him*, to the Ellsworth Air Force Base.

I know Lon Chaney was a great outdoorsman—how did he enjoy going to South Dakota and making Chief Pontiac?

Chaney enjoyed living amongst the Sioux Indians on location in South Dakota for Cohen's *Battles of Chief Pontiac* with Lex Barker. (Photofest)

He spent all his time with the Indians, he was with the Indians all the time. He was playing Chief Pontiac and he wanted to "get the feel of the Indians and their lives"—he didn't want to live in a suite at the Hotel Alex Johnson in town, where *we* all were. So we built a big teepee for him, and he lived out there with the Indians. And he put himself in his role. He took *Chief Pontiac* seriously. And he did *not* drink during *Pontiac*, by the way.

Once you started making the movie, what were the Indians like to work with?
Terrible. 'Cause they would drink like crazy every night. There were two or three of 'em killed during the course of the shooting—killed at the Indian village, their deaths had nothing to do with us. We hired Indian deputy sheriffs to [maintain order] at the village, because the Indian men would get drunk at night and fight and this and that. We'd been told by the government Indian Office that we better have security, because of the alcoholic problem with the Indians. We also needed deputy sheriffs to keep the Indians *there*—otherwise, somebody we established in the movie *today*, tomorrow he's gone! Another thing I recall: The young teenagers who we used as braves, they were quite Americanized, and they resented being called Indians! When someone would say, "You five Indians over there..."—they didn't like that at *all*. They felt they were Americans, and that we were looking down on them.

The Indians were terrible to work with—but Chaney liked them?
Oh, yeah, he liked them. Lon was into history, the history of the Indians, and he knew the history of Fort Detroit. By the way, that's one of the reasons why Jack Broder liked the script: He was *from* Detroit, and this was [set at] Fort Detroit. And some of the story was true. The involvement of the German Hessian troops was true. Spreading small pox on blankets to kill the Indians, that's true too. And of course there really *was* a Chief Pontiac. That's where the Pontiac cars came from—do you remember Pontiac cars? If you look at that Indian head [on Pontiac cars], it looks just like Lon Chaney! [*Laughs*] No, seriously!

One day, we suddenly saw a couple white guys, in suits, on the location. "Who *are* those guys?" "I dunno ... they look like they could be union organizers...." So I said, "Dick ... go find out who the hell are they." Sure enough, they were union guys who had flown up from L.A.—somebody had squealed that, instead of bringing people in from L.A., we were using Indian laborers, to pick up the horse shit and everything. And they threatened to close down the set. So I told the Indians to get rid of 'em! Well, the Indians pushed 'em out of the way, "Get the fuck out of here!" and what have you! And they left! But when I came back to L.A., I was called in front of the Film Council and we were fined for using Indian laborers. They came all the way to South Dakota—on *our* cheap picture!

Was there any night life in South Dakota?
There was *nothing* to do at night except have a drink in the bar or something and go to sleep. We had to get up four-thirty, five o'clock in the morning.

Following his years with Jack Broder Productions, Cohen became a driving force in horror-exploitation circles via movies like *I Was a Teenage Frankenstein*. (*Left to right:* Gary Conway, Cohen, Angela Blake.)

Was there anybody there who claimed to be descended from Chief Pontiac?

You're forgetting, this was the Sioux, the Sioux in South Dakota. Chief Pontiac's tribe was out of Detroit. The tribe we hired was a different tribe.

And your director, Felix Feist?

He was a very good director who'd just done a hell of a picture [*The Big Trees*, 1952] with Kirk Douglas. But he had the rep of being a difficult director, and therefore, he couldn't get a job. He probably resented that he had to do a picture like *Battles of Chief Pontiac*. He wasn't difficult with *us*, but ... he was *too good for the film*, let's put it that way. Here we're making a shitkicker in ten days, and on location besides, with all the problems of location, and we had a pretty classy director. He was tough to push and handle, Felix was. But a hell of an intelligent guy.

Everybody I worked with was either down on their luck, or couldn't get a job—but had terrific credits! Who was the director of photography on *Pontiac*? Charles Van Enger again? Oh, I loved that old guy.

Legendary horror–SF movie writer-producer Herman Cohen lost his cancer battle on June 2, 2002, at age 76. This interview, conducted just a few months earlier, was perhaps his last.

And, again, Chaney was good in the picture, wasn't he?

Lon loved the part. He thought he *was* Chief Pontiac! In his speeches that he gave to his people before they went to war, he had tears in his eyes. Here is this two-bit movie we're making, and here's Lon Chaney with tears in his eyes doing his scenes. He thought he *was* the fuckin' Indian chief! He ate their food, by the way— the loaf of bread, the hunk of buffalo meat and the quart of milk.

Did you ever see him again after these three movies?

No. But, you know, that's the business.

And when you think back on Lon Chaney—what lasting memories?

He was a nice guy. He had problems. His father was a big silent star ... and he was living off his dad's name. He was a *good* actor. I mean, he did *Of Mice and Men*, and he thought he was going to be a big star after that. We had a couple conversations, when he would be drinking and talking about Hollywood and everything else. He was unhappy because of his career—his career went *no place* outside of Universal [his Universal horror films] and a couple others. He was a *damn good* actor, but nobody gave him the credit. So he wasn't a very happy man.

Did you hang out with him much?

Not much, no. Don't forget, I was in my early twenties, I wasn't gonna hang around Lon Chaney. And Lon Chaney wasn't gonna hang around *us*. And he never did. For instance, on *The Bushwhackers* we all went out together for dinner one night, John Ireland, Dorothy Malone, Myrna Dell, Wayne Morris, Lawrence Tierney ... but Lon wasn't one of the group at all. Lon was *never* with the actors. He just wasn't interested in being with the actors or the crew. He did his job, and that was *it*. That's the way he was. And when we were in Rapid City, he was with the Indians all the time. He just loved the area. We had a tough time even getting him into town, for production meetings and what have you. He *loved* it out there in the Indian village. He was an outdoorsman. He was *always* an outdoorsman. He went fishing, and he went hunting, and he went here and there. He became friends with some of the Indians. He could have been fucking some of the squaws, I don't know [*laughs*], but he was *always* with the Indians!

Lon Chaney *should* have been, and *could* have been, a hell of a top actor. He could have been a big star. But because of his father, and because of what he had to live up to, everybody wanted him for horror pictures. That's why he loved the part of Chief Pontiac, it was something different. That's why, the minute I offered him the job, he took it. And he was a *nice* man. A big, *big* bruiser—and a nice, gentle guy. I always find that, the bigger the guy is, the nicer they are. It's the little short scrappy one that wants to start trouble! Lon, he was just a nice guy.

Mike Connors

> *I remember doing silly stunts in those days that were absolutely ridiculous, but you did 'em. Much later in your career, you'd say, "Hey, I tell you what: [makes an obscene gesture] Go get yourself a good stuntman. I ain't gettin' in that water with the snake and the alligator—you're crazy!" But in 1955, I did it.*

One of TV's top stars in the cop and detective categories, Mike Connors first burst onto the scene in the late '50s as the undercover agent in *Tightrope*; he represented the long arm of the law again in the '80s as a federal man in *Today's F.B.I.*; and in the interim he had his best and longest-running role as the Los Angeles-based private detective *Mannix* (receiving five Emmy nominations and a Golden Globe).

Movie fans remember a whole 'nother Connors, however. This one was named Touch Connors. *His* "beat" was a dark and sometimes dangerous (for real!) low-budget B movie world of slippery characters like Roger Corman, Samuel Z. Arkoff and Sam Katzman. This ... is *his* story.

The actor actually began life under yet *another* name, Kreker J. Ohanian. Born and raised in Fresno, he lettered in high school football, basketball and track, but his athletic and academic pursuits were temporarily shelved while he served in the Army Air Corps during World War II. Following discharge from the service, he enrolled at UCLA, where he became interested in the theater. Once Hollywood took notice, he soon made his debut in a supporting part in the 1952 suspenser *Sudden Fear* with Joan Crawford. But the road from *Sudden Fear* to *Mannix* and TV super-stardom was paved with many unusual roles, from a gangster menacing Earth's last survivors on the *Day the World Ended* (1956), to a killer clad in animal skins and prowling by the African full moon in *Jaguar* (1956), to the Bond-like secret agent Kelly in the Dino de Laurentiis spy spoof *Kiss the Girls and Make Them Die* (1966). Mike Connors remembers these offbeat roles, and others, in this exclusive interview.

According to your studio bios, your early career plan was to follow in your father's footsteps and become an attorney.

That's true. My father was an attorney and, of course, every ethnic parent wants their kid to be a doctor, lawyer or a professor. So my mother—my father was dead by the time I started college—my mother insisted I become an attorney. I didn't want to, but to keep her happy, I went to college and law school.

One bio says you grew up in tough economic times.
When my father came to this country, to the East Coast, he was going to get his law degree here and go back to Armenia and try and help the Armenian people against the Turks—the Turks were massacring the Armenians in the old country. Then what happened was that Armenia got split up and part of it became Russia and part of it became Turkey. So he stayed here and he figured, "Well, I'll migrate to Fresno where there are a lot of Armenians, and practice law there and help the Armenians there that can't speak English." Many of his [Fresno] clients *had* no money, and they would pay him with fruit and vegetables and chickens. So it *was* tough times. We lived in ... I guess you would call it a ghetto-type area in Fresno where it was mainly Armenian and Greek and Italian ethnic groups that hung out. There wasn't a lot of money.

But still enough money for you to go to college when the time came.
No. After I graduated from high school, I went into the service, World War II, and got the G.I. Bill of Rights. And while I was playing basketball in the service, Wilbur Johns, who was coach at UCLA, came to me and he said, "When you get out of the service, if you're interested, maybe I can give you a scholarship." So I went to UCLA on a G.I. Bill of Rights *and* a basketball scholarship. That's how I was able to afford to go to college.

In 1961, you announced that you were going to make a movie about your father.
If I did, it was a false announcement.

The Innocent Hoodlum, *you said it'd be called.*
Yeah. That was a complete fabrication.

At what point did you switch from wanting to be a lawyer to wanting to be an actor?
While I was a freshman playing basketball at UCLA, we were playing a game before the varsity game, and the coach Wilbur Johns came up to me and he said, "There's a friend of mine in the audience with his son, and the son would like to meet you ballplayers." He took me over to the side and said, "This is Mr. Wellman and this is his son, Bill Jr.," "Hi, Bill Jr., how are you?" so forth and so on. Johns introduced each of the players to the boy. We then played basketball—and I played a pretty rough game of basketball at that time. After the game was over, Johns came to me and said, "That fellow you met, Wellman—he's a director [William "Wild Bill" Wellman]. He liked your voice and the way you played basketball, and he wants to know if you might be interested in being an actor." I thought it was a joke and I said [*scoffing*], "Sure, any time." [*Laughs*] So a few days later, Johns said, "I talked to Wellman and he says when he gets ready to do a picture, he'll give you a call." About a week later, Johns came to me again and this time he said, "There's a lady

Call him Kreker Ohanian, Jay Ohanian, Touch Connors, Michael Connors, Mike Connors—just don't call him when there are *snakes* around!

named Ruth Burch, a casting lady. They're looking for a new Tarzan and she called and asked if there was an athlete here. I mentioned the situation with you and Wellman, and she said, 'Have him come out and see me.'" So I went and saw her and she said, "You're wrong for Tarzan, but have you ever thought about acting?" I said, "No, not really." She said, "Well … *think* about it. And give me a call."

Who was Tarzan at the time? Who were they looking to replace?

Lex Barker. Anyway, the next day in a speech class I was taking, the speech teacher Estelle Harman asked me, "Would you stay after class? I'd like to talk to you." She said, "I'm casting a play, *All My Sons*, and you'd be perfect for one of the parts. Have you ever thought about acting?" I said, "*No*—but I'm sure thinkin' about it *now*." [*Laughs*] I called Ruth Burch back and I told her I'd be interested in acting, and she said, "Okay. I'm going to set you up with a coach." She sent me to a coach named Bob Paris—he had coached Clark Gable, and he was at the time coaching … she went with Howard Hughes…

Terry Moore.

Terry Moore. I told Bob Paris, "I have no money." …but I did have a postwar Jeep. "If you'll deliver some scripts and do some things for me," he said, "I'll coach you for free." So I delivered some scripts and so on for him, and I started working with him, [opposite people like] Terry Moore. But before I could work with Terry Moore, Howard Hughes had to okay me. One day, Bob Paris told me he wanted me to come to the Goldwyn Studio on South Santa Monica and Formosa. I went there, I went to the gate guard and I said, "Jay Ohanian here to see Bob Paris and Terry Moore." He said, "Well, just wait right here." I waited and I'm standing around and looking, and all of a sudden this old Chevy pulls up … stops … and the driver looks me over. And I look at *him* and I say to myself, "I think that's Howard Hughes…!" The car goes in, about 20 minutes pass and finally the guard says, "Okay, you can come in." Howard Hughes had said okay, and so I started working with Terry Moore. That's how my whole career got started.

Later on, I was doing a play at UCLA and a scout from Goldwyn Studios saw it and he offered me a chance to do a test. I went to the Goldwyn Studios, and they did one of those ["personality tests"]—look forward, look this way, look that way, how old are ya? what are you doin'? and so forth. And Goldwyn signed me to a 90-day contract. Well, when word got out that Goldwyn had signed me, every agency in town called me. I thought, "Gee, this is terrific," and I signed with Famous Artists Agency, which was a big agency. "Cubby" Broccoli was one of the agents handling me there.

So you were signed by Goldwyn ... but you never were in a Goldwyn movie, were you?

When my 90 days were up, Goldwyn let me go. Then I later found out what the ploy was: Farley Granger, who was under contract to Goldwyn, was giving 'em a bad time about money. So Goldwyn signed me and he told Farley Granger's agent, "I just signed a kid from UCLA that's the same age as Farley, tall, dark, same size, good actor ... and if Farley doesn't come around, *he's* getting the parts that Farley has." Well, the minute Farley's agent saw that Goldwyn had signed me, they made a deal and Farley came back and the Goldwyn people told me, "We don't need *you* any more."

So that's why I was signed by Goldwyn, to make Farley toe the line. But what it did was, it got me an agency [Famous Artists], which was great ... except that, at first, nothing was happening. So one day I'm sitting in the office waiting to go in to tell 'em that I was leaving, that I wanted a release. As I was sitting there, [agent] Henry Willson walked in. I had already met Henry through a good friend of mine, an actor-friend named Craig Hill who was under contract to 20th. Henry asked, "What are *you* doin' here?" and I said, "Well, Mr. Willson, I'm going in to tell 'em I'm leaving the agency." He asked why, and I told him that nothing was happening. He said, "Sit tight a minute." Henry went in, and then when he came out, he told me, "I'm handling you. Just stick with the agency, I'll take care of it." Well, what had happened was, Henry went in and Mark Fellman, who was an agent there, said that I didn't have a chance, that I didn't photograph good and so on. And Henry said, "I'll make you a bet that I can get him a job." (Henry didn't like Mark Fellman, he thought Mark Fellman was a phony.) So Henry came out and he told me to stick with the agency and he said, "Okay, now, the first thing we do is change your name. You got any nicknames?" "Touch—" Willson [*instantly*]: "*Great*! Touch, that's it!" Because at that time it was Rock Hudson, Rory Calhoun, Guy Madison, Race Gentry...

If you knew going into your career that you could have made a go of it with your real name Kreker Ohanian, would you have kept it?

Absolutely. *Absolutely*. It's the one big regret I had, that I let them talk me into changing my name. When Henry Willson took me over at the agency, he said, "There's already an O'Hanlon [working in Hollywood], George O'Hanlon, and Ohanian and O'Hanlon are too close. We gotta change your name." He came up with the Connors, and then the *Touch* Connors. And I hated it from Day One. Then when I got the *Tightrope* TV series [1959-60], I wanted to go back to Ohanian. And Columbia Studio said, "No, no, no. You've done too much as Connors, we want to keep Connors. You can change the *first* name." So that's how [Mike Connors] came about.

I notice that you've used the name Ohanian as a character name a time or two.
One time. After *Mannix* [1967–75], we did a pilot film, *Ohanian*, and my background was to be what I am, Armenian. Goff-Roberts, who produced and wrote *Mannix*, were also the writers-producers on this, and they asked, "Why don't we use your real name here, as the character?" That's how that came about.*

What memories of landing your first part, in Sudden Fear*?*
I had graduated from college and I was in law school by then. One day Henry Willson said, "I've got an interview for you out at Republic. It's a Joan Crawford picture. I'm gonna take you out, we're gonna meet the director and producer." So we go out there and the producer Joe Kaufman says, "Are you *kidding*? We're gonna put a green kid in with Joan Crawford, Jack Palance, Gloria Grahame? You gotta be out of yer heads." They wouldn't even give me a chance to read or *any*thing. So we left. But about a week later, Willson called me and he said, "Listen, you know that part? They've started shooting but they still haven't cast it. *I* can't get you another appointment, but if you can get out there some way and talk to them and talk them into letting you read or something…"

I left law school in my old 1936 four-door DeSoto for which I had paid $75, I went to Republic, it was about noontime, and I stood there thinking, "How am I gonna get *in* here?" Then I noticed that the people coming back from lunch, they'd just kinda walk in and wave to the guard. So I waited 'til a good group of about 15 people were going in, and I walked in with 'em and I waved [*laughs*], and I got in. Once I was inside, I asked, "Where are they shooting the Joan Crawford picture?" and I was told the number of the stage. I walked over—of course, it's the first time I'd been on a movie lot—and I looked and I saw on the door a red light and it said PRIVATE—NO ADMITTANCE, so I was thinking, "Gee, what am I gonna do *now*?" I stood out there for a while, and along came the producer, Joe Kaufman, who saw me and said, "What are *you* doin' here?" I was green, I said, "I'm waiting to see the director." He said, "I *told* you, you can't have the part," and I came back with, "*Hey.* You *mind*? *I'm* gonna talk to the director. Just mind your own business!" I knew he was the producer, but *I* thought the *director* was *the* guy—I was gonna let a fuckin' *producer* tell me what to do? [*Laughs*]

He looked at me like I was *nuts*, he said, "I don't *believe* you," and he walked in. A few minutes later, they broke for lunch, they came walking out, and there's David Miller the director. I guess Kaufman told him about me, 'cause when he saw me he started to smile and he said, "What do you want?" I said, "Give me a chance at bat, let me read for the part! How do *you* know I can't do it, you struck me out without being at bat." He said, "Okay, kid. I'll be back from lunch in a half-hour. Go in there and see the assistant, get a script and look at scene number so-and-so."

---

*Connors played Karl Ohanian in the pilot, which did not become a series but was later seen as a TV movie, The Killer Who Wouldn't Die [1976].

I went in, I got the script and I was lookin' at the thing 'til they came back. In those days, they had those little dressing rooms on the set, about six feet wide and about eight feet long, with a little couch in it and maybe one chair. Little, bitty dressing room. So in came Crawford, in came David Miller, in came Joe Kaufman. And there was a gal there working in the picture in a small part, Virginia Huston. I was told, "Okay, read this part," and so Virginia Huston and I did the scene. They said, "Okay, thanks. Wait outside." I walked outside, onto the set, and I waited. And Joan Crawford went by, she said, "Thank you, very nice"—she walked on the set. David Miller came by and he said, "Not bad, kid"—walked on the set. Joe Kaufman came out and he said, "Wellll ... it's against my better judgment, but they like you and they want you for the part. Do you have a tuxedo?" I said, "No, sir." "All right," Kaufman said, "go to wardrobe, get a tuxedo, you start day after tomorrow." That's how my first part came about.

Once you did get going with Sudden Fear *and other early parts, were you making a decent living?*

No, I didn't really make any kind of a living until I did *Tightrope*. That was the first significant money I made. Up 'til then, it was just struggling. In fact, almost every three or four months, I'd tell my wife Mary Lou, "If something doesn't happen by (say) Christmas, I'll quit. Go back to law school." And Christmas would come and I'd say, "If it doesn't happen 'til Easter..." "If it doesn't happen 'til Fourth of July..." And then, finally, things started to pop.

Working for Roger Corman and AIP in the early years of your career—what was that like?

[*Laughs*] God, how can you explain it? You'd rehearse maybe once or twice and shoot it and print it and move on. You did all those pictures in seven, eight, nine days—there was *no* time taken on these things. No money, no time taken, but it was experience and it was credits. That's the most I can say about *that*, I guess!

Everybody I've talked to about Corman's Swamp Women *[1956] talks about the hardships. Do you have a favorite story?*

Well, Roger took us into the swamps outside of New Orleans to shoot that. He got a place that used to be a hotel, it had been shuttered and closed for ... maybe years ... and [*laughs*] he re-opened it, put a bunch of old beds in there, and that's where we stayed! Out in the middle of nowhere! One of the things I remember: One night we were getting ready for bed and I hear this scream and this hysterical laughter. I get up and go in, and—it was either Beverly Garland or Marie Windsor's bed had completely collapsed, and she was on the floor!

Now, the *girls* in that picture had it much worse than I did. They were playing escaped convicts, the girls, and they captured me. They had to trudge through the mud, the swamps, pulling this rowboat, and I was sitting in the rowboat high and dry. Then towards the end, after I escaped, I had to dive into that dirty water—it had snakes and stuff in it, and it was just terrible. But to Roger, it was like [*shrugs*], "So you get bit by a snake—big deal!" It was a horrendous experience, I'll tell you—just the worst.

Was Roger "high and dry" throughout?

Yeah, he was well taken care of. I don't think he stayed in that hotel with us, I think he had to go [into town] and look at the dailies ... and get a decent meal ... and so on [*laughs*]! But, again, y'know, you did things in those days because you wanted the experience and the credit and the few bucks it brought you. I remember doing silly stunts in those days that were absolutely *ridiculous*, but you did 'em. For instance, in that picture, I was supposed to dive into the water and swim up to an alligator and knife-fight it and kill it. Now, just previous to that, we were in a rowboat, and one of the fellows rowing took a paddle and swung it at something in the water and hit it, and you saw this snake go flying. It was a water moccasin, which is deadly. So now, the next day I was supposed to dive *into* this swamp and swim out to this alligator. A big fucking alligator. I said, "Look, this is ridiculous." They said, "We're gonna tie the alligator to a tree across the bank, and it can only go so far."

Oh, sure!

"And then *you* dive in and you swim towards it, and when you get to a certain point, you stop."

And you have to hope that the alligator doesn't wriggle free—

And hope that you don't misjudge it. Much later in your career, you'd say, "Hey, I tell you what: [*makes an obscene gesture*] Go get yourself a good stuntman. I ain't gettin' *in* that water with the snake and the alligator—you're crazy!" But in 1955, I did it. And it worked out fine. But then they also had the biggest rattlesnake you've ever seen in your life. It was real big around and it was about six feet long. (I hate snakes.) I'm tied to a tree and that rattlesnake was supposed to crawl over my leg. The trainer says, "We're gonna get the poison out."

But that doesn't mean it won't bite you!

I'm a nervous wreck. So I'm watching and they milk the snake, and I notice now that the trainer is trying to get this snake and he's being very careful how he's going about it. I say [*whistles through his teeth*], "C'mere a minute," and I ask him, "If that snake has no poison, why are you being so fucking careful about grabbing that snake?" He says, "Well ... y'know ... sometimes..."

Sometimes there's some poison left!

At that point I tell Roger, "Roger, before I do this scene, you get somebody to tape that snake's mouth." They say, "Yeah, but we like it [untaped], you see the tongue and all that, and—" I tell 'em, "I don't care what *you* like. Either tape that snake's mouth, or get somebody else's legs." They finally taped the snake's mouth and the snake came over my legs. And I gotta tell ya, and Mary Lou will verify it: I had nightmares for weeks after I got back, about that ... big *fuckin'* snake [*laughs*]!

Before we get away from the jungle and snakes, were things any better making Jaguar?

That was for Mickey Rooney's company—it was with Sabu, and the gal in it

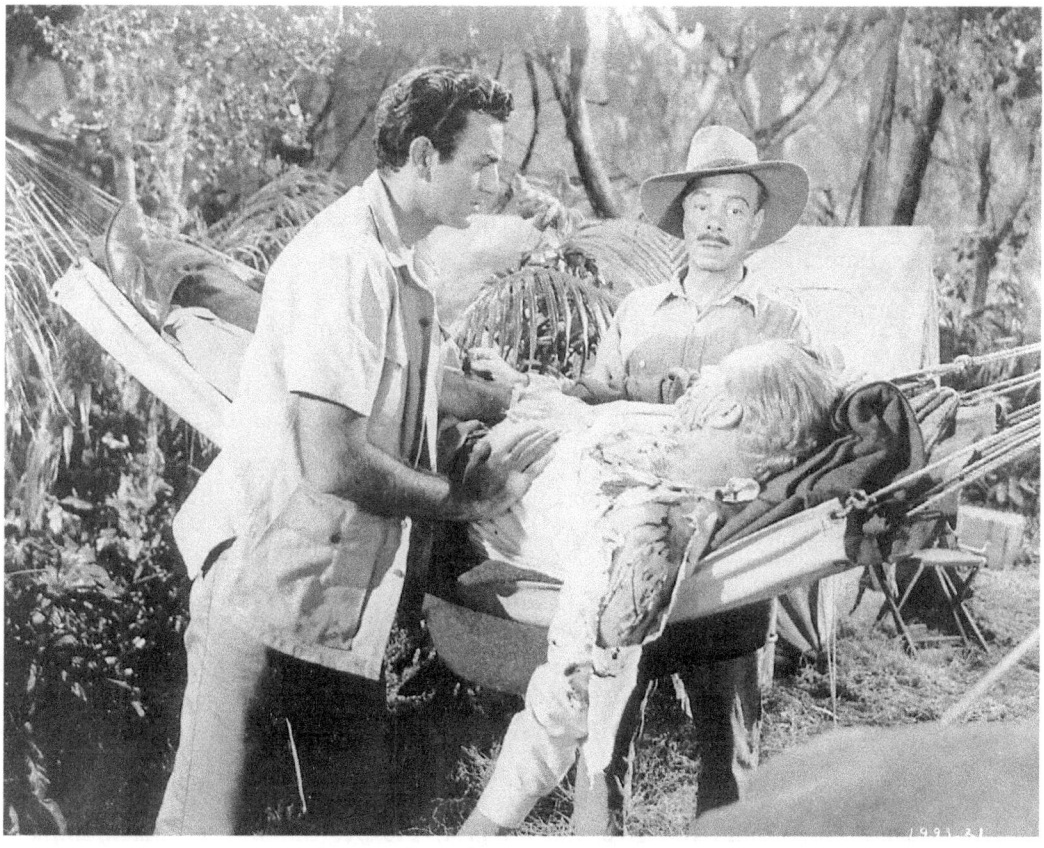

Wreaking hammock: The body of Barton MacLane is examined by Connors and Jay Novello in a grisly scene from *Jaguar*.

[Chiquita] was a dancer, from the Chiquita and Johnson dance team. Did you see the scene where I get knocked in the river and the piranha eat me? In the picture, I played a character who put on this jaguar outfit and killed people and made it look like the animals did it. So I'm in this outfit on a raft, Sabu and I are fighting, he throws me over the side and I go under and the piranha eat me alive and kill me. Well, the first couple times we try it, the tail of the jaguar outfit comes to the surface. They say, "Jesus, it doesn't look like he's being eaten alive, because the tail is floating up here!" Finally they put a weight on the tail, and then when I got pushed off the raft, that weight kept the tail down and I stayed underwater for, I dunno, half a minute or whatever it took to do the thing. That's how they got the shot.

There was also a snake in Jaguar.

They had a boa constrictor. And it was a big mother. But as long as the tail isn't anchored, those snakes can't apply enough pressure to squeeze a man. A stuntman was going to double Sabu in a scene with the snake. Well, somehow the snake got its tail anchored and got around him, and damn near killed him. Three, four guys got in there and grabbed the snake and pried, pried, and got the stuntman loose, and he was almost gone. They barely saved him.

As I told you, Mickey Rooney was the producer of that. He also directed me in a picture called *The Twinkle in God's Eye* [1955]. Mickey signed me under a contract, and I did a pilot film which was called *Daniel Boone*. But about the time we finished shooting it, Disney came out with Fess Parker [as Davy Crockett], so that was the end of *Daniel Boone*. But then I did *Twinkle in God's Eye* and *Jaguar* for Mickey's company.

Early on, if you could have written your own ticket, what kind of roles would you have played?

I'll tell you, my favorite actors in those days were Clark Gable, Spencer Tracy, Bill Holden. Those types of roles, I would have liked—the very natural-type acting. But I don't think I had really set a "niche." I knew the type of acting I liked, that very natural type of acting—but I just wanted to be successful. So ... whatever. I was willing to do anything that they'd hire me for.

Getting back to Roger Corman and AIP—did you get any direction from Corman, or just where to stand when you started talking?

It was pretty much "Do it quick." There wasn't a lot of acting direction going on. For him, it was where to set the camera and how to make the most use out of the time he had. You were pretty much on your own.

Most of your seven AIP movies were produced by Alex Gordon.

Loved him. Would you give him my best? He was the one guy that I think *every* actor liked—everybody that worked for that company liked Alex. He was just one of the top terrific guys. I believe he was responsible for a lot of actors coming back to do *more* pictures for AIP. A lot of people, had they dealt with Sam Arkoff on those AIP pictures, would have said, "Screw." But Alex was such a sweet, wonderful guy that, when he'd call and say, "Hey, listen, we got a new project...," you'd say, "Okay, Alex."

So you knew Arkoff and Jim Nicholson too?

I liked Nicholson, I think he was the real brains behind the actual picture-making. Arkoff was the businessman. Sam never met a man he didn't like ... *to screw* [*laughs*]! As far as I was concerned, he didn't have a lot of integrity. You never knew what he was gonna do. And he was always angling, maneuvering ... always had that phony smile on his face and a great big cigar. Well, the proof is that Nicholson couldn't even get along with him, they finally split. I'll never forget, I produced a picture for AIP back in the '50s called *Flesh and the Spur* [1957]. I raised the money, we shot the picture for $117,000. In color. Pretty good cast. No better, no worse than 90 percent of the pictures that AIP put out. We never saw a *dime* profit out of it. Now, AIP made millions off of that type of picture ... but *my* picture "didn't make a dime." So Arkoff's bookkeeping was [suspect]. And Arkoff would just smile and say [*sweetly*], "Well, y'know, that picture ... somehow it just didn't take off..." Then, in the '80s, I decided to produce another picture, called *Too Scared to Scream* [1985]. A friend of mine, a very wealthy friend wanted to get in the picture business, and he said, "I'll put up the money." I kept telling him, "It's not a good investment," but he said, "I don't care. I just wanna *do* it." So Tony Lo Bianco came to me with a script and he said, "I want to direct this," and the timing was right—it was a [horror movie script], and this was about when all those horror pictures were popular and making money. So we put together the project, got the money and we had a pretty good cast lined up: It was Anne Archer, myself, Ian McShane...

Maureen O'Sullivan.

Maureen O'Sullivan, John Heard ... a lot of 'em said they would work for scale because they knew Tony or they knew me and we gave 'em little pieces of the action. I didn't know whether I wanted to try and get distribution *before* shooting or after the picture was completed, so before we got ready to shoot I called Arkoff and I said, "Sam, I'd like to talk to you about something." Up until this point, there was no animosity or anything—I knew what he *was*, but... So I went in and I explained, "Sam, I'm getting ready to shoot this picture and I'd like a little advice about distribution, I know *nothing* about distribution. Do you think I should get distribution ahead of time, before we start shooting, or wait to take a gamble on it? Tell me a little bit about distribution." He said, "Lemme tell you *this*: Why don't *you* just stick to acting and let *us* stick to producing?" I said, "Well, Sam, I'm *gonna* produce—" and he said, "Well, you're making a big mistake, and... There's nothing I can tell you." And I left. *That's* Sam Arkoff. It would have cost him nothing to spend a few minutes and answer a few questions for me. I wasn't asking him to distribute it. If he'd *wanted* to distribute it and he'd said, "Hey, I'll give you so-and-so," I would have been willing to listen. But he just completely said, "Screw off."

Some time later, I got a call from him—they were going to honor him somewhere and so he was calling people, asking if they would make an appearance. I said, "I'm just really too busy," and I wouldn't go. I never talked to him again.

I don't blame you. You were the underpaid star of many of his earliest pictures—what a way to treat you later on!

I just never respected Sam Arkoff, I just thought he was not a man with integrity and not a nice man. And I wasn't alone in that feeling.

AIP's Day the World Ended *with Richard Denning, Adele Jergens, Raymond Hatton—what memories?*

Adele Jergens for many years lived just three doors away from me, she and her husband Glenn Langan. She was terrific, I loved her. Bawdy gal. And Raymond Hatton was just great, I enjoyed working with him. He told great stories about the old days and was a delightful old guy. But the best memory is that Denning and I became very, very good friends. In fact, we even went into business together many years later, when he was living in Hawaii. We formed a corporation over there and bought some land in Hawaii together. I loved him, he was just a sensational guy, and his wife Evelyn [Ankers], who by that time had quit acting, was terrific. We spent a lot of

Years before his name change to Mike Connors and long-running career in TV law enforcement, the actor (left) added a touch of menace to exploitation items like Day the World Ended **with its three-eyed monster star Paul Blaisdell (right).**

time with Denning and his wife, and as I say we formed this little corporation together, he and his accountant and myself. We at one time had ten bungalows set around a hillside on the Big Island of Hawaii, with a central pool and bar, and used to rent out those little cabanas to different people.

Does anything come back to you about the making of Day the World Ended?

I remember that, in the movie, practically the entire Earth was devastated by the atomic blasts, or whatever the blasts were. In the little house where we survivors were staying, we had all the curtains closed—and when we looked out through the curtains, we had to be *vvvvery* careful that the camera couldn't see out through the curtain, because there was nothing devastated *out* there! You'd peek out, this little peek like this [*Connors pretends to be parting curtains a fraction of an inch*], to make sure that [the camera] couldn't see [*laughs*].

You worked for Corman four times in one year, 1954–55—then never again.

I had co-starred in four pictures for him, $400 a picture. So I decided that I was going to call him and tell him I wanted a raise. I called him at his office—his office was a couple doors away from Scandia, which was a very terrific restaurant.

He had an upstairs *office near that restaurant.*

Right. In those days, to have a lunch at a restaurant like that was unheard of for me. So we came down the stairs *and*—instead of turning left to the restaurant,

Gangster Connors gets tough with moll Adele Jergens on the *Day the World Ended*. In real life, the two were friendly neighbors. (Notice onlookers, top left.)

we turned *right* to the STOP sign and crossed the street and went into Turner's Drug Store, where they had a sandwich bar! And we sat down at the sandwich bar and he said, "Order anything you like!" [*Laughs*]

I think I ordered a tuna sandwich and a cup of coffee, sitting on the stool at the counter, and I said, "Roger, I've done a number of pictures for you for $400 a movie. I'd like a raise." He said, "All right, you're right, Mike, you're right..." And he raised the coffee cup to his lips and he looked at me and he said, "I'm gonna give you ... uhhhh ... $1200..." "Wow," I thought, "1200!" If he'd said 500 a picture, or even *450*, that would have made me happy. As Roger took a sip of his coffee, he saw my eyes go big, and he put the cup down and he added, "...For three pictures." [*Laughs*] I said, "Roger! That's *still* $400 a picture!" and he said, "Yeah, but I'm gonna give you *three pictures*." And that was the end of my working for Corman.

Did you enjoy working as fast as directors like Corman and Voodoo Woman's *Edward L. Cahn would work you?*

It was good training, let me put it that way. It's much like the difference between shooting television and a feature today. I'll tell you another anecdote about working for AIP: I'll never forget, when I produced that picture *Flesh and the Spur*, one day Arkoff and Alex Gordon and I guess Jim Nicholson called me in the office. We hadn't started shooting yet, and yet I was told, "This is how we're gonna promote the picture," and they showed me artwork that depicted Marla English on an anthill,

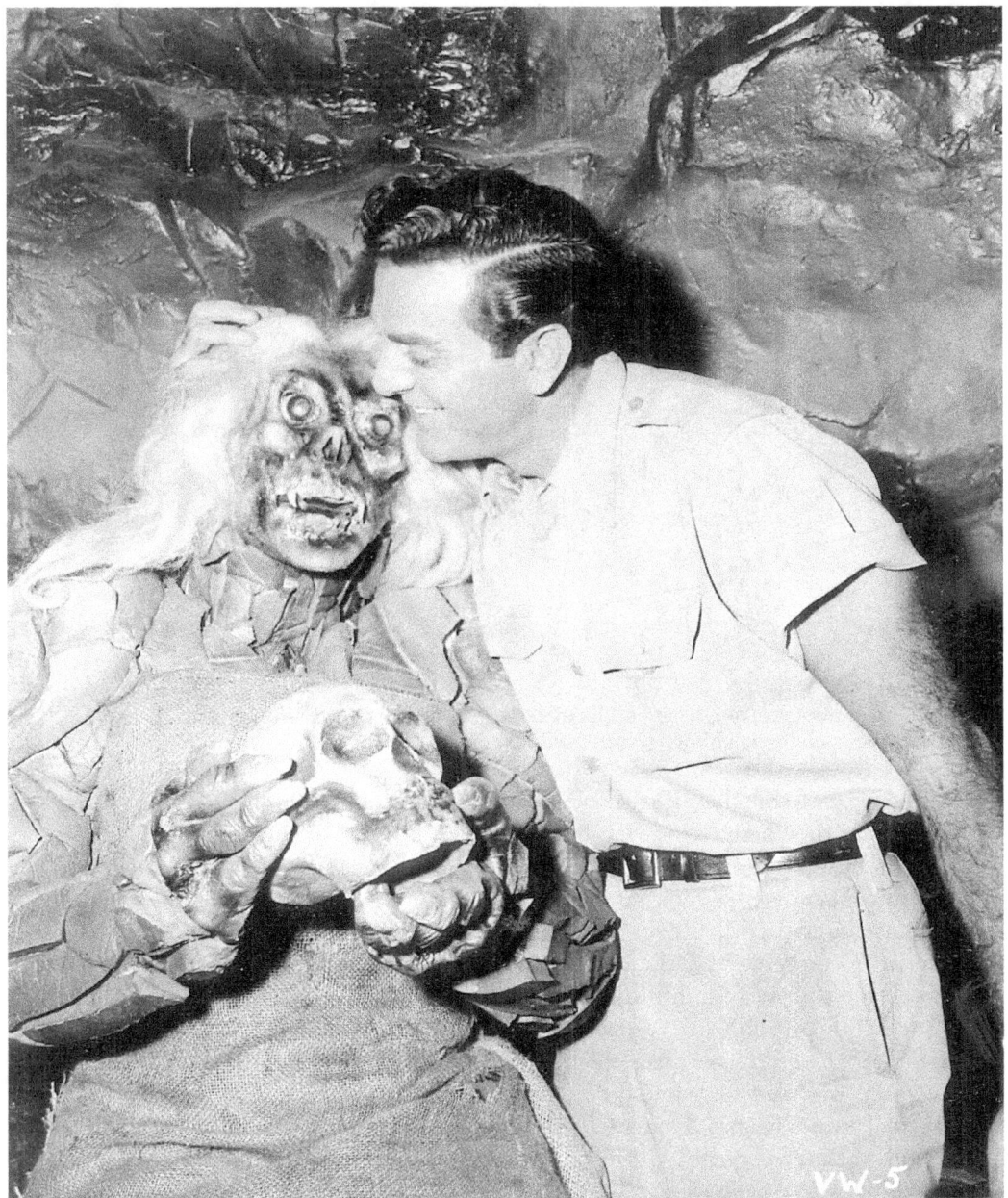

A Touch of romance: Connors makes time with a female monster (played by Paul Blaisdell) in a *Voodoo Woman* gag shot.

staked out, with Indians around her. "Fellas, that's beautiful," I said, "but we got no Indians *in* the picture. There are no Indians, there's no anthill, there's nothing like that in the script." They said, "Well, that's the thing we're talking to you about. We're gonna have to put in a scene." I said, "You mean, right in the middle of the picture, suddenly a bunch of Indians appear and grab her and put her on this anthill and disappear?" They said, "That's right, because this is how we're gonna promote the picture!" [*Laughs*] So that's what happened! AIP sold *all* their pictures on the promotions—the poster was always the most important thing.

Marla English was also in Voodoo Woman.

I don't remember a lot about *Voodoo Woman*. I remember that they had set the jungle up on a stage, and you could only shoot about ten feet at a time. Then they'd move the camera and shoot ten feet going the other way [*laughs*], and then ten feet sideways and ten feet *this* way. It was kinda difficult to visualize what you were trying to put over, it was tough to be seeing a jungle that was only ten feet by ten feet square and picture yourself deep in the heart of Africa! Marla, though, was terrific, I liked her *very* much. She stayed to herself quite a bit, but she was a very pleasant gal to work with.

Did you ever get into a movie that was so bad that you thought, "This is gonna hurt me"?

Yeah, about *five* of 'em [*laughs*]! Most of 'em AIP Corman pictures!

Can you name one where you reeeally thought, "This is not good, what I'm doing here today"?

I thought *Voodoo Woman* was going to be a joke. *Jaguar* was another one. *Sky Commando* [1953] with Dan Duryea was another one that, about the second hour of shooting, you knew it was going to be a disaster. It was a war picture using a lot of war footage. We were supposed to shoot that picture in six days. Well, the day before we would have finished, the camera department called and said the last two days of shooting were completely unusable—there had been a camera malfunction, or a hair in the gate, or I don't *know* what. Dan Duryea turned to me and he said, "Hey, guess what? We're gonna get a couple of extra days shooting, we're gonna *finally* make some money from [producer Sam] Katzman." The next day was the end of the original six days, and Katzman came on the set and he said, "Well, thank you very much, fellas, that's a wrap." We said, "W-w-what about the two days of scenes that are unusable?" He said, "Aw, don't worry about it, fellas, we'll put in more stock footage!" [*Laughs*] So in essence, the picture was shot, basically, in four days worth of production!

Was there ever a point at which you thought, "I've done so many B pictures, it's going to be too tough to progress beyond this"?

Yeah. Television is what saved me—doing that series *Tightrope* was what really changed everything around for me. We did 44 episodes and it was in the top 20, and the reason it went off the air was Jim Aubrey, who was head of CBS. We had a pharmaceutical company sponsoring us—in those days, *one* company sponsored a show, and they pretty much had the say-so as to what happens to your show and what you're doing—they either said, "We'll take it" or "We won't." This pharmaceutical company had bought a time, nine o'clock on Tuesday night, and they'd had that for years with CBS and never made a score. Every show they tried, bombed. *We* [*Tightrope*] came along, and we were a hit. And Aubrey said to the pharmaceutical company, "I want to change your show to ten o'clock on another night"! The pharmaceutical company said, "*No*! We've bought this time for three years and we've finally got a hit, and now you want to move it?? *No*." Aubrey said, "Either move it, or you're through." They got pissed off and they said, "Okay, we'll go to another network," and they left. That's why the show didn't continue. ABC wanted it an hour show, we did it as an hour and it didn't work as an hour. So ... the show went off the air.

Did it ever air on ABC as an hour show?
    I'm not sure. Also, when it went to an hour, they said that I had to have an associate, and I told 'em right from the beginning that it would not work. Because the whole premise was this guy, all by himself, "on a tightrope." But in those days, they didn't think it was possible for one man to carry an hour show, and so they wanted [to introduce a sidekick]. I said, "When he gets a sidekick, it loses the threat and the danger, and the whole premise is in the toilet."

Is it true that you were offered the opportunity to replace Raymond Burr as Perry Mason?
    What happened was, again I was used as a foil [*laughs*]. Raymond Burr was giving 'em a bad time, and he refused to come to work. So they called me and they said, "We want you to do a *Perry Mason*, and if Raymond Burr doesn't come around, *you're* the Perry Mason."

You become Perry Mason.
    Yeah. So I did one *Perry Mason* ["The Case of the Bullied Bowler," 1964] where they said that Perry was out of town and he called in his best friend to come over and take over the case, so I took over the case, and he wasn't in the episode at *all*. Well, about two weeks later, Raymond Burr signed the deal and he was back as Perry Mason.

At the height of the James Bond movie craze, you played a Bond-like CIA agent named Kelly in the send-up Kiss the Girls and Make Them Die.
    That was a lot of fun. We shot that in Rome and Brazil ... Rio de Janeiro. It was a wonderful experience. Dino de Laurentiis produced it. I had a two-way wrist radio ... if I put my heel down, a dart would fly out of my shoe ... Terry-Thomas was my driver of the Rolls-Royce and he'd pull over to the side of the road, press a button and a big billboard would come out and we'd be hidden behind the billboard [*laughs*] ... real James Bond-type stuff!

It's a spy movie that sort of "fell through the cracks," but it couldn't have been a cheap picture.
    No, Dino spent a lot of money on it. I'll never forget, we were getting ready to shoot and Dorothy Provine, who used to be under contract to Warners, was cast [as an undercover British agent]. De Laurentiis comes over to Brazil and he looks at Dorothy—Dorothy was kind of a plain, all-American gal. "Hold it," he says. "I'm taking her back to Italy, and we'll start shooting in a week." So I'm sitting in Rio

Going *way* out beyond the call of duty, Connors did stuntwork atop Rio de Janeiro's towering Christ the Redeemer statue in the spy spoof *Kiss the Girls and Make Them Die*.

de Janeiro for a week doing nothing, waiting for Dorothy. When she comes back, you would never believe the transition in her looks. They did something with her eyes, they gave her a new hairdo, they made her a wardrobe—and she comes back lookin' like the most sophisticated, beautiful thing you've ever seen. I mean, it was a shock. Then we started to shoot.

The high point of the movie—literally!—is your fight scene on top of the Christ the Redeemer statue in Rio.

That statue is on top of Mount Corcovado. The mountain is 2300 feet, and *then* the statue [almost 100 feet tall]. In one of the main sequences, Kelly is being chased by the heavies and he goes into that statue and up the stairway. At the top of the statue, at the head, there's a hole about the size of a manhole cover; he gets up through that, and a helicopter comes with a rope ladder and picks him up off of the top of the statue.

We had done all the fighting, the hanging over the sides of the statue—we'd done all of that. But for *this* [the helicopter stunt], I said, "I'm not gonna do *this*." They said, "We'll get a stuntman." Incidentally, we were the *only* company the government down there ever allowed to shoot on that statue, and they'd given us, like, two days. And at the end of the second day, the director Henry Levin said, "Mike, you're finished. The stuntman will be here pretty quick to do the last shot." That was the only shot we needed to complete the sequence, and it was the last we could use the statue.

At the bottom of this statue, there was a little bar and, since I was all through shooting, I was sitting there having a drink, waiting to see the stunt being done. This little Volkswagen drove up and out came this Portuguese stuntman. (The producers had trouble finding a stunt guy—most of the Portuguese are pretty small, and the producers wanted a guy that was on the bigger side.) He got out of the Volkswagen and he was standing by the car and a local man that we had hired as an interpreter was talking to him in Portuguese. And then I saw the stuntman get in the car, turn around and drive off [*laughs*]! I found out later that when the stuntman had been told what to do, he said, "What are you, crazy?" and he left! Jesus Christ, the whole sequence was dead without [that capper], what were we gonna do?

The helicopter was circling, waiting for the order to come in and pick up ... whoever. And so I said, "Fuck it. *I'll* do it." So I climbed up there—

You had to walk all the way up again?

Yeah! So I went back up there and I got out of the hole and I was sitting there, and it was really windy. I started to stand up, and I *couldn't* stand up—we had to wait 'til the wind died down. Incidentally, when you fly into Rio, the airliner circles that statue as it's coming in to land, and the pilot usually tells the passengers a little story about it. The story that he told when *I* came in was that, when they were building the statue, the natives didn't know that they *were* building it. The statue was unveiled for the first time at night, with a bunch of spotlights and stuff. On that night, at the unveiling, they turned on all the lights and there was this 100-foot-tall statue up there. Well, all the natives looked up and saw this light and they saw this Christ figure up there, and they thought—

The Second Coming!

Yeah! Anyway, the pilot told this story on my plane just before it landed. So now I was sitting up there on top of the statue and, sure enough, here comes the airliner [*laughs*]. It was just about level with me and I was waving at it, and I was wondering what the people on it were thinking, seeing me sitting up there!

Finally the winds died down, I got ready to stand up and the helicopter came. As it came around, I grabbed the ladder, hooked a foot into it. It kinda flew straight up and *stopped*, and then brought me right straight back down, and I got back *into* the hole and went inside the statue. But he'd lifted me off enough so that [the scene worked]. That was the first time I knew what people meant when they said, "I got weak in the groin": When I stood up there, I had that strange feeling.

But you weren't really scared of heights—needless to say, I guess, or you probably wouldn't have done the stunt.
Heights never bothered me in those days. Back then, I could climb over the edge of a building, do *anything*, heights didn't bother me. But *today*, if I get up on a tall place and look over, I get a funny feeling. It's strange how, with age, it's changed. Incidentally, I had a picture of me standing up there on the Christ statue, with my arms out *like* the Christ statue. *TV Guide* got ahold of the thing and they were going to use it, and then—I don't know whether it was [*TV Guide* founder Walter] Annenberg, but *some*body said, "I think it's a little too sacrilegious." And so they didn't use it.

Was the idea that, if Kiss the Girls *had been a hit, you would have continued as Kelly?*
I don't know what their thought was. Originally I was strongly considered for the role of Matt Helm [spy-hero of four 1966–69 movies beginning with *The Silencers*]. But what happened is, they signed Dean Martin to play Matt Helm and put me in *Kiss the Girls*—they were basically the same type of bigger-than-life character [Matt Helm and Kelly]. Unfortunately, the two pictures [*Kiss the Girls* and *The Silencers*] came out just about the same time and, with Dean Martin in the other one, of course our picture got lost in the shuffle. The Martin picture got all of the publicity and "push" and ours just kind of dwindled away.

Whose idea was it for Kelly to occasionally stop, sometimes even in the middle of action, and eat a banana?
I forget now *what* the reason was for that, I don't know why that was put in there. I don't remember whether that was lead to something that was cut out, or *what*.

What do you think of Kiss the Girls?
I think it was pretty well done. I think it *should* have gotten a little better reaction than it got. I thought it was funny, had a good sense of humor, and I was pretty happy with it. And, by the way, Terry-Thomas, that English actor with the gap in his teeth, he was wonderful. We'd be out in the middle of the jungle shooting and his wife would show up at lunchtime and she'd set out a blanket and spread his lunch out for him. The rest of us would be eatin' box lunches, and he'd be sitting out there with the silverware and wine and the this and the that. And he'd say [*Connors pretends to be drinking tea, pinky finger extended, English accent*], "Because we are in a barbaric country, we don't have to *act* barbaric." [*Laughs*] I loved it, he was terrific.

Murder suspect Harry Madsen keeps police lieutenant Connors at bay in *Too Scared to Scream*, **Connors' second stab at motion picture production.**

When you produced Too Scared to Scream, *you said that if it made money, you'd be happy to make another picture. And you didn't make another picture. Does that mean it did not make money?*

The fellow who put up the money, a guy named Ken Norris of Norris Industries, got his money back. But I did not enjoy the process of producing. I found that many times I had to say to the director Tony Lo Bianco, "You can't have another day on that location," *knowing* as an actor that he should have it, to make it *work*. But financially we couldn't, I didn't *have* the money. He'd look at me like I was crazy and I'd say, "Tony, I *know*. To do this thing right, you need more time there. Or you need *this* or you need *that*. But—we can't *do* it. I just don't have the money and I can't *raise* any more money for it." And I didn't like having to say no when I knew the answer should have been *yes*. So I didn't really enjoy it. Producing is not for me, unless you've got unlimited money and you can do what you want.

You were involved in President Reagan's presidential campaign, and during that time you became very interested in the inner workings of Washington. Are the law—and lawmakers—still an interest of yours?

I've become completely disenchanted with politicians, and I'm not into the political scene any more. For a while there, I got pretty active in it. But nowadays, after [former California Governor] George Deukmejian, the last person that I really felt was completely honest and above reproach, there are not many that I trust. I'm sick and tired of politicians only worrying about what's good for the party rather than the country and the people, and I just don't respect most of them.

What now career-wise?

I've pretty much retired. I do a few things now for charity—I just participated in a two-hour special for the legal system to help the mentally ill. And then I did another p.a. for a bunch of doctors who are going to Europe, mainly Armenia, to operate on the eyes of young kids free of charge—set up medical trucks and stuff. I did a fund-raising thing for them. But other than that, I'm not doing much, really. The last thing I did was a couple years ago, I did a movie [*Gideon*, 1999] with Christopher Lambert, Chuck Heston, Carroll O'Connor, Shelley Winters. It was about a bunch of people in an old folks home, and it was quite a good picture.

But you're still getting offers, I bet.

I've had a few offers to go and meet [people], about pictures and stuff. The last one I *almost* went to: They're shooting it now, it's a comedy, and the director's a big director, Barry Levinson. I was tempted because it was a cute part—not a big part, a small part. They wanted me to go in and talk to him about it, but I didn't go in. I just don't have the drive or energy to do it any more. I enjoy playing golf when my back lets me ... having breakfast with friends...

There isn't anything you miss?

I miss some of the camaraderie and all. But the business is so different now. It's not the same feeling these days when you go on a set—it's almost like it's everybody *against* everybody. At least, that's the feeling *I* get, which may be wrong. But [in the old days], if I heard that, say, Paul Picerni had gotten a good part, I was thrilled to death. [Picerni, co-star of the 1953 horror classic *House of Wax* and the TV series *The Untouchables*, set up and participated in this interview.] But today, it's almost like everybody *resents* the other guy getting something.

> **Paul Picerni speaks:** *This man is one of the most generous guys in the business. When he was doing* Mannix, *and a lot of guys like me were looking for jobs, he would give the casting director a list of his friends like Paul Picerni, Dick Bakalyan, Tige Andrews, whoever, and he'd say, "If ever a part comes up that these guys fit, I want you to put 'em in." As a result, every year I would do a* Mannix. *Not too many guys would do that.*

Well, to me, the business was a thing of friendship and people helping each other.

Susan Douglas on Five

> When Five *came out, people just pooh-poohed the idea ... people just didn't think that this [an atomic war] would be possible.*

"After the Bomb" movies became a recurring sci-fi subgenre in the 1950s–'60s, with entries ranging in cost and quality from mainstream dramas (*The World, the Flesh, and the Devil, On the Beach*), to the more exploitative, drive-in-style likes of *Panic in Year Zero!* and *Last Woman on Earth*. The first of the '50s films to explore the theme still holds up as one of the most intriguing: Writer-producer-director Arch Oboler's low-budget indie *Five*, shot on Oboler's own Malibu ranch, and starring William Phipps and Susan Douglas as two of the five fortunate(?) souls mysteriously left alive after a new type of bomb, one that kills without destroying, wipes out the rest of the peoples of the Earth.

Five's leading lady was born Zuzka Zenta in Vienna and studied dance as a child, before the war in Europe sent refugees fleeing for safety throughout the rest of the world. Arriving in New York with her mother in 1940, teenage Zuzka learned English from going to the movies (three a day) and changed her name to Susan Douglas. (Zuzka is Czech for Susan, Douglas she picked out of a phone book.) She acted on New York radio, the stage and in short subjects, then made her movie debut in 1947's *The Private Affairs of Bel Ami* with George Sanders.

Other film roles, including *Forbidden Journey* (1950) with her future husband, opera singer-actor Jan Rubes, followed before the diminutive (five foot) blonde landed the role of Roseanne—the Earth's entire female population—in *Five*.

Did you intend, right from the start, to be an actress?

I really wanted to be a dancer, and I took ballet lessons from the time I was about eight, in Prague. When I got to New York, a lovely person got me an audition with George Balanchine [founder of the New York City Ballet], and he said, "You're too short. You'll never make it. But you're such a beautiful interpretive dancer, why don't you consider acting?" I liked acting too—but I *really*, really wanted to be a ballet dancer!

How old were you when you talked to Balanchine?
　　I was 14 and I was still in high school, George Washington High School in Manhattan. When I graduated at 16, I began looking for a job. I started looking for auditions in radio, because radio was the *big* bread-and-butter time. It was easy to get auditions, because there was *so* much radio going on. Movie people weren't doing any radio, and theater people *were*. So it was theater people and those who started in radio, like I did. Radio was wonderful for all of us, because there were all the soaps. You'd run from one soap to the other. And in those days, you had to do a soap opera twice: You had to do it in the morning for the East Coast and in the afternoon for the West Coast, because it was live. There was really quite a lot of work, we worked all the time. Do you know a guy named Hi Brown?

I've met him, that's all.
　　Hi Brown was an incredible guy—he produced *so* many radio shows, and he was hysterical. You'd bump into him on the street and he'd say, "You want to do a show a week from tomorrow? I'll give you five dollars." You'd look at him and you'd say, "Come *on*, Hi…!" And he'd say [*off-handedly*], "If you don't wanna do it, I'll get somebody else. That's okay." [*Laughs*] A wonderful director, great sense of humor, he had a wonderful art collection, he was a wonderful guy … and the cheapest producer I've ever known!

Were you on some of the "better" shows, too?
　　Yes, a lot of them, including *Theater Guild of the Air*. One of the *Theater Guild*s I did was "Little Women" with Katharine Hepburn, and I played Beth. In those days, those shows were with an audience, and evening clothes, at a theater, and there was always a party afterwards. Lawrence Langer, who was the head of the Theater Guild for years and years and years, was at the party that followed "Little Women." The Theater Guild was casting a Russian play by [Leonid] Andreyev called *He Who Gets Slapped*, and he asked me to audition for the ingénue lead. I did and I got it, and that was really a big breakthrough.

That was your Broadway debut?
　　Right.

Was The Private Affairs of Bel Ami *your first movie?*
　　That was the first movie. But in those days, if you really wanted to make movies and be a movie actress, you had to sign a seven-year contract. After *Bel Ami*, that's what I was faced with—either a seven-year contract or … nothing! All the studios did the same thing, sign people for seven years. If you were lucky and you did well, that was terrific; and if you didn't do well or if you didn't do what they wanted you to do, they would suspend you without pay and *not* loan you out. It was very strange. For anybody young who is working now, I don't think they could understand what it was like. The director of *Bel Ami*, Albert Lewin, used to work for MGM, and through him MGM offered me a seven-year contract.
　　Anyway, I didn't really like [Hollywood] very much. I mean, it was fun doing

In her breakthrough stage role, Susan Douglas played the ballerina in Broadway's *He Who Gets Slapped*.

the movie and they were very nice to me, but it was not a place I was going to *live*. So I went back to New York, which I loved, and knew everybody, and did a lot of work. So … that was my experience with a big movie studio.

Your second movie, Lost Boundaries *[1949], was shot in Keene, New Hampshire.*
    A very, very interesting movie based on an actual story of a doctor in Keene

who was colored and passed as a white. (When we met the family, actually, I thought they looked Cuban.) He was a wonderful doctor and the town adored him, and when World War II came, he applied for a Navy commission. But when they found that he had gone to a black medical school, the Navy denied him the commission—in those days, they didn't give a commission to a black man. And when the town found out that he was black, they ostracized the family. The doctor had two children, a daughter and a son, and the son eventually committed suicide because he couldn't cope with it. It was terrible. Eventually they moved. That's the true story—the movie didn't follow it. Mel Ferrer played the doctor, and I played his daughter. It was quite a wonderful movie for me because they dyed my hair black, they gave me dark contact lenses (they wanted my eyes darker), and I was 22 playing 15. It was a great part, I loved it. It was shot in a sort of a semi-documentary way, and it did very, very well. *Reader's Digest* magazine was the co-producer of the movie.

The screen's number one cad, George Sanders, broke the heart of Douglas (et al.) in her feature film debut, *The Private Affairs of Bel Ami*.

Acting on prestigious radio series brought Douglas in contact with legends like Charles Laughton.

You and William Phipps were the stars of Five. *How did you get that part?*

I don't think Arch Oboler and I ever discussed how or why I got it. I just got a call from my agent, who said that he was sending the script of *Five*. I was living on 53rd Street between Lexington and Third Avenue at the time. I had just read a horrible script, something that we decided *not* to do, so I was anxious. I liked the script [of *Five*] a lot, I really thought it was very imaginative. I liked the whole idea of atomic dust rather than an atomic bomb, and all living matter is destroyed and all man-made things *stay*. And I was anxious to meet Arch Oboler anyway.

So, before Five *came along, were you aware of Arch Oboler.*
 Oh, yes. Have you ever heard any of his radio shows? He wrote wonderful stuff, and always ahead of his time, I felt. He was very respected in that medium, by *everybody*, because he did it so well. He came to New York and we went out for dinner, he said, "I'd love you to do the part" and I said, "I'd love to do it." That was that [*laughs*].

Oboler had the idea for Five *years before he made the movie. The first time he did that story was as a radio show with Bette Davis.*
 I never heard that show. By the way, I think it was unfortunate for him that he didn't have a big name in the movie, and that it was made at least two, three years too early. When *Five* came out, people just pooh-poohed the idea. And it was too bad, because later on ... what was the movie with Ava Gardner?

Oh, On the Beach *[1959].*
 On the Beach. Which wasn't the same as *Five*, but it was very similar. It was a big hit. But in 1951, when *Five* came out, people just didn't think that this would be possible. So Oboler didn't really get the attention that I think, a few years later, he would have had. And if he thought up the story some years *before* [he made the movie], it shows you his mindset. He was a very intriguing personality, very much ahead of his time. Even his radio shows were quite macabre and quite ahead of their time. Maybe because it was radio, people were more likely to believe [an end-of-the-world story], whereas with the film *Five*, there it was in front of your eyes. If audiences decided, "This is impossible," then of course it was sort of dismissed.

In preparing to shoot Five, *Oboler was supposedly offered plenty of star names, but he chose to make the movie with unknowns.*
 I can't believe that. That's just my opinion. I think, if he had been offered an Ava Gardner, he would have gotten her! Perhaps he offered it to a lot of "name" people, people who felt, "Oh, that's so improbable," and didn't want to be associated with it. For *me*, it just tickled my imagination, and I just thought it was a wonderful idea.

You shot the movie on Oboler's ranch in Malibu.
 That's right, up the mountain from Zuma Beach. Zuma Beach is a big beach, and going up from there, in the mountains, was the house where he lived. And on the *top* of the hill he had a guest house that was designed by Frank Lloyd Wright, a wonderful house. It was a six- or eight-sided house, and all around were big windows, huge—I'd never seen that many. That's where we were shooting, that was supposed to be my house in the movie. Oboler's house down below was a normal-looking, average house; I think he'd had it for many years. It wasn't a very

interesting house, the one below. The guest house above was architecturally very interesting, but the house down below was a relatively ordinary looking house. A long house, narrow and long.

The cast and crew lived at Oboler's house throughout the shoot.
That's correct. I stayed up in the guest house while we were shooting. The other four actors stayed down below at Arch's house—it had some extra bedrooms. And the crew stayed in a tent! They didn't have enough room [in Oboler's house]. They lived in a tent, and the actors stayed in the house. So it was interesting!

How many rooms in the guest house where you shot the interiors?
It just had sort of like a living room-dining room area, although it wasn't formal like that, it was just a large room. And then one room off it, which was the bedroom, and a bathroom and kitchen. That was it. There was very interesting, very rugged terrain all around us. They wouldn't let me walk anywhere outside alone because there were rattlesnakes. If I wanted to go somewhere, one of the crew members would go *with* me, with a little pistol. Actually, I have a picture of myself and the second cameraman with a pistol—he had just shot a rattlesnake. Very strange ... but very good for the "feeling" of the movie [*laughs*]!

The movie starts with you walking through the wilderness back to your house, with the wind blowing like crazy. Was that a wind machine?
No, there was a storm! There was an actual windstorm, and Oboler just shot me walking through the windstorm and it was great. The scene wasn't written specifically with wind, but it worked out very well. He was lucky. But remember at the beginning when she [Douglas' character] looks into the car and she sees a skeleton? I thought it was too early in the story for that.

Presumably the atomic dust just killed everybody, and you're walking back to your house from the city.
That's right. And the audience can't be expected to think that I've been walking home for *so* long a time that a body would have become a skeleton. I just thought that that was too early in the story ... unrealistic. Unnecessary.

How did you keep people off Zuma Beach when you were shooting scenes there?
First of all, we were there early. But also, it was not a beach that was that popular. Zuma Beach at that time was not that close to a lot of houses. We shot in the morning, and there just *wasn't* anybody.

Was it as cold on the beach as it looks in the movie?
No, it was the middle of the summer. But it was *so* windy, that makes it *look* cold.

Oboler's crew was made up of just a handful of students from USC.
Yes, and they were a wonderful crew. *Oh!* Their way of photography and what

they did with the mikes ... they were really marvelous. I think they all eventually went and worked on big movies—separately, not as a crew. There was a lot of friction between Oboler and the crew, because they had certain ways that they wanted to shoot things, and he wanted it a different way. There was a lot of compromising that had to be done. You can imagine, five vital, young, exciting students versus Arch Oboler. Since they also were getting peanuts, or getting nothing, they at least wanted to establish their capabilities. But Oboler was very much a dictator. So it was very interesting.

Was Oboler's wife around?
    Yes. Oboler was married ... *and* he had a girlfriend. All living together! Arch is dead, isn't he? Because otherwise I wouldn't tell ya [*laughs*]! He had a wife, and he had a secretary who was *more* than a secretary. And the three of them lived in the house.

And everybody knew.
    Everybody knew. And I don't think anybody cared. That was his way of life!

One of the Five *crew guys told me they once saw Oboler, the wife and the secretary, all three in one bed!*
    I never saw the three in one bed but I'm sure they must have been—it was definitely a *ménage à trois*! One of the crew guys told you that? Well, if anybody sees anything or knows anything on the set of a movie, it's always the crew [*laughs*]! A crew always knows everything on every movie! I've *nnnnever* seen anything like it, they are the most informed guys!

What did Oboler look like in 1950 when you made the movie?
    I'm trying to think who he would remind you of. Do you remember an actor named John Garfield? Well, Arch was not as handsome as a John Garfield type, but he *was* dark, short, wiry. Wore glasses. And he had a great sense of humor. He was a very sensuous guy.

According to an old article about Five, *it was made for about $75,000, and Oboler mortgaged his house to raise part of the money.*
    I don't know that, but that is very possible. I certainly can believe it was made for $75,000 because nobody made anything. *He* didn't get paid, he didn't have to pay locations, and the crew (who were all young, and quite wonderful), I don't think *they* were getting more than a hundred bucks a week. We shot it in four and a half weeks. *I* wasn't getting much either. I can't remember for sure, but it seems to me that on the whole movie I made $2000.

William Phipps, your leading man, says he got the minimum S.A.G. salary and a small percentage.
    I didn't get a percentage, but I don't think the movie ever made anything. It's called a percentage of nothing [*laughs*]! And even if the movie *had* done better, I'm

Five's a crowd when an arrogant German mountain climber (James Anderson, left) intrudes on Douglas, Charles Lampkin (background) and the other survivors.

sure Arch would have written everything off. Quite understandably. He didn't pay himself for the script, he didn't pay himself for directing, so if there *had* been some money made, he would have quite rightfully taken the money. If *I* were he, I would! I don't think my agent thought there was much point in trying to get a percentage. I did *not* know that Phipps had a percentage. I wish him well [*laughs*]!

Was it a union picture?

Oh, no [*laughs*]! There wasn't a union person on the picture other than us actors.

According to Phipps, Oboler wouldn't watch as a scene was being filmed, he would just listen.

I can't tell you that it was actually so, because when I was in a scene, I wasn't watching Oboler, I was doing the scene! Maybe Phipps, when he wasn't in a scene, maybe *that's* when he would observe Oboler. But it was close quarters when we shot inside the house, so it was hard for Oboler. In those days, there were no such things as the TVs where a director could watch as it was being filmed. The crew was on top of each other, there was hardly any room. So if he *did* just listen, it's understandable.

Phipps was an interesting boy. He got the part because of Charles Laughton—did he tell you that?

Phipps told me that Oboler saw him in a play directed by Laughton, and that Laughton said that Phipps was his best actor.

Incidentally, I worked with Laughton in two different episodes of *Theater Guild of the Air*. I did "Payment Deferred" with him, he played my father. We spent quite a lot of time together, because we went to Washington D.C. [to do "Payment Deferred"]. He took me to the Mellon Museum, and to go with Laughton to see paintings was just incredible. He explained and showed you things in a painting that I would never have dreamt of looking for. He was incredible. A very, very interesting man.

Have you got any anecdotes about the actors in Five?

No, not really. Because they lived down below and I lived up at the top, there wasn't as much camaraderie as there would be if we were all staying in the same place. We all ate dinner together down at Arch's house, and then one of the crew men would walk me up to the guest house, because of the rattlesnakes around. I went up to the guest house and there I stayed. It wasn't like I could run in and out or back and forth or anything. After dinner, I just was up there. So while they were having (I guess) a fun time, I was up in solitude [*laughs*]!

As far as working with the actors, what kind of director was Oboler?

He was very good. I think he liked the actors. And I think we all liked *him*. We all thought he was very good, and we were a little bit in awe of him, you know.

Phipps told me that Oboler hit one of the crew members one day.

He did. I was there. And afterwards, I went with the crew into L.A. We left. The crew packed up, they were leaving, and they asked me if I would go with them. I said yes. But we went back to work the next day.

So you all walked out on Oboler for a day?

We walked out, yeah. I don't really remember exactly what caused [the fight]. It was probably one of those "frictions": Maybe Oboler wanted a set-up in a certain spot, and *they* wanted a set-up in *another* spot 'cause they said it would work better and it was easier. Anyway, before you know it, Arch hit one of the guys ... and the guy hit him back. There were bloody noses and stuff, and the other guys had to pull them apart. It was awful.

The crew guy did hit Oboler back?

Oh, yes, they hit back and forth—both of 'em had a little blood flowing. And it was scary, because we were in such a desolate place there. I was scared by the whole thing. It happened outside, on the balcony of the guest house.

And everybody still got along together again after the fistfight?

Oh, yeah. Right after the fight, the other actors all stayed there at Oboler's—

I was the only one who went with the crew. I stayed overnight at the house of one of the crew members, Art Swerdloff. He was married and he had two kids. And we all came back the next day and nobody said anything about anything.

Swerdloff was the guy in the fight with Oboler.
That's right.

Even he cooled off?
Oh, yeah. Those things happen. We all had a nice dinner at Art's house, a dinner that his wife made, and we had quite a bit of wine. And the next morning, we just all got together in the station wagon and went back.

I'm not sure I'd have been as forgiving!
You know, when you're tired, and there are artistic arguments, things can happen. There was more friction between Oboler and the crew than Oboler and the actors. We all had our parts, we knew what we wanted to do, it was what *he* wanted us to do and we agreed. So…it was different. But every set-up for the crew was a different thing.

None of Five *was shot in a studio?*
No.

How did they make you look pregnant in some of your scenes?
We just put a pillow in … that's it! And, actually, I thought it looked quite all right. The only thing that really struck me as strange was, in some of the scenes near the end, I was supposed to hold a baby. I was supposed to *run* holding a baby. And when it came time to do those scenes … they gave me a baby! I asked Arch, "Why are we not using a doll? You can't even *see* it." He said, "No, no. I want you to 'feel' this baby." I said, "Could I meet the mother that's stupid enough to allow an actress to *run* with a month-and-a-half-old baby?" I mean, I was supposed to *fall* with the baby! I could never understand that! But Oboler was a stickler for things like that, and I suppose that, if the mother was willing… [*laughs*]! *I* would never let an actress take *my* baby and run through the woods and stumble!

Whose baby was it?
I have no idea who the woman was. Oboler said to me, "I don't want you to talk to her. You'll talk her *out* of letting us use the baby." [*Laughs*] I mean, use the real baby in a closeup, all right, *that* was bad enough, but we used that baby in all the scenes that you saw me running and stumbling. All that was this live baby. And in some of the later scenes, the baby was supposed to be *dead*! *That* was the part I couldn't understand. Arch kept saying, "Just hold it tight. Don't let it move!" It was mad!

The really fun part was when we went into Glendale to shoot the city scenes. Of course, we had to shoot it at about five in the morning, so there wasn't a living person around. And if there *had* been, Arch Oboler would have just asked them to move [*laughs*]! So it was fun shooting that part…

What time did you have to get up to get to Glendale by five A.M.?
   We actually went into town the night before, and stayed at a hotel.

Oboler had a hard time finding a company to distribute Five.
   I know. Nobody thought that anybody would go and see it because they wouldn't believe it. It wasn't believable enough in their opinion. So, yes, he *did* have a hard time.

After Five, *did you go back to New York?*
   Oh, I went right back!

Were you already married to Jan Rubes when you made Five?
   No, not yet. Jan was doing an opera tour, going through South America, and I was doing *Five*. The phone bills were heavy [*laughs*]! We got married September 22, 1950, right after I made *Five*. We got married in New York at noon and went to Montreal in the afternoon for the opening of a movie that night.

Which movie?
   The movie that Jan and I had met on: We made a movie in 1949 called *Forbidden Journey*, shot in Montreal. They had a big opening, and Joe Ferrer was the master of ceremonies. The three of us flew from New York to Montreal on our wedding day.

Did you stay in touch with Oboler as he looked for a distributor?
   Not really.

Were you involved in any premiere activities?
   They had a premiere in New York, and I went. I think I'm the only one who lived in New York, *they* all lived in L.A.

What were you called upon to do at the premiere?
   Oh, just stand up [*laughs*]! Just an introduction and a stand-up and a wave! It was at one of the theaters on Broadway, downtown. It was fun. But the movie didn't get any publicity, really. And this kind of a movie, at that time, would have needed a lot of pushing. Columbia just didn't do that. It didn't run long in New York.

You just saw Five *again, for the first time in 50 years. What was your reaction?*
   My reaction was very much like when I saw it originally. I think if Oboler had had a couple of "names," he would have done well with the movie. Watching it again also reminded me of the discussion I had with Oboler, after I read the script, about the character of my husband, Steven.* I felt that Steven should not have been with

---

*Throughout the movie, Douglas' character wonders whether her husband Steven might still be alive. In the final reel, she finds his skeleton in a waiting room at the hospital where she was being X-rayed when the atomic death struck.

An impressive theater display for Arch Oboler's *Five*, prominently featuring Douglas.

her at the hospital. For sure, no matter *how* distraught she was, she would have looked for him and seen his body before she left the hospital.

He would have been very easy for her to find, yes. But instead of looking for him in the waiting room where she knew he was, she walks home!

That's right! Also, I asked Arch, "Is Roseanne ill? Why would Steven have gone to the hospital with her and waited while she went into the X-ray room?" Oboler said, "Well, because she thinks she's pregnant." And I said, "Well, you don't go into an X-ray room to find out whether you're pregnant!" [*Laughs*] The business with the husband—we discussed that several times, but Arch wouldn't give in. He said, "It's perfectly okay. It'll be accepted." Fine!

But other than that, considering there were five crew men, and no makeup person, no costume person, no nothing, I thought it came off quite well.

Everybody did their own makeup?

Oh, yeah! And it was hard, because we didn't shoot in sequence. Not that it bothered me, except the bit with the lipstick. I said, "Why don't I not wear *any* lipstick?" I didn't care! I said, "It'll make it so much easier," but Arch said, "No, no. Wear the lipstick." I told him, "I'll never remember how much lipstick was left at the end of a scene, when three days later we do the *other* part of the scene." I would have preferred to play it without *any* makeup. Along the same lines, Bill Phipps had to keep cutting his own beard. But he kept it the same pretty much all the time, so that was a little easier.

So you're saying that the amount of lipstick you wear in the movie sometimes changes within the same scene?

A little bit. But I don't think anybody would have noticed it except me. I was aware because I remember being concerned about it when we were shooting. And so I was *looking* for it all the time.

And the performances?

I thought they were pretty good. I thought it was an interesting group of actors. I always liked the old man [Earl Lee]. Well, I liked them *all*. I always thought that, at the beginning, James Anderson played Erik [an arrogant mountain climber] with maybe *slightly* more of an edge than I would have liked to have seen. I thought he tipped off the audience very quickly, that he was the bad guy. Is he not alive any more?

Douglas and her future husband (singer-actor Jan Rubes) met on the Canadian-made *Forbidden Journey*.

No, they're all dead except you and Phipps. Just like at the end of the movie!

How funny. By the way, Jan watched it with me the other day, and he thought it was pretty good. He said, "Oh, you were so pretty!" [*Laughs*] Oh, God … 50 years. That's a long time.

Did starring in a movie help your career at all?

Not really. I came back to New York and went back to the radio shows—the soaps. Whenever I worked outside of New York and then came back, I would call those shows that I was on and tell them I was back. Sometimes I played the same part, sometimes I played different parts. On *The Guiding Light* I'd *always* played the same part, *Backstage Wife* I played the same part, and *Our Girl Sunday* too.

Jan and I wanted to have

children, that was a big thing. Jan was an opera singer and a concert singer and traveled all over, but we wanted to have children. Well, Procter & Gamble decided that they would let *The Guiding Light* be the first TV soap, they decided they would try it out and see how it would do. It was a 15-minute radio show and it became a 15-minute TV show, live. And they asked all of us that played the leads on the radio show [to work on the TV show] and we all said yes, we would do it. It was kind of a fun idea. Every day was like performing one act on stage, because it was live. And for Jan and me it was lovely because, if we were going to have a baby, then I would only be working from eight to 12 in the morning. (Other kinds of work, like the theater, were not very conducive to having a family. For instance, if you were in a play in those days, you'd have to go out of town—the plays were all tried out in New Haven or in Boston.) So for Jan and me, *The Guiding Light* was perfect. And indeed I had two of my babies while I was working on the show. The people on the show were really very good to me: My character on the show wasn't married, so for me to have a baby in real life [but not on the show], they had to do some rewriting. The first baby I had while I was working on *The Guiding Light*, my character was sick and in an oxygen tent for about five months. The second baby, the character had an accident and was in a wheelchair, so I was in a wheelchair on the show for five months, covered with a blanket. They had to write *something* that was *not* having a baby! When I had the third baby, Irna Phillips, who was the writer, the wonderful writer, she said, "Listen, Susan, I can't cope with this any more. I'm gonna kill the character." So they did. But I was on for seven years.

Apart from The Guiding Light, *were you on TV much in the '50s?*
   I did a *lot* of television. I did I-don't-know-*how*-many episodes of *Studio One* and *Robert Montgomery Presents* and *Kraft Theatre*. And they were *live*. You rehearsed for two weeks and then you played it, and there it was. Those were very good and big times for me. I played the lead on one of the *Kraft* shows with Jimmy Dean, one of his very first parts. Nobody thought he'd ever be as big as he was—he was very shy and very inarticulate at the time. Sweet, sweet boy, but none of us ever thought that he would do a lot, and we *never* thought he could do any theater because you could hardly hear him. He spoke like this. Very quietly.

After The Guiding Light—*is that when you and your family moved to Canada?*
   Yes. Jan was anxious to move to Toronto, so after I was killed on *The Guiding Light* and I'd had the third little boy, we moved to Toronto. 1959.

And you kept busy up there too?
   I spent a lot of time, the first few years, at home, but I built a theater and ran the theater, the Young People's Theater in Toronto. We were one of the very, very first, in 1963, that took plays to schools. And I've worked on TV and in a few movies since.

What does the future hold?
   Well, now I'm enjoying playing golf and tennis and tooting around when Jan

Today, says happily retired Susan Douglas, "I play with grandchildren and stuff like that."

does a movie. And I play with grandchildren and stuff like that. Here and there, somebody will call, a director or somebody, and say, "Would you like to...?" I did a small part a few years ago in *Black and Blue* [1999], a TV movie of the week, but it was because the director called and asked me if I would play a 70-year-old lady for him, and I said sure. I did a part in *Due South*—do you know that series? It's a Canadian series but it's popular here. I played a Russian spy in that. It was fun. But I don't actively look for anything. If a director calls and says, "Would you like to do something?" I'm delighted. But I don't actively pursue.

Five (Columbia, 1951)

93 minutes (89 in Britain); Screenplay, Production Design, Produced & Directed by Arch Oboler; Cinematographic Consultant: Louis Clyde Stoumen; Music Composed & Conducted by Henry Russell; Orchestrations: Charles Maxwell; Editor: John Hoffman; Sound: William Jenkins Locy; Photography, Editing and Production Assistance: Sidney Lubow, Ed Spiegel, Louis Clyde Stoumen & Arthur L. Swerdloff (Through Arrangement with Montage Films, Inc.); Executive Secretary: Geraldine Klancke; Music Editor: Betty Steinberg; Cliff House: Frank Lloyd Wright; Special Sound Effects: Gus Bayz; Poem "Creation" Written by James Weldon Johnson

William Phipps (*Michael*), Susan Douglas (*Roseanne Rogers*), James Anderson (*Eric*), Charles Lampkin (*Charles*), Earl Lee (*Mr. Barnstaple*)

Arnold Drake on The Flesh Eaters

> *I told [a potential investor in* The Flesh Eaters*], "Look, this is crazy, this can't work. Frank Sinatra is in no position to do this kind of film." And he kept saying, "Frankie owes me, Frankie owes me..."*

One of the bridges between the black-and-white, "family-friendly" horror films of the '50s and the no-holds-barred gorefests of later decades, director Jack Curtis' low-budget *The Flesh Eaters* (1964) stands tall in the annals of indie exploitation. The storyline is standard issue: A drunken Hollywood actress (Rita Morley), her pretty secretary (Barbara Wilkin), a handsome charter plane pilot (Byron Sanders) and a jive-talkin' beatnik (Ray Tudor) are marooned on an Atlantic island with a Germanic mad scientist (Martin Kosleck) who has filled the waters around it with voracious microscopic creatures. This bare-bones premise, however, allowed for a succession of bare-bones *victims* and a number of additional shock scenes of a sort then new on the horror film landscape, all staged and enacted in an unmistakable "comic book" style.

The comic-book influence on storyline, dialogue—even shot composition—was a key part of the contribution of Arnold Drake, *The Flesh Eaters*' writer, co-producer and storyboard artist. A native New Yorker, Drake began his show biz career creating radio and TV material for such diverse personalities as Milton Berle, Xavier Cugat and Frankie Laine, but his greatest fame grew from his work on the comics scene, where he has attained near-legendary status for his contributions to such well-remembered titles as *Challengers of the Unknown*, *Deadman* and *The Doom Patrol*. His comic-book sensibilities inform and enhance *The Flesh Eaters*, which he recalls from conception and Long Island production to exhibition.

Whose idea was it to make The Flesh Eaters*?*

Jack Curtis and I, and Terry, Jack's then-wife, set out to make a film ... but we didn't know *what* film we were going to make. Actually, we had wanted to make a film in Greece—*not* a science fiction film at all, but a melodrama with a "socially conscious" center to it. We were all set to do that, and then we were advised by an English producer who had worked there that the conditions were impossible, in particular the labor conditions. He said, "They will walk off in July and tell you they won't come back until you put money in the Christmas fund," things like that. He really shook us up with that, all of a sudden we had great misgivings. So we said, "Look, let's do something nice and fairly simple." There are few instances of more-mistaken words being spoken, because *The Flesh Eaters* turned out to be *not* very simple. But we decided to do a science fiction. I sat down and wrote a science fiction storyline, the three of us agreed on it, and then I wrote the script.

This was around '61? '62?
  1960, I think, was when it began.

Was The Flesh Eaters *your first screenplay?*
  Yes, it was. I've written four features, and three were produced. And thank God the fourth one wasn't [*laughs*].

I know Flesh Eaters *and* Who Killed Teddy Bear? *[1965] were produced. What's the third?*
  There was a film called *50,000 B.C. (Before Clothing)* [1963]. Softcore … a couple of girls running around without tops on. The world's worst comedy. Dreadful! The guy who produced it wanted to produce another film of mine, bought a script from me, and didn't do it—and I blessed him for that!

What were your influences when it came to writing Flesh Eaters*? Were you a fan of horror movies? Of horror comics?*
  I was into science fiction. I read Jules Verne as a kid, I was into H.G. Wells as a kid, I was into Conan Doyle. A lot of people don't know that Conan Doyle *was* a science fiction writer—he wrote four or five stories, including *The Lost World*, about Prof. Challenger. So I had those influences early on. Then in the late '40s I got into comics when I was going to school on the G.I. Bill, and when I needed extra money, I started writing 'em.

Who was Jack Curtis in 1960? All I know about him, outside of The Flesh Eaters, *is that he was a dubbing actor.*
  Yeah, and also a very good sound editor. And pretty good with a camera. Although he had not a great deal of experience, he had been [working with cameras] as an amateur since he was about 16 years old.

You and Jack Curtis and Terry Curtis—did you all live in Manhattan at that time?
  Oh, yeah. Terry, like Jack, had done a lot of voiceovers. Terry had also written a lot of subtitles, and had written dubbing scripts—in fact, Terry became very adept at writing dubbing scripts, which is not an easy thing to do. I tried my hand at it and I failed miserably [*laughs*], 'cause you've got to really be able to see those mouth

The men who made *The Flesh Eaters*, Arnold Drake (as rendered by Luis Dominguez art) and Jack Curtis.

movements and I *couldn't* with my 20-400 eyes. Terry was very useful in the making of *The Flesh Eaters*, but her *most* significant contribution, I would say, was a lot of money that she won on a quiz show [on *High Low* in 1957]. You remember the quiz show scandals? Well, Terry was involved with one of those shows, and she won $70,000. She put up almost half of that [for *The Flesh Eaters*].

Funny story that goes with that: Terry wanted to take advantage of the fact that she had won this money. She was an attractive young woman, and an actress, so she was looking for publicity. She said, "I feel that this is my 'moment,' I've gotta *grab* it right now. They're about to present me with this big check. I've got to find some way to get some extra publicity out of it." So I said, "I don't think that should be *too* difficult. Lose the check." She said, "What do you mean?" I said, "Whoever finds a check like that can't cash it, a $70,000 check. So if you lose it, it really isn't lost." She asked me, "Well, how would I *do* that?" I said, "Put it in your handbag, then give *me* the bag. I'll take a bus ride and leave the bag on the bus." She said okay and we arranged this story that she would be at her beauty parlor when she suddenly realizes that she is without her bag and she calls the police. I left the bag on the bus; when I got off, I think the only person left seated on the bus was this rotund young black man who, as it turned out, found the bag. He immediately went to the network and told them he found the bag with the $70,000 check. And Terry's picture wound up on the front page of *The New York Post* the following day [*laughs*]. So that's how we cashed in on Terry's quiz show. Incidentally, the [*High Low*] producers had the young man who found Terry's bag on the bus make a guest appearance on the next episode, for p.r. purposes. I was there in the studio, and I had to skulk around in the shadows because I feared that he might remember the guy with the leather hat who was sitting where the bag was and say, "Hey, that's the guy who dropped the bag!"

You must have been chagrined to see him there. It sounds almost like a situation out of some old sitcom like The Honeymooners.
I *was* indeed chagrined!

As soon as you started talking about Terry winning the money, you mentioned the quiz show scandals. Does that mean she did not win it on the up and up?
That's what it means. But I also want you to know that *I* was not aware of that for a number of years. She and Jack were able to keep that from ev-er-y friend and ev-er-y relative—they *had* to. They were wise enough to realize that *no one* was to be trusted, not even your partner. *Especially* your partner [*laughs*]!

I see "Vulcan Productions" in the opening credits of Flesh Eaters—*was that the name of your production company?*
Yeah. It got that name because our lawyer, a guy named Jack Rabinowitz, had in his desk drawer a couple of names that he knew were "clear" for incorporation. When we came to him and said, "We gotta get incorporated and we need to do it quickly," he said, "Okay. You're Vulcan Productions."

Who cast the picture?
The three of us did. We knew we wanted Martin Kosleck right off the bat. And we also had a male and female lead cast, because we were friendly with a married couple named Rita Morley and Ken Harvey. So we signed Rita to play the actress and Ken to play the pilot, and Kosleck to do what Kosleck was doing all of his life. Not play Joe Goebbels [*laughs*], but pretty close! Then we went down to Greenwich Village and we bought tickets to three different off-Broadway shows, one ticket each. We would all go to watch the first act of one of the shows individually, and then we'd meet some place and exchange tickets and watch the second act of *another* show [*laughs*]! As a result, we were able to screen about 20 actors and actresses, and that's where we found Ray Tudor, the guy who played the beatnik. He was marvelous, he was a helluva piece of casting.

Was he playing a beatnik in the play you saw him in?
No, he wasn't, but I've clean forgotten what he *did* play. He didn't play a beatnik but it was pretty clear that he could. Barbara Wilkin was in a production with Kosleck—Kosleck was doing *Tis Pity She's a Whore*, a seventeenth-century melodrama, and Barbara was in that. We knew we wanted Martin, we went to see Martin just to talk with him backstage, and there we saw Barbara. So we asked her to come up.

"Come up" where? Did you and Jack Curtis have an office?
We later had offices on 57th Street but we didn't have them yet. So we were using Jack's apartment—Jack was living on 56th at the time and we were using that

as our office. If you could stand the stench from about 13 cats. They never cleaned up the crap! There were two hallways in that apartment, one of 'em was the cat's john and *no*body walked through there! Barbara came up and she read for us and she impressed us. We didn't have to have her read very much because we had seen her in *Tis Pity* and we saw her on something on public TV. She was real pretty and we knew that she could act ... a little bit. Roles like that don't *require* more than ... a little bit.

Sideline story: We're getting ready to go on location, and we're still short of money. We had a call out for casting Barbara's role, and actresses continued to come up even after we thought Barbara would probably do. And one *verrry* attractive woman—more attractive than Barbara by far—came up there, explained that she had no acting background, but said that she was a quick learner. And that her boyfriend was willing to put up as much money as we needed to finish the film.

"Okay," we said, "let's talk to him. There are ways and means to get a performance out of you, and if *any*body can do it, Jack Curtis can do it." She said, "Fine— but you'll have to go to Chicago to talk to him." The boyfriend took care of my tickets and, I think, my stay at the hotel. His first name was Chester. We talked, he and I, for a brief time ... he served champagne, if I recall correctly. He was in a suite right over Lake Michigan. Probably cost $300 a night *then*, so we're talking about maybe $2000 a night today. I gave him a quick idea of what the film was like and why I thought we could do it so inexpensively and why I thought it might be a real breakthrough film, all of that stuff. My favorite line was, "The star of our film is our *budget*," 'cause he kept asking, "Well, who's your star?" When I got done talking, he said, "Y'know, I like it. I think you guys might make a helluva film. And Frankie *owes* me." I said, "I beg your pardon?" "Yeah, Frankie owes me from way back. I'm gonna call Frankie."

Meaning Frank Sinatra.

Of course. I said, "You gotta understand, this is a *very* low-budget film. You're talking about a man who's just made a couple of very *high*-budget films." He said [*firmly*], "I *told* you. He *owes* me."

Chester was talking about getting Sinatra involved as an investor—not as an actor— right?

Oh *yes* as an actor! Oh, yeah, that's what was so insane about it. I told Chester, "Look, this is crazy, this can't work. Frank Sinatra is in no position to do this kind of film." And he kept saying, "Frankie *owes* me, Frankie *owes* me..." Chester was going to invest, but he said, "I'm gonna guarantee my money by getting Frank [to star]." I said, "We're talking about two different *worlds*, Chester. You can't make them *meet*!" [*Laughs*]

By the way, Chester dropped a couple of hints that he was probably in gun dealing. Probably. I thought dope when I first got there. But then, maybe dope with the right hand and guns with the left. At any rate, Chester had a lot of money, and apparently a fair amount of influence in a number of places. So he said, "Okay, it's a deal. I'm gonna get Frank to come in, and I'm gonna put up whatever you need."

I went home with my head swimming, saying, "This is *not* the film we started out to make. To do it with Frank Sinatra is gonna require a full union crew. We're gonna have to change our *whole* approach to this thing. Now we're talking about at least 700,000. ... But if *Chester's* willing to put up the extra 600,000..."

Anyway, the word from Chester was, "You will hear from my accountant." We waited several days and finally we heard from the man, and he said, "We've decided not to go with this venture." I'm sure Frank Sinatra said, "Are you out of your *brain*?" [*laughs*]—I'm sure that's the *first* thing that happened! I said to the accountant, "You made the mistake of looking us up in D&B [Dun & Bradstreet]? You should have looked us up in BD—Bad Debts! I think you would have found we were *permanent* there!" By that time, I was kind of annoyed—who the hell did he think he was dealing with? Two young people who were trying to make a picture with less than $100,000 are gonna be in Dun & Bradstreet?! So that was the end of that, we never got that beautiful girl. Maybe we were better off, 'cause ... Barbara was okay. I think she "works." Not great, but she works.

Any memory of how much you were paying these people?

The actors were paid minimum and a very small "piece" of the gross, to make up for the fact that they *were* only getting minimum. One of the extraordinary things about *The Flesh Eaters* is that, though it was made for about $95,000, it was done completely union. We went to the local electricians' union and said, "Look, we want to make this picture and we want to make it in New York, but we *can't* do it under your rules, it's impossible. You guys have to recognize that New York's never gonna be a real 'film city' if you're gonna adhere to these rules. There's no reason for anybody to move from Hollywood to New York if you've got the same kind of stringent rules here that they have there. They save nothing that way." Well, he *agreed* with us, and he said, "There's not a helluva lot that we can do about changing the rules right now, *but*—if you will get 50 miles out of the city, you will find you're dealing with union locals that are a lot easier to handle than *we* are." We asked for a suggestion and he said, "I'd try Long Island if I were you." So that's how we wound up in Montauk, and how we went completely union, because out there they didn't give a damn. As long as we had at least one licensed union electrician on the job, that was all they cared about. And we did *that*. So that's the story of how we were able to do a union film on a $95,000 budget.

You mentioned getting Ken Harvey to star in the picture—which he didn't. Why did he drop out?

Ken Harvey came to us about a week before we were to go on location, and he informed us that he had just been offered the job of stand-by for the lead in a new Rodgers and Hammerstein called *The Sound of Music*. And though he realized that he probably wouldn't get to play the role very often, just to be able to rub shoulders with Rodgers and Hammerstein was more than he could possibly ask for, and would we please let him out of his contract.

Theodore Bikel played the lead in Sound of Music. *Did Ken Harvey look like Theodore Bikel?*

He *was* a big guy. I told him, "Ken ... you're a friend, we're gonna let you go. But ... I understand Theodore Bikel hasn't had a sick day in his life..." [*Laughs*] By [bailing out] at the last moment, Ken had breached a very significant rule in "the book"—by "the book," I mean his own union. But we saw no point in trying to pressure him because we'd have an unhappy actor on our hands if he decided to go along with it. So Jack, Terry and the rest of the cast went on location while I remained in New York screening some more actors until I found Byron Sanders, the fellow who eventually played the lead. Nice guy.

In the credits, Carson Davidson is listed as the photographer—but every time I see a behind-the-scenes Flesh Eaters *shot, Jack Curtis is working the camera.*

The fellow we hired, Carson Davidson (known as "Kit," of course), had received an Academy Award nomination for a short documentary called *3rd Ave. El* [1955]. "Kit" was basically a documentary maker, a very good one, and an excellent color photographer. (In those days, if you were a documentary maker, you *had* to be a good photographer. 'Cause you didn't have the money to hire somebody!) But he hadn't shot black-and-white in years, and when he went onto the set and started shooting, it was pretty bad. So we replaced him with Roy Benson, a professional magician who was Jack's first cousin. We hired Roy originally to work on our props and special effects and stuff like that, but when we had to part with Carson Davidson, we realized that Roy *was* an expert photographer and so we said, "Roy, why don't *you* handle the cinematography?" He said, "Great!" Well, we knew that Roy was a heavy drinker but what we *didn't* know was that he drank whenever he was terribly anxious. And the assignment of a feature film, which he had never done before, made him so anxious that he just *got* drunk and *stayed* drunk. So we couldn't use *Roy*. At this point, we were on the set, we were a week into shooting, and we had rented a motel out there, we rented the whole place for a month. And so were into it for a fair amount of money, probably 30 or 40,000. So Jack said, "Let *me* try"—and he did. And it turned out that he was really quite good.

You rented an entire motel?

Yes, and we were fortunate in *getting* that motel. The motel was brand-new, about 300 feet back from the water. Nothing in between it *and* the water but a lot of beach. It was owned by a college professor and his wife who had arranged to build it as their retirement investment. That first year, they didn't do too well, because they were new on the scene and also because Montauk was not the kind of center that the Hamptons are. Not *then*—it is *now*. At any rate, when we showed up and became interested in renting that place, they were overjoyed, because our rental put them into the black. So their first year, they made a profit they never had expected. We rented that whole establishment, which meant everybody had his own room and a little kitchen, and then we made arrangements with the restaurant across the street to feed dinners. My wife Lillian prepared lunches and did all of the food shopping for us.

Why does Carson Davidson get credit as photographer if he did so little—or nothing?

Because he "covered" us. The reason for some of those names in the credits

Barbara Wilkin proves that some flesh looks more edible than others.

[names of people who didn't work on the movie] was union coverage. I don't recall now whether we paid them or *what*, but there were people whose names we got to use if we needed somebody to cover us on a particular front. This was one of the ways that we made a "union" film on that kind of low budget. You wanna talk about "handmade productions" [*laughs*]—*this* was a handmade production. A homemade, handmade production!

I can't help but notice that a lot of the shots look like panels out of a comic book.

I had a lot of experience in writing storyboards, 'cause I had been writing comics for years. So what I did was, I sat down and I did a storyboard of the entire script. On the back of each script page, I did a storyboard facing the next page. We introduced that concept to low-budget movies, and it helped a great deal. And, to "match" scenes, we were very early users of the Polaroid camera. You know the problem of matching scenes: A guy in one scene is smoking a cigarette, so when you shoot another part of that very same scene days or weeks later, he should still be smoking it, right? And is it in his right hand or his left hand, and so on and so forth. All of that's usually taken care of by the script girl. Well, we decided that, better than a script girl would be Polaroids. So every time we knew that a scene was going to be intercut, we would inform the actors that at the end of that scene, they must hold position. And while they held position, I would shoot a Polaroid. That went into the book, and we were later able to match scenes very easily as a result. That was something of an innovation.

Approximately how long did shooting take?

Well, we had two shooting sessions. There were these two bright fellows [Curtis and himself] who decided to make a movie on the tip of Long Island during September ... Hurricane Season ... without taking out insurance. Talk about windy! And lots of sand flies, which the women hated. And, of course, we got hit [by a hurricane]. At that point we were about two weeks into shooting, and we were wiped out—the sets were destroyed, etc., and we said, "Okay, we're going to have to come back again next year." So the film was actually shot over a period of a year—two weeks in '60 and two or three weeks in '61 is what I recall. In all, it probably took us five weeks to shoot it. We shot about one-and-a-half-to-one, which is ... kinda fabulous. Low-budget Hollywood films shoot three and four to one, and the *high*-budget—forget it! If it's Stanley Kubrick, it's a *thousand* to one!

Did you use a wind machine to get the sandstorm in Martin Kosleck's first scene? Or for the tent interior where the whole tent is shaking?

I don't think we ever used a wind machine. We created the wind effect on the tent by having people flapping the tent. And it *was* pretty windy most of the time we were out there, so it wasn't hard to get a sandstorm. You didn't have to rub two sticks together to get a sandstorm [*laughs*]!

Where were you when the hurricane hit? Were you shooting, or was it the middle of the night, or...?

As I remember, it hit in the late afternoon. We tied everything down as best we could and hoped and prayed. The next morning, we were pretty well wiped out.

When you say "the sets were destroyed," I'm afraid I don't know what "sets" you mean. You mean the tent??

Yeah, the tent, and we had that thing that I put together that was a mock-up of a giant solar battery. Things like that. We were wiped out and there was noth-

ing that we could do about it because there were actors' schedules to be considered. If we *had* gone back to work immediately, we would go way over schedule, and the actors would be [screwing up] *their* schedules. So it just had to be cancelled, and worked in again the following year. By which time we knew a good deal more about what we were doing.

Did you stay at the same motel the second year?

No, we did not. We stayed at another place, on Old Montauk Road, if I remember correctly. It was more a hotel than a motel.

Did you shoot in Hurricane Season the second year?

I don't remember whether we were able to get out there in the spring, before the season began, or whether we went back again in the fall. I think we probably tried to avoid Hurricane Season the second year. I read an interview with Martin Kosleck where he claimed that we were there in the fall both times in order to avoid the cost of being there on-season, but I *think* he was wrong.

Where did you get all the dead fish we see on the beach?

Our first idea was to make a

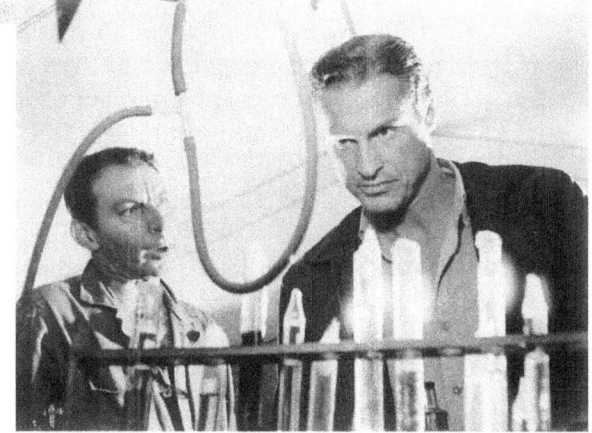

Even the *Flesh Eaters* still photos show the Drake influence, looking like comic book panels.

deal with one of the many fish supply houses out on Montauk, to give us barrels of fish skeletons. Well, what they gave us were these semi-filleted things which did not look at all like fish skeletons. Our prop man was a guy named Larry, who went on to make some softcore porn. But at *that* time, Larry's job was to turn those things into skeletons. Well, Larry couldn't find a way. Finally he tried lye, and the lye did the job—but all the bones came apart. For the one closeup of a fish skeleton, I think Larry did that with a knife—he managed to carve away most of the stuff. But when you see a long shot of fish skeletons, that's something that Lillian and Arnold Drake did that winter, sitting in their living room with a couple of scissors and a bunch of sheets of white cardboard. We cut out fish skeletons ... *hundreds* of fish skeletons ... which we then scattered around the beach for the long shots. And for the close shots, we used the real thing [actual, semi-filleted fish]. So that's the story of the fish skeletons.

Was everybody good about "pulling together" under these low-budget circumstances?
Pretty good. There was some friction, but generally speaking it was pretty good. Martin, who had a drinking problem, did not drink at *any* time during working hours. But the moment we were done working, *bam!* he was into it [*laughs*]! But he held off, he was very professional in that sense. So, yeah, there *was* friction, but it was nothing great. There was *far* less friction than you'd have on an average Hollywood picture, you can be sure.

You said the word "friction" three times, so you're begging the question...
You must recognize that Ken Harvey's wife Rita Morley was very self-conscious about the fact that her husband had done what he did, that he had left us in the lurch. She had a chip on her shoulder, and "the best defense is a good offense," so ... that's what she practiced. That was a source of irritation. I think she particularly focused on me because she didn't *know* me—she knew Jack and Terry fairly well but she didn't know me at all. So it was a lot easier to focus on me.

Were you bothered by beachgoers or passersby?
Not much. Long Island has probably 40 miles of the best beaches in the world, and that includes Hawaii, where Lillian and I spent a month a while back. *Continuous* beaches, just about no interruption whatsoever. Back then you could find a lot of very remote areas; *today* it would be much harder. Montauk's become quite a spot now, and Lillian and I often vacation there.

Do you ever revisit the actual Flesh Eaters *spot?*
Oh, sure!

How much of the Flesh Eaters *shooting were you around for?*
I was there for almost all of it, except when I would run back to town to raise more money. But otherwise I was there for the entire shooting.

What did you do nights, out in the middle of nowhere?
We worked. We worked 'til like two and three in the morning, Jack, Terry and

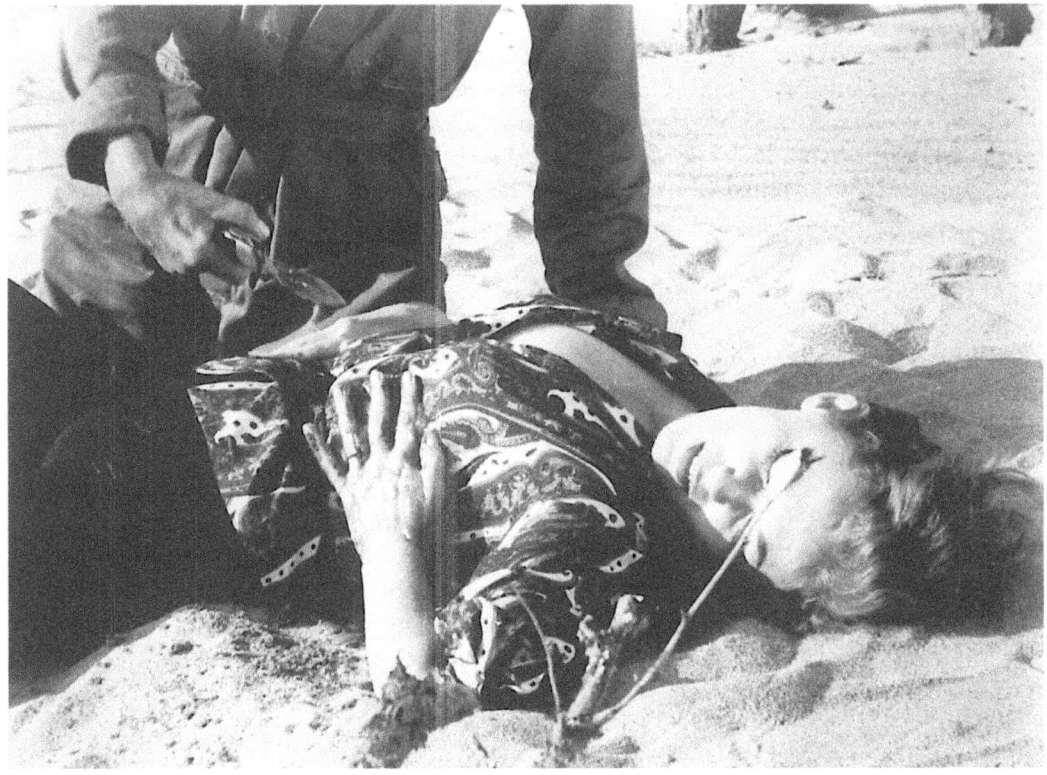

Cleavage *and* carnage: Knife-wielding Martin Kosleck disposes of buxom boozer Rita Morley.

I. We got half-drunk in order to be able to continue working on an 18- to 20-hour-a-day schedule, so there was a lot of vodka consumed, which helped us not to scream at each other when we felt like screaming at each other. We would line up new shots and figure out why something wasn't working and how we could correct it and so on.

Jack Curtis—I'm told he had only one hand.
That's true. He was born that way. But he played a pretty good piano.

With one hand?
Right. Well, he had the stump of the other, and he used that to play bass notes. And then with the right hand, he played melody. And pretty good! He had a good musical ear. And a very handsome man.

He was in his mid–40s when he passed away in 1970—how did he die so early?
[*Pause*] Well, basically, I think it was the result of a lot of alcohol over many years. But in the end, it was pneumonia. I loved Jack ... Jack was as close to me as a brother. Lillian felt pretty much the same way about him. We kinda helped Jack and Terry get together—they had their first date in our home. And it was very sym-

bolic that on that date, Jack took off his prosthetic and hung it up in the closet. That was always very meaningful to me.

He permanently stopped wearing it in real life.
Yeah. He came to terms with it. He assured himself that the reason he had it was that he was an actor—he appeared on stage, and now he was starting to appear on TV, and he needed another hand. But that was only partially the reason. I think the reason was ... he had not come to terms with it. And when he met Terry, I think, he decided, "This is the time to recognize who I am."

Why did he drink?
You would have to ask his missing left hand why he drank...

How large—or small—was the Flesh Eaters *crew?*
Probably five. Maximum five. Jack and Terry, and Roy Benson, and Lyn Fairhurst, an Englishman who'd worked in British films. I don't remember how we *got* Lyn—Jack found Lyn somehow or other. Lyn was quite useful, a sort of jack-of-all-trades kind of fellow.

In an interview, Fairhurst said that an actor named Christopher Drake, who's briefly in the movie, also worked behind-the-scenes.
That's true. He was Martin's boyfriend, which is how we got him, through Martin. Actually, we *wanted* to use him as the pilot and we tested him. But he was, again, so anxious that he got plastered, and wound up screaming all the lines. We knew that if we could work on him and get him sober long enough, he *might* be able to do it—but it was too big a risk. So we did not use him for that, but we used him for a bit role.

Was he considered before or after Ken Harvey?
After Ken Harvey.

Martin Kosleck's final closeup in the movie, after he's shot himself—is that him, or...
It's a life mask.

What was Kosleck like?
Martin was okay. As I said, he was an alcoholic, so he could be difficult after hours. But during working hours, he was splendid, wonderful to work with. The only time I had any difficulty with him was when we finished shooting him but we still had about a week to go on the schedule. We "released" him, but he said, "Do you mind if I stay?" We said, "No ... but we can't *use* you." He said, "Well, you've got a scene there where you see my legs approaching a body..." I said, "Yeah, but *I'm* gonna do that, Martin. We'll just use *my* feet instead of *your* feet." He said, "*No! No!* In a film that I make and where I play the character, I want *my* feet, *my* feet, only *my* feet!" So [*laughs*], I said, "Okay, Martin, but you know we can't pay you for that." He said, "Oh, *that's* all right, I understand that. You're paying for the hotel for me

A baddie off-camera as well, Martin Kosleck held up the producers for more money before he would agree to dub his scenes.

for the week and so on, so that's okay." Then when it came time to do the dubbing … Martin refused to dub until we gave him that week's pay. That was the only time I ran into a problem with Martin.

Did you pay him?
Oh, yeah, we had to. He would not dub his voice if we didn't do it. We dubbed the entire film.

I know it's Kosleck's voice—but do all the other voices that we hear belong to the actors that we see?
No, not all. Remember the dockside scene where the old fisherman [Darby Nelson] refuses to go out to the island with the supply boat? Jack dubbed him. Darby Nelson wasn't an actor, he was an assistant cameraman who, Jack decided, looked like an old fisherman. I think that's the only one who did not dub himself. That scene, incidentally, was the one scene that I wasn't present at—that's when I was back in town raising money. While I was away, Jack decided that the island atmosphere was getting claustrophobic, and he felt that he needed a point in the film where he could "breathe" a little bit. So he figured, "I'll do a cutaway to these two fishermen, and get away from the island for a minute." And so he put the scene together himself.

He wrote it and shot it? Out on Long Island some place?
Yeah. I looked at it and said, "Good job."

Are you in the movie?
Well, you will recall the pre-credits sequence on the boat with the boyfriend and girlfriend [Ira Lewis and Barbara Wilson]. The boyfriend turns on the radio, and Jack Curtis is heard saying, "And now for a real hot number from the Teen Killers!" The Teen Killers is what we called the group—except it *wasn't* a group, it was *me*! I wrote a song called "Pete's Beat," and there's a story behind *that*. I had written a couple of shows in the Army, and I wrote one of them with a guy named Jimmy Osmun. Real good jazz pianist, good musicologist. For *The Flesh Eaters*, we needed a number in that spot and we couldn't afford to buy one. So I called Jim and I said, "Have you got *anything* that's already recorded, that I could set a lyric to?" So he said, "Yeah, I cut a boogie woogie on an organ and we had that recorded." He

played it to me over the phone, and I said, "You know, it's got a very similar chord structure to 'The 1812 Overture.' I'm gonna write a lyric based on 'The 1812 Overture' and we'll see how it works." *That's* what I did, I wrote, "A guy named Pete who was the clumsiest gink/ Was on the dance floor when his girl spilled her drink..." And "The 1812 Overture" went right along with it. We went into a studio with *his* organ recording, and I whistled [whistles the intro to "Pete's Beat"] and introduced it that way, and then I sang, "A guy named Pete who was the clumsiest gink..." So I'm the whistler and singer, and Jim Osmun is the organ player.

And the name of this supposed group was "The Teen Killers."
Yeah. Because that's how we felt about teens at the time [*laughs*]!

In the end credits, an actor is credited as playing "Cab Driver," but he's only in the movie for a split-second. Was a scene cut?
Probably. What we were trying to do was to get the thing off the ground as quickly as possible. We had a preface which we thought would suck 'em in—the boy and girl on the boat, and that ending with her hand filled with blood. I think that preface said, "Hang arouuund...!" [*Laughs*] *Then* it got into a lot of talk, and we were *afraid* of that talk. We wanted to get as quickly as we could to the island. So I think we snip-snip-snipped a lot in order to do that.

Who made the Flesh Eaters that we see in the movie?
There were two. Just to confuse you, the big one in the movie [the building-sized Flesh Eater that rises out of the ocean] was small in real life and the small one in the movie [the Volkswagen-sized Flesh Eater on the beach] was big in real life. The big one, the one on the beach—that was the work of Roy Benson, the magician. *I* made the small one. Since we were using a blue drop-out [optical effects] process, when I painted that Flesh Eater, I used everything except blue. Well, if you use everything except blue, what you get are reds, oranges, pinks and so on. My daughter Pamela, ten or eleven at the time, said, "It looks like a birthday cake!" [*Laughs*] So it became known as "The Birthday Monster"—which she sometimes wore on her head!

Funny thing about the beach Flesh Eater: We had to truck it up and down for use in different areas, so we would put it on the back of this pickup truck and haul it wherever we needed it. Well, the wind would get under it and threaten to lift it out of the truck—it was a dome, and if wind gets under a dome, it's gonna take that thing right up in the air. Therefore, every time we took the thing out in the truck, somebody, very often myself, was assigned to sit *under* the monster and hold it down. We'd be driving along the highway and there'd be a pile of cars behind us, 'cause they were all curious as to what that thing *was*. And every once in a while, I would lift the monster up and I would *waaave* at them and then drop it [*laughs*]!

Do you know how Roy Benson made that Flesh Eater?
He did it with a fabric which he soaked in a chemical that softened it up [presumably celastic and acetone]; you could then mold it into anything you wanted,

and when it hardened, it was like a piece of wood. Roy built some kind of form and then he molded this stuff over the form and then removed the form. As I mentioned earlier, Roy was a magician, but perhaps more important he was a good "mechanic" of stage magic, a "designer" of stage magic. He helped other magicians to do their tricks, built things for them.

What about the effects shot where Ray Tudor's dead body is on the raft and there's a hole right through his midsection?
    In that scene of Ray on the raft, you see the backbone and the ribs [in the hole]. *I* painted the backbone and the ribcage on his body—I *personally* painted it. It was a pain in the ass: I knew I was gonna wind up doing it, so I had gotten myself a book on anatomy for precisely that reason. I was ready to use some plates from there, ready to copy those—but Jack decided he wanted [to shoot the scene] a day or two before I was prepared to do it. I said, "Okay, I'll wing it." So what you see there is kind of a wild interpretation of what *I* thought the backbone and the ribs would look like. It's like no ribs and vertebrae anyone ever saw [*laughs*]! But I think the shock was such that nobody examined the bones too closely, except maybe a couple of nerdy interns at the Hospital for Joint Diseases.

You just painted it on the guy's belly? Surrounded by a color—probably blue—that would disappear in an effects shot?
    Exactly.

Besides Montauk, where were some of the places you shot?
    The waterfront area at the beginning of the movie, where they charter the seaplane—that was 23rd Street in Manhattan.

And the Nazi flashback sequence?
    We didn't shoot that. That was added by Mike Ripps, the distributor of the picture, and it was shot probably in the South, which is where he lived. Do you know anything about Mr. Ripps?

My interviewees tell me he was a loud "dese, dem and doze" type. A real character.
    I think the term is *nut* [*laughs*]—that's what a psychiatrist would say. You and I might say a schizophrenic, but a psychiatrist would say, "He's a *nut!*" We needed a distributor who was willing to put some money up front, because we had run over budget. I told you the picture cost $95,000 and that's what we paid out in order to get the picture into the can. But we wound up owing over $27,000, so actually it cost more like 120,000 if I'm not mistaken. We ran over budget and we needed a distributor who would guarantee the money that we owed—that was our first demand. And there were very few distributors who were willing to do that. We had made the unfortunate choice—I won't say it was a *mistake*, because I don't think we *had* a choice. But we had made the unfortunate choice of shooting it in black-and-white. And that was a point in time at which TV was beginning to go over to color, and most every film was being produced in color—everybody was producing in color

to make sure that the theater owners would not turn them down. So we produced one of the last black-and-white films, aside from the "artistic" films that are made in black-and-white. And as a result, the distributors didn't want to handle it—that was the primary problem. They thought it was pretty good, we got a pretty good reception from them, but they said, "We can't sell it because it's black-and-white." *So*, we wound up making a deal with this crazy man Mike Ripps, who had a device that he would use where he would seat you under a lamp, a bright lamp, and question you from off in the darkness, like out of some Hitchcock film he had seen [*laughs*]. I realized that he was strange—*very* strange. But Jack said, "*I* don't care if he's crazy, as long as he puts up the money."

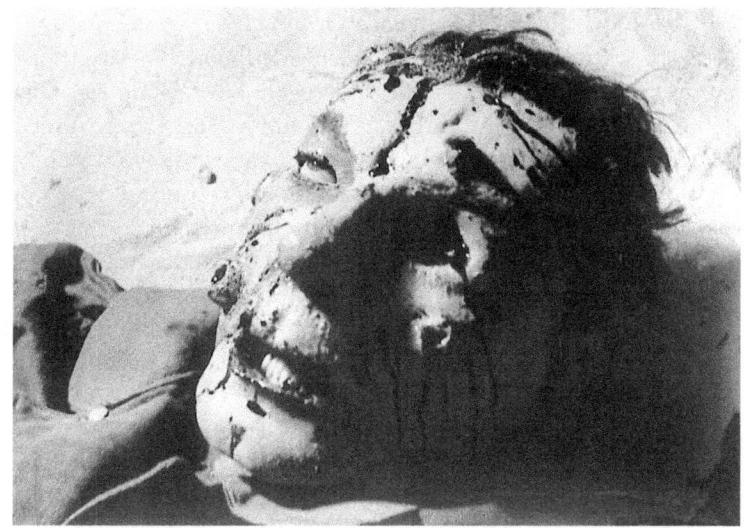

The Flesh Eaters meet their maker (Martin Kosleck)—who then meets *his*.

Where was the room with the light bulb?

I don't remember where it was—it *may* have been at his hotel, but I'm kind of fuzzy on that. We were both questioned, Jack and I.

He came up to New York, you didn't go down to him.

Oh, no, he came up here. He showed us what he had done in the past [publicity-wise] for pictures that he handled, he showed us some old-fashioned, wild, crazy publicity. And we said, "That's what we think *The Flesh Eaters* needs, *that* kind of garish, outlandish approach." Ripps did a pretty good job of promoting it, particularly in the South. The [box office] reports that we got back were probably ... 70 percent bullshit would be my thought. According to him, he made a little less than a million dollar gross; I would say that he probably grossed more like two. No way to know that. Well, we knew somebody who worked for Ripps, and after he left Ripps, he said to us, "Yeah, he screwed the hell out of you." But at any rate, that was the story of *The Flesh Eaters*. It got a lot of mileage for a low-budget film, and became something of a cult item. It became *much* a cult item in England, I'm told. It couldn't be shown in public theaters there, because of their code, so it went into these "clubs" that showed pictures that were restricted in England. And *in* those clubs, it became something of a cult favorite.

The Flesh Eaters is in "Supramotion." What exactly is Supramotion?

A word [*laughs*]. Look, we needed *some*thing. In those days, movies were color, and most were widescreen. They were advertising *this* kind of screen and *that* kind of screen, Wide and Super-Wide and Super-Super-Wide and all that shit, in order to get people to come out of their houses and stop watching TV. Since we had a little animation in our film, we claimed that it was a new process called Supramotion. That's all it was, it was a tag to stick on.

At some point, someone started the foolish rumor that, to get the effect of the little Flesh Eaters in the scene where Kosleck is depositing them in the beatnik's glass of booze, we punched holes in the film. The *true* story is: Originally we were going to make this film for 60 or 65,000. We knew we couldn't manage to do that after we got wiped out by the hurricane. We *had* to go back to convince our investors … *not* to put up more money, but just to allow us the right to *raise* more money. So we decided, "Well, the best way to do *that* is to show 'em what we've got. That should encourage them mightily." Jack said, "Yeah, but we don't have any animation in there yet. It's going to look 'flat.'" So at that point, we decided to punch holes in *that* particular shot and get the effect that we did … brilliantly. But of course, when we got to making the actual negative, the monsters were done by animation, it was not done by punching holes. Otherwise you would have had to poke holes in all of the 120 or so prints that Ripps made—a lot of holes! So that's the end of *that* rumor.

What about the music score?

One of the unusual things about that film, and as you know by now there are a whole *bunch* of unusual things about that film, is the fact that a full symphony orchestra plays our score. How we *do dat?* Well, we priced it in New York and it was just impossible, we couldn't possibly come close to it. But we found out that if we went over to Germany, we could hire a symphony orchestra for half the price that we would pay in New York. And we could afford to send the composer and the arranger [Julian Stein and Noël Regney] over there, to handle the scoring, and send Jack to help them coordinate the music with the editing. And what we had now is a picture made for 95,000, 96,000 cash and about 27,000 in debts—with a full symphony orchestra playing an original score! I think that probably had never been done before! In most low-budget films, you will hear an organ playing in the background, or you will hear Tchaikovsky or Rimsky-Korsakov being played by an Iron Curtain orchestra, recorded off the air, for which they paid *zilch*! That's not what we did. We paid our way, we just did the best that we could under the circumstances.

Julian Stein was the music director on the long-running stage show The Fantasticks, *and Noël Regney later wrote the Christmas song "Do You Hear What I Hear?"*

Noël Regney was a marvelous arranger.

Did anybody worry that the movie was going to be too gory—or did you figure you could just take out some of it later, if need be?

We were a *little* concerned about it, but we knew that was the way it was going, that was the trend. I think it was a good thing that we did it the way we did, because since it took us about three years to get from the first word to the screen, by the time we got there, things *had* changed quite a bit.

Horror movies had gotten gorier, you mean.

Yeah. We knew a fellow named Radley Metzger who owned The Charles, a theater on Avenue B and 12th Street in the East Village where he was showing art films and old American classic films, and he offered us the theater for a sneak preview. "Oh, goody!" we thought—*that's* not easy to get. So we did a sneak preview at Radley's theater, and we came away with about an 80 or 85 percent approval in the reviews that we got back from the audience. I think that's probably average—audiences like to be kind. But 15 or 20 percent were these *scathing* reviews—really scathing. Then we stopped and said to ourselves, "Schmuck! You went down into Greenwich Village, you went into an area where a bunch of artists and schoolteachers and social workers and do-gooders hang out, and you show 'em this kind of film—what do you *expect* them to tell you, except that you are 'destroying the minds of our children!'"

This sneak preview was before Mike Ripps came along?

Yeah.

Drake isn't sure that *Flesh Eaters*' distributors gave them a fair shake $-wise, but feels that "it was profitable in the sense of experience."

Radley tells me that a middle-aged man happened to have a heart attack that night in the theater—do you remember that at all?

No, I don't. Maybe there was, I don't recall.

Well, according to Radley, you thought it'd be great to play that up in the publicity!

[*Laughs*] That could have happened, I guess. Anybody who'll lose a handbag on a bus will try to cash in on a heart attack! It may absolutely be true.

Lyn Fairhurst told an interviewer that Jack Curtis intended to do five more horror movies.

Jack did want to do more horror films ... we *both* did. And we should have. We made the mistake of deciding that it would be easier to import a film and dub it. So we did that, and lost money on it. It was a huge mistake.

Was it a horror movie?

No, it wasn't. That's why we lost money [*laughs*]! It was a film called *We Are All Naked* [1966].

You didn't get all the money you should have gotten, you told me, but was Flesh Eaters *still profitable for you?*

It was profitable in the sense of experience. That was the major profit that we got out of it. We certainly learned more making this picture than we could learn in four years at a university, studying filmmaking. Back in those days, universities were just teaching technique in classrooms.

The movie—how do you feel about it after all these years?

About a week ago, I got the VHS copy you mailed me and ... I really didn't want to look at it again. I thought to myself, "It's gonna be old-fashioned, dusty and musty." Well, I finally decided to run it off the other night, at midnight. What better hour? And—you know something?—I was impressed with it, I really was. Lillian and I sat down and looked at it and said, "Son of a bitch ... it still *works*! The goddamn thing still works!" I thought it was going to look very antique, I thought the dialogue would be pretty corny, and I thought that the low budget would show itself all over the place. It really doesn't. One of the reasons is that I chose to put my people on a desert island, so we were not involved with the question of what kind of clothing they wear and how old-fashioned the clothes look. Or the cars, or the houses, or anything like that. Five people on a desert island today look like they did 40 years ago. So that's one of the reasons that it does not show all the signs of wear that most pictures do. The actors all come off fairly well—Barbara and Rita are fine, Byron worked out well, and I think Ray Tudor was great. Jack's direction is superb and that his editing is magnificent. And I think my script *works*, and you can't ask much more from a script for *that* kind of film than that it works. The picture never stops, it goes boom-boom-boom-boom-boom, which is what I learned from writing comics: The story must never stop.

The most important thing in making a film and in living a life is to keep remembering what your goal is. Try not to alter it. And if it changes, then ask yourself, "Do I really want to *do* this?" We knew what we wanted to make, and we made it. I think it's a fun movie, I still kinda like it. For two semi-experienced fellows like ourselves, I think it was a helluva good product, I really do. I don't think I'd make it much better today. A little bit, but not much. It was a drive-in movie, basically, and I think we did exactly what you were *supposed* to do with a drive-in movie.

Drake's earliest *Doom Patrol* stories have been compiled into the new DC Comics hardcover *The Doom Patrol Archives* Volume 1.

ARNOLD DRAKE

The Flesh Eaters (C.D.A., 1964)

Vulcan Productions, Inc.; 87 minutes; Presented by M. A. Ripps; Associate Producer: Bernard Cherin; Produced by Terry Curtis, Jack Curtis & Arnold Drake; Directed by Jack Curtis; Screenplay: Arnold Drake; Photography: Carson Davidson & (uncredited) Jack Curtis; Music: Julian Stein; Orchestrations: Noël Regney; Production Manager: Lyn Fairhurst; Camera Operator: John Carroll; Camera Assistant: Fred Portnow; Editor: Radley Metzger; Dialogue Supervisor: Film-Sync; Sound: Titra Sound Corp.; Sound Engineer: Martin Garcia; Rerecordist: Robert Sherwood; Sound Effects: Laverne Owens & Cinemascores, Inc.; Laboratory Supplies: Will—New York; Skin Diving Equipment: Richard's Aqua Lung Center; Supramotion: Wylde Films, Inc.; Special Effects: Roy Benson; Optical Photography: B&O Film Effects; Technical Consultant: Evan J. Anton; Songs: "It's a Wonder" by Gloria Regney & Julian Stein (Sung by Anita Ellis); "Pete's Beat" by Arnold Drake & Jim Osmun (Sung by Arnold Drake); "Mars Calling" by Noël Regney

Martin Kosleck (*Prof. Peter Bartell*), Byron Sanders (*Grant Murdoch*), Barbara Wilkin (*Jan Letterman*), Rita Morley (*Laura Winters*), Ray Tudor (*Omar*), Christopher Drake (*Matt*), Darby Nelson (*Jim*), Rita Floyd (*Radio Operator*), Warren Houston (*Cab Driver*), Barbara Wilson (*Ann*), Ira Lewis (*Freddy Miller*), Jack Curtis (*Voice of Radio Deejay/Voice of Jim*), Arnold Drake (*"Pete's Beat" Whistler-Singer*)

Robert M. Fresco

> *My "bent" was more toward imagination as opposed to "How do we scare 'em?" I didn't want to do a* Creature from the Black Lagoon *or giant ants that were gonna kill you. That wasn't what I was about.*

Robert M. Fresco is the producer of an Oscar-winning documentary and an Emmy-nominated PBS special; a documentarian who brought cameras into the American courtroom and helped pave the way for Court TV. But before he could apply his energies to these and other, equally prestigious pursuits, the Burbank-born Fresco first had to "break out" of science fiction—the genre in which he was typecast by Hollywood in the monster-mad 1950s. An early stint on TV producer Ivan Tors' *Science Fiction Theatre* led to an association with director Jack Arnold and the job of writing *Tarantula*—a box office hit which in turn led to *The Monolith Monsters* and uncredited writing chores on *The 27th Day*, *The Alligator People* and the made-in-Lapland *Terror in the Midnight Sun*.

Eventually the grind of writing "Medium Shot—Monster" took its toll on Fresco, who moved on to worthier vehicles. But the skeletons in his closet (the succession of movie monsters he created in his mid-to-late twenties) continue to dog his trail via cable TV and home video. Once ashamed, now amused by his sci-fi/horror stepchildren, Fresco here recalls their conception, along with the rogues' gallery of producers and directors who brought them into the world.

How old were you when you joined the Screen Writers Guild?

I joined the Screen Writers Guild on March the 20th, 1951, when I was not yet 21 years old. As I sat there on the bench, the guy who went in before me to become a member was Hal Kanter, who went on to make millions as a comedy writer. Well, I *haven't*!

At what point in your life did you figure out you wanted to be a writer?

I think I was about two [*laughs*]—I started writing as a kid. And movies always fascinated me. My parents were European-born and they loved French films and

German films. The first film I ever saw, I was seven years old: They took me, first-run, to see *Grand Illusion* [1937]. All these years later, I see it about once a year and I always cry! So, yes, I always knew I wanted to become a writer. Actually, I had *four* ambitions: I wanted to write films, I wanted to *make* films, I wanted to teach and I wanted to be an architect. And I've done three out of four—I haven't built a house yet, but I've "played at it." That's not bad for one lifetime.

My first office was in an office building on Beverwil and Pico—I rented it for $25 a month in 1951. I'm glad I did it because I "lucked" into a kind of writers' cabal. My "next door neighbor" there was this wonderful writer named George Zuckerman, who wrote a lot of the good Douglas Sirk films at Universal; George was kind of a mentor and became a dear friend up until his death a couple of years ago [1996]. Other writers clustered around us—there was Harry Essex, who was a journeyman screenwriter; there was Larry Roman, the screenwriter and playwright, the guy who did *Under the Yum Yum Tree* and lots of movies; and there were a bunch of others. So there was always somebody to go to lunch with, somebody to talk story with, somebody to give a script to for a reading.

At first I floundered around—I was writing on instinct, I didn't know what the hell I was doing. But by the time I was 23 or 24, I sorta did, and that's when I got into TV. I got into it through Ivan Tors and *Science Fiction Theatre*.

How did you hook up with Tors?

George Zuckerman introduced me to Ivan, he and Ivan were friends—they'd both been screenwriters at MGM. George watched me struggle in those early years and he'd read what I wrote every once in a while, and finally he said, "You know, you're pretty good now, you can *do* it. Why don't I talk to Ivan?" I said, "Fine. Be my guest!" That was that.

What was Tors like?

Ivan was a very interesting man. Ivan was very Hungarian, married to a beautiful, beautiful woman, [actress] Constance Dowling. He started out in Hollywood as part of its European émigré community, but he wasn't in the top rank. But he had ambition, he wanted very much to succeed. He used *Science Fiction Theatre* as his entrée into television, and he ended up with a couple of series—*Sea Hunt* and *Flipper* and so on. He was a good guy, I liked Ivan. He was an honest man. I mean ... he fudged a little [*laughs*], but they *all* fudged on credits. When we get to Jack Arnold, I'll tell you a story or two. They all fudged on credits and money, but that was Hollywood.

Were you enough of a science buff that you were able to come up with the ideas for your Science Fiction Theatres, *or were they "written to order"?*

No, I always had originals. And [as for his SF movies], they were more fantasy than science fiction because they were about the *ideas*, they weren't about the gimmicks or the monsters. *Tarantula* was about a search for a nutrient, it wasn't about how to make a giant spider that was going to look through the window at Mara Corday in her nightgown. Not that that was *bad* [*laughs*]—she looked pretty good in those days! But my "bent" was more toward *imagination* as opposed to "How do we scare 'em?" I didn't want to do a *Creature from the Black Lagoon* [1954] or giant ants that were gonna kill you. That wasn't what I was about. (I didn't realize that I was a humanist until I started making documentaries. *Then* I realized I was a humanist, and I knew I was *doomed* [*laughs*]!)

How much were you paid for a Science Fiction Theatre *script?*

I think in those days it was $750—that's the number that flashed through my mind when you asked. Certainly under 1000. They had limited budgets, and they shot those things in two or three days. By the way, those *Science Fiction Theatre* people did something interesting: They shot in color, even though there were no color TVs then. They shot it in color and then they struck black-and-white fine grains and used those as the negatives. And they put the color negatives away knowing that *someday* there'd be color, and they'd be like money in the bank. Very smart.

You wrote three Science Fiction Theatre*s.*

Yeah, I did a bunch of them for Ivan, and they were good, and one of them was directed by Jack Arnold. That's how we met.

"No Food for Thought," which later provided a kind of basis for Tarantula.

That's right. Jack was doing this sort of thing because he couldn't do anything *else*. He had produced and directed a documentary [*With These Hands*, 1950] on the Triangle Shirtwaist fire of 1911, and it went up for an Academy Award. He was very proud of that, as he should have been. But in 1955 when I met him, he was making his living directing *wonderful* garbage, *Creature from the Black Lagoon* and blah blah blah. He was directing this "No Food for Thought" that I had come up with for *Science Fiction Theatre* and it had a marvelous cast: It had Otto Kruger, a classic actor who had been a star. It had Vera Miles, who was about to be in *The Searchers* [1956]. (Vera had the same agent I did, Milt Rosner, so whenever she wasn't working, he'd throw her in whatever he was doing.) And it had John Howard, who was a good actor, a former leading man-type. Jack said to me, "Hey, stay on the set," so I did—he had me on the set all three days. And we liked each other. He liked the script and he liked the quality of the dialogue, and one day he said, "You know, there may be a *movie* in this." I said, "Okay with me." Then he added, "But you gotta put a *monster* in it." There was no monster in "No Food for Thought," believe me, it was about a bunch of scientists developing an artificial nutrient. And the lab animal in the show was not a tarantula, it was a mouse named Moses [*laughs*].

So Arnold was the one who instigated things.

Yes, he suggested that we do something. I brought him up to my office after the episode was done and we had lunch a couple of times, and talked. And I came up with the idea of the spider instead of the mouse. He went away and I developed the story, seven pages. According to the screen credits of *Tarantula*, it's a story by … I believe the order is Jack Arnold and Robert M. Fresco, although maybe it's Robert M. Fresco and Jack Arnold.

Robert M. Fresco turned a *Science Fiction Theatre* teleplay into the screenplay of *Tarantula*—substituting this hairy arachnid for a mouse named Moses in the process.

No, it's Jack Arnold and Robert M. Fresco.
    Yeah, that's what I thought. But he never wrote a word. We sold that to Universal for, I think, $7000, so he made some money on the side there. But he got me the assignment to write the screenplay, of course. Universal liked Jack—he'd already done *It Came from Outer Space* [1953] and *Creature from the Black Lagoon*, so he was "hot" in that strata.
    I wrote the script, and I had a very good time doing it. I wrote it in the Writers Building at Universal, "C Building" it was called, and I didn't want Jack to see what I was doing until I had the first act, which ran about 30 pages. I had this crazy secretary and I said, "Listen, I want to do something [goofy]. Are you willing to...," and she said, "Sure." She typed it up and we pasted it together so that it was like a scroll. I laid it out in the hall of the Writers Building, and I told Jack, "You gotta read this walking." So he walked his way up the story pages!

Why did you do that to him?
    I don't *know* why—I was a 24-year-old punk, I guess. But I was having fun and I was pleased with what I'd written. And Jack liked it. But what I didn't know ... and when we get to my "favorite" producer...

Bill Alland [the producer of Tarantula*]?*
That piece of shit. When we get to him, I'll tell you what happened. I didn't realize that the fix was in.

Anyway, Jack and I got along, and again he was happy to have me around while the film was being shot. I wasn't on salary, but I was in and out. There was one wonderful moment: There's a scene where the tarantula is attacking the house and the claw of the tarantula hits Leo G. Carroll, the British actor who co-starred in the film. Of course it was a fake claw and it was cushioned and all that, but they dropped it as they were shooting the scene, and they really hurt Mr. Carroll, they cut his forehead. Nothing *serious*, no stitches, but he had to go to the infirmary. That happened in the morning. He and Mara Corday and Jack were having lunch afterwards, when I was also in the commissary. I left the writers' table, the big round writers' table in the corner, and I walked over to Mr. Carroll and I apologized for my spider having hurt him [*laughs*]. And he "responded in kind," he was funny as hell. He was very nice.

You ready for the most trivial question you'll ever be asked in your life?
Can you guarantee that, Tom?

Honestly? I think I can.
Okay, go.

In real life, the disease is acromegaly. Why did you change it to "acromegalia"?
'Cause I probably fucked up [*laughs*]! Listen, let me tell you my standard operating procedure when I got to Universal. Every time. I would call the library and I would say, "Please send me a copy of *Merck's Manual of Medicine*." And I would sit there, drinking coffee and leafing through every hideous disease that could afflict the human race. And I came up with acromegaly. *I* don't know why I called it acromegalia, I have no idea. But I'm sure I'm quite capable of having screwed it up!

Were you on the set every day?
Not every day, but ... often. I think they shot the damn thing in about 12 days—a couple of weeks tops.

Did you go to Apple Valley, where they shot the desert exteriors?
[*Laughs*] Oh, let me tell you about that—I'm glad you asked, because I completely forgot about that. Thank you for reminding me! Jack had been a pilot in the war, and he found out that I was a civilian pilot. So, prior to production, we flew ourselves to Apple Valley to scout locations. He got Universal to pop for a day's rental of a Cessna 170, a four-seater, and the two of us flew all the way out there, we had lunch in Palm Springs and flew ourselves *back*! He was the pilot, I was the co-pilot. It was fun. My one location flight, and I helped fly the plane [*laughs*]!

Jack was a very good pilot. And an interesting man. He was a talented man, and *so* ambitious. He didn't want to do monster movies. *The Mouse That Roared* [1959]—films like that were *reeeally* his schtick. Jack wanted to do caustic comedy.

He was very nervous, very, very tense. He had a long, thin nose, flaring nostrils, and he always looked like he was ... *sniff, sniff* ... ferreting out his next meal, and he leaned [forward] a little. He was very intent. He was *not* a bad guy. He had his eye on the buck, but he really was someone who, in another incarnation and another time, could have been much more of an artist than he let himself be, or was able to become. I have fond memories of Jack. He muscled in on [the story credit and money] for *Tarantula* but ... that was just normal. Everybody did that. And the next time we worked together was *The Monolith Monsters*, which I thought of as a disaster from beginning to end.

Are you going to tell me about Bill Alland now?

Oh, I'll tell you about Bill Alland. With displeasure [*laughs*]! You remember, I was 24 years old and I had my eyes on the stars. I'd been raised as a clean kid in a dirty world. I mean, I wasn't a *baby*—I joined the United States Army the day I was 18 and I went to Ranger School. So I wasn't a fool or a virgin, but I *was* an optimist. One day early on, Jack says to me, "Well, now you're gonna meet Bill Alland," and he takes me to Alland's office and introduces me. Then Jack gives me a *look*—I realized later it was a warning look, but I didn't know it at the time. Then he turns on his heel and exits, and I'm surprised that he left. Well, he's left me in the lion's den: I find myself in this oversized office with this man who starts telling me how terrible the story is. How unhappy he is that he has to be involved with it. Who doesn't really have any confidence in my ability to write it. It was a pure "I'm gonna fuck with his head" kind of meeting. I was completely taken aback, because it was so surprising and so upsetting. I held my own, but I couldn't understand what was goin' on. Well, what was goin' on was, Alland was saying "I'm the boss and you better believe it" and a nyah nyah nyah and a scowl and a this and a that.

I don't know if you know who Bill Alland *was*. He was the chief *fink* in the McCarthy era. He turned in more people than any other single person in the movie industry. He was a real shit. He wasn't doing it because he was speaking his conscience, it was because he was saving his *ass* at the price of other people's careers.

Alland was a sailor. Now, *I'm* a sailor—I love to sail, it's one of the thrilling things in my life. And Alland, when people were starving because of the shit he had done, *he* had enough money to buy a sailing yacht. Forty-something feet. He gloried in being a member of a yacht club and sailing this yacht. And I kept thinking, "It ain't *right*..." Oh, he was a shit. He was a nasty little man. I later realized that every studio had a bunch of these people on contract. That was *their* way of keeping their names and their employees' names out of *Red Channels*, that nasty publication that named names and named people who had never done anything but had the same name as someone who *also* had never done anything but had been *accused* of something! That's *true*, by the way—I'll tell you a story about that. I had a friend named Don Martin, who was a jobbing screenwriter—not brilliant, but he wrote and wrote, he used to write Republic movies and Columbia B movies. And he had the same name as a *radio* writer named Don Martin, who had been named as a Red. The Don Martin I knew was completely apolitical. The *other* Don Martin was *not* a Red. *My* Don Martin—forget the other Don Martin, *he* was ruined. *My* Don Martin didn't work for seven years.

You share screenplay credit on Tarantula *with Martin Berkeley.*
　Martin Berkeley—[real name] Marty Berkowitz. He was another person who was on the Universal payroll to keep them looking good in the eyes of the John Waynes and Adolphe Menjous and the Ward Bonds. Marty Berkeley finked on all the Screen Writers Guild guys. He was a dirty word to most people. He was a big Brooklyn kid trying to be English. Tattersalls and tweeds, tweeds that had enough hair so you had to comb 'em every two days. Bespoke shoes. Suits from Savile Row. Think of Rex Harrison as Henry Higgins. A really horsy English gentleman—he played the part perfectly, you would have thought that he was born in Buckinghamshire instead of Brooklyn [*laughs*]. And he had one of the most beautiful automobiles. Parked in the parking lot next to my old Ford, he had a Jaguar sedan, as big as the old Bentleys. I went to his home once, and he had a picture of Hitler over the john and he had an American flag next to his desk, just in case anybody questioned.

Why was he brought onto Tarantula*?*
　To get a credit and make some money. He paraphrased my scenes. He didn't change a single character, he didn't change a single name. It was a joke. He just sort of … rewrote lines. He did just enough to get the credit. (Somewhere I have the original and the final script, and there's really no tangible difference.) And I realized the fix was in from the beginning: Alland was just waiting for me to walk out so he could bring in Berkeley. But I was learning the ways of [*singing*] *Hol*-ly-woooood, and that was part of my upbringing.
　I can't believe, looking back, how vulnerable I was. I mean, the Robert M. Fresco who's got the Academy Award and the Cannes Film Festival and all the documentary festivals and the Guggenheim Fellowship is *not* the same guy who stood in Alland's office and listened to him give me shit. *I* didn't realize he wanted me to walk out so he could put Berkeley on the script. So he was stuck until I was done and fulfilled my contract and left with a smile on my face—and the next thing I know, Jack tells me, "Marty Berkeley's on it." I ask, "Why?" He says, "Well … because." I ask, "What do you mean, 'Because'?" and he says, "Well … he and Alland are buddies."

I like some of Jack Arnold's movies but I don't like the way he came across in his interviews—like a real credit-grabber.
　Of course he did. Look, Arthur Ross and Harry Essex wrote *Creature from the Black Lagoon*, but you wouldn't think so if you talked to Jack Arnold. That's 'cause he was desperate. You know who he was? Sammy Glick, the character in the great Budd Schulberg novel *What Makes Sammy Run?* Sammy Glick, the ultimate hustler who ends up on top of the heap *all alone*, 'cause he's alienated everyone on the planet. There was a lot of that in Jack. He just never did it to *me*. I mean, he did it to me [taking undeserved story credit and money on *Tarantula*], but that was the

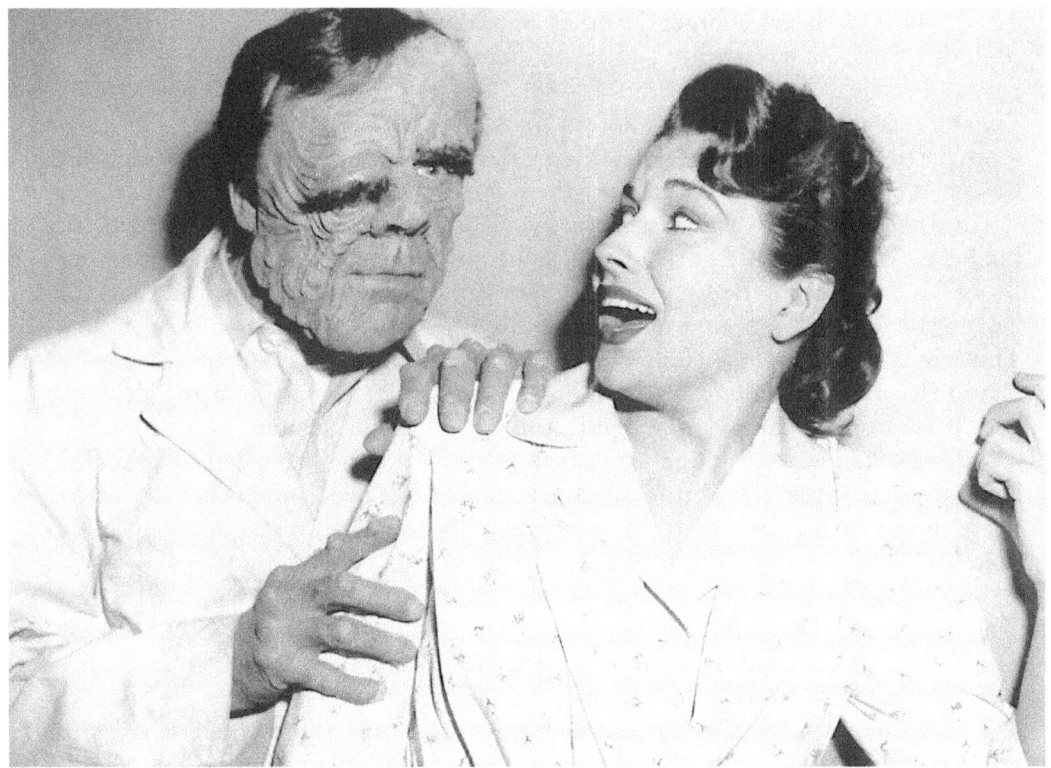

Acromegalic scientist Leo G. Carroll scares a scream out of lab assistant Mara Corday in a *Tarantula* **posed shot.**

price of admission and I knew it. I remember discussing the situation with my agent Milt. He shrugged and he said, "You wanna do the screenplay at Universal?" I said yes. He said, "Okay. Put Jack's name on it." So I did. And that was it.

You say "Jack never did it to me"—well, he did do it to you. I'm looking right now at a Jack Arnold interview where he says he wrote Tarantula. *Doesn't mention you once.*
    He says he wrote *Tarantula*? No shit... [*Pause*] That's interesting. Well, take my word for it—not a word [did he write]. Not a word. He didn't even invent the spider, we just talked out the idea of what kind of a *thing* to have that could grow, what could we possibly have as a lab animal that could get big and frighten somebody. We didn't want to have a giant mouse [*laughs*]!

Them! *was a recent hit—did that have any influence on the selection of your giant creature?*
    Weren't those ants? With Jim Arness, right? Oh, I'm *sure* that that was the inspiration. Look, I thought the whole *idea* [of *Tarantula*] was ridiculous, but it was $750 a week. I'll tell you what Jack and I *wanted* to do: There was a book that Universal owned that he wanted to direct and I wanted to write: *Badge of Evil* [the basis for Universal's 1958 film *Touch of Evil*, written and directed by Orson Welles]. I

wanted to do that so badly, the drool was coming down my face. I knew what those characters were, I was writing dialogue on my own. Jack wanted to direct that film and I wanted to write that film, and we tried, and we got shit. I knew what I wanted to do, I would have made a hell of a script, and I think we would have made a good film. Didn't happen.

Did you go to the previews of movies like Tarantula*?*

Yes. It was at a theater in southwest L.A., and we were all there. And there was a line of dialogue that [during production] I realized was no good and I said, "Jesus, don't shoot that, Jack." And he said, "No, no. I'll shoot it and we'll cut it later." But he didn't, it was still in there. There's this moment where our hero John Agar is about to do something completely stupid, he's gonna go where he shouldn't go, and the girl looks at him and she says… "Be careful." [*Laughs*] I did what *you* just did— I laughed. At the preview. I was sitting behind Alland and I laughed. He turned and he *spit* at me, practically. (He didn't spit, but he went, "*Hey*! Be *quiet*, for God's sake!" He was just *furious*.) He didn't have enough sense to realize that it was a shit line and that it shouldn't be in the movie.

And it stayed in?

Jack didn't have any courage. That was one of the reasons Jack never [made it]. Jack didn't take chances. He wouldn't stand up to Bill Alland and say, "That's a terrible line. The writer said it's a terrible line, I agree with him, let's cut it." But he was a *good director*. He had a profound sense of movement, he had an understanding of lighting, he was a good director. But he didn't have the balls. That's why, I guess, he had to lie and boast. I don't want to speak ill of the dead, but I'm telling it straight.

By the way, just to "wrap up" on *Tarantula*: Ed Muhl was running the studio in those days, and he believed in these smaller films. He was a very interesting guy, very dour-faced guy, always well-dressed, blue suit, dark hair—he looked like Ed Murrow. I remember … God, I must have been callow and raw in those days … I remember, we'd just come out of a screening of something, I think it was a screening of one of George Zuckerman's films, *Written on the Wind* [1956] or something really nice. And, half-ashamed, I said, "It's no *Tarantula*," or something like that. He said, "Don't put it down. That little movie of yours, it cost a couple hundred thousand and it's made four, five million. This studio keeps its doors open on movies like yours. Those are the things that pay the bills around here." I always remembered that. He was not condescending at all. It didn't have to be a big god-damn movie with Charlton Heston and Anne Bancroft, he was very happy to make small movies.

Next sore subject: Whose idea was The Monolith Monsters*?*

Theirs. I will not take credit. They just wanted a monster movie, and they said, "How 'bout rocks that grow?" I said, "You gotta be kidding!" But it was $750 a week and it was getting back into Universal, where I still had hopes of writing that other movie [*Touch of Evil*]. Universal was doing detective movies and war movies, and I

"How do you make a movie about rocks that grow?!" was Fresco's lament throughout the scripting of the lamentable *The Monolith Monsters.*

wanted to break out [of monster movies]. I thought, "I'll get a detective movie. I'll get a Jeff Chandler movie. I'll get *some*thing to break me out of 'Medium Shot—Monster.'" It didn't happen. So I wrote *Monolith Monsters*. I did what I could, but … it was a hack job. I *enjoyed Tarantula*. It was silly, but it had grown out of a good idea, a humane and decent idea. But *Monolith Monsters* was just a put-together. And whoever directed it [John Sherwood] did it with his left hand. If you look at that movie, it's listless. A terrible movie.

Who was it who sat you down and told you to write a movie about "rocks that grow"?
   I can't remember. It could have been Ed Muhl's idea, transmitted to me by [producer] Howard Christie, but … I really can't remember.

I notice that you borrowed some plot points from Tarantula. *There's the desert and small town setting, a corpse that baffles science, a newspaperman not allowed to write about what's going on—*
   Listen, I was desperate! How do you make a movie about rocks that grow [*laughs*]?! How can you be against a thoughtless thing? It didn't make sense. The whole time, I kept saying, "Look, you want some stories? I'll give you *ten* stories.

I'll *give* you the stories, you don't have to buy 'em. We'll just do the scripts." "No, no, no, we're gonna do this one. We want these rocks and the desert and the blah blah blah blah." I kept saying, "You're crazy!"

Again, the story credit goes to "Jack Arnold and Robert M. Fresco."
If you believe that, there's this bridge…

Is there any possibility that "rocks that grow" was Arnold's idea?
No. I certainly didn't come up with that idea, and Jack didn't either. *Some*body did, somebody in the studio. Jack and I had had a successful run with *Tarantula*, it had made money and they said, "Let's use the same team and make another one." It was imposed on us.*

So, just like on Tarantula, *he didn't write a word of the story.*
He *couldn't*, he wasn't a story man. I remember looking at Milt again [discussing Arnold's undeserved co-credit and co-payment] and Milt saying, again, "You wanna do the screenplay at Universal? $750 a week…" and me saying, again, "Okay … I'll put Jack's name on it…"

Norman Jolley gets co-credit with you on the Monolith Monsters *screenplay.*
Norman Jolley was the writer who came in to try and save the script after I barely finished. I scraped into the end of that script—I think the last pages were draft, because it was almost impossible for me to finish. It was awful. I was drinking coffee, staying there 'til two in the morning. I had a terrible time finishing that script, I finished it by my fingernails, and I'm sure it wasn't any good. So they brought in Norman Jolley—I didn't know him. He was a journeyman screenwriter, undistinguished but okay. We talked over the script, I said, "Good luck," and that was that. He didn't change that much of it. I thought he could improve it more than he did—he really *didn't*. So I challenged the screenplay credit [insisted that Jolley hadn't done enough to deserve co-credit]. And I lost, they said he changed it enough. I just wish he'd done *more* [*laughs*]! Made it a better movie! I thought it was hopeless.

I don't like the movie but I do very much like the special effects at the end, the rocks coming toward the town.
The special effects people were wonderful at Universal—you look at that Tarantula's claw and you cringe! They did a beautiful job on those things, they were great. But I certainly wasn't responsible for anything in *Monolith Monsters* except *boredom* [*laughs*]!

Yes, I remember that part of it!
So do I! I tried to see it last year. I couldn't finish it. I was groaning and my

---

*Arnold was originally set by Universal to produce and direct The Monolith Monsters, *but relinquished both chores in favor of directing a bigger Universal picture,* The Tattered Dress *(1957) with Jeff Chandler and Jeanne Crain.*

The Merck Manual *furnished Fresco with a myriad of maladies to inflict upon his sci-fi movies' characters. (Pictured: "Stone Man" Phil Harvey from* The Monolith Monsters.*)*

wife Judy looked at me and I said, "Baby, do you *really* want to see this?" She said, "Not really." And I said, "God *bless* you!" and I turned it off *real* quick [*laughs*]!

I can't stand the fact that the Monoliths are threatening to destroy the entire planet—but everybody in the little town is more concerned over some little girl who's sick.

Everything was wrong. It was a wrong-headed film. It should not have been made with that premise. It was just terrible. It was like one of those situations where you put on shoes and you know they don't fit and the suit is too tight and the tie's the wrong color and you say, "*I* can't go out in this," and they say, "No, no. You look fine." And you look like hell! That's what it was like, it was just terrible. But now I laugh about it.

That was it for Universal. I'm not surprised they didn't hire me again after that! Oh, God … what else?

You don't get a screen credit but you wrote for a movie that was made in Lapland, Terror in the Midnight Sun.

There was a very talented director doing television at Universal named Virgil Vogel. I wrote a bunch of *Wagon Train*s, and that's where I met Virgil—he directed a *Wagon Train* that I did that had Cameron Mitchell starring in it. Virgil and I cooked up the story for *Terror in the Midnight Sun*. He had a house in the Valley with a pool and a luscious wife, and we used to sit in his pine-paneled den and say, "Well, what do *you* want to do?" and we worked it out. (We also used to sit around his pine-paneled den looking out at his wife at the edge of the pool!) The film was going to be produced by two haughty Swedish brothers, Gustav and Bertil Unger, who were among the founders of the Hollywood Foreign Correspondents Association, a society of about 30 or 40 people that later became the Golden Globes. I only met them once or twice. These guys wore monocles, they were kind of nuts, and they were *unbelievably* pretentious—hubris to a fault. Bullshit artists is what they

A Kong-sized space monster runs amok amidst Lapland's frozen wastes in *Terror in the Midnight Sun*.

were, but they managed to get some rich Swedes to back 'em, and they made this movie. I recently saw the picture for the first time, and I thought Virgil did a pretty good job of *filming* it.

That's the one bright spot in that movie, I think—the fact that some of the photography is striking.
Virgil didn't look very imposing—he was not a large man, and he didn't seem terribly secure. But he was a very talented fellow. He worked beautifully with actors. On that *Wagon Train* I mentioned, Cameron Mitchell played a dowser—but he was a fraud. [*In a singsong voice:*] But because of the faith of a little boy, he *wasn't* a fraud, he actually found the water … *that's* the kind of crap I used to write. Anyway, Virgil did a *beautiful* job with Mitchell, he got a *lovely* performance out of him. Virgil *always* got good performances out of people, and he had a very good eye. He *should* have been a more successful director than he was.

So you're telling me you thought Midnight Sun *was … okay?*
[*Pause*] No! [*Laughs*] I don't want to lie to you, Tom, you're a nice guy! I couldn't believe the hairy monster, and I couldn't believe the fact that there wasn't a "third act." The outlines of what I wrote were there, and a few of the lines, but that's all. Everything else was gone, and of course the end of the *movie* was gone. There *was* no end of the movie, it just *stopped*.

Arthur C. Pierce gets sole screenplay credit. Why isn't your name in the credits?
I have no idea.

The 27th Day *with Gene Barry?*
Helen Ainsworth was the producer, and she hired me. She was a partner with Guy Madison in his production company—Guy Madison was hot stuff in those days. Helen Ainsworth was this large, very pleasant woman who had connections and money. Most doors are 80 inches tall and 30 to 36 inches wide; that was Helen Ainsworth. (She wasn't that tall, but that's what she looked like.) She had impeccable manners, had a beautiful education, and was very nice to me—hey, I was making a grand a week, a lot of money in those days. But then she sort of disappeared from the scene, because there was this movie her company was making in Italy with Guy Madison, so she was on a plane to Italy most of the time. That's when the executive producer, Lew Rachmil, took over. He'd been a big cheese at other studios, but he was on the skids when I worked for him. Lew was not a very nice man but … that's all right. He was "old Hollywood."

You wrote the picture at Columbia?
Yes. When I was a little kid, we had family friends who were at Columbia, so I used to go there then. At that time, it was Poverty Row. Then as the years went by, they did bigger and bigger films, and at some point [executive] Harry Cohn built this lovely modern building there. But he didn't want his writers to be distracted, so on the floor where his writers were gonna be (which I believe was the third floor),

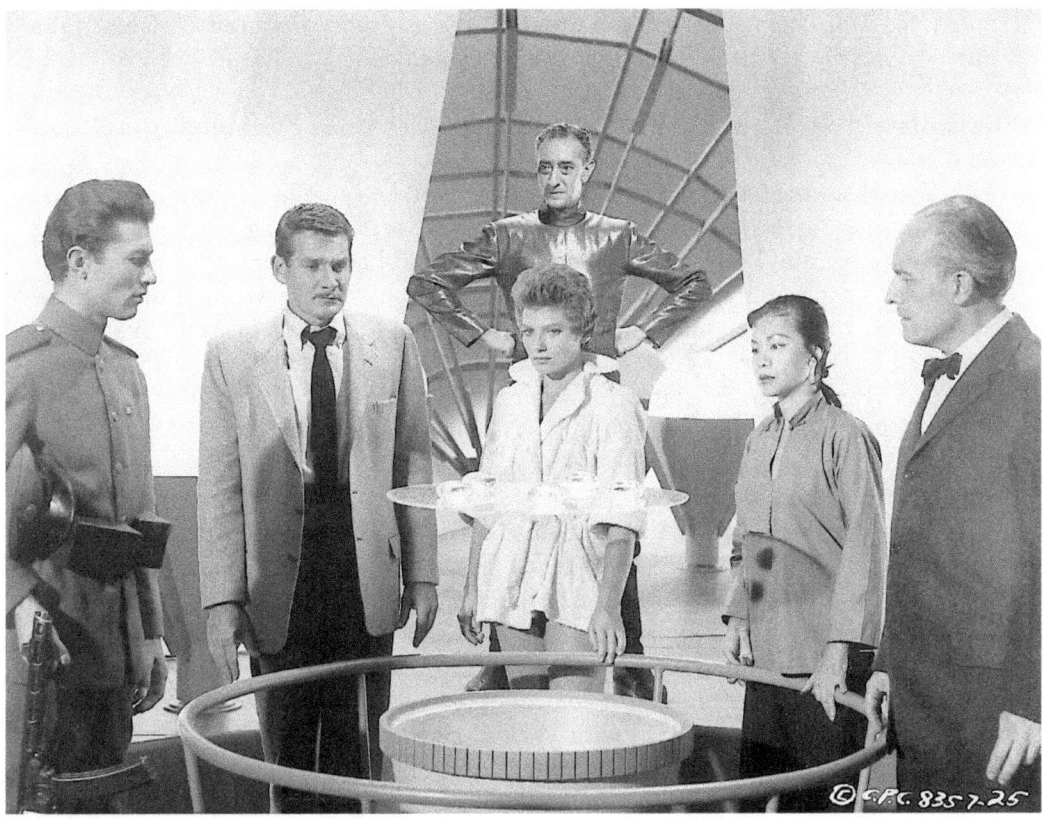

Spaceman Arnold Moss presents a cross-section of Earthlings (Azemat Janti, Gene Barry, Valerie French, Marie Tsein, George Voskovec) with weapons of mass destruction in *The 27th Day*. (Photofest)

there were big, *beautiful* offices ... but no windows. He actually did that. He felt writers shouldn't be distracted. "I'm paying 'em good money, they shouldn't look out the window." That was Harry Cohn. Whom I met exactly one time. He had one of the coldest sets of eyes I've ever looked in. But he had good taste. Look at the people he hired. Look at the chances he took.

Look at Lew Rachmil!

[*Laughs*] Rachmil was the kind of man who would walk in as you were sitting at the typewriter. He'd walk up to you so close that you felt his tie on your neck as he looked over you to see what you were writing. I didn't like it much. I *took* it, but I didn't like it. And Rachmil didn't like me much. I've never been good at sucking up, and Rachmil was the kind of guy you had to flatter. I was courteous, I was respectful, but I didn't butter him up. I didn't know how. Had I known, I wouldn't have.

What did you think of the premise of 27th Day*?*

It was an interesting premise, but it was full of holes, and there wasn't a lot you could do. And I was superseded on that by the guy who produced *Gunsmoke*, the guy who got the credit. What the hell was his name?

John Mantley—who also wrote the novel The 27th Day *that the screenplay was based on.*
Yeah. I started with his novel, and when I left, he came in. He was not a pleasant man, but I guess he was pissed that anybody was touching his stuff. I hadn't come in "over" him, I was just assigned his novel and I adapted it. It was a fair adaptation and I thought it "worked." Well, he tried to change everything I did. For my adaptation, I had taken and amplified and featured [elements of Mantley's novel] because I felt they were interesting. I'm talking about *his* stuff, *his* inventions, which I shined up. But then he came in and he got *rid* of them, in order just to change things! Even though they were *his*! He was one of *those* guys.

Well, at least you had a nice office.
It was the largest office I'd ever had, and I'd had some pretty big offices at Universal. In fact, it was the largest writer's office I'd ever *seen*. The area that had the desk and the typewriter was on a pedestal level—you stepped up to it. It was magisterial. I expected Louis B. Mayer to be sitting there glowering at me. And there *I* was. Without a window [*laughs*]! But, I tell you, I had fun—you know *why* I had fun? Because I made friends with somebody on the lot. They were filming a John Fante script, *Full of Life* [1956] with Dick Conte and Judy Holliday. And the guy who played Conte's father was from the Metropolitan Opera, Salvatore Baccaloni. He and I became friendly. I was walking around the lot one day 'cause I didn't have a window, and I had an Italian-esque name, Fresco. He started talking to me in Italian and I said, "Wait a minute—I'm a Jew!" But we became friends, and we would have lunch together once a week. Watching that man eat was one of the great educations of my life [*laughs*]! He was really a basso buffo and he had the circumference to go with it. God, he'd break into song and the glasses would shake. He was hilarious, he was a very nice man and he was nice to me. That's a sweet memory.

Why are you uncredited on 27th Day*?*
I thought the credit wasn't worth fighting for. I *could* have gotten a credit, but I remember looking at my agent and saying, "The hell with it. It isn't worth it." I shrugged it off and I walked away. I was getting to the point where [the succession of] science fiction assignments were beginning to give me an ulcer. I never quite *had* the ulcer, it was incipient, but ... if someone would say science fiction, I would wince.

You ready to wince?
Go!

The Alligator People.
Boy, did I wince! But, you know who was fascinating? Robert L. Lippert [producer of *The Alligator People*]. I was once commissioned by *Collier's* to write some-

thing about this man, because I was fascinated by the people that he was able to attract. He'd made a deal with Fox to release his pictures. Half of it was non-union, he broke every rule in the book, but Fox released them. And Lippert had all kinds of talent working for him, James Clavell and so on, and these people were doing it for 37 cents! Then—my usual luck—by the time I was ready to turn in the story, *Collier's* went belly-up [*laughs*]! But I admired Lippert and I thought it was worth doing a story about this strange man.

Lippert was one of these guys who said, "I'm goin' to be a movie producer so I can go to bed with women." He was gonna be a little Orson Welles. He had started [as an exhibitor] during the War, up in the Bay area. The shipyard workers needed something to do, they'd come off the midnight shift and they'd be hungry for booze, hungry for food, hungry for entertainment and wide awake. So Lippert would rent the strangest places and make movie theaters out of them. By the late '40s or so, he was a millionaire and he owned movie theaters, and then he thought, "Well, I'll make my own movies." Another funny thing Lippert did was, wherever he went, he bought the building. There'd be offices and stores on the first floor, and you'd go up a staircase and there'd be a fancy layout—his production company upstairs. He changed location a time or two while I was involved, 'cause this assignment [*The Alligator People*] went on for a *long* time—longer than I would have liked.

How did you get the job of writing that for him?

I can't remember any of that. What I *do* remember is how difficult those people were. Getting the script written took a few months. It should have been done in three *weeks*, but they kept changing their minds, they didn't know how serious they wanted to get or how much they wanted to spend. I didn't get a lot of guidance. I would write something and they'd say, "Well, yeah, that's okay, but ... what if you were to blah blah blah?" Pretty soon I was goin' nuts. But they were doing interesting things, which is one of the reasons that I stuck around. As I mentioned before, they had James Clavell doing films for them—he did *The Fly* [1958] for them. There was some class there and some good ideas, so I stuck it out. I blocked out a couple of [*Alligator People* drafts] and they were never quite right, and I was getting frustrated. And, again, my ulcer started getting me. Finally I looked at the producer Jack Leewood one day and I said, "I'm startin' to *suffer* here, and I don't like it. And I don't think it helps your script, and I don't think it's gonna get a lot better. You give me a free hand and I'll give you a good script, *or*..." Finally they paid me money to go away. It's the only time that ever happened. It wasn't a lot of money, I think it was $5000 or something. They gave me that money and we parted amicably. Who *did* the script? Who got the credit? I can't even remember.

Well, you're uncredited. The story is Orville H. Hampton and Charles O'Neal; the screenplay, Hampton.

I knew Hampton; I don't know who the hell Charles O'Neal was.

He wrote a lot of old movies. He was the father of Ryan O'Neal.

Really? Oh, that's interesting. I knew Ryan O'Neal came from a Hollywood

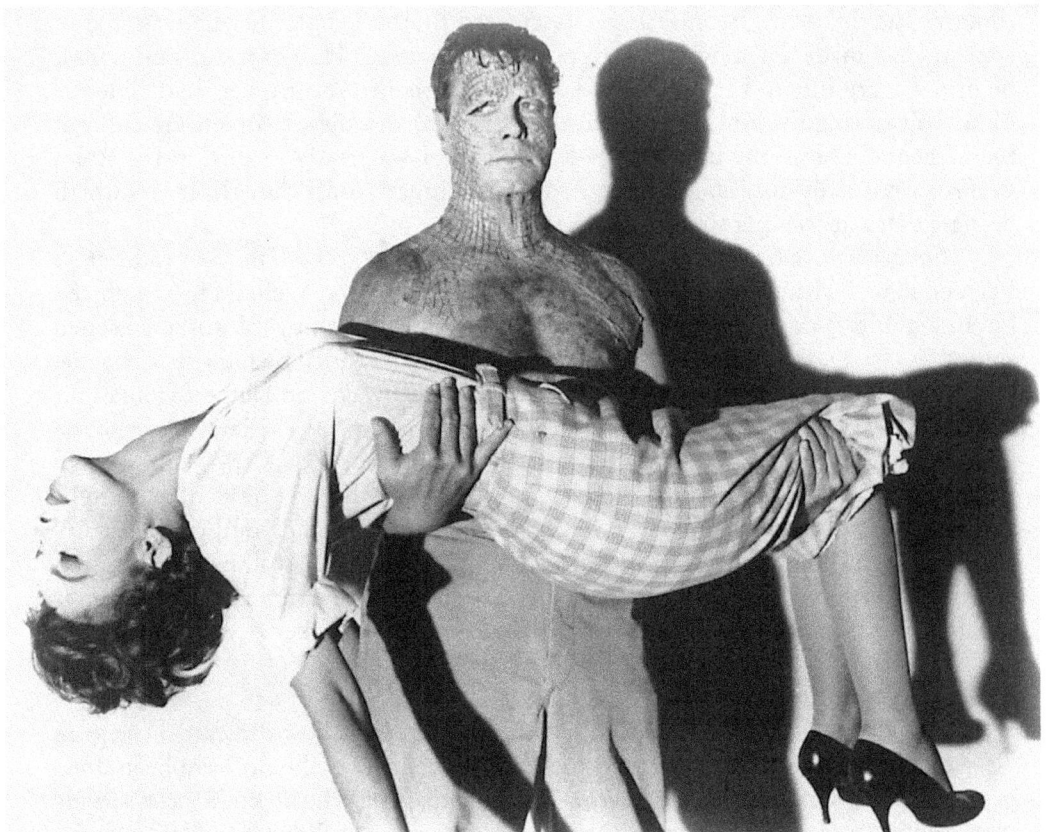

Richard Crane, well on his way to becoming one of *The Alligator People*, does the Beauty and the Beast bit with screen bride Beverly Garland.

family, but I didn't know who and what. I knew Hampton from the Guild, or *some* place; we'd shaken hands. But we never met on the film. It was a friendly experience, don't get me wrong. There were parties, I remember being at James Clavell's home and all that, people were friendly, it was a decent environment. Lippert was sleazy, but he was fascinating, and he really intrigued me as a character. I could see doing a movie about a Robert L. Lippert, with*out* making him a monster [*laughs*]. He was just this middle-aged businessman who wanted to get into the young girls. He wasn't the first—*or* the last.

The plots of The Fly *and* The Alligator People *have a few striking similarities. Were you influenced by* The Fly?
No. When I started *The Alligator People*, *believe* me, it wasn't like *The Fly*. The last thing I would do is emulate somebody's else story. Whoever ended up writing it took that tack.

And did you get to meet Roy Del Ruth, the director of Alligator People?
Roy Del Ruth was fascinating. I met with him at the old Nibbler's, a famous

hangout deep in Beverly Hills [to talk about *Alligator People*], and we got along. But he wasn't in control of anything [on the set], he was there to make sure the actors knew their lines. By then, all he did was tell stories about his great movies. But he was a very nice man and I had a lot of respect for him.

Alligator People was my last [science fiction credit], I was at the end of my tether with science fiction. By this time I was about 29, and I was so *sick* of spiders and of alligators and of writing "Medium Shot—Monster" that I almost had that ulcer. I mean, I don't think I ate anything stronger than cottage cheese and drank anything stronger than a glass of sherry a *year*. I couldn't eat *lettuce*...! The time had come to change my life around. So in 1959, I got involved with a series for ABC called *John Gunther's High Road*. Remember John Gunther? He was an author who wrote *Inside Europe, Inside Asia*, Inside This, Inside That—he was a guru for his time. I worked on that for, I don't know, part of a year. Prior to that, I used to spend money made from writing "Medium Shot—Monster" and try to make documentaries. I was just feeling my way, and losing thousands here and there. But *John Gunther's High Road* was the first time that I was seriously involved with professional [documentary] filmmaking, and I found that I *loved* the documentary and that I had a knack for writing for it and that I had a knack for editing it. That led to my being hired by David Wolper in '60 or '61, when Wolper was the leading independent documentary producer in the country. He gathered together all kinds of people and we made all kinds of wonderful TV films for two or three years. He had a series called *The Story of...* on ABC, and I became the writer of the series and the associate producer.

*You did a film on the Soviet invasion of Czechoslovakia [*Czechoslovakia 1968, 1969*] which won an Oscar, and also a four-part PBS special called* Trial *which received a number of awards.*

When I was working with Wolper and doing *The Story of...*, we couldn't do the story of a lawyer because we couldn't get into a courtroom. And when we did the story of a Congressman, we couldn't get onto the floor of the Congress. That pissed me off—I thought, "What are we, still in the star chamber days? That's *wrong*." So I determined that I'd try to bust that. It took me a lot of years, but in 1969, we got permission to shoot in the courtrooms of Denver, Colorado. It was a local Black Panther vs. the cops. Remember, this was '69–70 America, Stokely Carmichael time and Black Panther time. The cops were harassing the local Panther, the Panther was calling the cops mother fuckers and [*sarcastically*] "a wonderful time was had by all." And when the Black Panther went on trial, I was able to put a cameraman in the jury box, I had another cameraman across the room, and we filmed the trial. We also filmed running interviews every day with the cop, the defendant and the judge—Zita Weinshienk, the first female judge in the history of the state of Colorado. We did very well with *Trial*—we were nominated for an Emmy, we won the EBU [European Broadcasting Union] award at the Cannes Film Festival and so on. And *Trial* led to a lot of good things—well, it led to Court TV, which I didn't even *dream* of. (That was a $50 million mistake!) But I didn't do it to make money, I did it to let the air into the courtroom. And what it did directly lead to, which makes

Waltzing with Dinosaurs: Veteran monster movie scribe Fresco (and friend) in a recent shot.

me quite proud, is the televising of the Congress. So now we get to see the monkeys in their cage [*laughs*], and I think that that's a service to the country.

By the way, there was a "wonderful" moment in the history of *Trial* which deals with science fiction. After *Trial* came out and it was incredibly well-reviewed, won all kinds of awards, I was on 13 [New York City's Public Television channel] for a show about whether cameras should really be in courtrooms everywhere. There were all these eminent lawyers, William Kuntsler was one of them. And this idiot woman who introduced me, instead of starting with the stuff that was cogent, *Trial* and *First Camera* and other things, she started at the bottom and she said, "And Mr. Fresco is the author of *Tarantula*." Of course, the people there never *looked* at me again, they felt I was some kind of alien who had wandered onto the set [*laughs*]. "Hey, what the fuck are *you* doing here? We're talking about serious stuff!"—and, of course, I'm the guy who'd *done* it [gotten cameras into courtrooms]! It was funny.

I've interviewed a number of writers of the old science fiction films, but none of them did the kind of "serious stuff" you've done afterwards.
  I got serious, right? Well, I was so fuckin' sick of science fiction. But you know what I've got in my head *now*, of course, don't you? A marvelous science fiction film [*laughs*]. I mean, a really good one, a really interesting idea. The kind of thoughtful thing that has to do with people's aggression towards other people and an attempt to fix that, an attempt which of course goes wrong, as most attempts do. But not violence for violence's sake. One thing that pleases me is, in every-god-damned-thing I've ever written, I think there have been three punches thrown, and they were always amazingly legitimate. I mean, I did *Wagon Train*s and a bunch of *Bonanza*s and all that stuff, and there were never any arbitrary fistfights, never threatening with guns. I've never used violence or the threat of violence in anything I've ever written, and I'm pleased with that. One of the reasons I don't have millions of dollars!

So are you embarrassed to be doing an interview focusing on your science fiction movies?
  Well, it's interesting: I used to be ashamed of them. And now I'm not. I've put them in context. It was a kind of growing-up for me. I couldn't break out of them. I tried, I'd do all kinds of originals. I could always get a thousand bucks a week writing "Medium Shot—Monster," but they wouldn't take an original. You have to remember that the '50s and early '60s were terrible days in terms of original film and filmmaking, it was all very, very "routinized." A film like *Marty* [1955] was looked upon as something from Mars. I got tired of science fiction, I was *ashamed* of it.
  But I don't feel that way any more. I mean, I'm pleased that I did it, and I get an *immense* kick out of friends of mine calling me after Halloween and saying, "You won't *believe* what I saw on the blah blah blah channel!" Something fun, like *Tarantula*, or something hideous like *The Monolith Monsters*! And I still get a few hundred dollars a year in residuals—my father used to call 'em "residentials," because they helped pay the rent. It tickles me that I'm still getting paid for something I wrote in 1954, when I was 24 years old.

Alex Gordon on The Atomic Submarine

> *When I finally saw [the one-eyed monster] on the screen, in rushes, I was fit to be tied. I said it was so awful and it looked so cheap that I didn't want a monster in the picture.*

In August 1958, the U.S. Navy submarine *Nautilus*, the world's first nuclear-powered vessel, made a historic undersea journey from Point Barrow, Alaska, to the Greenland Sea, passing under the ice cap of the North Pole. The "top of the world" exploits of the sub and its daring crew did not go unnoticed by Hollywood moviemakers: Just one week after the *Nautilus* reached its destination, the movie capital's trade papers were announcing that producer Alex Gordon had already registered the title *The Atomic Submarine* and was preparing the picture for production.

Of course, Gordon being the past producer of such horror hits as *Day the World Ended* and *The She-Creature* (both 1956), the crew of his soundstage sub contended with more than just arctic ice and cold. In the screenplay by Gordon's producing partner Orville H. Hampton, the men of the submarine "Tiger Shark" are on the trail of an underwater flying saucer and its occupant: A giant, tentacled stalk with its (one) eye fixed on the conquest of the Earth. In this interview, Gordon talks "in depth" about the battle to bring *The Atomic Submarine* to the screen.

According to 1958 press clippings, the journey of the Nautilus *inspired you to make your movie.*

That had something to do with it, yes, it *was* based on the idea of something like the *Nautilus*. But actually I had made a submarine picture before, *Submarine Seahawk* [1958] with John Bentley, the British actor, at American International, written by Orville Hampton. And I was always interested in submarines and old submarine pictures—*Submarine D-1* [1937] and others like that. Hampton and I thought it might be an interesting idea to try a submarine picture. Also, we knew we could buy stock footage and we wouldn't have to actually go *out* on a submarine, but instead just build a submarine *set* on the soundstage. That would make it easier budget-wise to make a submarine picture. When we made *Submarine Seahawk*, it was possible through my brother Dick [movie producer Richard Gordon], and Dick's connection with Seven Arts, to obtain stock footage from the Warner Brothers pictures *Destination Tokyo* and *Air Force* [1943], spectacular footage. It was rather funny: In their review of *Submarine Seahawk*, *The Los Angeles Times* said, "Particularly impressive is the inclusion of the authentic footage of the Battle of the Coral Sea, making *Submarine Seahawk* look much bigger than it actually is." But of course [*laughs*], even in the Warner Brothers pictures, it wasn't authentic footage, it was special effects!

Anyway, after *Submarine Seahawk* I thought, "Well, that seemed to come out pretty well. Let's try another submarine picture." Orville Hampton and I had formed a company called Gorham Productions—**Gor**don and **Ham**pton—and we thought we would do two projects, one a submarine picture, the other a picture called *The Beetle*. At just about that time, after *Submarine Seahawk*, I severed my connections with American International. I wasn't getting any money on my percentages on my AIP pictures, and I realized it would just go on like that. They were now making deals with many other producers, and I was being sort of shoved into the background a little bit. And also, they expected *me* to come up with some of the financing for my pictures. I wasn't really in that end of it, I didn't think that I *should* be responsible for that, because AIP was putting the money that my past AIP pictures had made into pictures that I was *not* involved with.

The Beetle, of course, was never made. What would that have been about?

A treatment was written by Orville Hampton, and actually it was the old "steal" on *Them!* [1954]: A group of scientists are looking for treasure in Egypt and they come upon this giant beetle which apparently is a throwback to the old days.

You once wrote that Atomic Submarine *was suggested by [special effects men] Jack Rabin and Irving Block.*

I forget now how I first met Rabin and Block—I think they came to *me*, because I was identified with some special effects pictures. They said they had an idea of a combination of a submarine picture and a horror picture. So we were discussing it, and they said that they would come in for a *very* good price and do a lot of special effects on deferment and so on. There were some script rewrites, and then when the script was done and we all sort of liked the way it came out, I took it over to Allied Artists, to Allied's president Steve Broidy. He said that he liked the idea of the picture, if we could make it for a *price*. "Let's budget the picture and see how we come out," Broidy said, "and then see if we can work out a deal."

Did you do the budgeting?

No, I got my regular production manager Bart Carré to make a budget for the picture, and he came out at $135–137,000, depending on the cast. I went back to Allied Artists and they said that they would put up 60 percent of the budget, and then recoup it in first position. And we would have to come up with the balance of

Producer Alex Gordon's *The Atomic Submarine* was an attempt to cash in on publicity surrounding the then-new *Nautilus* submarine and the sci-fi movie craze. (Left to right, Dick Foran, Arthur Franz, Paul Dubov.)

40 percent, and be in second position. That was their regular deal for independents on my level. Also, we would have to supply a completion bond. So the picture was budgeted for eight days of production, plus however long it would take to do the special effects. The special effects costs were limited to between $25,000–27,000. Oh, and Allied Artists said we would have to use part of the regular crew that they

had on salary for their various pictures, so we would need to use Edward Morey, Jr., who was production manager on virtually *all* Allied Artists pictures.

Instead of Bart Carré, who was usually production manager on your movies.

Bart Carré was still tied up with American International Pictures, so he couldn't have done it anyway. Bart said, "Look, I can't go over to Allied Artists with you because I'm doing more AIP pictures. Use Clark Paylow." The crew was a combination of a few Allied Artists people but mostly "our" people [Gordon regulars] like Harry Reif the set decorator, who was on all my pictures, and Judy Hart the script supervisor, who was the daughter of Edward L. Cahn and was script supervisor on the pictures that Cahn did at American International. And I selected [director of photography] Gilbert Warrenton—Bart Carré had suggested him, and I immediately was thrilled to have him. He went back to the days of the silent *The Cat and the Canary* [1927] and Mary Pickford and so on, and he was terrific. What was great about him was the fact that he took just as much care shooting that picture with umpteen setups a day as he did on some of the *big* pictures he'd worked on. This was something that always impressed me about Hollywood crews: For the most part, they took just as much care with B pictures as they did with much bigger pictures.

Warrenton later photographed Master of the World *[1961] for director William Witney, who complained to me that he was "so god-damn slow."*

Incredible! Somebody should have told Witney that Warrenton turned out *our* picture, with all the effects and the lighting and all that, in eight days.

Before we get even further ahead of ourselves—how did you go about raising your end of the money?

Henry Schrage, who had co-produced a couple of Bert I. Gordon's pictures, had recently broken up with Bert Gordon. He agreed to put up some of the money that we needed for our 40 percent of the budget, and in return for that, he became a co-producer. He wanted a better credit than he had on Bert Gordon pictures. Schrage put up $19,000 but we actually needed more than that, we needed...

40 percent of 135,000—whatever the heck that is!

[*Laughs*] Yeah, that's right. Through connections with Dick, I flew to New York to try and get a man named Peter Gettinger, a well-known finance man for independent movies, to put up some of the money and a completion bond. And would you believe that the day I flew, I got complete laryngitis! When Dick took me in there to talk to Gettinger, I could hardly talk! I was croaking—it was very embarrassing! And Gettinger told me, "Look, you made a *lousy* deal with Allied Artists. I'm not going to put up any money *or* a completion bond."

I'd heard that a man by the name of Theodore Ticktin had put up a completion bond for one or two pictures, so I went to see him and he was a *very* nice man. Now *there* was a person you could really talk to—*and* a very good financing man. He was actually a builder here [in California], building and buying real estate and so on. He was interested and we got on very well with him, and he (I guess) thought

I had an honest face [*laughs*]. Anyway, to make a long story short, he agreed to put up a completion bond for us. That was, of course, a great break. Then I got a couple of friends of mine to put up a little money—one was an agent, Allen Connor, and another one was a personal friend, a businessman. One put up $5000, the other $7500 to help us with some of the 40 percent on our end.

Allen Connor the actor?
Yes, in the 1930s, he was in some Republic pictures; the one that people usually remember is the serial *S O S Coast Guard* [1937] with Ralph Byrd and Bela Lugosi, where he played the brother of the leading lady, Maxine Doyle. Then he became an agent with the Wallace Middleton Agency.

What did your total budget come to?
$137,931. The above-the-line, the story, cast, director and everything, came to $23,554. Below-the-line, $104,957. So a total of $128,511. So we had to have the figure between the 128,511 and 137,931 as deferments. Naturally my producer's fee, my $5000, was deferred, and Rabin-Block was the other deferment.

Then the rest of the money came from Allied Artists.
Right. Allied Artists was interested in a lot of small independent pictures, pictures which were exploitable, and where they only needed to put up 60 percent of the money and had first position. They figured they would certainly make *that* back, even if the *producer* didn't get any money! Those who were in second position were often left empty-handed.

Being in second position—that's when it got "iffy"!
That's when it got very iffy! As I mentioned, I was told by certain people that I didn't make a very good deal with them. But I had no real clout at the time. Steve Broidy was a very tough person to deal with. He was considered a great humanitarian and he was on all the boards of all the benevolent societies and motion picture charities ... but sitting across a desk from him, he would talk very loud at you and was very pushy, like a steamroller pushing over you if you came up with any thoughts. He was one of these "booming" people, it seemed he couldn't just speak in a normal voice. A lot of big movie executives were like that—I guess they were trying to intimidate you. And, frankly, I was a bit intimidated by him! Also, it didn't work that I reminded him that I was the one responsible for bringing Monogram's "Rough Riders" Westerns from 1941-42 to England. Originally they weren't going to be shown over there because of the "Bacon or Bogart" situation.

You're going to have to explain that one!
Due to World War II, there was at that time a restriction on importing American pictures. In Parliament, someone had said, "Look, what do you prefer, bacon or Humphrey Bogart? We've got to limit the number of pictures that can come in. We need the convoys for food and weapons and things—we can't use that much shipping space importing movies!" So I wrote Pathé Pictures [the British distributor of

Monogram Pictures], I bombarded them, urging them to bring in the Rough Riders. I said Buck Jones, Tim McCoy and Raymond Hatton, the stars of the Rough Riders series, were still big names in England, and promised to help to promote them through my Westerners Club [a fan club devoted to Western stars]. And finally they *did*, they brought in *Arizona Bound* and *The Gunman from Bodie* [both 1941], the first two, and then they brought in *Forbidden Trails* [1941], *Down Texas Way*, *Ghost Town Law* and *Below the Border* [all 1942]. Those Rough Riders pictures were shown in England, and Monogram made quite a bit of money out of it ... but when I brought it up, Broidy brushed that aside. He wasn't the type that you could talk to about something like that. He was just business. And his second-in-command, his "hatchet man," George Burrows, was even tougher. Burrows was the financial man.

Were you able to make it in eight days, as planned?
Eight days. And then Rabin and Block had several weeks for their special effects.

Your parting of the ways with AIP wasn't 100 percent pleasant. Did you have an "I'll show them*" attitude in the back of your mind when you went off on your own to make movies?*
It wasn't really an "I'll show *them*" attitude, I just wanted *out*. And I wanted to try to do better, try to "upgrade" a little bit. At that point, the AIP experience was water under the bridge.

I assume you did the casting...?
I always did my own casting on *all* my pictures, down to the bit parts and extras and everything. Allied Artists, however, had a casting director who was a rather miserable kind of a person, very tough to talk to, very unpleasant, named Joe Rivkin. Although he had a good reputation in the trade, he was one of those rough, tough-talking people (with the bad language and everything) who worked for several studios. And he took a particular delight in wanting to impose his casting choices, which I didn't like. George Burrows, Broidy's second-in-command, said Rivkin would do the casting and get us a good cast, and I said, "No, no. I always do my own casting." Burrows said, "Well, you better work *with* Rivkin, then, because we have to *approve* the cast." By that, I think he meant the leads, the first four or five people.

Well, I thought of John Agar, with whom I had worked on *Flesh and the Spur* [1957] and *Jet Attack* [1958], but his agent quoted too high a price. So then I took Marshall Thompson and Arthur Franz to lunch. They were close friends [of each other]. I knew Marshall Thompson because he had done several pictures with my brother Dick, so I got in touch with him and with Franz and I had lunch with them at Frascati's on the Sunset Strip, a great French-Belgian restaurant I liked. I told them, "I would love to have *both* of you in the picture [Franz as Lt. Comdr. Holloway, Thompson as Comdr. Wendover], but unfortunately in this particular case I can't *afford* to have both of you, I can only have one of you." So Thompson said, "Then take Arthur." He didn't *say* that Arthur wasn't working too much lately and

Arthur Franz nearly mutinied when producer Gordon wouldn't allow him—and his kids!—to screen the daily rushes.

needed the money, but ... he inferred it. So I said fine, I'd be delighted to have Franz. And Allied Artists approved Arthur Franz.

How much would actors on the Franz-Thompson level have commanded in 1959?
    I think they wanted 1500 each. We settled for 1000 with Arthur Franz. Then, for the other parts, I began looking through various agents' books. I didn't think of

Dick Foran right away, but when I saw his picture, and they said that he would work for a week for a thousand dollars [as Comdr. Wendover], I thought, "That's pretty good!" And he'd already worked in an Allied Artists picture or two, so they approved him. As it turned out, I had much more fun talking to Dick Foran than I would have with Marshall Thompson, who was a rather reserved type and not all that interested in his old pictures and all that. Brett Halsey they all thought was a very good idea, too—I'd used him in *Submarine Seahawk*. He was a *very* nice guy who was going at the time with Italian actress Luciana Paluzzi. Allied thought his was a very good name, that was fine.

Did Luciana Paluzzi visit the set?

She visited quite a bit. I don't know if she didn't trust Brett with the ladies [*laughs*] but, yes, she *did* visit quite a bit and she also came to a showing of it and was very complimentary. She was very, very nice-looking, very much Americanized, and they seemed to be very happy together when they were on the set.

Anyway, then I came to my famous "supporting casting." Paul Dubov, Allied didn't care; he had worked *very* well with us on several other pictures, including *Day the World Ended* and *The She-Creature*, and was always on time and knew his lines and everything. So that was great. Bob Steele they also didn't object to; that role was further down the castlist, they thought he was okay. I liked Bob Steele and used him wherever I could. When I suggested Victor Varconi, they sort of did a double-take [*laughs*], but they didn't object. Of course, I was thinking of Varconi back to when he was playing Admiral Nelson in *The Divine Lady* [1929], things like that. So *he* was accepted. Jean Moorhead had been in my picture *Motorcycle Gang* [1957], a very attractive girl, very nice. Joi Lansing was someone Rivkin proposed, and I gave way to him. I was told that she was Frank Sinatra's girlfriend—or one of many [*laughs*]—and she'd work one day for 250 bucks. They probably wanted to use her in order to keep in good with Sinatra and especially the William Morris Agency, who represented her. I said, "That's fine," even though 250 bucks was a lot of money for us—we would have ordinarily paid a hundred bucks for that role. She turned out to be a *very* sweet girl, didn't bother us at all, had no airs. The guy who did the saucer voice [John Hilliard] I think may have been suggested by Spencer Bennet, our director. I think Spence knew him and had used him on some narration at Columbia, or wherever.

And, getting special "and" billing, Tom Conway.

Tom Conway I *loved*—he was a terrific guy, a terrific actor, and he had a great sense of humor. I'd already used him in *The She-Creature* and *Voodoo Woman* [1957], and I had *started Runaway Daughters* [1956] with him but then, unfortunately, he got sick and we had to replace him with John Litel. In a way, I felt I owed him another picture, because we made a multiple deal with his agent Wallace Middleton, and Conway had even flown over from England especially to do *The She-Creature* for us, when we were in trouble. So I really wanted to use Tom wherever I could. (And, also, he needed the money.) So I got *him* in it, and of course he was a *very* good name for Allied Artists.

Joi Lansing wearing considerably less in this *Atomic Submarine* portrait shot than she does in the film.

As always with you, familiar faces even in the tiniest parts.

Selmer Jackson, who played the admiral—of course, nobody could object to him, he'd played so many Army and Navy men! Jack Mulhall was an old pal of mine and I tried to get him in wherever I could. Sid Melton was somebody that Henry Schrage wanted, so I threw him a bone. I *hated* Sid Melton on-screen, the kind of roles that he always played—the loudmouth. I didn't think he was the least bit funny. And he was also the kind who, on the set, wouldn't leave you alone for a *moment*—he was always suggesting bits of business and additional dialogue and so on. He was a nice guy personally but it was just *too much*, he was always after you!

Edmund Cobb and Frank Lackteen were two actors I used whenever I could, and I *told* Joe Rivkin, "Of course I always use Edmund Cobb and Frank Lackteen." He knew who they were and he said, "You can't have them on the submarine, they're much too old." I said, "I know that, I'm just gonna have 'em like as extras, walking by in the submarine yard." He said, "That's ridiculous, that's throwing money away. We'd have to pay them $100 each [an actor's minimum one-day salary], and nobody'll even recognize them. If anybody is to walk by, it can be an extra at 20 bucks." I said, "Well, I *insist* on having them in there." This was really going to be an issue, you know! I told him I would pay it out of my own pocket, but to no avail. He said [*flatly*], "*No.* I'm going to tell Steve Broidy that that's a waste of money."

So the next morning at six o'clock, I was outside the Allied Artists gate, in the brush there, waiting to "ambush" Steve Broidy. I knew that at nine o'clock, Broidy was going to come in. I waited from six o'clock 'til five to nine—and it was cold! And as Broidy's car drew up and as his driver stopped at the gate, I got on the running board of the car. I had my courage back—I was now fighting for somebody *else*, not for myself. I said, "Mr. Broidy, before anything else, before you go to your office, I've got a problem that I've got to solve and it means a lot to me. Do you mind if I walk with you to your office?" He said okay. So Broidy walked in with me as the driver put the car away, and I said, "Look, this is so stupid, we're arguing here about a situation of Edmund Cobb and Frank Lackteen…" He knew them from Monogram Pictures. "I use them in virtually every picture. It's a question of [Lackteen and Cobb] working as actors, not as extras, so it's a hundred bucks each. I will pay that out of my money, but I want them in this picture." Broidy said [*in a weary voice*], "Why is Rivkin making all this fuss about it? *Certainly* you can use them. As soon as I get to the office, I'll call him and tell him to … to shut up!" [*Laughs*] So after that, I felt a little better about Broidy, I felt, "Okay, he *is* all right to sit on the Board of Directors of those humanitarian organizations—he's not as bad as I thought at first!"*

Where was the picture shot?

Entirely at Allied Artists' studios at the corner of Sunset and Hollywood Boulevard. They had a series of bungalows and one soundstage, so that's where we were shooting it. It was all shot on the one soundstage.

Was Spencer Bennet your first and only choice as director?

Actually, we initially wanted Edward L. Cahn and we did *go* to him, Orville Hampton and I. But he was exclusive with Edward Small by then, so we got Spencer Bennet. I was very happy with Bennet, who was a good friend and a wonderful, likable man. And he worked fast! He was not as good a director as Eddie Cahn, I think,

---

**Funnily enough, after all this fuss, the footage of Cobb and Lackteen walking past as extras did not make its way into the final cut!*

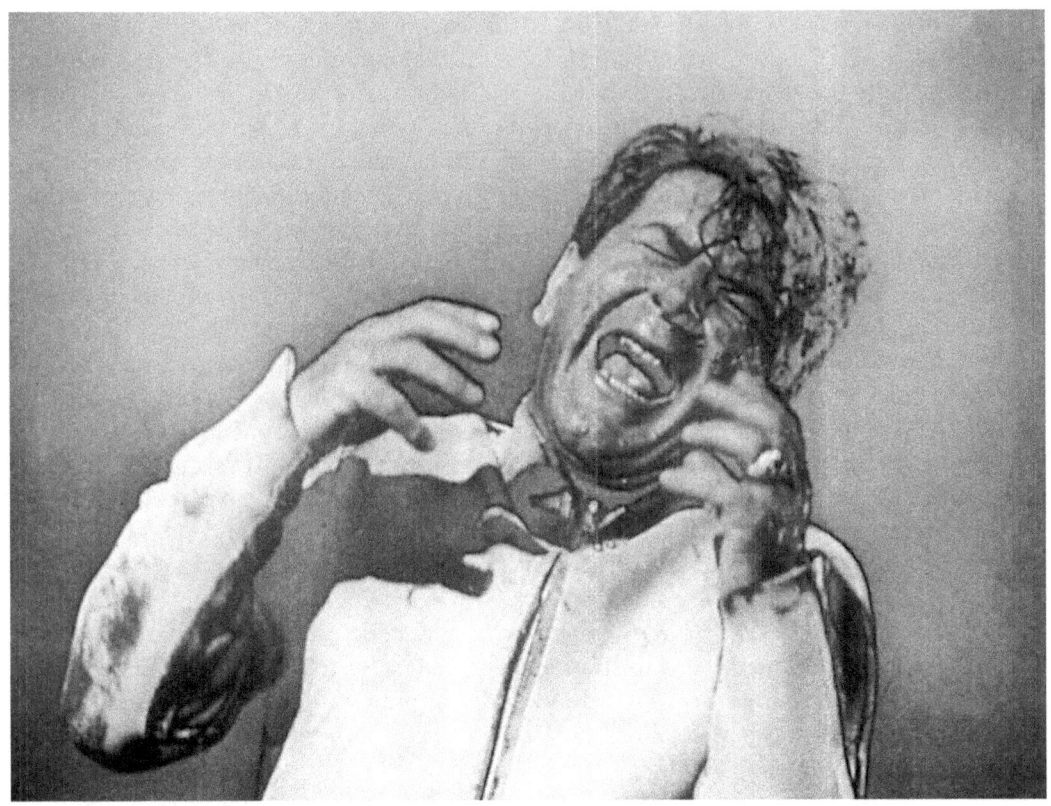

The saucer alien turns up the heat on Paul Dubov.

because he didn't direct the actors at all. If they spoke their lines, that was it [*laughs*]—that was good enough for him! Eddie Cahn did try to direct the actors, especially when he was working with people like Marla English, who needed a little help.

Were you pleased with the set-up at Allied Artists and the sets and all?
   The submarine set was marvelous. That was the set decorators and Warrenton with his lenses and lighting. In fact, when my wife Ruth came on the set, she said, "That set is so small ... how can you get anybody *in* that set?" And Warrenton said, "Come here and look through the camera." When she looked through the camera, it was like you were in a real submarine. It was the same with *Submarine Seahawk*.

Who came up with the name Tiger Shark *for the submarine?*
   Tiger Shark was my idea, because of the [1932] Edward G. Robinson picture, one of my favorite movies.

The DVD of Atomic Submarine *is so sharp, I can see a copy of* Argosy *magazine on a table in one scene. Was that some sort of in-joke, or...?*
   I believe we were hoping to get some kind of a publicity plug in *Argosy*, some kind of mention or coverage.

Representing the interior of the flying saucer with just a black set and a narrow walkway ... did you think this "worked"?

I thought that black set and narrow walkway worked very well. When I first saw it, I didn't think for a moment that it was impressive, but once it had the lighting and everything, everybody agreed that it was very effective.

I'm assuming it was done that way because there wasn't much money going around.

Yes, it was. But even with no money, [the set designers] still wanted to give it whatever they could—inventive lighting and so on.

You mentioned your wife Ruth a moment ago. You gave her an "Assistant to Producer" credit on the picture.

She was actually the dialogue coach, because Victor Varconi, who had a strong Hungarian accent, found it very difficult to speak the lines that he was given. It never even occurred to me when we first had the script, but there *were* a lot of technical explanations, a lot of technical verbiage from Varconi, when they're all sitting there, talking about things. And he had a lot of trouble with the pronunciation and memorizing those lines. Ruth said, "Why don't you let me take him aside and coach him, go over the lines with him? That might help him." (She had done this before, she had worked in a little theater group for quite a while.) And it did help Varconi. Then, when a couple of the *others* said, "Can I read lines with you too?" I said, "Let her get some kind of a credit." So that's how she got in on that.

And the rest of the actors? Any problems from any of them?

Well, Arthur Franz was a strange man. He was "up" on his dialogue, he never kept you waiting, and he said all his lines and everything, hardly ever fluffed. But he wanted to come and see the rushes—and even bring his *kids* to see the rushes! I said, "I'm sorry, Arthur. Allied Artists does not allow actors to see rushes"—I made it appear that it was all Allied. If Allied *had* allowed it, I would have *maybe* given way, I don't know, because he was so emphatic about it. But I didn't like the idea of actors seeing rushes either, because they may want to do something over again, so on and so forth. As I said, Franz would do all his stuff very professionally, but then if I wanted to sort of approach him on something, sometimes he'd shun me and sit down all alone on the stairs, waiting for his next shot. It wasn't easy to have little conversations with him, like with the others. So he was not too friendly, but I thought he came off well in the picture. Brett Halsey was a very sweet man, very nice. He was always with the girls, but he was a nice guy and worked very hard and knew his lines. Bob Steele, of course, was like "family," and we had a great time.

Dick Foran was an absolute delight. I was talking to him about all his Westerns and serials and all that. Real nice guy. He rather underplayed his part in the picture; he could have given it, I think, a little more emphasis. But that's all right. After principal photography was completed on the eighth day on time and schedule, we had a little party on the soundstage for the cast and crew, and I decided to pull a surprise on Dick. I had in my record collection a 78 RPM record of Foran singing "The Prairie Is My Home" [from one of his 1930s Warner Brothers West-

Dick Foran, Western star of the 1930s–'40s, suited up for atom-age naval action.

erns] and "Mexicali Rose." I bought it in England as a kid and brought it with me when I came to America after the War. As everyone was having drinks and buffet meals, I put on the record over the loudspeaker, waiting for Foran's reaction.

Dick was talking with some people and suddenly stopped in mid-sentence. With a look of utter surprise, he exploded, "My God, that's *me* singing!" When both

Gordon "regular" Tom Conway got special "and" billing for his role as scientist Sir Ian.

sides had been played, he rushed up to me and said, "Where on Earth did you get that record? I've never *heard* it before!" It seems that, around the same time Dick recorded "Mexicali Rose," it was also recorded by Gene Autry, and Autry's became a gold record for him immediately. The Gene Autry version was such a big hit that the record company shelved the Dick Foran one, except in England. It was a fun moment that has stayed in my memory.

To me, Tom Conway looks a lot older here than he does in his other pictures for you. Was that due to his drinking?

I don't really remember that Tom Conway looked so much older, but if he did, it was due to his illness, because this wasn't too long after *Runaway Daughters* ... and he was having other health problems too. He didn't really have a drinking problem. Perhaps he did drink a little too much at times, but never on the set when we were working. But sometimes, when we were at his house, he *was* inclined to take that extra drink. Whether that had anything to do with his illnesses or not, I don't know, but anyway, he wasn't too well. But he was definitely "with it," he knew all his lines and didn't fluff.

Did you get along well with Rabin and Block?

I got along with them *until* I saw the so-called "monster." They made a miniature figure of the one-eyed alien, about a foot and a half high—about the size of the figure that was used in *King Kong* [1933]. They never showed it to me, I never saw it until after they shot it. I kept asking, I wanted to see it, and they (probably realizing what my reaction would be) refused to show it to me. So I was mad as hell. And then when I finally saw it on the screen, in rushes, I was fit to be tied. I said it was *so* awful and it looked *so* cheap that I didn't want a monster in the picture. So we went to Steve Broidy—Rabin and Block and Hampton and I. I don't think we actually took the puppet with us, I think we just took the few feet of footage that they had shot. I said to Broidy, "This is going to look very, very bad. It's not a good special effect. I don't think we ought to show the monster, I think we ought to just suggest it." And Broidy said, "No, we gotta have a monster in the picture." So I had to agree to do it. And, actually, I *will* say this for Rabin and Block: When it was photographed for the picture, the way the cameraman did it, it doesn't look at all bad and I was satisfied. Especially with the sound effects, and the diffused alien voice, and the set and all. So I changed my mind, I now think it was adequate. But at the time, of course, I was very, very upset and disappointed.

When you told Broidy it was very, very bad, were Rabin and Block within earshot?

Oh, yes, they were sitting right there [*laughs*]! I told him I thought it was a lousy monster!

Did Gilbert Warrenton also photograph Rabin and Block's effects footage?

No, Rabin and Block did all that in their lab.

Rabin and Block get a co-producing credit.

They didn't co-produce the picture *except* if you want to say that their special effects made it a "co-production" venture. You might say they deserved their credit because they did produce the special effects.

How about your other co-producer, Henry Schrage? Was he involved in the making of the movie?

Schrage was strictly a money man. He had nothing to do with the actual production of the picture, but he wanted a credit. And Hampton also had nothing to do with the picture at all except the script. "Gorham Productions," Gordon and Hampton, was formed to make films, but it was dissolved after we did *The Underwater City* [1962] at Columbia Studios because Hampton got a deal working for Edward Small, making a whole bunch of pictures there. So Hampton and I had to dissolve the company.

And Allied Artists was pleased with it when you screened it for them?
Yes. One of their executives, Ben Schwalb, said, "It's a good little picture…," indicating that it was all right for Allied Artists.

Jack Rabin once told an interviewer that Atomic Submarine *was "a horrible picture."*
I'm surprised, because he later came to us wanting to do another project.

Whose idea was the "Electro-Sonic" music? How well did you think that worked?
The composer Alexander Laszlo was recommended to us by Bart Carré, and he [Laszlo] had the idea for the Electro-Sonic music score. He gave us a sample of it and we liked the idea, so we worked with him. I think it worked all right. I like "full" music scores, I'm not crazy about [electronic] music, but I thought it came through all right for this picture.

Did Atomic Submarine *have a preview, the way so many of your AIP pictures did? What was the audience reaction?*
It was previewed in Seattle. It was on a single bill there, in a first-run theater for Allied Artists. I wasn't present because I didn't know they were going to do it. I probably couldn't have gotten up to Seattle anyway. But it was very good, the reaction.

You can't really tell from the poster of Atomic Submarine, *and you definitely can't tell from the trailer, that it's sci-fi. Was Allied Artists trying to sell it as a "straight" submarine action movie?*
I never thought about it, but I suppose the poster *doesn't* really indicate that it's sci-fi. If you look at the lobby cards, however, there *is* an indication that there is some terror there. There's not a big emphasis on it, they don't show the one-eyed creature and all that. But I don't think they were trying to sell it as a straightforward submarine picture.

The trailer promises "adventures beneath the waves" and that kind of stuff. No indication of the flying saucer, the monster, nothing.
Well, you're probably right then, maybe Allied Artists *did* try to sell it as a straightforward submarine picture.

Was it profitable for Allied Artists and you?
It was *not* profitable for us, although everybody got their money back. At first we weren't getting any money, of course, because Allied Artists was getting their 60

Top: The flying saucer (as seen on *The Atomic Submarine*'s view screen). *Bottom:* Arthur Franz (in round portal) gets an eyeful of the saucer's Cyclopean occupant.

percent back first. After they had recouped their 60 percent and it came to our 40 percent, they began falling further and further behind in their reports to us. I had to keep calling about the reports, which were supposed to be quarterly. And there was no money. Sometimes they'd send us (like) $300 when they were supposed to send (like) $3000. This was going on and on, and I kept calling and calling and calling, and there'd be no reply. Their lawyer was Steve Broidy's future son-in-law Jack Sattinger, and I had the most *terrible* time with him. He was a Jack Carson look-alike and a Jack Carson "type," and I had a love-hate relationship with him. I *liked* the guy personally, and whenever we were face to face he was very nice. But he never returned my phone calls. Whenever he said we would have a contract, or this piece of paper, or that piece of paper, or that he would call me back, he never would. I sat by my phone literally all *day*—I didn't have an office, I was working out of my home at the time, and I was really in very bad shape there, my nerves were really on edge because this was a touch-and-go situation and I had people "on the hook" and that kind of thing. I went through a year or more of just terrible times. And later I realized that Allied Artists had money problems. They were pulling all kinds of [shenanigans] in order to try and get their house in order financially—but then they went broke, went into bankruptcy, and actually went out of business.

Finally, through our lawyer, I got a report of what they owed us, and it was something like $8400. We were entitled to that, that was part of our return, but with them in bankruptcy, we had to get a judgment against them. That took another I-don't-remember-*how*-many months. Finally we got a judgment against them and they were forced to pay it, but our lawyer took half of it.

But everybody who put up any cash on the picture eventually got paid back in full. Schrage was paid first, all the others got their money back too, Rabin and Block got their deferment, everybody got paid fully. I was last with my producer's fee, and *that* went to paying some [other outstanding debts], so I never really got any money out of the picture. When Dick arranged for a VHS home video deal on the picture, we got some money, but that also went towards paying what we still were "out" on expenses, personally. So when you ask, "Was it profitable for Allied Artists?" it *was* profitable for Allied Artists. But not for me and my co-producers!

Did the "recent" movie The Abyss *[1989] remind you a bit of the plot of* Atomic Submarine*?*

As soon as I saw that, I thought, "That's a direct steal from *The Atomic Submarine*." And there was another picture, made by Charles Band, where they used a one-eyed creature that was a direct steal.

Rate your horror-science fiction pictures, in order of preference.

I'd say probably *Day the World Ended* ... *The She-Creature* ... *The Atomic Submarine* ... then *Voodoo Woman*. The script of *Atomic Submarine*, of course, isn't the greatest, and some of the lines are a little... [*trails off, laughs*]. But I think the acting, for the most part, is okay. No great shakes, but it's competent. And there are so many diverse characters—Tom Conway is so different from Victor Varconi, and Varconi from Dick Foran, and so on. Arthur Franz, I think, is okay, and also Brett

Producer Gordon poses with posters of his subsea sci-fi adventures.

Halsey. But I'm not complaining. Thinking of all the grief we had to get it on the screen, I think it's adequate in its category.

The Atomic Submarine (Allied Artists, 1959)

A Gorham Production; 72 minutes; First day of shooting: June 18, 1959; Released in January 1960; Associate Producer: Orville H. Hampton; Co-Producer: Henry Schrage; Produced by Alex Gordon (In Association With Jack Rabin & Irving Block); Directed by Spencer G. Bennet; Screenplay: Orville H. Hampton; Story Ideas: Jack Rabin & Irving Block; Photography: Gilbert Warrenton; Special Effects Designed & Created by Jack Rabin, Irving Block & Louis DeWitt; Electro-Sonic Music Composed & Conducted by Alexander Laszlo; Art Directors: Don Ament & Dan Haller; Assistant to Producer: Ruth Alexander; Editor: William Austin; Production Manager: Edward Morey, Jr.; Assistant Director: Clark Paylow; Set Decorator: Harry Reif; Properties: Max Frankel; Chief Set Electrician: George Satterfield; Sound: Ralph Butler; Production Associate & Dialogue Supervisor: Jack Cash; Wardrobe: Roger J. Weinberg & Norah Sharpe; Makeup: Emile LaVigne; Script Supervisor: Judith Hart; Sound Editor: Marty Greco; Music Editor: Neil Brunnenkant

Arthur Franz (*Lt. Comdr. Richard "Reef" Holloway*), Dick Foran (*Comdr. Dan Wendover*), Brett Halsey (*Dr. Carl Neilsen*), Tom Conway (*Sir Ian*

Hunt), Paul Dubov (*Lt. Dave Milburn*), Bob Steele (*Chief Griffin ["Griff"]*), Victor Varconi (*Dr. Clifford Kent*), Joi Lansing (*Julie*), Selmer Jackson (*Admiral Terhune*), Jack Mulhall (*Secretary of Defense Justin Murdock*), Jean Moorhead (*Helen Milburn*), Richard Tyler (*Don Carney*), Sid Melton (*Yeoman Chester Tuttle*), Ken Becker (*Seaman First Class Al Powell*), Frank Watkins (*Operator*), Everett Creach (*Seaman*), Pat Michaels (*Narrator*), John Hilliard (*Saucer Voice*)

Brett Halsey

> *[In the Sicilian church where we shot* Demonia*], they had all these bodies on shelves on the wall! All very nicely dressed in their funeral finery, but having been there for maybe hundreds of years. ... Then there was a trap door in the floor, and we were told, "There's hundreds more down there." ... Everyone was kind of afraid to open that.*

Brett Halsey's career has gone through a record number of phases: In the 1950s, he went from boyish, toe-in-the-dirt roles in movies like *Ma and Pa Kettle at Home* to star of "wild youth" and sci-fi adventures; in the '60s and '70s, he could be found everywhere from European-made swashbucklers, Westerns and spy flicks to the top American soap operas like *General Hospital*. More recently, he became a regular in the gore-splattered films of Lucio Fulci (*Touch of Death*, *Demonia*, more). Taking advantage of his lifetime of film and TV experience, Halsey now juggles a Cinema Arts teaching job at the University of Costa Rica, acting assignments—and reminiscing about his many genre roles for this exclusive interview.

The son of a roving building contractor, Halsey (real name: Charles Oliver Hand) picked up his education in schools up and down the California coast. The nephew of famed Admiral "Bull" Halsey (and also related to the illustrious jurist Learned Hand), he was under contract to Universal at the start of the '50s and to 20th Century-Fox at the end—and, while freelancing in the interim, played his first sci-fi leads in *Return of the Fly* with Vincent Price and *The Atomic Submarine* (both 1959). In his subsequent European movie career, he has worked with all of Italy's top horrormeisters: Fulci, Mario Bava, Riccardo Freda and Dario Argento.

The dashing screen roles, the globetrotting lifestyle and the succession of glamourpuss wives (including Luciana Paluzzi, Heidi Bruhl and "Miss Germany" Renate Hoy) might turn the average actor's head, but Prof. Brett Halsey is friendly, funny and resolutely down-to-earth as he settles in to discuss the people and the productions that made him an international exploitation movie legend.

Having the wandering life that you did as a kid, where did you go to school?

I went to high school in San Francisco, and I graduated from Santa Cruz High School. I didn't go to university because at 19, I went under contract to Universal. Actually, I didn't go to university until I started teaching at a university [*laughs*]! My students all have more degrees than I do!

Would you have gone on to college if the Universal offer hadn't come up?

Yeah. But it got to where I was working and doing well, and in my teenage mentality I thought, "What the hell. I'm earning more money than most college professors, why should I quit?"

When did you first realize you had the urge to act?

I believe it happened when I was doing a church play when I was about five years old, playing King Midas. As a young child, I was performing in front of all these adults, and they were all *listening* to me, I had their attention, and it was as though I had some power over all these adults. And I *liked* that. I didn't realize it at the time, but I know now that it was right then and there that I became an actor.

How did you get your foot in the door at Universal?

That's one of those "Hollywood stories," like Lana Turner on her drug store stool. I was going to school, the Don Martin School of Radio and Television in Hollywood, studying acting. My plan was to get into radio and then into television and then into the movies ... or something like that. But I was also a page at KNX Radio on Sunset Boulevard, just east of Vine. *The Jack Benny Program* was done out of there. Well, Jack and Mary Benny were always really nice to me, they took a liking to me. One afternoon my supervisor came to me and said, "Mary wants you to work the Sponsors' Booth." The Sponsors' Booth was a glass booth overlooking the stage, where special guests would sit instead of sitting in the audience. I was there working the Sponsors' Booth and Mary came and she had a big smile. Next a man came, and she introduced me to him; I said, "How do you do?" I was polite to everybody, that was my job.

A couple days later, I got a call at school that they wanted to see me out at Universal. I called around to people I knew, and nobody knew why. I went to Universal and they said, "We're interested in you. Do you have any scenes?" I said, "Well, I have radio scenes." They said, "Okay, get one of your radio scenes and come back tomorrow at two o'clock." I went back tomorrow at two o'clock and they said, "We've decided to put you under contract." And I said, "...*Really?* Why?" And the casting director said [*flatly*], "I don't *know.*" [*Laughs*] Well, what happened was, the man that Mary introduced me to was the president of Universal, William Goetz. I had no idea who he was. Obviously she said, "Help the kid," and he said he would. I didn't know how it had all happened until, oh, about a week later, I guess, when Mary told me. I signed in October 1952—50 years ago this year.

So when you went back to Universal with your radio scene, did you have to play it for the guy?

Brett Halsey was a busy contract player at Universal in the days before B movie stardom.

Uhn-uh. No, he had received orders, "Put him under contract." Having me come back with that radio scene—that was "the routine," they had to at least "go through the motions." So that was it, I was under contract. And *that* [a contract] was something that *all* young actors were trying to get. At that time, most of the studios had "new talent" programs, and young actors from all over the world would compete to be accepted. In effect, what it *was* was, we were paid to go to school.

My interviewees tell me that Universal was one of the best places for that kind of stuff in the '50s.

Among my contemporaries, we seem to agree that Universal was *the* best.

Walk me through an average day at Universal when you were not working on a picture.
We had classes five and a half days a week—Saturday mornings we had horseback riding. We'd usually go to classes—dance and diction and acting and so on—in the morning, and then more classes in the afternoon, after we'd had lunch in the commissary. Sometimes they'd put us in films, if they needed to fill small parts. They also used to put us in their musical shorts. Another part of our school was doing looping on pictures, "walla walla" and so on. And, depending on the directors, I would often go to movie sets and just sit and watch.

Among the other actors and actresses there, who were your friends at Universal? Who did you gravitate to—or who gravitated to you?
Well, the friendship that has really lasted since then is with Clint Eastwood. We were pretty good pals, and have remained so through the years. There was John Saxon ... Tony Curtis ... Tony was a little bit ahead of us, Tony *and* Rock Hudson were like a class ahead of us.

They were still taking classes too, while you were there?
Yeah, more "specialized" classes. Rock more than Tony. And I remember Russ

Johnson, who was the Professor on *Gilligan's Island* ... Dick Long ... Jack Kelly ... Anita Ekberg ... I guess she came out with the biggest career, out of *our* class.

How would an actor find out that he'd gotten a part in a picture?
You'd have to go audition. The director had to *want* you—Universal didn't want to impose us on directors. The directors were told to use us unless they *really* didn't want to. I don't think I was ever refused.

All I Desire [1953] with Barbara Stanwyck—was that your first film?
Yeah. My first *whole* film. Before that, I had done a couple musical shorts. The first one was with Andy and Della Russell—Andy Russell was a Mexican pop singer, pretty famous in the States. Then I did another musical short, with (I think) Xavier Cugat.

When you started at Universal, your name was still Charles Hand. Changing it to Brett Halsey, whose idea was that?
The publicity department. Halsey is because of my great uncle the admiral, and Brett was just a name *they* picked out. It sounded good to *me*.

And if that's what it took to get in the door...
Exactly. I was such a kid then, I wouldn't have argued if they wanted to call me Abe Goldberg [*laughs*]. "Okay! If that's what you want, that's what you want!"

Among the directors at Universal, any favorites?
Budd Boetticher was one of my favorites, although I never worked for him. I'd had no experience on a movie set before I signed, so he allowed me to be on his set every day that I was free, when he was shooting a picture called *East of Sumatra* [1953] with Jeff Chandler and Suzan Ball. Just to learn. He would talk to me, explain things to me—he kind of took me under his wing. And Jack Arnold was a kind of a pal. He would associate more on a social level with the students than any of the other directors. Jack was an all-around good guy and would show up at our parties.

The students threw parties for themselves at Universal?
Oh, yeah! It was a very congenial, collegial group.

What memories of Arnold's Revenge of the Creature *[1955]?*
That was the only science fiction I did at Universal. We shot at night, that scene where Bobby Hoy and I had our fight with the Creature. Bobby was a pretty good actor, but his problem was, he made so much money as a stuntman that he couldn't *afford* to act [*laughs*]. We did all of that *Creature* thing on the back lot.

There was a beach on the back lot?
Yes, there was a lake, and we used parts of the lake. Hell, they'd use it for the *ocean*, sometimes. It was a pretty big lake—pretty big, I mean, for a studio lake. I got pretty badly beaten up by the Creature. Not in *life*—I mean, in the movie!

Halsey (with flashlight) and Robert Hoy make the mistake of getting between Beauty (Lori Nelson) and the Beast in *Revenge of the Creature*.

When Hoy gets thrown into the tree by the Creature, was that him, or did he have a stuntman?

Bobby played the part *and* he did his own stunt. They had a large crane there on the beach, with wires coming down from high up on it, and Bobby was suspended on those wires when he swung away from the Creature and into the tree. As I recall, they took the precaution of rehearsing first, but it was still dangerous. Bobby was an experienced stuntman, so he knew to take as many precautions as were possible in those rough-and-tumble times.

Had you seen the first Creature*?*

Oh, sure. *Creature from the Black Lagoon* was one of Universal's *major* releases at that time, we *all* saw it. I probably went to the premiere.

The Creature "in the flesh"—still scary and effective?

[*Pause*] No! It just was a guy, in a *great* suit. You know, when you're working on the set, and the guy playing the monster sits down, has a cup of coffee, smokes a cigarette—

It spoils the "illusion"!

Sure! Anyway, we shot all night, and by the end I looked really bad, my face was covered with "blood" and stuff. And I just wanted to go home, I didn't want to stop and take a shower or wash up. So I figured, "To hell with it, I'll do it when I get home." But, driving home, the looks I got from other cars were really spectacular [*laughs*]. I looked like I'd just been half-beaten to death!

You're under contract, being "groomed" at Universal, probably all of 21 years old ... and then, all of a sudden, they let all their contract players go.

Yeah, they phased out the "new talent" program. After the government forced the major studios to divest themselves of their chains of theaters, the studios no longer had the power to control as they had before. Also, actors were becoming more independent. The studios could no longer control their actors, and it became the way sports is today, with the players going from team to team. In the old days, if you were at a studio, you were there for your career. Then the business went to hell with television coming in, the antitrust decree and so on—all the studios went waaay down. And "new talent" programs were a luxury they didn't feel they could afford any more.

Did you feel this was a big blow to your career, going from being under contract and being groomed at Universal to cheap TV shows and "j.d." [juvenile delinquent] movies?

It was a blow to my career and it was a blow to my *ego*, because [Universal] really took *care* of you—it was a very paternalistic sort of thing. Now to be out on my own, with my agent, going to auditions and all that stuff, it was a bit of a shock. But I had to make a living, so I got used to it. Hell, that's the way *most* actors were working.

At one point during your j.d. movie career, you were in your mid-20s. Did you still feel you were right for teenage roles?

Actually, I never thought about it. *High School Hellcats* [1958] was my first one. One of the disappointments of that picture: my *first* movie with star billing, and they spelled my name wrong!

B-r-e-t!

All it did was piss me off. My first starring role, they misspell my name. Well, by the time anybody noticed, the ads were done and there was nothing you could do about it.

Did you enjoy the j.d. pictures?

Yeah, they were fun, I really did enjoy shooting them. I was the star, so I was treated nicely, even though they were quickies. I have some good memories. And I *learned* a lot, working with directors like Ed Bernds [*High School Hellcats*] and Charley Rondeau [*The Girl in Lover's Lane*, 1959]. These guys were all oldtimers who knew the business inside and out. We'd shoot these pictures in eight, ten days. And no problems—we just *did* it. The hours, as I recall, weren't any longer or more difficult than TV today.

In your early pictures, you often played self-sufficient, very responsible young characters. So how come your wife once told a reporter, "Being married to Brett is like raising a child"?

Which wife was that?

Renate. Your wife at that time.

Well ... we didn't have a great relationship. But she may have felt that way, I don't know. I'm trying to remember ... I don't remember much about our relationship! We had a fairly volatile marriage. She may have had that honest feeling—and maybe she was right [*laughs*]! The last time I saw her was a couple of years ago, at our daughter Tracy's wedding.

According to your old publicity, you raced cars in the '50s until you had a bad accident in Mexico.

The racing started off as a publicity thing, then I "got into it," I got driving Jaguars. I was in this Mexican road race and I lost it in the mountains, on a curve, and almost went off the mountain. At that point, I decided that ... it's not the life of an actor to be risking his life in these stupid cars. So I stopped that.

Were you injured, or just the car?

I was okay. The car was *badly* injured [*laughs*]!

Did having famous relatives like Admiral Halsey and Judge Hand work to your advantage, or it didn't make any difference?

I don't think it made any difference at all. But I'll tell you one story: I was shooting a Western called *Gunman's Walk* [1958] with Van Heflin and Tab Hunter. Playing small parts in it were four cowboys, and I was one of the four cowboys. My name wasn't even listed in the screen credits, but it was a good job 'cause it ran all the way through the picture. We were on location in Arizona and one day around lunchtime, the admiral came drivin' up to the set. Everyone went nuts: "What the hell is the *admiral* doin' here?" buzz buzz buzz, "He says he's come to have lunch with his nephew"; buzz buzz, "*Who's* his nephew?" "Brett Halsey"; "*Who's* Brett

Halsey??" [*Laughs*] All the brass, they wanted the admiral to have special lunch with them, but, no, no, he'd come to see *me*. His daughter was there, and we just went off and had a little private sort of thing—which pissed everybody off! But it sure raised *my* stock with the company!

Speaking of Admiral Halsey ... in a 1962 TV Guide *article, an "unnamed friend" of yours said of you: "I sometimes get the feeling that he's sort of bugged by the specter of Admiral Halsey and Judge Hand, that he knows he comes from good stock and that he really ought to be doing something worthwhile with his life." Some friend!*

I don't know where *that* came from, that was a stupid thing to say. I felt I was doin' just fine [*laughs*]! Listen, Tom, *you're* in the business, you know that if you can't think of something to say, say something negative. I've had enough negative press to understand what it's all about.

By the late '50s, you were a B movie star in B movies—and yet every now and then you'd make unbilled appearances in bigger pictures, I Want to Live! *[1958] for example. Why did you take these minuscule parts amidst all your starring roles?*

Grocery money [*laughs*]. See, when I was starring in all these movies, they used to pay $500 a week—that's $1000 apiece for the pictures, 500 a week for two weeks. (*And* I was being told, "You're really screwin' us. We're makin' these pictures in eight and ten days, and, y'know, a week is six days, so ... you're being overpaid.") So I wasn't getting rich doing all these j.d.s, I just had to do a lot of work. Speaking of *I Want to Live!* [director] Bob Wise told me that he ... well, I don't know if *he personally*, but he said they auditioned 200 actors for that role [a sailor in a scene with star Susan Hayward]. That was amazing. So I felt that I had accomplished something, getting that role, even though it wasn't a big one. Working with Susan Hayward, I was *very*, very nervous. She was the first female star that I had to kiss on screen. And she was kind of nervous, she wasn't relaxed, she was kind of ... "tight," I guess, is the best way to say it. She was very *nice*, but tight. We had a party scene where we were standing on this balcony, and as I was handing her a hamburger, I moved my arm and I knocked a Coke off a railing, and it spilled allll over her dress. I about *died*. I must have turned dead white. She looked at me and she looked at her dress and then she looked back at me and she said [*with concern*], "Oh, Brett! Did you get any on you?" I said [*stammering*], "N-n-n-n-no…" She said, "Oh, that's good. I'll go change…" She was *so* sweet about it. And I almost died.

You were not yet under contract to 20th Century–Fox when you made Return of the Fly, *correct?*

Correct. By that time, 1959, I'd done a series of these low-budget hot rod pictures and so on—and I wasn't making any money. I was a minor movie star, but…

Also minor paychecks!

[*Laughs*] Yeah! So when they offered me *Return of the Fly*, I said, "Okay—but I'm not gonna do it for a thousand dollars." They went back and forth, and finally Robert Lippert, the head of Associated Producers [the indie company that made

Return of the Fly for 20th Century-Fox release], called me in to his office. "Look, Brett," he said, "I want you to do this picture. It's *important* for you to do this picture. But I'm not gonna pay you any more money." I thought about it, and because he was a big man at the time, I felt, "Well, maybe I guess I better." So I did it, and Lippert was right, because as a result of *Return of the Fly*, I was put under contract at Fox.

Did you see the first Fly *when it came out?*

I *had* seen it. I liked it. I thought it was a good picture. Herbert Marshall played the police inspector in the original, and we were supposed to have him in *Return* too, but he was ill and couldn't do it. That's why John Sutton played the inspector part in ours.

Who thought of you for Return*? The writer-director, Edward Bernds?*

Possibly. I don't know. That's a good *thought*, though. Apparently Lippert knew who I was, because he "pushed" me.

Any reservations about starring in a monster movie?

[*Scoffing laugh*] No! I'd been doing these hot rod pictures. *Return of the Fly* certainly wasn't a step *down* for me.

What was Bernds like to work with?

Wonderful. Ed Bernds was really a nice man, good director. He was one of those directors, and there've been a few, that I never could understand why he wasn't doing A pictures. Anything positive you could say about a director, you could say about Ed Bernds. He was really innovative. But he didn't have much *time*. I thought it was remarkable that we shot that picture, *on* the lot at Fox, in ten days. It was unheard-of. And in CinemaScope! Black and white, but it was in CinemaScope. To shoot that picture in ten days on the lot, I thought was remarkable. And, incidentally, I met my future wife Luciana Paluzzi while we were shooting it. I think. Or maybe just before.

Vincent Price?

That was my first time meeting him. I became friends with Vincent and his wife Mary. He was busy and I was busy so we didn't spend a *lot* of time together, but when we did, it was a good time. And working with him was a good experience. He was a pro, he'd been around forever, and he was generous with his knowledge, and happy to help. I was still learning. Even though I'd done a lot of pictures, I hadn't done much *good* stuff.

What memory of your other co-stars? And of the circus giant who took over for you once you became the Fly?

David Frankham [the villain] was very professional. I was surprised that he didn't have a bigger career later on. He was a nice guy and a pleasure to work with, and I felt that David would do more in the business. I don't know what happened to him. Danielle De Metz [the ingénue] ... a sweet girl. Later on, I moved to Rome, and she did too, and I'd see her around. She was there looking for work, but how much she found, I couldn't say.

And the circus giant [Ed Wolff]?
All I know is that there was a big problem, because he was a giant but he couldn't move. Any time he had to run or something like that, it was very difficult, because he wasn't well, physically.

Once your character became the Fly, you had practically all of the rest of the picture "off," correct?
Yes. In fact, that was one of their selling points for me to do the movie, they said, "Look, you only have to work up 'til this point in the story..." And, by the way, the white Jaguar XK120 in the movie, the one Vincent Price drives—that was mine. We just used that for fun. I was into fancy cars.

(A), were you a person who went to see his own movies, and, (B), did you go see Return of the Fly?
(A), I would say *most* of the time but not all of the time. There are still some pictures out there that I haven't seen. (B), yes, I saw *Return of the Fly*. I've always liked it. When I studied the script, I "believed" it. By *that* I mean, I believed it *could* happen—someday, something like that [matter transmission] *could* happen. I believed in the picture as we were shooting it and so I felt good about it, and I felt good about the result.

You mentioned that Return of the Fly *led to a Fox contract—how do you know that?*
Well, they *told* me. It was really strange to go from that little ten-day little wonder to *The Best of Everything* [1959], my first picture as a Fox contract player, a biiig Fox production. When you're working in the Bs, if you have an hour off, if you're supposed to be back at one, then at one you're supposed to be back and working. I remember going back to work from lunch on my first day on *Best of Everything* and no one was there [*laughs*]! On a picture like that, they'd just kind of drift in, the hour didn't *mean* a hell of a lot!
To this day, I marvel at the fact that we could do these science fiction pictures so quickly, and that they were successful. And are *still* successful, in a certain niche. We shot *The Atomic Submarine* in *six* days ... that's *amazing*!

I don't know why Hollywood seems to be going backwards—you can't shoot a TV commercial in six days any more.
That's right.

Just days before you went under contract to Fox, you were in The Atomic Submarine *for producer Alex Gordon.*
Alex was a really nice man. I'd already done a picture called *Submarine Seahawk* [1958] for him. I don't know how I initially got hooked up with Alex—I prob-

Halsey braces for subsea action in *The Atomic Submarine*.

ably just went on an audition and got the job in *Submarine Seahawk*. But he was always like a friend, not just a B-movie producer. He was a wonderful personality, always smiling. I enjoyed working with Alex a lot.

The Atomic Submarine was directed by Spencer Bennet. What memory of him?

Only that he was extremely efficient. We didn't have much of a personal relationship, but I felt that I learned a lot from him. He didn't waste any time, but he wasn't *pushy* about it. He knew exactly what to do. And he was also good with working with the actors. When you're in a hurry, as all these movies were, it's seldom that the director would have time to work with his actors.

So in B movies in the '50s, you would say that, in general, the actors were on their own?
Pretty much. What we would do sometimes is, we would rehearse (say) in the director's office before production started. If there was any real acting to be done, rather than just action or something, that's what we'd do. That way, we would have a pretty good understanding of what *he* wanted and what we could *do*, before we ever started shooting. That's really the only way you could shoot that fast.

Most of your Atomic Submarine *scenes were with Arthur Franz.*
Arthur Franz was a nice man, but my impression was ... he was bitter about his career. That he wasn't a happy man. I think he felt he should have had a much bigger career, and that working in these [sci-fi pictures] was a real comedown for him. He was very professional and there was no problem ... but I just didn't feel I was working with a happy person. And that's too bad, 'cause he was a good actor.

Did you look to make friendships on sets of movies like these?
Let's put it this way: If a person was open and friendly, then, yes, he and I would become friendly. But if he was "closed," well, to hell with it! You don't have *time* for babying personalities. On *Atomic Submarine*, working with Dick Foran, who was *such* a big [B Western] star when I was a kid, was a thrill. I would get a real charge out of working with people like Dick Foran and Bob Steele, who was another cowboy star from the old days. He was playing a really small part in *Atomic Submarine* and I was playing a starring part, and I felt like, "This is *wrong*. This is *Bob Steele*—my God, I must have seen 40 or 50 of his movies!"

Why did you leave 20th Century–Fox after working under contract there?
Because Fox was going broke. That was *Cleopatra* time [Fox's notorious 1963 money pit of a production]. They cleaned out almost all their contract actors, and they sold the back lot, because they were going bankrupt. Oh, I was very happy at Fox, I would have stayed. But they were letting *everybody* go.

Your last genre film in the U.S. was the horror anthology Twice-Told Tales *with Vincent Price.*
Vincent and I had become pretty friendly by that time, so it was nice to work again with Vincent. For me it was a short job 'cause the picture was a three-parter and I was in only one of the parts. I think we shot our part in, I don't know, four or five days. I don't have any special memories of it, other than it was a pleasant shoot. Sidney Salkow, the director, and I were friends, and later we were friends in Rome— he was living in Rome part of the time while I was there. *Twice-Told Tales* was a picture I didn't see 'til years later, because soon after making it, I left Hollywood, I went to Europe.

How did you get your start making pictures aboard in the early '60s?
Prior to *Twice-Told Tales*, while I was making the TV series *Follow the Sun*

[1961-62], I got an offer to go to Italy and make a movie, but I wasn't available. Then later on, practically the same day that *Follow the Sun* was dropped, another offer [of an Italian movie] came. I've always been fascinated with Europe, and ... I dunno ... the adventure of it fascinated me. So I went to do that picture, *Seven Swords for the King* [1962].

How did you feel, stepping for the first time onto the set of a picture in a foreign country?
How did I *feel*? Well ... terrific! It was a totally new experience, it was exciting.

And you spoke the language?
No, no, no...

Well, there's one difference between you and me—I'd feel very insecure any place where I couldn't speak the language.
I didn't feel insecure. We shot part of that picture in Spain, and there was one scene where there were five different actors, each acting in his own language. And *that* was confusing, because naturally I didn't understand the other languages. Learning the lines, I had to learn *every*body's lines, and then count to know when it was my turn to speak. *That* was a new experience!

I came back after that one and I'd enjoyed the experience very much. It was an adventure picture, it was a lot of fun. When I came back, I did *Twice-Told Tales*, and *while* I was doing that, I got an offer to go back to Italy to make three pictures in a year. There was a U.S. tax benefit for staying away for 18 months, and most Americans who went over at that time tried to work it out so they would stay away 18 months and wouldn't have to pay taxes on the money they earned. So ... I went. And, y'know, some years later, I was *still* there, working.

Were you still married to Luciana Paluzzi at this time?
No, but I met Heidi Bruhl, the German actress, while I was working on a film called *Jack and Jenny* [1964] with Senta Berger in Berlin. We married and set up a household, had a couple kids. We lived in Rome, although she worked mostly in Germany.

Before we get too far away from Seven Swords for the King—*what were your impressions of director Riccardo Freda, who later became known for his horror movies?*
We did two pictures [*Seven Swords for the King* and *The Burning of Rome*, 1963], and we really got along. Freda was a master of what he did. He died just a few years ago [1999]. He was great fun, he had a real sense of humor. I think it was on *Seven Swords for the King* that he got me about half-drunk at lunch one day, just before I had a big dueling scene. And that cured me forever of drinking when I have action to do, because it scared the hell out of me. Not that I was going to hurt my*self*, but that I was gonna hurt somebody else. But the interesting thing with Freda was, after two pictures he called me one day and he said, "The next picture, we're gonna do *Romeo and Juliet*." Now, Freda was a great action director, but that's as far as it went.

I said, "You want me to play Romeo?" He said yeah. "Well, you know," I said, "I don't have much schooling in Shakespeare. I don't know if I can do that. How much time are we going to have?" meaning how much time for rehearsal. And he said, "Four weeks."

I said, "Four weeks rehearsal ... well, maaaybe I can do it in four weeks, but I'm not too sure..." He said, "No, no, no—we're not going to have *any* rehearsal. We have four weeks *shooting*." I said, "Riccardo, I just can't do it. I've done a lot of crap, but I'm not gonna embarrass myself by doing Shakespeare with no rehearsal." He was so offended, he didn't speak to me for about ten years! I really offended him by turning him down. But, what the hell, I'm not gonna stick my neck out that far knowing it's gonna chopped off.

Also, isn't Romeo a teenager?

Yeah, he was about 14, I think [*laughs*]. Another problem right there!

How many other languages do you now speak?

I get by pretty well in Spanish and Italian. And I can *survive* in German. I made two films where I acted in French [*L'Heure de la Verite*, 1965, and *Bang Bang*, 1967]. But I'm not a linguist, it's a struggle for me.

Looking over your list of credits, I see what looks like every country in Europe, I see South America, the Middle East...

Canada...

You're like the Richard Kimble of movie actors [laughs]! Who's chasin' you, man?

Well, I've always liked to travel. My mother tells the story that I used to run away a lot when I was young—I mean, *really* young. Five years old, I'd just go out of the house and go on a streetcar or something. So I've always been kind of a vagabond at heart, I guess. While I was in Rome, my agent Sandy Leiberson would come up with scripts for me. And my first question wasn't about the script, it was mainly about, "Where does it *go*? What's the location?" 'Cause if I liked the location, then I wanted to do it. So I've always enjoyed new places, new locations. The picture *Spy in Your Eye* [1966] with Dana Andrews and Pier Angeli, we shot that in Rome ... in Berlin ... in Beirut ... Amman, Jordan ... Athens ... so *that*, for me, was a great picture! And working with Dana Andrews was pretty good too.

That was going to be my next question, what was he like at that point in his career?

[*Sighs*] Well, as an actor, he was great. But he was still having problems with alcohol. His wife was with him to try and keep him clean, and she did a pretty good job. But sometimes he'd ... lose it. It didn't really affect his work except... [*Pause*] Well, y'know, like anyone else, if you're drunk, you're not as sharp as you could be. But he was an actor to be admired—I don't want to just dismiss him as another Hollywood drunk, he wasn't that at all. He did have his problems, though.

Pier Angeli was another one who had her share of problems.

Yeah. But she was a pro and we never had any trouble with her. Her problems,

I think, were more with pills. She killed herself not too many years after that picture.

I believe you did make a reappearance in Hollywood after several years overseas—but only briefly.
After I'd been away for five years, I came back, and I didn't realize that my career here had pretty much *died*. If you're out of sight, you're out of—

You're outta luck!
Out of luck, yeah! I got back, and I thought I was still near the top of what I was doing. But the people here didn't know if I'd died, or *what*! I still thought of myself as a movie star and now [in Hollywood] I didn't get that kind of treatment. I felt kind of uncomfortable about *that*. I'd been home about six, seven days when I got an offer to go *back* [overseas] to make a picture right away. So I said, "To hell with *this*," and I went back again.

You worked with a famous horror director—Mario Bava—but not in one of his horror films.
Bava, in my estimation, was a better director than the material that he got. And I wondered why he would do some of the stuff that he did, particularly [the sex comedy] *Four Times That Night* [1972]—that was a disaster, and I'll tell you the story in a minute. I've no real evidence, but just from things that I picked up, I think Bava was in need of money. I don't know exactly *why* I think that, but I remember him mentioning something about a problem he was having with a house, and money seemed to be an issue. So I think he did a lot of work 'cause he needed the money. Not that he didn't want to *do* those projects, but he could have done more with them if he'd had more money.

Now, what happened with *Four Times That Night*: Dick Randall, that's a name you've probably run into. Dick produced a number of low-budget, crappy pictures. He was the kind of guy who was interested in the deal, not the project. Anyway, on *Four Times That Night*, Dick brought a guy named Putnam, I don't remember his first name, into the deal, and Putnam put up a lot of cash. And there was a producer in Rome, a line producer, who was putting the physical elements together. And what *he* did is, he took the money, Putnam's money, and he used it to pay off debts from two of *his* old films! So it came time to start *Four Times That Night*, and there was no money. To Randall's credit, he did scrounge up enough money to make the picture, but we didn't have the money that we really *needed*. There were shortcuts taken, and we were doing this picture not knowing that we were ever going to be able to finish it—there was a constant cloud of, "Well, are we gonna come to work tomorrow or not?" How that relates to Bava is, it put a lot of pressure on *him*, to keep the thing together. Well, we did make the picture, and I saw it recently, saw the DVD. It looks all right. You wouldn't know that we had the problems that we did. His son Lamberto was very efficient and helpful when working as his father's assistant.

How did Mario Bava act under pressure? Did he get stressed?

Bava *would* get stressed, I suppose, but he was very good at handling it. He was the type of really good director who was "captain of his ship." And if the ship was going down, he was there at the wheel and trying to keep everything going. You wouldn't know if Bava was stressed or not. I also did a Western with him called *Roy Colt and Winchester Jack* [1970], and we had a lot of fun with that because he took a shot at comedy with it. Some of it worked and some of it didn't, but it was a pleasant experience. And Bava was more relaxed and had more fun on that one. Bava was a reeeally nice man, the kind of director you want to work for because you *trust* him. There are other Italians who ... I don't know how they ever got the job. You knew that they didn't know what they were doing. Bava was a real pro, and he knew how to handle his people, and he was fun. It's nice to work with someone who knows what they're doing, and is relaxed with it, and knows how to keep his *people* relaxed.

Riccardo Freda was like that, Lucio Fulci was like that. Fulci was different, though, Fulci was a kind of a madman. But he was a big phony about being a madman. I remember times when he'd come to work in the morning and he'd come in and he'd be screaming, like going down a line, yellin' at this one and yellin' at that one. He'd get to me and he'd say, "...Good morning, Brett. How you feelin'?" "Fine, fine." "Great. Let's have a cup of coffee later"—and then he'd be off screamin' at somebody else! So he wasn't sincere in his rudeness, I don't think. I never did think so.

The poor souls who did *get screamed at—did they* know *that he wasn't sincere in his rudeness?*

I don't know. Because the other people were all Italian, and I was generally the only American. I don't know why, but he was just more courteous with me than he was with other people.

What was your first picture with him?

It was called *Devil's Honey* [1986], shot in Sitges, which is just outside Barcelona. He was *very* ill. He hadn't been working for a long time, he had some problem with his stomach or something. They had to really baby him, and he was eating only gruel. His daughter Camilla was taking care of him. But then, later on, Lucio and I developed a pretty good relationship. Until the end.

Well, before we get to the end of Fulci, let's talk about the beginning. Devil's Honey, *what did you think of that picture?*

I haven't seen it. I play a doctor who can't save a kid who was in a motorcycle accident—he dies on the operating table. His girlfriend [Blanca Marsillach] kidnaps me and tortures me in revenge. I understand that, after we finished shooting, they went back with [the actors who played] the young girl and her boyfriend and shot some sex scenes. So I don't know how it did finally come out. I'm kind of curious to see it.

*Touch of Death *[1988] *might be the goriest of your Fulci flicks. Maybe a bit too gory?*

Well, I really liked that picture. I mean, I liked the idea of it. I tried to play it

Revenge against Halsey is sweet for *Devil's Honey* co-star Blanca Marsillach.

… not for comedy, but for *irony*. I thought it was kind of amusing, the way this fellow [Halsey's character, a gambler murdering wealthy women] enjoyed the killing. So, rather than play it just as a straight crazy guy, I tried to make him a little bit amusing.

That's one picture I would like to do over again. I wish we'd had a better script. It's such a good idea, and I don't think that that idea was very well executed. It could have been done *much* better. With a better script, and thinking it through a little better. Thinking through the *storyline*. Not the *way* we shot it, but *why* we were shooting it, *what* we were shooting. We shot that in Rome.

On a Fulci film, did you ever make suggestions as to the direction?

Well, yeah. Fulci didn't mind collaborating. As I said, it was my idea to make that character in *Touch of Death* "lighter" than he was written. He was written as just a bad guy, a crazy guy. But very quickly Fulci fell in with the idea of lightening it. There were no conflicts about it at all. In fact, I can't remember conflicting with Fulci about *any*thing that we ever discussed.

Did he have many suggestions for the actors?

I don't remember him being much of an actor's director. He was more involved in the movement, in the broader picture. One of the lessons I learned, something I use when teaching: He always said, "If the actors aren't moving, the camera moves."

Halsey knows that wielding a blade helps when delivering a *Touch of Death*.

Fulci believed that, to keep things interesting, if the actors were static, then he should try and move the camera, on a dolly or a crane or something. Always keep some movement in, quote, *moving* pictures, unquote. He was very good with his camera. For a low-budget director, he had a really good "eye," a good technique with his camera.

Were you actually around for the shooting of the gory scenes in Touch of Death*? The cutting-up of the body and that sort of stuff?*

Much of the time, yeah. It was especially interesting because I was married at the time to an Iranian woman, Firouzeh, who didn't know anything about movies. So I took her to watch this ... and Fulci particularly delighted in demonstrating his talents to this total outsider [*laughs*]! She was horrified—she thought it was just awful!

How were some of the gory scenes done?

For the scene where I use the power saw to cut up the woman's body, I think the closeups were real meat—pork or something. When I put the woman's head in the microwave, that was just a wonderful makeup job on the actress herself.

Ultra-gory horror films like these—what's your opinion about them, and their impact on their audience?

Well, I guess it's like everything else: The more they have special effects, the

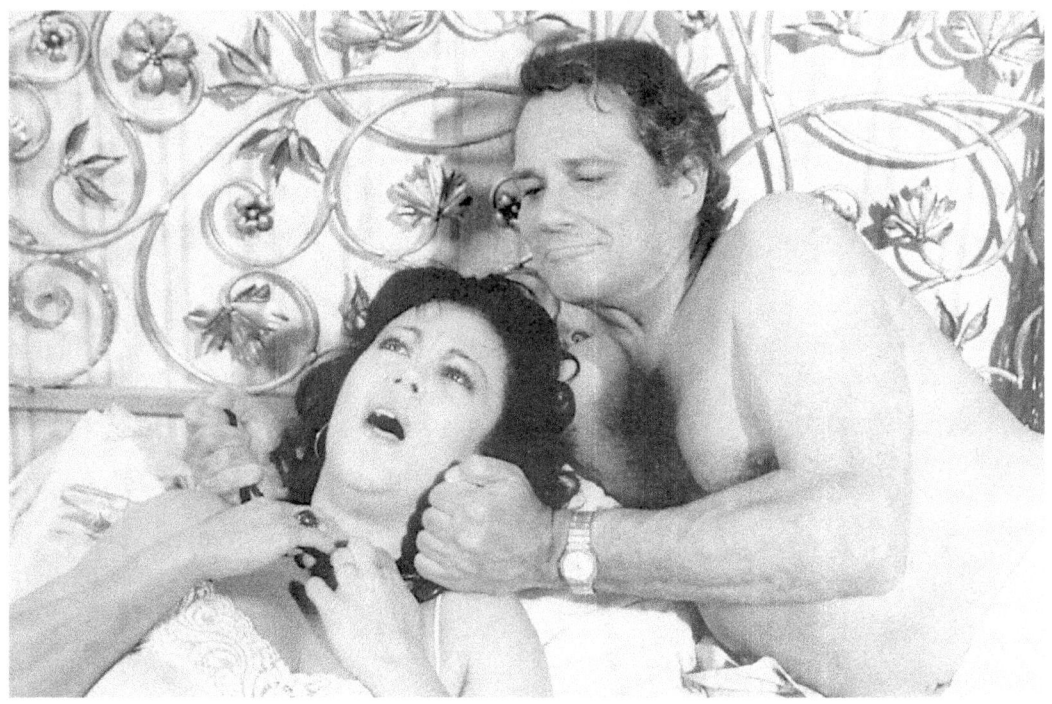

A ladykiller in real life, Halsey became a different sort for Lucio Fulci's *Touch of Death*.

more they *do*. The impact ... it's more graphic, like sex is more graphic on television. It just seems they keep pushing the envelope to see how far they can go [with gory special effects]. With an "X" now, Christ, you can tear a body apart with the computer, whereas they had to build models and things before. I look at some of this stuff, like what I did with Fulci, and it's kind of primitive, the effects, compared to what they're now doing.

If you had young children or grandchildren today, would you let them see these movies you've done?

Young children? No. But, see, to me, they're kind of campy. I'm not frightened by the effects. Maybe you might be frightened [by pictures like] *The Silence of the Lambs* [1991], because that's so real. But I think these campy horror pictures are just so *un*real that you shouldn't really be afraid. Although I ran *Demonia* [1990] the other night — some of my students were here — and they were kind of grossed out by some of it. I guess people *are* affected by it. But personally I never took 'em very seriously.

How is the set of one of these Euro-movies different from being on the set of, say, The Best of Everything, *a Hollywood production? Obviously they're lower-budget, but in what other ways is it different?*

Organization. One of the things that was remarkable to me: We could have worked in the morning, but everybody just kind of screwed around, took it easy, had

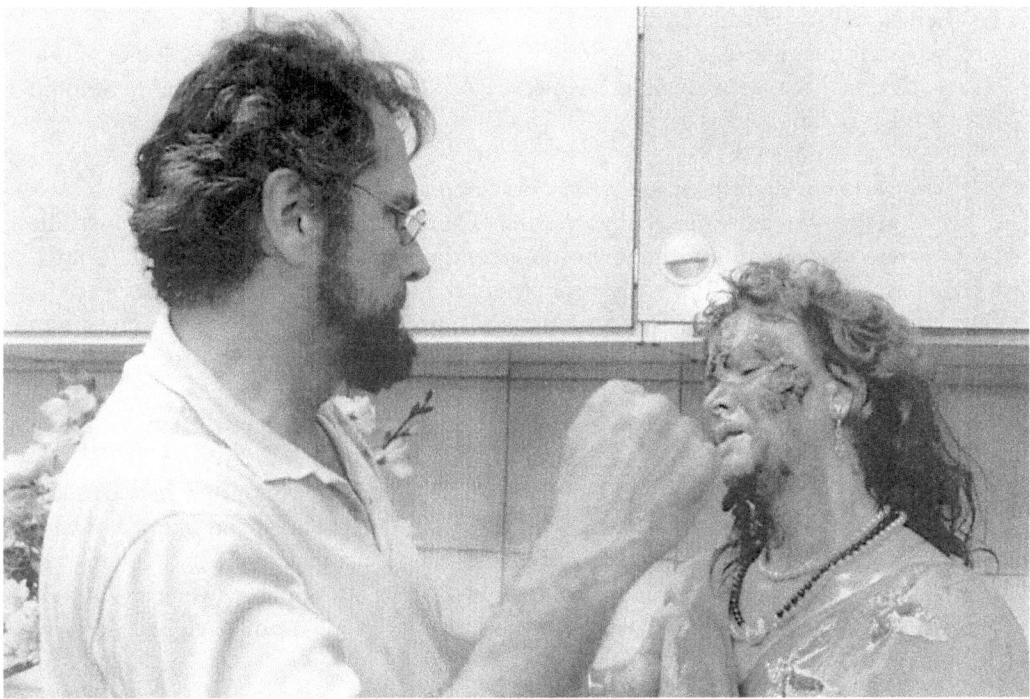

Halsey says that the gory effects in movies like *Touch of Death* make the movies "so *un*real that you shouldn't really be afraid."

coffee, talked about it, maybe got a couple of shots. And *then*, after lunch, the production manager would all of a sudden realize that we hadn't done half a day's work, that we still had almost a whole day's work to do in half a day. So we'd rush rush rush rush in the afternoon to compensate for what we *didn't* do in the morning. This went on picture after picture, and I never could understand why they couldn't figure out that, if we did a morning's work in the morning, we wouldn't have to rush so much in the afternoon!

These are Italian movies you're talking about here, or...?

Yeah, mostly Italian films. But I did quite a few Italian-Spanish co-productions, so it kind of slops over into Spain as well. Another thing that was remarkable to me when I was working in Spain was that, generally speaking, American actors had a reputation for being a bunch of drunks. Especially in Almeria, which was a center for all the "American" Westerns. In that area, ours was never the only picture shooting, and so there'd be other American actors on other shows. We'd get together after work in the bar and have a drink, sit around, shoot the shit. And, from that, we American actors had that "drunk" reputation. But here's what I noticed: In the morning when you'd go to work, the first thing that the crew would do was go to the table where they had the coffee and the other stuff set up, and they'd always have brandy there. The Spaniards—*especially* the Spaniards, but also some of the Italians—would start drinking first thing in the morning, and just drink all day long!

Whereas the American actors never would, because we were doing action. We had to be so careful that we *couldn't*. So it was remarkable to me that they looked upon *us* as drunks because we would have some drinks after work, whereas *they* would drink all day long [*laughs*]!

Where were some of the places that Fulci's Demonia *was shot?*
Oh, that was amazing, *really* amazing. There were three notable locations. The site where we were doing the archaeological dig was near the ocean on the southern coast of Sicily, near the town of Sciacca. The dig was there, and so was the amphitheater. Then there was a castle; and also a church which was some miles away, up in the mountains. It was one of the *weirdest* things I've ever seen: We were in this little village waaay up in the mountains in Sicily. The village was so isolated, it was one of those places where everybody looked like they were related—walking down the street, you'd see the same face all over the place. Anyway, in this village's old church, there was like a basement and a *sub*-basement where they had all these bodies on shelves on the wall! All very nicely dressed in their funeral finery, but having been there for maybe hundreds of years. It was just spooky as hell. There was no air, so people would get sick if we shot in there too long. How we ever got permission to shoot in there, I have no idea. The church must not have had any clue what we were doing.

There were corpses out in the open air?
Yeah! Picture that you're in a cavernous room. This room was, say, two stories high, and there were bodies on the floor level, and then there were niches in the walls as well—there were bodies up the walls too. You had these decaying bodies in their suits and fine dresses.

Are we talking skeletons here, in some cases?
Oh, yeah, yeah—in *all* cases! Some of them were in coffins, some not. And all the coffins were open, there were no closed coffins that I can remember. And there they were. The people who ran the church in the old days just put the bodies in there, and they would disintegrate or ... whatever! It should be on a tourist tour. In that room, there were probably 50 corpses. And then there was a trap door in the floor, and we were told, "There's *hundreds* more down there." But we didn't open that, 'cause everyone was kind of *afraid* to open that. No one even wanted to *see*!

I'd have been afraid to breathe—I wouldn't have gone in there without a gas mask!
Well, after the first day, people *were* wearing surgical masks. It was really eerie. And, because Fulci's so famous for his effects and his dummies and things, people must have thought that he *created* all that. But it was ... all ... real.

One scene in Demonia *involves a fire in that place—but that couldn't have been shot in the church.*
Oh, no, that was shot in Rome, in a studio.

So—except for all the dead bodies—you enjoyed Sicily?

To me, Sicily's amazing, because it has everything that California has, and *should* have an economy like California. Except it's so Mafia-ridden that no one can *do* anything. You can't build a hotel or run a business, because the Mafia will be in there and taking over in no time flat. It's really a bad situation for the people there. There is a newspaper, a Sicilian newspaper—I used to call it *The Daily Mafia*. I'd buy it in the morning, and invariably—I'm not exaggerating—*almost* every morning, on the front page, there'd be a photograph of some guy slumped over a steering wheel or something, somebody who'd been shot by the Mafia the night before. Generally in a car. They never bothered foreigners or tourists or anything, it was always their own people. Not in any way was it dangerous for us to be there. But it's a violent society, and that's too bad, because Sicily could be just a marvelous place. There's a whole story to be told about that, how the Mafia runs Sicily. And they still do. I don't know how they're ever going to change it.

You were going to talk about "the end of Fulci."

Yes, the end... I went to Rome and I called him, and he didn't call me back. I called him, I don't know, two or three times, and I was really surprised that I didn't get an answer. Well, I found out later, looking at somebody's list of the films that I had made with him, that I was supposedly in a film that I had never even heard of. People said, "Oh, yes, you're in it," and I said, "No, I'm not. I never made that picture." What happened was, Fulci made a movie [*A Cat in the Brain*, 1990] and he used clips from other movies—including a lot of footage of *me* [from *Touch of Death*]. And no one told me about it. They didn't even send me a copy of it, I haven't seen it, I don't know anything about it. So I assume that he didn't return my calls because he thought I was looking to be paid [*laughs*]. But at the time I was calling him, I didn't even know about it!

Why did he do that to you? Did he, like Bava, have money problems?

Bava and Fulci, they were different. Fulci could have a million dollars in his pocket, but he was "broke." What I'm saying is, he was *very* tight with money. I believe he *had* money, but I think he was just one of those people who never has *enough*. Because he had a reputation for being fast and loose with deals and so forth.

In Cat in the Brain, *he plays himself, a guy who's directed too many gory horror flicks and whose mind is maybe becoming affected. Do you think there could be anything even faintly autobiographical about it?*

He *was* a little quirky, but I'd say no. It probably occurred to him as an idea for a film that could be made very cheaply, because he didn't have to *pay* anyone. Fulci was really a frustrated actor. People used to think that he acted in his pictures to save paying an actor. But I think it was more than that, I think he loved acting and being in front of the camera.

Did he do a good job as an actor?

He played in *Demonia*, he played the detective, and he did a pretty good job of it.

I didn't mean his performance, I mean ... did he ever forget his lines, did he blow takes?

No, no. Well, he was so economical in everything he did, he wasn't gonna cheat him*self* by taking extra takes!

Dario Argento—how well did you get along with him?

I never worked for Dario as a director. He wrote *Today It's Me ... Tomorrow You!* [1968], my first Western there [in Europe], and then he produced a TV series called *Giallo*, an Italian series that I acted in. "Giallo" means mystery in Italian. We were friendly, even though ... Dario was really kind of weird. I think drugs were his big deal. He was always kind of ... "out there" ... barely touching down every now and then. The last time I saw him was in Toronto, at a film festival where they were showing one of his pictures. We went to dinner and had a nice time. Strange kind of guy, but harmless in terms of being a *bad* person or anything. He could have had a better life, I think, if he'd been a little "cleaner," taken better care of himself.

Amidst your Fulci films, you did a horror picture for a director named Luigi Cozzi, The Black Cat *[1989] with Caroline Munro.*

Frankly, I don't remember too much about it. I think I played some sort of a monster, but I just don't remember...

Do you remember getting paid? Munro says she wasn't.

I got paid, I didn't have any problems like that. As a matter of fact, I don't think I had any problems at *all* except with the director. After you've done a lot of films and you're working for a director who thinks he's discovered the secret of life, you just kind of put it on cruise control and do the job, and leave it at that. Like a picture I did in Egypt, a Canadian picture called *Search for Diana* [1993]. You've never seen it because it hasn't been released and never *could* get a release. The director was just totally incompetent. I remember one day they called me from my trailer and I got to the location, and the camera crew was kind of laughing a little. I said, "What are you laughin' about?" They didn't say. The director came over and he explained the shot to me, and I said [*with annoyance*], "*You* can't do *that*!"—and the cameramen all broke up with laughter. Because they *knew* that as soon as the director told me what we were going to shoot, I would say, "*You* can't do *that*!" and they were just waiting for the explosion!

Some of your fans might not know that you're also a novelist, and that one of your novels was loosely based on your moviemaking experiences in Europe.

Well, mainly in Rome. That's an interesting story how that book [*The Magnificent Strangers*] got started: When I was living in Rome, I *knew* I was living in a motion picture historical period, even a social historical period. Like Paris was in the '20s and San Francisco in the '50s, I knew it was something unusual. I was always kidding with people, I'd say, "Oh, that's a good one, *that's* gonna go in the novel." Then eventually, after I'd come home to Los Angeles, I was talking to a writer about this story and he said, "Hey, that's a *good* story. I think I can get you a deal with that." He took me to Charles Bloch, who was then the West Coast representative editor for Bantam Books, I told *him* the story, and he said, "Yeah, I think we might be able to do something with that. Write an outline." So I did. He said it was okay, and he introduced me to the president of Bantam. Well, *he* read the outline, and he said [*sneering*], "You're just another one of those fucking actors who thinks he can write. I want to see some chapters." So I wrote the first five chapters ... and they bought it!

Like most people, when I said "I'm going to write a novel," it was just one of those pipe dreams that maybe you're gonna do someday. But all of a sudden, here I was with a check in my hand and a contract that said "Brett Halsey—Author." The contract *also* said that, if I didn't give them the book, I have to give the money back.

Now there's an incentive!

That was probably the *greatest* incentive [*laughs*]! So I wrote it, and I had some great reactions to it. I remember one woman—I won't mention her name, but when the book came out, she said, "You son of a bitch—you *son of a bitch*! How did you know what my husband and I were saying in the bedroom? You had it practically verbatim. How do you *know* all this??" I said, "Hey—I know *you*. And I know *him*. And I just figured what you *might* have said. So ... thanks for the compliment!" [*Laughs*] But she was really pissed off about it.

So you actually did base it on people who recognized themselves when the book came out?

What I did is, I just would take someone who I knew, and use that as like the basis for a character. And then I would add to it. For instance, one of the leading men was based on *two* people, one who had an interesting story and the other who had more of an interesting character. I just put them together—what the hell, it's my book, I can do anything I want! So, yes, the characters were loosely based on real people. I remember one fellow who I didn't treat very well, and I was amazed that he really felt complimented by the fact that he was in the book! And I made him out to be a real bastard.

I'd had a similar thing happen to me in *The Best of Everything*. My character was modeled after a real-life person. The character was a guy who was in love with this girl, and then he married a rich girl instead, but he wanted to keep the *first* girl as his girlfriend, and she didn't go for it—that's basically the story. Written by Rona Jaffe. Well, this was based on real people as well, and I met the real-life girlfriend who was dumped. She complimented me, "Oh, that was so wonderful, the way you played that son of a bitch. I really admire what you did." Then a few weeks later, I was at *another* party and I met the *guy* that I played, and he said, "Oh, that was great, you played me so well...!" He was so proud of the way that I played him. I thought, "Boy, you people are all *nuts*!" [*Laughs*]

Your second book Yesterday's Children *was a look at the private lives of performers in a soap opera.*

I call that "a soap opera in novel form about people making a soap opera," that's basically what it was. I had some success with that. So I've done those two and I've been working on a third for a couple of years—I haven't taken the time to get seri-

Halsey is now a film teacher at the Universidad de Costa Rica where, he laughs, his students have more degrees than *he* does!

ous about it. I want to do a historical novel about early California. My great-great-great-great-great grandfather was the first alcalde in Los Angeles, so there's some family history there. I'm interested in Mexican California. Actually, I'm interested in Mexico, too—I'm reading a really big, thick book now on the life of Pancho Villa. So history is kind of a fascination for me, especially California history.

And these days you're "a professor of cinema arts."

I'm into my sixth year teaching at the University of Costa Rica, which with 30,000 students is one of the major universities in Latin America. I'm teaching acting and directing for the camera, which is something I wish I'd paid more attention to when I was more seriously pursuing my own acting career. I still act when the opportunity presents itself. In the last couple of years, I've done some Spanish language TV and a movie.

Last year [2001] I went to Cuba, where I gave a master class at the International School of Cinema and TV, near Havana. I get the feeling that the political situation there is much the same as it was in East Berlin before the Wall came down. I'm hoping to be around to see what will happen after Castro's gone. And last *week* I gave a guest lecture on film acting and directing at the Universidad de Latina, here in Costa Rica. I'm really enjoying my life as an honored professor in the upper echelons of Latin American academia. Not bad for an old actor who never went to college!

What language do you teach your classes in?

Well, I call it Spanglish. There's a real lack of good textbooks in Spanish, so all the textbooks that I've gathered are in English. So I work in both languages.

Looking back over the life and the career that you've had—what kind of a journey do you feel you've had?

There's two sides to it. I've had a wonderful life, and my career provided that wonderful life for me. I *might* have had a better career if I'd been more attentive to my craft as an actor. In my six years as a teacher, I myself have learned a lot more about my craft than I knew during my heyday. My studies and experience combined with my natural instincts guided me toward what I had to do as an actor, but I didn't always understand *why*. In order to teach, I've had to figure *out* why and learn how to *explain* why, and that's given me a better understanding. I know now that if I'd been more serious about my acting, I might have had more of an A-movie career.

But then, on the other hand, I wouldn't have had some of the adventures. And I wouldn't have the children that I have, children that I'm very proud of, because I wouldn't have met their mothers and so on. So ... all in all, I'm pretty satisfied with the way things have gone. And I don't think it's over *yet*—as I mentioned, I still work. In fact, just yesterday I did a voiceover for a documentary here. And when I was in Toronto in January, I did a commercial for Budweiser beer.

Which played during the 2002 Super Bowl.

Yes it did. So I don't think it's over yet. It's just that, right now, I'm doing something else [the teaching]. I look at my contemporaries: Some have done better. Some have done *much* better. Some didn't do [as well]. And ... well ... some are dead—I guess that's about the ultimate [*laughs*]! But all in all, I'm satisfied with the way my life has gone, by and large I'm happy with my life. If I had it all to do over again, what would I change? I can't think of what I would change.

Not a single thing?

Well, I *might* not have done a picture, or I might *not* have turned down something. But nothing monumental. I don't want to say that I'm *proud* of my life, but I'm certainly not ashamed of anything.

John Hart

If I could start all over again, I'd just be a cameraman. Oh, hell, yeah! You're makin' a ton of money, and it's a trip to burn up all that film that somebody else is paying for.

Tall and athletic, and possessed of "movie star" good looks, John Hart acted on the stage of the renowned Pasadena Playhouse as a young man, then made his screen debut in a supporting role in director Cecil B. DeMille's big-budget 1938 *The Buccaneer* (the first of many Paramount credits). With these physical assets and early acting credentials, the native Los Angeleno seemed bound for bigger and better things. But military service slowed his momentum. Returning to Hollywood after World War II, he found himself back at the proverbial starting line.

Hart soon fell into the low-budget Western and serial rut, serving with distinction in many youth-oriented productions: He was the perfect embodiment of radio-comic strip hero *Jack Armstrong* in a 1947 sci-fi serial, took over the TV role of the Lone Ranger and donned the purple costume of comicdom's The Phantom. But his Phantom serial was never seen by the public: After filming was completed, the moviemakers were forced to re-shoot most of the production with Hart now prowling the jungles in a new outfit and with a new moniker, Captain Africa (in *Adventures of Captain Africa*, 1955).

In this interview, Hart (now retired and residing on a California mountainside) recalls some professional ups and downs, his fellow actor Lon Chaney, Jr., a few offbeat career bypaths and the heroic serial and television roles that have earned him a measure of cult status.

When you came back into the movie business after World War II, you had to work as a stuntman at first.

After the war, I came to Hollywood, and nobody knew me any more [*laughs*]! Nothing! But I had known Jon Hall very well, so I started back in working in a Western with him. We were the same size and kinda looked alike, and I did stunts for him. As a kid, I'd worked as a cowboy during the summers and I had grown up with horses, so being a cowboy was nothin'. But I *really* wanted to be an actor. Then

I began to get stunts with bit parts. In the Westerns, believe it or not, most of the leading men hated to learn a lot of lines, so the bad guy did all the talking. I started getting wonderful bad guy parts, and if [in addition to acting] I'd get shot off a horse or beat up or whatever, that was *another* 100, 150 bucks. You know who Frankie Darro was? I worked on a picture called *Teenagers Go West* [released as *Vacation Days*, 1947] where I was this evil deputy sheriff, and here were all these kids—and I'm about three feet taller than any of them. And at the end of the picture, one of 'em, Frankie Darro, beats me up [*laughs*]!

I did quite a few shows like that, and then I got the lead in *Jack Armstrong* for [producer] Sam Katzman. And that was a high-budget serial for the time—a five-week shooting schedule instead of two. I said to myself [*exuberantly*], "*Now* I'm on the road."

John Hart as a Paramount contract player at the start of his screen career.

The entire cast of Jack Armstrong *must have been in great shape by the time it was finished. In every other scene, everybody's running, running, running!*

Oh, God, I'll say! All that running and climbing on rocks and leaping around, I think that was shot at Iverson's Ranch—there was a good bit of location work on *Jack Armstrong*. [Leading lady] Rosemary LaPlanche was wonderful; she was a former Miss America [1941]. She was just a sweet, pleasant person, and a competent actress. I kept track of her; she was married to a TV producer and we stayed in touch, sort of. She died at an early age.

Going into Jack Armstrong, *had you ever heard of the character before?*
Oh, sure, on the radio—in fact, I used to know the theme song!

What was Sam Katzman like?
He was an absolute genius at making low-budget pictures. He never made a real *good* picture, but he never didn't make *money*. He had a coterie of actors and stunt guys who were very loyal to him. He *hated* drinking—anybody who was a boozer didn't work for him. I always was there on time and I always knew all my lines, and Sam knew that. I could just walk in there, if I couldn't make a car pay-

Hart thought *Jack Armstrong* would blast open Hollywood doors for him. It was followed instead by a return to bit parts and stuntwork.

ment or something, and say, "Hey, Sam, can you use me in something?" He never let me down, I'd always get to do something big or little or … whatever! So ol' Sam was always a friend. There were some really nice guys there and we had a little kind-of "stock company" for Sam. But [*laughs*]—but it was *allll* low-budget stuff!

Did you know him socially at all?
    Katzman loved horse racing and spent a lot of time at Santa Anita. I rode out

to Santa Anita once with him and a couple other guys and, honest to God, he lost thousands of dollars that day. And the trip back was very grim [*laughs*]—nobody said a word! When you worked for him, he was stingy as hell, but person to person he was generous. And he loved lobster. An actor named Rick Vallin and I used to dive, and if we got a good bunch of lobsters, we'd give some to Sam. I went to Sam's house many times, I'd swim in his swimming pool—he was a nice guy. His brother Dave was like his production manager, and Dave's son Lennie Katzman became a big, big producer.

On TV, yes.

Lennie learned the business from the ground up. *Dallas* was his big show, and he did a bunch of others. And I could always say, "Hey, Lennie…" and he'd say okay and I'd get to do something for *him*. He put me on *Dallas* as a senator at a trial, and I sat there for at least a week or ten days making a nice fat salary. There were three or four senators, and I had the script right in front of me—I used the script like they were the "trial papers"! That was a lovely job.

When you were a kid, did you like serials?

I remember being a *big* movie fan. Boy, we hit that damn theater every Saturday, and then we'd go home and kind of "act out" the movie we'd just seen. My mother was a drama critic, and so I also started going to the theater when I was, oh, 13, 14 years old. I saw almost everything they did at the Pasadena Playhouse, and then later I worked in a few shows up there. That's where I made a lot of friends, Robert Preston and Lloyd Nolan and J. Carrol Naish and Akim Tamiroff and so on.

Once you became a serial star, would you ever go to a theater to see a chapter with an audience?

Well, *Jack Armstrong* played in a theater that was a few blocks away from my grandmother's house. So, yes, I went a couple of times, and it was kinda fun.

Listen [*laughs*], the life of an actor is terrible. It's either feast or famine. I thought when I did *Jack Armstrong*, "Now I'm not gonna have any trouble gettin' jobs." Well … nothin'! After *Jack Armstrong*, I went right back to doing bit parts and fights and saddle falls—oh, God! Three months later, I was out scroungin' around, tryin' to do *any* damn thing. That's how I got into some more Westerns— I did shows with Johnny Mack Brown and Wild Bill Elliott, and always played the bad guy. I did all the riding and the fighting and got shot at the end! I also did some *Red Ryder*s with Jim Bannon, I played the bad guy in two or three of those. It was a lot of horsebacking and fighting and stuff. I used to be a pretty good boxer, so I could do some good fights.

You got the job of playing TV's The Lone Ranger *when the producers decided to replace the original Masked Man, Clayton Moore. Do you know why he was dropped?*

I have a theory about that, and I think I'm right. We're going back to '49, '50, when TV was just getting started. Clayton was the star of a top, high-rated show, *The Lone Ranger*. Jack Chertok was the producer, and he was the cheapest son of a

"The All American Boy" (Hart) and Princess Alura (Miss America runner-up Claire James), used for knife-throwing target practice in *Jack Armstrong*.

bitch I ever worked for in Hollywood. Oh, God! So I think they were probably paying Clayton the Screen Actors Guild minimum, or barely a little bit more. And once he did 100-and-some shows for 'em, I'm sure that he wanted to get paid [more]—and so they decided, "Well, we'll get somebody else." See, the credits were at the end of each episode—it wasn't like his name was at the beginning [*Hart hums "The William Tell Overture"*], "*The Lone Ranger* starring Clayton Moore." No, they didn't do that, they'd go right into the story, and then at the very end of the show they'd run the credits real fast. Unless you were looking, you wouldn't *know* who had played the Lone Ranger.

So he was replaceable.
    That's right.

You acted on the show before you became the Lone Ranger.
    Yeah, two or three shows—I was a bad guy again [*laughs*]!

Do you happen to know how you were picked as his replacement?
    Because I had been on there and they'd seen me. And then they ran all these Jim Bannon *Red Ryder*s where I had good heavy-duty parts and did a lot of horse-

backing. I was a good-lookin', young, husky guy who could do all this stuff, and *also* do lines. I was a pretty good actor! Now that I'm sitting up here in my old age, I think, "God damn, I never really got into what I could do *really* good…" [act]. I was a good, competent actor. But, you know, they see you in *one way*, and that's *it*. Riding horses, shootin' and fightin' or whatever it was.

I don't know how many guys they looked at to do the Lone Ranger, but they picked me. When I first started out, I got a lot of bad advice about playing the part. I *tried* the bad advice for about one or two shows and then I said, "The hell with that, I'll do it my own way." They wanted me to be like a stiff Army major, and it was all wrong. So I just forgot that and slipped into the part, and everybody loved it. I made 52 episodes.

And were you accepted right away by everybody? There were no "Clayton Moore loyalists" looking at you sideways?
Oh, no! Everybody was glad to see me, that's for sure.

What was Jay Silverheels [Tonto] like to work with?
Jay and I became very good friends. I love to act and, boy, *The Lone Ranger* was about all the acting you could want. The scripts ran around 34, 35 pages and they shot every episode in two days, so that's like 16, 18 pages a day we were doing. I'd have to get up at five in the morning and start memorizing dialogue, 'cause the Lone Ranger talked and talked and *talked* [*laughs*]! A bunch of the townspeople would come out and tell me and Tonto that the bad guys were intending to rob the bank, or what*ever* the trouble was, and then they'd all leave. Tonto would look at me and say, "Uhhhhh … what we do now, Kemo Sabe?" I'd talk to him for about another page of dialogue, and then he'd jump on his horse and he'd say, "Me go!" and ride out [*laughs*]!

Near the end of the day, Jay had a thermos bottle with a little Scotch in it. He'd laugh at me—I'd be out there struggling with all this dialogue, and he'd shake his thermos bottle at me [*laughs*]! I *never* never would drink when I was working—there was plenty of time afterwards. I starred with Lon Chaney, Jr., in *Hawkeye and the Last of the Mohicans* [the Canadian-made 1950s TV series] and, God, he drank a fifth by noon and another fifth by the end of the day!

Did you know Chaney before you went into the series?
No, but I'd seen him around casually. I'll tell you what: At the end of almost a year up there, I didn't know him much better than I did before [*laughs*]. I lived on the outskirts of Toronto in a big apartment house—I had a lovely apartment overlooking Lake Ontario and I could see Toronto off in the distance. Chaney took an apartment upstairs, and we went back and forth to work together in his "motor home": He had a nice big camper on the back of a pickup truck. And that was his dressing room, too [*laughs*]—he kept himself comfortable! The studio drivers drove it.

Anyway, Chaney liked Jim Beam. If anybody went to the States and didn't come back with a bottle of Jim Beam for him, he was highly incensed—he was really pissed off about it [*laughs*]! So I kept a bottle of Jim Beam, I put it on the kitchen sink. And when he'd come down to get me in the morning, he'd have a couple of slugs out of that bottle.

Out of your *bottle.*
Out of my bottle, yes. Then he'd have *his* bottle for the day, and he'd sip away at it all day long. You could tell what time of *day* it was by the bottle [*laughs*]! I never, in all my years of working, would take a drink while I was working—God, you had too many lines to learn and too much stuff to do, you couldn't get loaded. But [back in Hollywood] Chaney used to run around with Broderick Crawford and a couple of other guys, and they were just drunk all the time. And yet Chaney was never *late*, never didn't know his lines. He got a little "juicy" by about three in the afternoon, but he was a professional actor and knew his part and did a good job. He was never out of control.

He apparently was like that for most of his career—drank and drank, then drank some more, but never got too "juicy" to do the work.
I think he was pretty frustrated with his career, all the monster pictures and stuff like that. We got along *very* well, and I *learned* things by working with him—you learn just by working with a pro, back and forth. We had a lot of scenes together, and he made it easier. He was great.

Do you think he was happier in shows like Hawkeye *than in his monster pictures?*
Yeah. But I think he would like to have done some bigger, "straighter" things. He had a *terrible* family—oh, his father and his mother, he hated *them* and I guess they hated *him*. He had an unhappy childhood.

This is something you know from reading about him, or he told you this?
Oh, he used to talk about it, so that's no secret. Like I said, he wanted to get into some nice "A" pictures as a straight actor. He certainly could have done it. He was a wonderful actor.

The "motor home" you mentioned—was that Chaney's own?
Yes, he had somebody drive it all the way up there.

And studio drivers had to drive it back and forth to the location.
I don't know whether they *had* to, but they were *wise* enough to have [someone other than Chaney] drive the truck [*laughs*]! That kinda made it nice, 'cause we could take it easy. It'd be about an hour's drive up and an hour's drive back, and after a long day I could stretch out and rest a little bit, in the back there with him.

How did you keep warm on those wintry Canadian locations?
Ol' Chaney used to hunt a lot, and he knew about some very expensive padded thermal underwear for hunters. I'm sure he got the studio to pay for this, but he sent away and got each one of us a set of this underwear. Then I had Canadian Army

Arctic boots—they looked like Indian mukluks. There was a double-felt lining. I'd be out there and the temperature would be eight or ten degrees, and I'd be warm as toast! And I had some Eskimo sealskin gloves that were pretty good.

You mentioned Chaney being a hunter. Did he do much hunting up there?

No, he didn't get a chance to. See, Toronto was like L.A.—you don't go huntin' in L.A., you go a couple of hundred miles. It was that way in Toronto too, and he just never could get away long enough to do it. But he *talked* about it a lot.

At the end of months of co-starring with Lon Chaney, Jr., in the TV series *Hawkeye and the Last of the Mohicans*, Hart laughs he "didn't know him much better than I did before."

We made friends up there—people used to bring me elk fillet. I'd put it in my icebox and slice off a slab and cook it in butter every once in a while. Oh, *man*, it was good! And they had Canadian lake trout that are almost like a salmon, it's a pink meat. Boy, they're good too. Chaney liked to cook—he loved to cook game and fish and stuff. He'd cook all that stuff, and I'd sometimes have dinner with him, I guess in his apartment. But I don't remember his apartment much at all, so I guess I only did it a few times. He'd get to drinking, you know, and... [*Laughs*]

Chaney had a wife who'd come up, a wife who'd wander in and out. She was just a dear person, and I guess it was very stressful—she never stayed very long [*laughs*]! Her name was Patsy. She'd come up for a week and then go back to Los Angeles. I kept track of her after he passed away; she lived down here in Point Loma, not too far from where I live, and I used to phone her up once in a while just to see if she was all right. She finally passed away a few years ago.

You did some of your own stunts on Hawkeye, *but Chaney had a few years on you. Did he also do some stunts?*

[*Laughs*] Yeah, what there *was*. He was a wrestler, an Olympic wrestling coach. Did you ever see *Of Mice and Men* [1939]? Then you know he was a giant, husky, *strong* guy. And, in *Hawkeye*, he *still* was. We'd have all these Indian battles, and the producers would get these poor kids out from Toronto who wanted to get in the movies. They'd come out there, *not* dressed for the cold or anything, and they'd have to fight Chaney and me. Chaney would be about three sheets to the wind, and he'd grab these kids up and *slam* 'em into a tree...! [*Laughs*] And one day the "Indians" quit fighting, they wouldn't fight any more!

And in general, you two running over hill and dale and that sort of thing—he could keep up with you?

Yeah, yeah. But neither one of us could *see* too well—I needed glasses. We'd be way down in the forest and there'd be a mark they wanted us to trot up to. Chaney would say, "Can you see the mark?" And I'd say, "I'm not sure ... I think *maybe* I can see the mark..." [*Laughs*] But once they started shooting, as we got closer, we could see the mark. That was kind of funny.

What hours did you work?

We had to leave the studio at six, so I'd get up about five to have a little breakfast. Chaney would hit my door about 5:30 and have a coupla slugs out of the bottle, and we'd jump in his truck and off we'd go. We wouldn't get back until dark. Then, as winter came and snow was all over—hell, it was damn cold, yeah!

I'll tell you *one* thing Chaney and I did that was a lot of fun. In those days, the Blue Laws were enforced in Toronto—there was absolutely nothing to do on Sunday, except go to church! No movie theaters, no stores, no nothing. The only entertainment was, they had a double-header Junior A hockey game. Now, Junior A was like the minors in baseball, but these guys jumped from Junior A to the pros (the *good* guys did). They had teams from all the little towns all around, and they played a double-header every Sunday afternoon. So Chaney and I would go to that, and we got to be real hockey fans. It was wonderful.

What kind of money were you and Chaney making?

[*Laughs*] I got about 800 bucks a week, and so did Chaney. That's nothin', to do the lead in a Top 20 show. That's why I was sooo disappointed when that show wasn't picked up [for a second season]. We took it seriously and worked like hell. I *never* would take a drink when I was working, I took my job quite seriously. Sometimes there were just *pages* of dialogue, but I never didn't know my dialogue. I was a good professional actor.

You met your future wife when she appeared as an actress on an episode of Hawkeye and the Last of the Mohicans.

I was 38 or 39 then and I'd chased around Hollywood pretty good for a long time, but I always kinda wanted to be settled. So when the series looked good and I felt good about it, I thought, "Jeez, I'm gonna find me a nice little gal and get married and have a family" and all that sort of thing. I'd never felt that way much before 'cause I'd never felt any *security* about taking care of a wife. One day this darling little actress came out there ... did her scenes ... and I asked her for dinner. And that was it! We got married in February 1957.

The funny thing is, when she was a little kid, *she* was just a dyed-in-the-wool fan of *Jack Armstrong*—if her folks wanted to threaten her, they told her they wouldn't let her go to see *Jack Armstrong*, so she behaved. About three years after we were married, we were at a cocktail party somewhere, just havin' a good time, and somebody started talking about, "Hey, John, when you were Jack Armstrong…" My wife's jaw dropped and she *looked* at me and she said, "*You* were Jack Armstrong?" She never knew it!

I read in one of your old interviews that Chaney was the best man at your wedding.
It was a Friday, and I had to work [in an episode of *Hawkeye*]. It was a mine cave-in scene, and the director *knew* I was gonna go get married, but he kept shooting it over and over and doing all kinds of junk to make me late. That director was a real … well, I won't get into *that*. I finally got home, got in the shower, put on a suit and got goin'. And Chaney came with me—he *was* the best man.

There's a snowstorm, and I have to drive about 30 miles to this church in another little city. And of course, as I told you, Chaney drank a fifth by noon and a fifth by six o'clock every day. He had the ring—you know, the best man's supposed to have the ring. I'm driving along and I say, "Chaney, you got the ring?" He just looks at me and he says, "I got the ring." Doesn't show it to me. You're a little nervous when you're gonna go to get married, so we go another five or ten miles and I say, "Chaney, you *sure* you got the ring?" "I got the ring!" Again, he doesn't show it to me, he doesn't pat his pocket or *anything* [*laughs*]. Well, we get to the church and I go up to the minister who's going to perform the ceremony, and I tell him, "I don't know whether this guy's got the ring or not!" The minister said, "Don't worry, I've got one if he doesn't." Anyway, everything went very well, Chaney *did* have the ring—but the son of a bitch wouldn't show me!

You mentioned that Hawkeye *was a Top 20 show. Why didn't it last longer?*
I never found out the whole story. *Hawkeye was* a Top 20 show, and I thought, "At last I have a little security." After shooting the first bunch of episodes, Chaney and I came back to L.A. and we thought, oh, boy, we're in a Top 20 series. And I bought a nice house that I knew my mother could live in when I went back to Canada to make some more. Well, the dumb shits never made another *one*! They got in a big hassle, the producer and the sponsors and the networks, and it all went in the toilet. That's life in Hollywood, it just happens like that.

Did you keep in touch with Chaney after Hawkeye *was cancelled?*
Yeah, we kept in touch a little bit. My wife and I went to see him once on a ranch and, oh, he got *so* drunk it was just awful. My wife and I got the hell out of there.

His ranch?
Or *some*body's ranch he was livin' on. And then he wanted to buy a fishing boat, and he wanted me to run the fishing boat. Well, that was nice … but that isn't what I was tryin' to do [*laughs*].

Chaney was *such* a good actor, he always did his scenes real good. But such a strange guy. We were up there from July [1956] to March or something, damn near a year, and (like I told you before) I don't think I knew him any better when we parted than when I first met him. I learned about his habits and his thinking and stuff, but I don't think I knew *him* any better.

A lot of folks still remember you very fondly from Hawkeye.

I go around to conventions and they always like to have a panel discussion. They get several hundred people in the audience in a little auditorium, and whoever the stars are sit up in front and take questions. It was the funniest thing: I was at a convention, I don't know where the hell it was, somewhere in the East, and right next to our Q&A room was a funeral parlor. And while we were in there, they started playing the music and they were having a funeral over there! Anyway, we carried on and answered questions, and some kid in the back was waving his hand. I said, "Okay, what's your question?" And he said, "Hey, Hawkeye—did Chaney ever turn into a monster on ya?" I said, "Yeah. Every day at five o'clock!" [*Laughs*]

Getting back to your serials, you were in a 1955 serial called Adventures of Captain Africa *which actually started out as a serial about the Phantom.*

This was another Katzman deal. It was made as *The Phantom*—the whole 15 chapters were shot, made, in the can and probably edited! And then they found out they couldn't get the rights to *The Phantom*! King Features probably wanted a couple of million dollars or something [*laughs*]—too much for Katzman, *he* wasn't gonna pay 'em that! So they cut in a bunch of junk [action footage] from some other serials he owned and they called me back and they put me in a different suit, a god-awful-lookin' thing with a leather aviator's helmet [*laughs*]! And I did my whole part over again in seven shooting days. They changed the script around and I just talked and talked and talked all day long. And it was released as *Adventures of Captain Africa*, when it was intended to be *The Phantom*. I actually saw some of that—it's just terrible. They cut in stuff from *The Desert Hawk* [1944] and other old serials, and it didn't hardly make any sense.

Throughout Captain Africa, *you get into fights with wild animals and you're able to control animals. But did you ever see an animal at any time on that shoot, or was it all stock footage?*

[*Laughs*] Well, there was that gorilla! That was actually some poor guy in a gorilla suit. That was it!

In one of the better cliffhanger endings, Captain Africa is caught in quicksand.

Did you ever hear of vermiculite? It's like a chemical sawdust, and they use it in construction and stuff. It's very light. For [movie quicksand scenes], they dig a hole and dump in a bunch of vermiculite and water it, and it looks like quicksand and you can sink down in it. I did that a few times.

The director on Captain Africa *was Spencer Bennet.*

Spence was great. When he got ahead of schedule, he'd get real excited and he'd be great as long as everything was rolling along. But then when things would get bad, he'd get a little weird [*laughs*]! But *very* intelligent—he knew how to do

In an early, never-released version of the serial that became *Adventures of Captain Africa*, Hart played the legendary jungle hero the Phantom.

these quickies. (You know, it takes a special skill to make these low-budget pictures!) Everybody liked Spence, he was very nice and very good to work with. I don't know anybody that had a problem with him ... unless they were really stupid or somethin'. He and I were real good friends.

Is it frustrating to play characters like the Lone Ranger and Captain Africa, where you wear a mask through the whole thing? To bust your hump starring in something and yet audiences never even know what you look like?

Well [*laughs*], when you're an old trouper like me, you don't give a damn. I *loved* to act. And if I could keep acting and get paid for it, I felt, that was wonderful.

In addition to all your acting roles, you've also worked behind the camera quite a bit.

I had my own little film company—I made school films and lots of travel films, a couple in Europe and three in Hawaii. It was a good way to travel around on somebody else's nickel, but I never made much money out of it. I made one school film called *Animals Can Bite*. I made this for about $16,000, and it grossed just about 200,000 bucks. (I only had a little piece of it.) Then I started shooting stuff for Universal, like pickup shots. I had a bunch of cameras, including a 35mm Arriflex that sounded like a coffee grinder but it worked real good, and I'd go out and shoot all this stuff for Universal.

Jungle king *Captain Africa* (Hart) lays the smackdown on one of his simian subjects.

For features or TV, or both?

Well, whatever they needed. They'd tell me they couldn't find a shot of some weird thing, so I'd go *shoot* it—a school bus going across an open field, the bus depot in downtown L.A., taxi cabs at night, the list goes on and on. Later I got a job on *Quincy* [the Jack Klugman TV series]—I wound up on *Quincy* for three years, supervising the post-production. Mostly the editors and the pickup shots and the inserts. I had been my own film editor for years and I got real good at all this stuff. Then when *Quincy* shut down, I worked a year for Marvel Productions—they did all the Saturday morning cartoons. I was the dubbing supervisor for *Defenders of the Earth*, *G.I. Joe*, *Transformers*, a whole bunch of shows.

And you enjoyed doing all this?

If I could start all over again, I'd just be a cameraman. Oh, hell, yeah! You're makin' a ton of money, and it's a trip to burn up all that film that somebody else is paying for.

In 1973, you starred as a monster-making scientist in an awful "blaxploitation" picture called Blackenstein.

It was just so low-budget, so awful. [Writer-producer] Frank Saletri, the guy who put the thing together, was a lawyer. Boy, was *he* weird. But I *knew* him, and I kinda had a lot of fun with him. He always carried a gun, because he'd get really bad guys out of jail and stuff. He was all mixed up with a bad element. And he was dating [actress-mobster moll] Liz Renay—sort of. I don't think she gave a damn about him too much. So that's how we got into *Blackenstein* ... God Almighty!

And you got the starring part—
Because I was bummin' around with Frank Saletri! I was the only real actor he knew! But *Blackenstein* wasn't really a Guild picture and I didn't want to get in trouble with the Guild because they have the best health insurance. My poor wife was in and out of the hospital all the time and, my God, they paid all the bills. They must have spent a million dollars on my wife—for 20 years, she used to go to the hospital for two or three weeks twice a year, taking an intravenous treatment that you can't do at home. So I was worried, I didn't want anybody to know about *Blackenstein*. To keep myself [in the clear], I told Saletri he'd have to pay me Guild minimum wages, and he did.

At least you shot at a nice, fancy mansion.
That was a *beautiful* mansion! It had a great winding staircase and, oh brother, it was some place! It's on the way to Malibu, on the coast. I don't know how many millions of dollars it took to build it. The rich guy who built it, his kids were all a bunch of spoiled rich kids, and they all fought over who owned it and they were trying to sell it, and in the meantime they rented it for movies. I've seen that mansion in several movies—God, it was just a beautiful house.

What memory of the big guy who played Blackenstein?
He was a poor soul ... not very bright. Saletri got him out of jail and *made* him work in the picture [*laughs*]! I don't think he paid him a damn thing! Of course, the guy loved being an actor, being in a movie, getting all made-up—he thought it was great. He was not too bright a guy, but he looked good for the part, with the makeup.

The monster actor—what was he in jail for?
I haven't any idea, I never did know. But Saletri had him under his thumb. He could be in the picture or go back to jail. I remember one time Saletri took us to a big restaurant in the Valley called the Queen Mary, and—I shoulda known—it was a gay joint. They had guys there who dressed up [in women's clothes], and some of 'em looked just like beautiful girls—you know how they can *do* that? They danced and they were very sexy. Well, I went away from our table to go to the bathroom or something, and on the way I saw the big black monster guy—he's got one of these gay "girls" and they're locked in a lip lock in the hallway [*laughs*]. I thought, "That dumb son of a bitch doesn't know that's a *guy*!" Oh God ... I laughed so hard, I had to go home!

How did Saletri pick this *place? Was* he *gay?*
I think he was AC-DC. He always had girlfriends, but I think it was kind of

a front. It never made any difference to me. And, as I said, he was mixed up with a *lot* of bad guys, and he had guns all over his house. His guns, they were kinda hidden, like so he could grab one [at any given moment]. He had 'em planted around the house. I used to go by and have a lot of laughs with him. He never drank but he always kept anything *I* wanted. He made that one picture *Blackenstein*, and I think later on he dabbled in a couple more. But somebody did finally shoot him and kill him, right in his house, a couple of years afterwards.

Was Blackenstein *shot on 16mm? It looks so cheap...*

No, it was 35mm. They didn't shoot it in three or four days, they gave it a *little* time, but nobody knew what the hell they were doing, really, they just shot a bunch of stuff. I don't think I ever sat through the whole thing. The guy who directed it, Bill Levey, I think he went on and did other things. He wasn't the world's greatest director, I gotta tell you. The black girl who played my lab assistant, Ivory Stone—*she* was real nice and a pretty good actress. I thought maybe she'd get somewhere, but I never heard of her again.

Saletri got *Variety* or one of the other big trade papers to review the show, and of course the review was terrible. It said how god-awful the picture was, and it said, "The only professional actor in it is John Hart. The poor man must be desperate for work." [*Laughs*] I've still got a copy of that review some place!

You accepted roles in movies like Blackenstein, *as well as some minuscule bit parts, partly just to make sure that your Screen Actors Guild health coverage continued, correct?*

You have to make x-amount of dollars to keep that [health insurance] up. If you don't work for a long time and you don't make enough, you can lose your insurance. This is why I did *any*thing, even if it was Guild minimum. I did some crap that never got on the screen; *I* didn't give a damn. If it was Guild minimum, count me in—I had to keep up my insurance. I recently had quadruple bypass, which I'm sure was at least a couple of hundred thousand dollars; and then I had to have my neck rebuilt, *another* 50,000 bucks. And they just pay for *everything*.

I was watching a Mamie Van Doren movie the other day, Vice Raid *[1959]. A fight breaks out in an office; you come in a door, throw one punch and get knocked out. And that was your whole part!*

Yeah, that's right. Then there was a TV series called *The Gangster Chronicles* [1981], and I was cast as a senator. I never did a goddamn thing! I bet I had three lines! I'd show up, get paid, have a lunch [*laughs*]—I never even saw it!

Do you work any more?

No. I'm 82 now [1999] and I had a terrible open heart surgery—and now my knees are giving me a bad time. But I'm really pretty damned healthy for my age. And I've got a nice wife and I've got a nice home up on the side of a mountain in North San Diego County, near Mount Palomar.

I'm sure you never planned it this way, but your claims to fame are things like Jack Armstrong *and* Captain Africa *and* The Lone Ranger. *Do you ever watch any of this stuff on your own, at your age now?*

    I got cassettes of most of the *Lone Ranger*s and most of the *Hawkeye*s and sometimes, whenever visitors want to see them, I put them on. *Hawkeye* was my favorite show because we made it in Canada and we had four days instead of the two days we had on *Lone Ranger*. We got it done and it was pleasant, and I had more *scenes*—scenes with *real people*, instead of playing the Lone Ranger.

David Hedison on Voyage to the Bottom of the Sea

> Voyage to the Bottom of the Sea *debuted on a Monday night, and the next day, Tuesday, in* The L.A. Times, *the headline was "ABC Sinks to New Depths with [*Voyage*]." ... A devastating, horrible review! Had* Voyage *been a play and had the review been in* The New York Times, *we would have closed in one night!*

It's an indelible memory for every sci-fi-loving baby boomer: Battening down the hatches every Sunday night at seven and setting sail for TV adventure aboard the U.S. Navy's glass-nosed atomic submarine *Seaview*. The series, of course, is *Voyage to the Bottom of the Sea*, the Irwin Allen underwater adventure with the late Richard Basehart as *Seaview* creator Admiral Nelson and David Hedison as the ship's captain, the intrepid Lee Crane. It's still popular, still airing on TV all around the world even as it nears its fortieth anniversary—and was, in fact, recently named by *New York Post* TV critic Adam Buckman as the ninth greatest show of all time and his "personal favorite of every sci-fi fantasy show that has ever aired." Swimming against the tide of popular opinion, however, is star Hedison, who feared (even before the 20th Century–Fox series left port) that it would be less than shipshape; watched it take a crash dive in quality in later seasons; and in fact let out some whale-sized whoops of joy at news of its cancellation!

A native of Rhode Island, Hedison was active on the New York stage before being brought to Hollywood by 20th Century-Fox. Acting under his real name Al Hedison, he debuted in (appropriately enough) a submarine adventure, *The Enemy Below* (1957), then the following year played the title role in one of the '50s' most successful sci-fis, *The Fly*. Five years after changing his name to David Hedison for his first Fox series, the 1959 spy drama *Five Fingers*, Hedison found himself being courted to do a second (*Voyage*).

He describes his initial resistance, and four seasons of subsea spooks, spies, dinosaurs, lobster men ad absurdum, in this exclusive interview.

Prior to Voyage to the Bottom of the Sea, *you worked with Irwin Allen on* The Lost World *[1960].*

Going into *The Lost World*, I had met with Irwin Allen, and he liked me a lot. I read the script, and I thought, "I don't want to do this." Jill St. John in pink tights and her silly little dog and ... [*sighs*]. There was no reality to any of it. It sort of started out interestingly enough, but when we got into the dinosaurs and all that ... Jesus! But they did have good people in it, like Claude Rains and Michael Rennie. Come on, if they were going to do it, I figured, what the hell, I'll join the team. I was stupid. I should have gone on suspension. But I did it. And I was *very* unhappy making the film. Then, about a year later, Irwin sent me the script of the movie *Voyage to the Bottom of the Sea* [1961] because he wanted me to play the Capt. Crane part. I thought, "I will no more work for this guy on this kind of film again—" [*laughs*]. "*Never!*" I just thanked him for it and I said I was working on something else, I wouldn't be able to do it and so forth and so on. I got out of it, it was fine, and that was the *end* of it. Bob Sterling got the part.

Did you see the movie when it came out?

I didn't. There was a screening at the studio, and I may have seen about 20 minutes. I didn't walk out because it was bad, I just left because I had something I had to do.

Then, a few years later, Allen starting pushing for a Voyage *TV series—and again pushing you to play Capt. Crane.*

This sounds like I'm bragging, but I don't mean to brag, I'm just trying to tell you the truth of the situation: Irwin just *insisted* that I play that part. And again I turned it down—I made up all kinds of excuses. I thought this was not the direction I wanted to go. I was hoping that another offer would come along, something better, the kind of thing *I* wanted to do.

I went back East, and Irwin called me back East and he said, "It'll be wonderful for your career! All the people will see you on television!" blah blah, so forth and so on. I said, "It's not the kind of thing I want to do, Irwin. I want to do, like, a doctor show, or a *this*, or a *that*. Something with a little character. I don't want to work with photo effects and all that stuff." So I turned it down again. Then I went to Egypt—Alexandria and Cairo—for an international television festival, because *Five Fingers* was very successful there. Also there were other stars like Terry Moore and Bob Conrad and so on and so forth. Roger Moore was doing [his TV series] *The Saint* so he flew in from London; that's when we first met, 1963. On my way back home, I stopped off in London and my agent Jean Diamond called and she said, "Roger Moore thinks you're very right for a part in a *Saint*." So I stayed in London and did it. Anyway, while I'm there, my phone rings—it's Irwin Allen. He just followed me all over, *he didn't give up*! I said, "Irwin, I told you, *I don't want to do it*." And that was it—finished.

You thought.

I *thought*! Two days later, four o'clock in the morning, he calls again ... wakes me up in the middle of the night. He tells me he's got Richard Basehart to play the Admiral. So now I start thinking, "Jesus Christ, if he's got *Richard Basehart* to do this shit..."

I should mention that, during *The Saint*, I got an offer from the BBC to appear in Tennessee Williams' *Camino Real*. I was all excited because there were going to be some terrific English actors in it and I wanted to work with them. Then Roger Moore and I got into a conversation about the fact [that Hedison could do either *Camino Real* or the pilot of *Voyage*]. Roger said, "Well, there's really no choice, I would think. *Camino Real* will go on the air and that's the end of it. But something like *Voyage* could continue for a long time. Might be a lot of fun, it might be successful, you'll make a little money..." He kind of talked me into it. Actually, it was the combination of Roger encouraging me to take it, and also when Irwin said Richard Basehart was playing the Admiral. So I called Irwin and I said, "Okay, we're on" ... I called the BBC and said, "Sorry, I can't do *Camino Real*, I'm going back home tomorrow" ... and off I flew to Hollywood, California. That was the beginning of it—I was on *Voyage* for four years. But for *years* I wondered, "*Why* the hell did Irwin insist? *Why* did he want me for it so much?" I figured it was because he liked me. And he *did* like me. We used to *fight*, but he *liked* me! Then, one day just a few years ago, taking a nap, it finally hit me why. And I'll tell you why later.

From the time you were placed under contract by Fox in 1957—were you under contract there right through the end of Voyage?

No. Starting in '57, I was there for five years under contract—a seven-year contract. But then my option was dropped, and everybody *else's* was, too. Because there was no one there! We were all dropped during the period of 1962–63, when *Cleopatra* [the mega-budgeted Elizabeth Taylor picture] came along, and the studio was losing all kinds of money. [Fox president] Spyros Skouras sold off half the lot because they needed the money—desperately! They just couldn't *have*, or take *care* of, contract players any more, and they just dropped all of us. I think the only one they kept, because he was still working, was Gardner McKay, the star of [TV's] *Adventures in Paradise*, because that series went on for another year or so.

When you went under contract to work on Voyage, *were you under contract to Irwin Allen or to Fox again?*

I was under contract to Fox *and* ABC. It was a five-year contract for the series, with increases in salary. Like 20 cents every year [*laughs*]!

How did you feel when you were first let go by Fox in '62?

It's funny—I thought it was all for the best. After all, there was no work. I was so totally excited about *being* there when I was put under contract in '57, and with my first two films, *The Enemy Below* and *The Fly*, I thought I was off to a good start. But then, in the years between, there were inferior films, *The Son of Robin Hood* [1959]

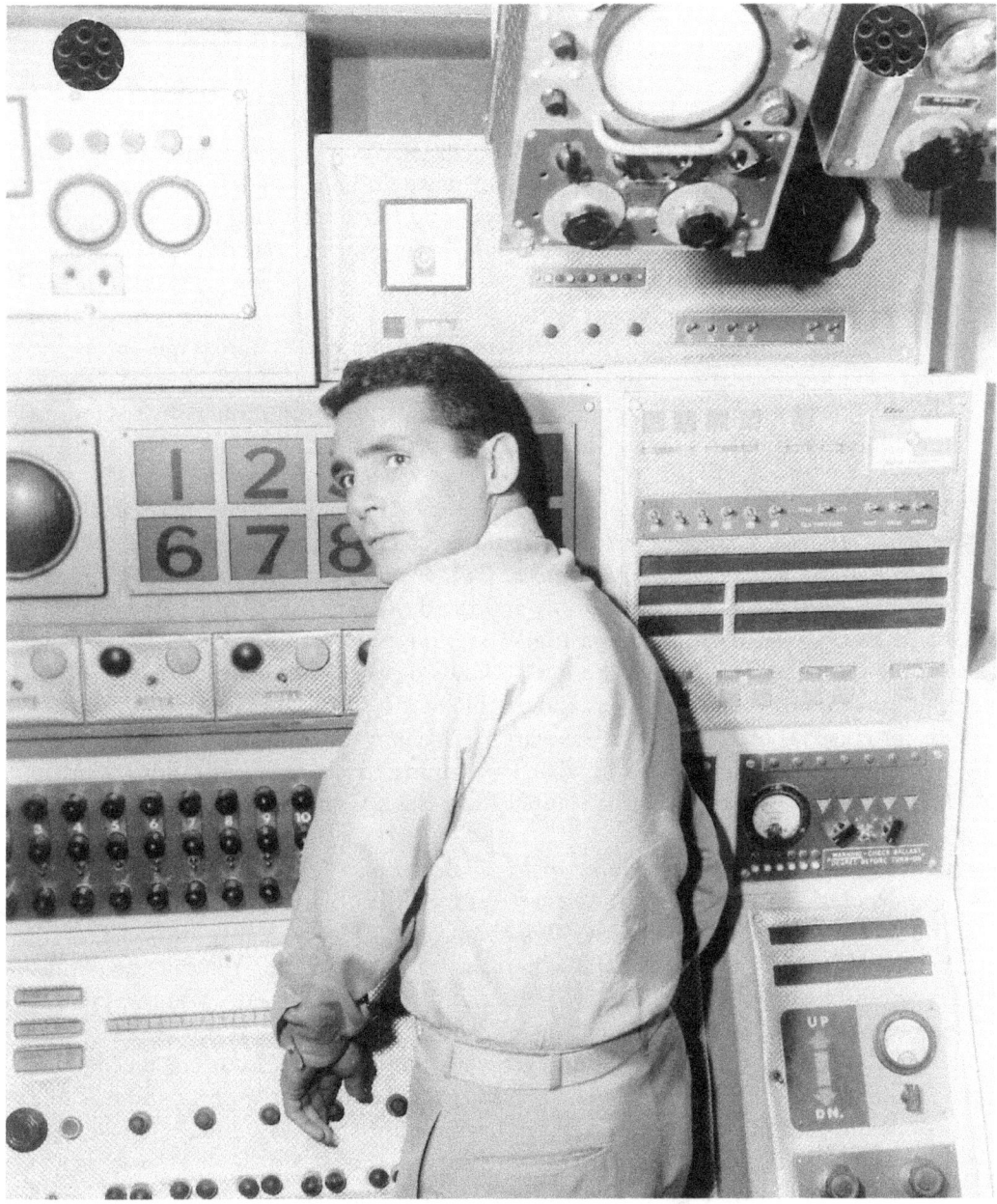

Badgered by producer Irwin Allen into enlisting as the *Seaview*'s captain, David Hedison endured four years of submarine series stardom in ABC-TV's *Voyage to the Bottom of the Sea*.

and *Marines, Let's Go* [1961] and *The Lost World*, and I thought, "I better get my act together and try to get some better work—"

There at Fox.

There at Fox, or ... *any*where! After I was let go, I began freelancing, and I was doing *The Greatest Story Ever Told* [1965] for George Stevens when Irwin started in with me about the *Voyage* TV series.

And you finally gave in when he said the magic words "Richard Basehart."
   The day he told me that Richard Basehart was playing the Admiral, I figured, "Christ, if *he* can do it..." Also, I thought it would be a wonderful experience to work with him. So I got right down to work and I created a long biography of Lee Crane, I went back to Fox with it, and—oh, Irwin wanted none of it!

Wanted none of your Crane biography?
   I would go see the writers, and Irwin would practically throw me out of the room. He knew what he wanted—he just wanted "Action!" "Go!" "Move!" "Run!" "Jump!" He wanted nothing comedic, no characterization, nothing. Just standing there looking good and saying your lines and being as heroic as possible.

You once told me that, as you were preparing to do Five Fingers, *you consulted an acting coach to "run" scenes and get a feel for the character, so I know you took your TV work seriously. But I never would have guessed that you'd prepared a biography for Capt. Crane!*
   Oh, I did, I took it very seriously and I had this whole bio going! As I remember, Lee Crane had grown up on the Vanderbilt estate and his father had worked for the great Vanderbilt, and Lee got all kinds of wonderful education. It went on and on and on and on and it was a lovely bio and something that the writers could *use* for episodes of *Voyage*. And—aaaaargh!—Irwin wanted *none* of it! Even though the writers seemed interested in what I was going to say, Irwin just didn't want to know. He knew exactly what he wanted from Capt. Crane and the Admiral.

So you brought the bio to the writers and Irwin Allen?
   No. I was in a room with the writers—it was Allan Balter and Billy Woodfield—and Irwin walked in. [*In a whiny Brooklyn accent:*] "Heeey! What are you *doooing* here??" When he saw me with the writers, he was just a wreck! "You can't dooo this! We know what we're doooing!"—he just went on and on. I said, "Y'know, I've got some good ideas here," but he didn't want my ideas, not at all. It was crazy.
   We argued for four years ... and yet we got on very well. I was at a recent convention with Bob May, the guy who played the Robot on *Lost in Space*, and he came to me and told me that he used to see Irwin and me arguing. Finally he went to Irwin one day and he asked, "Irwin, why do you and David shout at each other? Why are you always arguing?" And Irwin said [*shouting*], "Becawse I *lllove* him!" [*Laughs*]

Did you get along with Allen better on The Lost World, *or did you find things to fight with him about then too?*
   He more or less left me alone on *The Lost World*. But *Voyage to the Bottom of the Sea* was really much more "personal" for me, because in a way it was my show and it was Richard's show. It meant more to me, and I wanted to get everything right, on target. Anyway, it didn't work that way! Funny thing: Irwin would have these

lovely dinner parties at his house, and I'd be invited. I would go to his house, and I'd be the only actor there from any of his shows. I remember I went to, like, a New Year's Eve party there—these were important parties with wonderful people. He might have some of the oldtimers like Peter Lorre and Groucho Marx, but he would never have any of the younger people, and I'd think, "Jeez, I'm the only [young actor] here...!" I thought it was quite an honor. For some reason, he liked me.

Voyage's first two seasons featured a number of espionage and spy stories, but eventually it became a monster-of-the-week series. Which was the better direction for the show?
Oh, the first two years, by all means. They were by far the best.

Because they had more of the espionage stories—
Yes, and more believable, more interesting characters and all that kind of stuff. When they got into the monsters, I think the show just [fell apart]. I'm sure some of the kids loved it, but *I* thought it became idiotic. There was no sense to it at all. I'm surprised that it went into a fourth year—we weren't at all sure, after the third year, that it would be picked up. I thought to myself, "I'm sure it won't be," but it *was*. I was disappointed [with the series] because I think it *could* have been like *Star Trek*, it could have had a much more lasting value, particularly with someone in it like Richard Basehart, who I think was brilliant. It could have gone on much longer and there could have been more substance, more characterization. But ... that never happened. Any time Richard was out a day, because he was sick, or whatever, they would just give me his lines. And the same with me—if I were out for maybe even a *half* a day, they'd give *my* lines to Richard. Or to *Kowalski* [one of the minor crewmen]. Or to *anybody*! And there was none of this "Oh, come on, I can't. Those are Richard's lines, that's *his* character, those lines shouldn't be coming from me"—because it made *no difference*. They were totally interchangeable. We were all playing the same kind of character and saying the same kind of words. You just had to bring as much of yourself to the part as you possibly could. The show was just total action, there was nothing that had anything to do with a person or his personality. Irwin could have brought in issues of the day and so on, but ... no. It got to be way-out. *Too* way-out.

When you bring up Star Trek, *you're saying that* Voyage *could have had science fiction elements to it, but they should have been intelligent science fiction elements—is that right?*
Sure. *Star Trek*, I thought, was fairly intelligent. And a lot of fun.

All the supporting roles on Voyage *were played by pretty obscure actors. Was there an effort made for some reason to get "lesser-knowns" ... or were they all the budget could afford?*
I think it was because of the budget. They got *good actors*, I thought, but those good actors weren't allowed to do anything interesting. Or they weren't given a specific character. They were just all saying the same lines and running around and being very "bravura." And that was it.

You know, here I'm complaining, and yet the show was a big success. Did I ever tell you about *The Los Angeles Times*, their review? When *Voyage* debuted, it was part of what ABC called their "Wide World of Entertainment." *Voyage* debuted on a Monday night [Sept. 14, 1964], and the next day, Tuesday, in *The L.A. Times*, the headline was "ABC Sinks to New Depths With *Voyage to the Bottom of the Sea*." And the review started, "If this is part of ABC's 'Wide World of Entertainment,' then stop the world, we want to get off!" How would you like reading *that*? And it also said things like, "The actors must have been cringing at the lines they had to say"—it went on and on and on! A devastating, horrible review! Had *Voyage* been a play and had the review been in *The New York Times*, we would have closed in one night!

That must have been discouraging, so early on, when you probably held out some *hope that it'd be a decent show.*

No, I felt sure it was not going to "work"—the pilot ["Eleven Days to Zero"] was horrible, I thought. And yet it worked! Irwin was thrilled, of course. And I guess we were happy too, Richard and I. Yes, we *may* have thought, "Well, *maybe* we're gonna do some good stuff." And then we did start making some good episodes, things that Balter and Woodfield would write. (They were the key writers and they came up with some *terrific* stories. That was the first year, and also into the second.) Then, in the third and fourth years, again for budget reasons, *Richard and I* became the "guest stars." In one episode, the Admiral would suddenly go crazy, there'd be a story around that. In another episode, I would turn into a werewolf. And we were just goin' nuts.

One day, Richard and I had a meeting at my house, which was off Benedict Canyon on a street called Yoakum Drive, and we called Irwin and asked him to come over. He did, he came, and it was just the three of us there in my small living room, having coffee. And for the first time, Richard *really* opened up, because it was just the three of us, nobody else around. He was literally pleading: He said, "Irwin, we want to aaaact! We want to make these characters real and responsible, we want to *this*, we want to *that*." I got into it too, of course, and, oh, we were just so passionate about the whole thing. But Irwin didn't really understand where we were coming from. He said, "By *character*, do you mean, like, you're in the control room and you have a cup of coffee, and all of a sudden the ship rocks and you spill the coffee over your shirt?"

Oh, God...

That's what he said. I said [*patiently*], "No, no, Irwin, that's not exactly what we mean..." It was *that* kind of conversation, it was *vvvvery* frustrating.

He thought you were asking for more "bits of business."

Yes, "business," and all that stuff. But it wasn't that at all.

Mark Goddard, who was on Irwin Allen's Lost in Space, *told me that one of the things that frustrated him was: It was a popular show with kids, but not a soul he knew ever watched it!*

Opposite: Hedison even felt that the deluxe *Voyage* pilot "Eleven Days to Zero" (with guest star Eddie Albert, left) was "horrible."

His *peers* didn't watch it, that's right. And as far as *Voyage* goes, I don't think that *I* knew many people who watched it. But I knew kids were watching it, kids and young people. The fan mail that we got, it was just incredible. People from all over the country were just going nuts for the show. My fan mail started toward the end of the first year, and it got *really* heavy. I remember, about the third season, going to Irwin because Richard Basehart was making a hell of a lot of money and I was getting piddle-dee-dee next to what Richard was making. And I was receiving a lot of fan mail, and they were writing [episodes] for me, and whatever. So I went to Irwin and I said, "Listen, I really think I should get some more money." And there we went again, a shouting match. Finally he said to me, "There *is* no maw, Basehart's *got* it awwwll!" [*Laughs*] The deal on *Voyage*, the ownership of the show, was: 25 percent went to Fox, 25 percent to ABC, 25 percent to Irwin and 25 percent to Richard.

Besides the 25 percent, do you happen to know how much Basehart was making?
They paid him *so* much money. He started off with 10,000 a week, which was a lot of money then, and after the series went on the air, [his salary] just kept going up up up. He didn't want to lose any of *that*, and so he stuck with the show, thinking that maybe it would change. Every now and then, an acting thing would come along that would make Richard very happy, a particular episode. That was something he looked forward to and enjoyed.

What was he like as a person, that you admired him so much?
Before I started the series, I called the house and I asked if I could come up and meet with him. He said sure. I went to his house on Lloydcrest Drive, off Coldwater Canyon, we talked and I said, "First of all, I want to tell you that it's really an honor to work with you. I've admired all your films, and I think if we work hard and work together, we'll make something very interesting out of this series." He agreed with me. And we got on famously—once we did the pilot, he and I became such good friends. But he was more of an introvert, very quiet, and I was more of an extrovert, I was always kidding around. He would leave the set and go into his dressing room and read a novel, and when they'd call him, out he'd come, he'd be prepared, and he was just absolutely wonderful.

And off the set, you were friendly too?
He invited me to his house every Thanksgiving—it'd be Richard and his wife Diane and his children and whoever else was there. By the way, for Thanksgiving, we'd only get a Thursday and Friday off, we didn't get a week off like they give you today. And for Christmas we didn't get much more, about one week and that was it. I would always go over there on holidays because we really hit it off very well, I spent a lot of time with Richard and his family. When he died, it was just devastating.

Were you married during the Voyage *years?*
No, I wasn't, I got married right after *Voyage*, as soon as it finished.

Hedison forged a friendship with *Voyage* co-star Richard Basehart which lasted until the latter's death.

Preparing for this interview, I re-read some past interviews with Voyage *guest stars. And a couple of them complained that Basehart put down the material and snickered at it—and they said that made the job tough for them.*

It's true, he did put down a lot of the material. He would be so upset with some of the scripts—he just couldn't believe that we had to utter some of those lines. And he would let it be known to his fellow actors. He wasn't putting *them* down, he was just putting the material down. But apparently, from what you're telling me, it did make them uncomfortable. Which I can understand. If I were a guest star, I would feel the same way. Richard would get frustrated when bad scripts would come along.

And there were a *lot* of them. I mean, there are bad scripts and there are bad scripts ... but these were just unbelievably bad. "Why? Why? Can't we afford something *better* than this?" Well, maybe Irwin couldn't work with too many writers—Irwin didn't like to have to deal with them, to have to say, "What's *this* all about? What's all this talk? What's *this*? What's *that*?" And he would cut, cut, cut things.

I still wasn't even ten years old when Voyage *went off the air—and even at that age, some of the stories struck* me *as too dumb!*

You probably said to yourself, "What are they—kidding?" It was really, really amazing.

In 1964, the officers and crew of a Navy submarine wrote to TV Guide *complaining about how the* Seaview's *crew always panicked in emergencies, and this reflected very badly on the Navy.*

Oh, it did, I quite agree with them. We were doing an over-the-top drama, because this is what Irwin liked. If there was any danger, he liked all kinds of emotion and terror and yelling and carrying-on. Of course, in real life they would never do that on a ship!

I'm told that there was talk at one point about replacing Basehart because, like so many actors of his generation ... he was "better in the morning than in the afternoon." I know you know what I mean.

Yes, he had a problem with drinking. He'd be all right in the morning, but I guess if he went out to lunch, maybe he'd have one too many or something. He still gave his all—he didn't come back on the set and cause a scene. But maybe he just was a little *slower*, or whatever. It's just too bad. I think it was one particular episode ["The Menfish"] where he didn't do too well, one where he was ... not well, and they brought Gary Merrill in and *he* played the Admiral. And then there was talk of Gary Merrill continuing on with the role. But they brought Richard back—thank God. Then, in the final year, Richard was fine. And then he got into Zen and he just totally stopped drinking—didn't drink at all. I would meet him and see him, and never would he have a drop of liquor. And he was content and happy.

If they had fired him—would you have stuck around?

If they had fired him, I think I would have walked myself. I would support him—I'm very loyal that way. I was very loyal to Richard, he was a great actor, and I said, "For one little incident, you can't fire somebody." It was as simple as that. I would have stuck by him to the end. I went into Irwin's office and I told Irwin, "This is ridiculous. Gary Merrill is a wonderful actor, but there's no *way* you can replace Richard now. Richard and I have a rapport, Richard's wonderful, the fans love him. He's just got to be given another chance."

Why did Basehart drink? Was he unhappy?

I don't know. Maybe the frustration of seeing some of the material, the scripts—maybe he would drink to forget. [*Mimes Basehart reading a script:*] "How can I *play* this?? Grrrrr!" Or maybe he thought the drink would give him some inspiration. But it never bothered *me*, because we always worked so well together that I could always see the problem. I could never lose my temper with *him*.

In the first year of Voyage, *you had the great "Bomber" Kulky, the wrestler-turned-actor, as the crew chief.*

He was *wonderful*. God, you didn't even have to *write* anything for him, you could just *look* at him and you'd know he was "a character." He had such a great sense of humor and he got on well with everybody. But after the first season, he died, and that's when we got Terry Becker [as the new chief]. I got on very well with Terry. He was *another* one who was very creative and wanted to *do* things—he also would talk to Irwin.

Was there compensation just in being on the Fox lot during that time in the 1960s when a lot of popular movies and TV series were being shot there?

Not really, because I was working so hard. I would go right to the set and I'd get out late and go home. There was really no compensation. Maybe you were invited to a screening, or you met certain people. I worked with Vincent Price on *Voyage*, and I really enjoyed him. Vincent was also in *The Fly*, of course, and people sometimes ask me, "What was he like to work with on *The Fly*?" And I have to tell them, "I don't know," because we never worked the same days! But I did get to know Vincent on *Voyage*. We were working on an episode called "The Deadly Dolls" and I was kidding around and making jokes—I was up to all kinds of nasty pranks. And Vincent looked at me in shock and he said, "David, I don't recognize you. You're so funny! When we were doing *The Fly*, you were *soooo earnest*!"—those are the exact words he used, "soooo earnest"! And back when I did *The Fly*, back in '58, I *was* terribly earnest. Terribly boring. Took it all *very* seriously. So I admitted to him, as I just did to you, that I took everything so seriously in those days. So we had a lovely time on *Voyage*. In fact, I was such a cut-up and we were having so many laughs that he invited me to his house for dinner—Richard and Diane Basehart and me and my date. Anne Baxter was there, too, and some of the other Fox people. It was really nice.

What other interesting actors did you meet through Voyage?

I talked to George Sanders ["The Traitor"] just a little bit, but he was very shy and didn't say much of anything. So I sort of left that alone. Victor Jory ["Fires of Death"] was a lot of fun, he was always kidding around, saying silly things and making us laugh.

And, in addition to the oldtimers, you'd occasionally get an up-and-comer like Robert Duvall ["The Invaders"].

He was very nice. He was a good actor, just starting out then, and I loved what he was doing. And John Cassavetes ["The Peacemaker"], he and I were giggling and laughing all through that thing. We had such fun. I liked him so much. He was *so* talented, had *so* many great ideas. And, oh, it would have been so wonderful if they had gotten more women on the show. But you know what *that* meant: That meant that they would be in hairdressing and they would take an extra ten minutes or something. And Irwin didn't want any of that, he wanted to get started *right away*. The men would have a makeup call for seven-thirty and we were on the set at eight. And off we'd go. "No, no—we don't waste any time here..."

Not only weren't there any female regulars, there were less and less female guest stars as the series went along!
Maybe a woman playing a heavy would appear in an episode, but that would be *it*. I could never understand it.

Susan Flannery—who just won an Emmy for her soap opera The Bold and the Beautiful—*was once "up" for a regular role on* Voyage.
I had no idea about that. But I wouldn't be surprised, because she was very good in the show. I remember one episode, I think from the first year, where she was *very* funny: She was kidding around with the material, doing things between takes, and she was a lot of fun. Everyone on the set loved her, she was a lovely girl. And I haven't seen her since.

Were all the Voyage *sets at 20th?*
Yes. On Stage 10 or 11 was where the submarine was—all the rooms and the cabins and everything else. In the first year, we went [on location] to Catalina a lot, did a lot of water stuff there. But mostly it was the 20th Century-Fox back lot.

Being that it was an "Action!" "Run!" "Jump!" show, were there any accidents or injuries that you recall?
Oh, no, no, nothing serious, because we had a great effects department that really knew what they were doing. Maybe a hurt knee or a couple of scratches every now and then, but nothing major at all.

Who was your stuntman?
His name was George Robotham. He would come and do all the dangerous stuff—but a lot of times he didn't, because I love doing a lot of the stuff myself. On "Man Beast" [an episode where Hedison turns into a monster], I remember they called George in, and he was paid for nothing that week because I wanted to do everything myself.

Director-wise, any favorites?
The ones I enjoyed working with—and so did Richard: One of the favorites was Leonard Horn, who is now dead. Another one was Sutton Roley, and Harry Harris—I *loved* Harry Harris. Oh, there were so many, I can't even think of them.

John Brahm?
He was good, he was very professional, he knew what he was doing. But I had more of a rapport with Sutton and Leonard and Harris, 'cause I'd always kid with

Susan Flannery (with gun), a guest star in the episode "Time Bomb," was later considered for a continuing role on *Voyage*—until Irwin Allen decided to keep it an all-boys club. (*Left to right:* Hedison, Flannery, Ina Balin.)

them. And they always came up with interesting ideas. And there was another one—*damn*, I liked him a lot—he directed "Man Beast." Jerry Hopper.

There are folks on record saying that Irwin Allen didn't have a creative bone in his body, that he just surrounded himself with good people. Would you go along with any of that?

No, I wouldn't say that. He *was* very creative, insofar as—look at what he did! Listen, Irwin was a great *salesman*. How the hell do you think *Voyage* got on the air? How do you think it *lasted* all that time? It was Irwin's enthusiasm and his love for the show. Look what happened with the movies he made, *The Poseidon Adventure* [1972] and *The Towering Inferno* [1974]—he got big stars to do them, and they were very successful. So you cannot say that he wasn't creative.

When there was a problem on Voyage, *would you go to the producer of that particular episode, or would you go right to Irwin Allen?*

Oh, no, no, never to the producer. You *had* to go to the top. Any time there was a maaajor problem, I'd go running into Irwin Allen's office and discuss it with him. I remember one day when we had just finished an episode and I got out early, around five o'clock. I went home and I was sitting by the pool and reading the script for the new show we were going to start shooting the next morning. And ... I went crazy. It was *so* bad. Not only was the script bad, *my* part was weak and *very* bad— it wasn't anybody I *recognized*! So I went storming into Irwin's office—screaming and yelling. "All this *time* I'm trying to *explain* to you what I'm trying to do, what this character should *be*, and now *look* at this *shit*, what *is* this?" rrrrrrr, rrrrrrr, rrrrrrr [*dog-like growling noises*]—I was raving! Next thing I knew, he was on the phone, calling all the writers in, but I kept going on, I was ranting and raving. (Irwin finally said, "Aw right, aw right, yuh don't have to beat a dead hawss!") The next day, when I went to work, there were a few pages there to do. The script was in the process of being re-written. By the time we got into a momentum, it was like noon— we hardly did anything. And Irwin came on the set and he said, "Yuh know something? This is awll yer fawlt! This is *awll yer fault*!" God...

Do you recall anything about the plot of the episode, so I can figure out which one it was?

Gee, I wish I knew. I don't remember. But ... it was a pretty bad one [*laughs*]! It could have been "Cradle of the Deep"—*that* was a loser. And there were a couple of other real clunkers, I just don't remember the names. Of course, towards the end I didn't even bother screaming any more. By then, there were scripts like "The Lobster Man" and all those other stupid things.

Were there any episodes that you did think gave you good opportunities?

Oh, yeah, there were a couple that I had fun with. One was called "The Phantom Strikes," and it was so successful they did a sequel later in the season, "Return of the Phantom." Those were with an actor named Alfred Ryder, who played a German submarine commander who'd come back from the dead. He wanted to take over the body of Capt. Crane, and in some way he managed—he sort of hypnotized the Admiral to shoot me, they took me right to sick bay, and then you could see the shadow of Ryder going into my body. I thought it would be fun to do a German accent, but unfortunately I couldn't go into a German accent, I had to copy *Alfred Ryder's* German accent. So I kept listening, listening, listening, trying to get his "sound," and I think I did it pretty well. If I *do* say so myself [*laughs*]! So those were two that I really enjoyed, I thought they were both great fun. Then there was "Man Beast," which I thought was a lot of fun. "Mutiny" in the first year I thought was interesting. And "Doomsday," I got a lot of fan mail on that one.

You mentioned that Voyage *was always long hours...*

Oh, yeah, the first year particularly. We'd go in early in the morning but we'd work 'til like ten o'clock at night, 11 o'clock at night, sometimes 'til midnight, trying to get that first year going. And we *did* it. The second year was bad as well, but not *as* bad. Then the third and fourth years were easy. We'd get out by seven o'clock.

All my years of interviewing have made me aware that the "glamorous" life of an actor is often up-at-dawn, work-'til-midnight, up-at-dawn again. How can—not just an actor— how can a human being live like that, with just work and sleep in his life?

It's hard work, but it gives you good money—for the most part.

Hedison felt that *Voyage*'s plots got sillier every year—and who can blame him?

Money you ain't got time to spend!
    That's right, you *don't* have time to spend it. But *that's* good too, because then it piles up! But any *real* actor knows that the absolute wonderful thing that happens is when you do a play. Once you've done all the hard work [of preparation], then all you *do* is, you know the lines, you know what you're going to do basically, and you go on. And you have a different audience every night, which shades your performance. I've often felt so lucky that I started out on the stage, that I got great training with Uta Hagen, with Sandy Meisner at the Neighborhood Playhouse, with Lee

Strasberg at the Actors Studio. Working on stage all those years before "the big moment" came, which was [the off-Broadway production] *A Month in the Country* [1956] that Michael Redgrave directed. There was all that *stage* experience—I loved it! Then I came out to Hollywood and I had to learn a new craft, basically.

After your movie-TV career began, did you do more plays?
Oh, of course! And doing them made me so content. You would get practically nothing [money-wise] for the play, usually, and then you'd come back and you'd have to do a TV show or something, to make a little money to pay the mortgage—that was never any fun. The *real* fun was working in the theater, and working with a good director, and working with a wonderful actor or actress. That's the *joy* of this business—well, that's *me*, anyway. A lot of very famous people have never *been* on the stage, and they don't *care* about it. They just love *movies*, and they're very good at that.

Do you remember where you were, and how you felt, when you learned that Voyage *would not be coming back for a fifth year?*
[*Softly, conspiratorially:*] Oh, I was so happy. [*Laughs*] Where *was* I? I was Positano in Italy, a little town south of Naples, a tourist place, a glorious, beautiful town. That's where I had met my wife Bridget in 1967, when I was scouting locations for a film [the never-released *Off Season*]. Then I went back there in '68 to *do* the film, and I invited her to come spend some time with me. And during that trip in '68, I think it was around March, my agent Dick Clayton called me and he said *Voyage* was not picked up for a fifth year. I knew it *wouldn't* be—after that stupid fourth, I knew it couldn't be picked up. I figured, "Four years, 110 hour shows—well, that's a pretty good run." So I said, "Okay, Dick! Great! We'll move on!"—then we had a huge party that night, to celebrate the fact that it was cancelled. Oh, my God, we were so drunk and happy! It was fantastic. We had a great time at a place called the Buca di Baca, a restaurant. "*Yeeeeah*, it's *cancelled*! I don't have to go back to that *set*!" Alexandra Stewart was there, the actress in *Off Season*, and Robert Wolders, who was in it, and the producer, Harry Millard. And a lot of townsfolk.

Harry Millard the actor?
He was an actor—in fact, he did a guest shot on one of the *Voyage*s in the first year, "The Human Computer." I think we were the only two people *in* that episode—they had me alone on the submarine, but yet of course there was also a villain aboard, stalking me down. *That's* the part that Harry played. Then Harry, who wasn't doing that well as an actor, decided he wanted to produce, and that's when he came up with this idea to do a film. Originally we were going to do it in Acapulco, but the director had *been* to Positano and thought that would be a much better location. Had we gone to Acapulco, I would never have met my wife!

Do you happen to know what Richard Basehart's reaction was to the cancellation of Voyage?
I think he must have been relieved too. There's no way they would have changed

the format. If that kind of show were on today, *I* wouldn't be watching it. I'd watch something else, like *West Wing*—the kind of shows *I* like.

If there had been TV in your youth, would you have watched Voyage?
Oh, sure! Oh, yeah! I'd be watching it, absolutely.

After the show ended, did you keep up with Richard Basehart socially?
Yes. And about a month before Richard died [in 1984], I had lunch with him, and he *still* hadn't seen any part of his 25 percent [his 25 percent ownership of the show]!

Did you get together because he was sick?
Oh, no, no, we just got together for old time's sake and we had lunch at a place we used to go to when we were doing *Voyage*. We sat down and we talked about everything he was going to be doing and what was up, and it was a very wonderful, pleasant, three-hour lunch. The Beverly Hillcrest is what that place is called today—it's on the corner of Pico and Beverwil Drive.

Ever work for Irwin Allen again?
Yes, I did. He called me for a pilot of a show with Robert Stack, it was called *Adventures of the Queen* [1975], which was the Queen Mary. I remember telling someone, "I'm doing a TV pilot with Robert Stack, *Adventures of the Queen*," and he said, "Which of the two of you plays the Queen?" [*Laughs*] Irwin was the producer, but it didn't sell.

You had no hesitation about maaaybe going into another Irwin Allen series?
It was different, a different part. I figured, "What the hell?"—a lot of time had passed [since the cancellation of *Voyage*], and I hadn't done that much work.

Back at the beginning of this interview, you said you figured out why Irwin Allen wanted you so desperately for Voyage, *and promised to tell me.*
Just recently, it finally hit me. "God damn it," I said to myself, "*I* know why he wanted me so badly. Because he had all this *stock footage* on me!" [*Laughs*] Irwin could use stock footage of me from *The Lost World*, he could use stock footage of me from *The Enemy Below*, he had that foolish [electronic] board from *The Fly*, he had all these things, "pieces" of David Hedison, all over the place! And he *used* them—he did a *Lost World*-type segment, you remember ["Turn Back the Clock," 1964]? A lot of my stuff from *The Lost World* was in that. So these days I'm thinking maybe *that's* why he was so insistent! This dawned on me just a couple years ago—the fact that Irwin Allen kept insisting on me crossed my mind, and suddenly the light bulb came on: "Hey, *wait* a minute. It *wasn't* because he loved me so much...!" [*Laughs*]

Do you watch an episode now and then—and, if so, why?
Well, I *don't*. First of all, it's on [the Sci-Fi Channel] at seven o'clock in the

morning. I get up very early, but I don't watch *Voyage*! I haven't seen it in a looong time. But, it's funny ... I go to these celebrity shows and people come up to me and they say, "You know that time on *Voyage* when you did *this* and then you did *that* and duh duh duh duh duh..." and they tell me the whole story. You don't want to hurt their feelings so you shake your head up and down, smiling—but I don't remember a bit of it! It's so strange! But the fans remember ev-er-y-thing, and I've started getting some really wonderful fan mail [from *Voyage* fans] again in the last two years.

Why do you think the fan mail has started up again?
Because they're playing it all over now. I'm getting a lot from Germany, and from France. And from Czechoslovakia! Some of these people write such lovely letters—it's the first time they've seen the show, and they're very excited by it. And it's playing again here, of course, on the Sci-Fi Channel.

Even though I know what your answers are going to be—what was the best thing about Voyage, *and what was the worst thing?*
The worst ... the terrible scripts. I can't say "all" the scripts, but ... *some* of the terrible scripts. That was really the worst. The best thing about *Voyage* was ... *Richard ... Basehart*. Absolutely the best.

Russ Jones on Dr. Terror's Gallery of Horrors

> *[Dr. Terror's Gallery of Horrors] was fun, but I knew it wasn't gonna look good on the résumé!*

For horror fans who prefer their terror tales in bite-sized, multi-course helpings, the mid–1960s offered a tantalizing bill of fare: Movie-wise, the start of a series of horror anthologies from England's Amicus Productions and, in the print medium, the debut of Warren Publishing Company's black-and-white comic books *Creepy* and *Eerie*. And also, for the dedicated drive-in denizen, a five-part monster mash with inspirational roots in Amicus *and Creepy-Eerie*: producer-director David L. Hewitt's *Dr. Terror's Gallery of Horrors*. An ultra-low budget and rushed shooting schedule resulted in a film that was perhaps more laughfest than frightfest, but the presence of veteran players John Carradine, Lon Chaney, Jr., and Rochelle Hudson gave it a (light) veneer of respectability, and the macabre story "tags" were steeped in the memorable *Creepy-Eerie* comics tradition. Not surprising, since the stories were supplied by Russ Jones, creator of *Creepy* and *Eerie*.

Canadian-born, Jones was a Marine by age 16 and then, after the service, a young TV actor (*Wagon Train, Cheyenne, Lawman, 77 Sunset Strip*). He now entered the world of comic books, working with the legendary Wally Wood and then, on his own, creating *Creepy* and its sister 'zine *Eerie* for publisher James Warren. Leaving Warren's employ, Jones relocated to England and went under contract to a Hammer Films producer. This was the point at which Hewitt approached him about collaborating on *Dr. Terror's Gallery of Horrors*—and the rest, as they say, is exploitation movie history.

What was the inspiration for Dr. Terror's Gallery of Horrors? *Was it* Creepy *and* Eerie, *or was it the Amicus multi-story movies, or...?*

I think you nailed it right on the head, I think it was a combination of the two.

Dave Hewitt liked Milton Subotsky's Amicus film *Dr. Terror's House of Horrors* [1965] very much, *and* he was a *big* fan of *Creepy*.

Do you remember where you were when you were first asked to get involved?
  I was in London, under contract then to Tony Keys at Hammer, mostly doing storyboards and rewrites and things like that on Tony's projects. One evening I was home, 22 Chesterford Gardens, Hampstead NW3, and I got a telephone call from the States, from Sam Sherman. I knew Sam from the Warren days — Sam was the editor of *Screen Thrills Illustrated*. Sam called and said that a nice guy, a Hollywood producer-director by the name of Dave Hewitt needed some stories for a movie, and would I be interested?
  Dave and I hooked up, talked on the phone, and he told me a very amusing story. He had contacted Jim Warren and told Warren that what he wanted to do was a screen version of *Creepy*. Well, Warren apparently gave him kind of a rough time on the phone. Things were going well for Warren at that particular period in time, and he asked Dave, "How *old* are you?" Dave said, "Twenty-nine," or something like that. Warren responded, "Well, I've got *neckties* that are older than that!" and hung up on him! So, kind of frustrated, Dave got in touch with Sam Sherman, and that's how the whole thing happened. I spoke to Dave, and he told me what he had in mind; I wasn't particularly busy at that time, and Dave had a picture to make and he didn't have a script. I had some cast-off stories that I had done, and I fired them off to him in the mail. The next thing I know, I was contacted again and told that it was a go and invited to come to Hollywood and work on the picture.

Sam Sherman thought to suggest you to Hewitt because of your Creepy *connection, I assume.*
  Yes. And also Sam knew that I had more than a passing knowledge of the picture business, and how to put scripts together. So it just all fell together … if you want to *call* it that [*laughs*].

Hewitt told me that his original plan also called for the movie to be hosted *by Uncle Creepy.*
  He did speak of that. I believe that Verne Langdon [vice-president of Don Post Studios] was set to create the makeup appliances.

These "cast-off stories" you say you sent Hewitt — for what purpose had you originally written them?
  I was putting together basically the same sort of thing Dave was: I was planning on taking them to Amicus and talking to Milton Subotsky about [using them in one of their horror anthology films].

So now you're coming out to Hollywood for Gallery of Horrors, *and…*
  The airline ticket arrangement was made, and getting from London to New York was not a problem. Getting from New York to L.A., however, was a nightmare. There was an airline strike, and I think the only carrier operating was Amer-

ican Airlines. It took me a full 26 hours to get from New York to L.A. It was misery, it was just hanging out in airports and bars and ... [*sighs*]. That was an arduous trip, to say the least.

You had more than one layover?
Oh, *many*. I remember being in the Dallas–Fort Worth Airport *forever*. Also Chicago and Memphis and Nashville and—

Memphis and *Nashville??*
Yeah. That *really* hurt [*laughs*]! Anyway, [associate producer] Gary Heacock picked me up at LAX at some ungodly hour of the morning and I went *right* to the soundstage. It was like three o'clock in the morning, and they were still filming! The segment they were working on was "Count Dracula"—at three o'clock in the morning, they were in the midst of shooting the scene where Jonathan Harker [Roger Gentry] arrives at Dracula's castle. And I remember that a giant piece of wood, a big two-by-four, probably 15 feet long, fell and hit the director of photography Austin McKinney smack on the head. It had been propped up against a flat. The impact was quite impressive—it knocked him out. He came 'round and went right back to work, but it had split his scalp and he was bleeding right up until they wrapped that morning. "The show must go on!"

How many of the stories had been shot by this time?
That was *it*, that was the first one they were shooting.

The picture, according to the credits, was shot at Hollywood Stage.
6650 Santa Monica Boulevard. The Hollywood Stage actually was quite okay. I've heard a lot of people say naughty things about it, but shortly thereafter I produced an in-house film for Busch Bavarian Beer there with Jack Benny and Edward Everett Horton and Joe Flynn and quite a few luminaries. Hollywood Stage was good enough for Jack Benny, *he* didn't complain, so it wasn't as bad as you might have heard. Actually, the dressing rooms and everything were quite comfortable. Ray Dorn [*Gallery of Horrors*' co-producer and art director] was the owner of Hollywood Stage. Ray, I'd say, was in his forties, and he was primarily a construction fellow— he did all the set execution and would follow an art director's elevations and floor plans and all of that. He was very good, he had a very good crew, and they could do it quickly and economically. They built the sets for *Gallery of Horrors*.

So you'd sent Hewitt the five stories, and by the time you got to Hollywood—
No, I actually sent him three stories. *They* threw together the [script for the] "Count Dracula" segment, which was the one that they were in the midst of filming when I first got there.

That one looks to have been based on an Archie Goodwin story in Creepy #1, *"Pursuit of the Vampire!"*
How "Count Dracula" was constructed, how they came up with the tag [Harker

In addition to scripting *Dr. Terror's Gallery of Horrors*, Russ Jones also had a small acting role in the "King Vampire" segment.

turns out to be a werewolf and he kills Dracula], I don't know. It could have been a rip-off of Archie's story but I can't say for certain because I don't know. That was also an EC ending in about 20 stories in the '50s.

Let's take the rest of 'em story by story. "The Witches Clock"?
That was one that I sent from England.

"King Vampire"?
Sent from England too.

"Monster Raid"?
That one I wrote out here [in Hollywood].*

So "Spark of Life" was the third and last of the three you sent from England.
Correct.

Was the picture non-union?
Yes and no. An S.A.G. bond had to be put up, so to that extent it was an S.A.G.

"Monster Raid" was loosely based on the Creepy *#3 story "Return Trip!" by "Arthur Porges" (a Jones pseudonym).*

picture. And there were some IATSE people, like the director of photography Austin McKinney. Austin was a member of the union and he was out of work, so he was doing this "on the sly," thinking that nobody would ever *see* it.

We have to put all of this stuff into perspective. In 1966, as always, the film business was in transition. This was the era of *My Fair Lady* and *The Sound of Music* and all those "roadshow" pictures. What the lesser companies, the small guys out in Hollywood were doing was relying on the drive-ins. If you could get a distribution arrangement for your picture with Pacific Drive-In Theaters, who would take just about *any*thing, you would make enough money, just from Pacific Drive-Ins, to make the whole thing quite viable. *Gallery of Horrors*, I think the whole thing, above the line, below the line and every *other* line you can cross, came to under $30,000.

Where did you do your writing of "Monster Raid" and whatever else you wrote there?

At Hollywood Stage, in one of the offices. As the pages were being written, Dave Hewitt's wife Jean would grab them and she would re-type them and have 'em mimeo-ed off and handed out to the different departments. We were working on such a tight schedule, it was really an experience for me. I was used to doing what *I* thought were fast pictures [the Hammers]. I went from pictures like those, pictures done in six weeks, to an 80-minute film [*Gallery of Horrors*] that was being done in five days. That's a lot of minutes per day!

A page of script gets pulled out of your typewriter ... how long before it's on the soundstage being shot?

In some cases, pretty fast. I'd say within a couple of hours.

What kind of a guy was Hewitt? How did you like working with him?

I liked him. But his investors, I think, for the most part, were of rather dubious character. Dave was assigned to make these movies. *His* background was opticals and special effects, and he was very *good* at it. But as a director, he was not. He didn't "have the germ," he didn't have a director's instinct. The film just kind of ... made it*self*.

I did half-an-interview with Hewitt about 20 years ago. We talked for an hour or more ... we parted on excellent terms with him promising to be around in a few days to finish the interview ... and I'm still waiting. He made himself unavailable to me from then on, and the interview never got done!

Yes, he's a peculiar guy, actually. He was that way about *paying* you, too. You had to actually come in and almost threaten physical damage if you weren't paid [*laughs*]. He was a bit of a rogue. But so likable, it was hard to get mad at him.

Hewitt did tell me in that half-an-interview of ours that you used to work for James Warren and that, by 1966, you "hated him."

Oh, I never hated Warren. We had a falling-out. It all had to do with money. It always *does*, doesn't it, unfortunately? Dee Gee, my wife at the time, and Jim did *not* get along. He can be, shall we say, a little bit hostile toward women. Consequently, Dee Gee and Jim didn't hit it off. *Just prior to our getting married, we had a party, and she refused to invite him to it. He got very angry about this. And Warren is a very vindicate guy. To this day.* Last year, 2001, I was asked to do an interview in *Comic Book Artist*, a big publication on the comic book industry, for *The Warren Companion* [a reference guide to Warren's magazines]. But Jim told them that if I was to appear in that issue, he *wouldn't*, and that he wouldn't let them use any of his material. I thought, "My God, it's been almost 40 years. Can't we let this little feud go away??" I hold no malice at all toward Jim, I had simply *quit* [Warren Publishing]. And he, somehow or another, couldn't handle that. Plus, I embarrassed him by field stripping an M1 rifle. Jim claimed to have been a big hero during the Korean War and I field stripped an M1 rifle and he couldn't put it back together again [*laughs*]. Well, I *do* things like that, you see, when I suspect that people are having me on!

Gallery of Horrors *features lots of stock footage from AIP's Poe movies. You must have known what footage you'd have available to you before you wrote the stories.*
    No, Dave did. Dave was a genius at "knowing where all the bodies were buried" when it came to stock footage.

How much were you paid for your work on Gallery of Horrors?
    In the neighborhood of 2500, 3000, something like that. Plus all expenses while I was out there. I rented a house in Reseda, and when we worked late, I stayed at a motel in Hollywood.

Uncredited, you play a small part in the "King Vampire" segment, as a passerby who's mistaken for the vampire and beaten by several Londoners.
    I did it because the actor slated for that little role didn't show. I still had my S.A.G. card so ... well, *you* know how it goes. I was enlisted to put on somebody else's wardrobe that they'd gotten from Western Costume, which didn't fit at all, and I ended up being the guy that the angry populace (four!) kills in error. Incidentally, "King Vampire" was originally a Jack the Ripper story that Dave Hewitt changed. At the tag of the original story, the Scotland Yard inspector [Ron Brogan] is talking about being baffled and we find out that the secretary who works for him, her name is Jackie, is actually *Jackie* the Ripper.

Any idea why Hewitt changed it?
    No. I have absolutely no idea why he did a great *many* things he did [*laughs*].

Before we get to John Carradine and Lon Chaney and Rochelle Hudson, I have to ask ... where did they dig up the other "actors" they used in the picture?
    People like Ron Doyle and Roger Gentry and so on? Ron Doyle ["King Vampire," "Monster Raid," "Spark of Life"] was a guy Dave Hewitt had met somewhere. Doyle had done a number of *F.B.I.* shows [the Efrem Zimbalist series *The F.B.I.*], he was like a semi-regular. He did a lot of work for Quinn Martin. Except for his pompadour and very loud voice, he was adequate, I think. Ron Brogan ["King Vam-

pire"] was very well-known as a Shakespearean actor, his background was theater. Roger Gentry ["The Witches Clock," "King Vampire," "Monster Raid," "Count Dracula"] was one of those guys who worked in a multiplicity of miserable movies. I don't know if Roger is still around or what he's doing, I haven't seen him in … forever.

Keeping in mind that these actors were working practically around the clock, and didn't have a lot of time to prepare … how would you rate the jobs they did?

Mediocre. I think with *direction*, they could have [done a better job]. But it wasn't like we were shooting fifteen-to-one or anything like that. A *lot* of this was one-to-one, or maybe *two*-to-one. And so I can't really fault anybody.

Why is it the same actors over and over in the five stories? Wouldn't it have been better with an all-new cast in each segment, à la the Amicus movies?

Absolutely! That was done to save time and money.

Carradine and Chaney—what memories of meeting them?

Oh, I knew John anyway—we used to hoist them [drink] together. And I knew Lon, too, that's why he was *in* it. John was a neighbor of mine when I was living in Oxnard. He had a boat called *The John Dark* up there, and we'd hang out at an establishment called The Lobster Trap where (the more John got into his cups) he used to sing. He would sing "sea songs." He worked on a couple TV shows that I was also in, a *Wagon Train* for one, and we got to be friendly. Later on, whenever a picture [came up], I would always throw his name forward. Like when I was in London, and Dave and I were talking on the phone, I mentioned Carradine, and that's how it all happened.

Chaney also did a couple of episodic television things and that's where I first met him—I *think*. (We're going back a lot of years, remember!) He and I used to hoist a few as well. Lon was very different: Carradine was quite an intellectual … and Chaney wasn't. But he was amazing in the incredible ability to tell stories. I used to just love to sit back and listen to him rant on about his days at Universal and all the adventures that he had there. Great stuff.

His days at Universal making the monster pictures?

Yeah, during his halcyon days there. He was just fun to be around. Of course, it was sad to see what happened to him. I mean, he was about 60 when he did *Gallery*, and by that time he'd pretty well committed suicide with the booze. He couldn't wear makeup; he'd sweat so much that he had to change shirts every five minutes. So he was not in the best of health. But he was an amazing guy to *watch*. He called himself a mugger, he said [*imitating Chaney*], "I, I, I'm not an actor, I'm a *mugger*." And, yeah, he *was* to a degree. But he had some amazing attributes that you'd have to *be* there to appreciate. One of them that *I'll* never forget: He was a pretty tall guy. I'm an honest six-three and he was just a little bit shorter than me. But Ron Doyle was probably no taller than five-seven or five-eight. Yet when Lon would work a scene with Ron Doyle, he had this incredible ability to "shape shift"

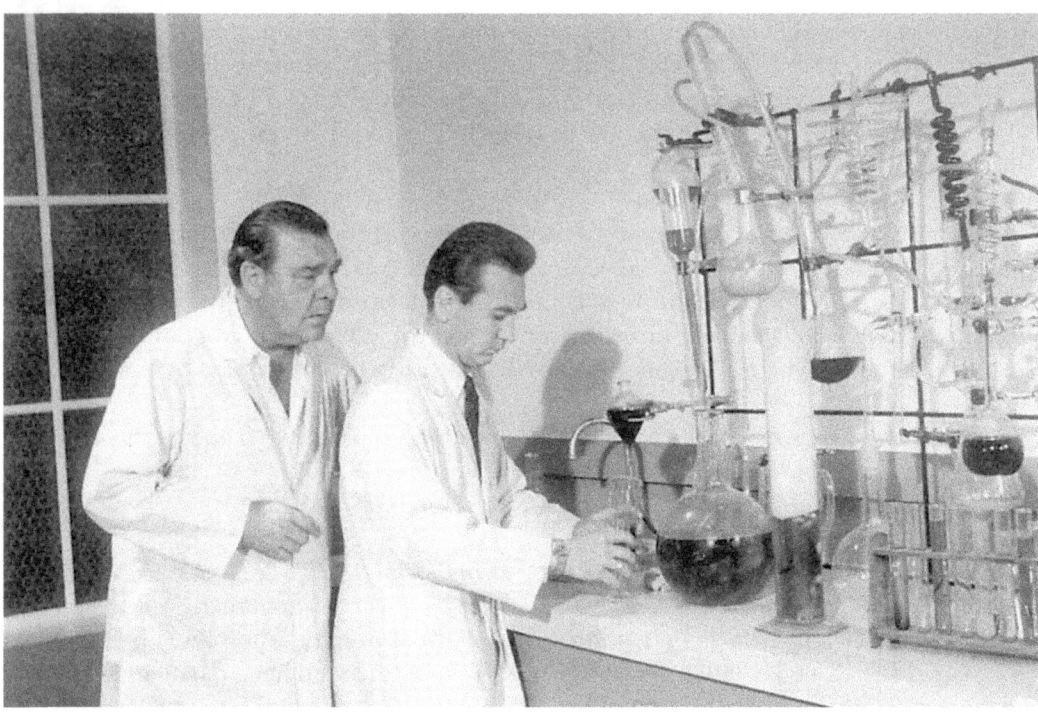

According to Jones, Lon Chaney, Jr. (left), could "shape shift" down to the same height as his *Dr. Terror's* co-stars like Ron Doyle.

and *shrink* [*laughs*]! And it didn't look like he was *doing* it! And if they were going to do a match cut, he knew *just* when he should (say) raise his hand. He was just spot-on with his [position and movements] from a medium to a closeup, or a full shot to a medium, or whatever. I thought that was a pretty amazing attribute. And his lines, he rarely blew them. He was prepared, and thoroughly professional.

Any idea how much he and Carradine were paid?
  I know exactly how much they were paid: Chaney got 1500 a day, Carradine got a grand a day.

A grand a day, 1500 a day, it all sounds great—but how many days did these guys work?
  [*Laughs*] Chaney worked a day and John worked two.

John worked two days because he had to also do the intros to all five stories, after the rest of the picture had been shot?
  That's absolutely correct.

Why more for Lon?
  I think it was because Chaney had a higher "TVQ" [degree of familiarity and appeal to TV audiences] than Carradine did.

Chaney on the set—did he seem to be enjoying himself?

Oh, we had a great time. My memories of that movie are mostly about him, because he was just so much fun to be around.

Dave Hewitt told me that Chaney was a practical joker on the set.

At the end of "Spark of Life," the two medical students [Ron Doyle, Joey Benson] think the body covered by a sheet on the operating table is that of the dissected killer, but it turns out to be their teacher Dr. Mendell, i.e., Chaney. Well, when they least expected it, Chaney sat bolt upright and *screamed*. I thought that Ron Doyle was going to have a heart attack! It took him about a half an hour to get composed again [*laughs*]. Lon was *always* doing stuff like that—*always*. He was a great practical joker.

And the drinking? Did that affect his work?

I have heard stories about his drinking, and I am sure that some of them are probably based on truth. On this particular shoot, he was drinking, but it didn't interfere with anything that he did. In fact, he finished early.

And Carradine? What was it like to have him around for "The Witches Clock"?

John was always fun to be around. He was another guy who would be telling you stories—all about his days with Barrymore, and his Shakespeare company way back when, and he loved to talk about films. I would quiz him on movies like Fritz

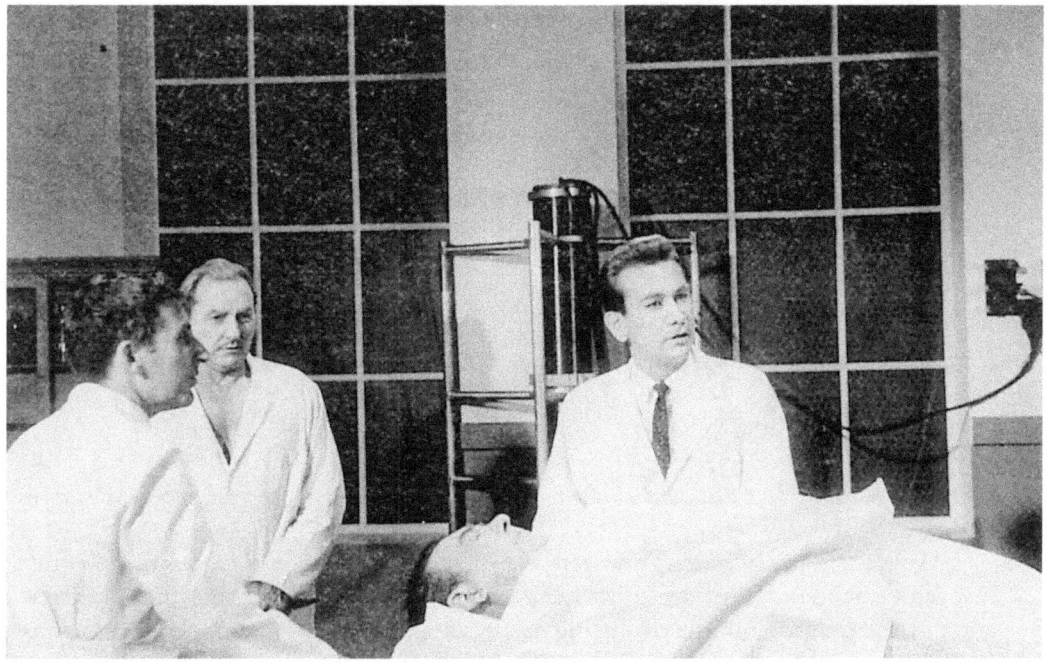

Practical joker Chaney (on operating table) is about to scare the yell out of his co-stars (*left to right:* **Joey Benson, Vic McGee, Ron Doyle**).

Lang's *Man Hunt* [1941] and a lot of the other pictures that he'd done at Fox. John was just a font of information.

You had time, even with writing the script and all, to visit the set and hang out with these guys a little?

They had a huge conference room, and between set-ups, everybody would kind of duck in there and have a Coke or, in Chaney's case, have some "iced tea."

"Iced tea" in quotes.

Yes, in quotes! That's also where he had his fresh shirts all stacked up, because he didn't want a dressing room. (He was very easy to work with.) The minute I knew that everybody was just kicking back and talking about the old days ... who could miss *that*? *I* couldn't! In fact, right there in that room, Carradine and Chaney and I, we worked out a whole storyline for a picture I had in mind. It was a story about some actor who's hung up with the fact that he played a werewolf in all his pictures and now he's beginning to really think that he *is* one. And it's also about this Shakespearean actor who's tagged as Count Dracula. I don't remember the details of it, but it would have primarily been about these two out-of-work thespians who actually *become* what they were well-known for, and I remember that it had some clever twists and turns. It really could have been a hoot. But, of course, nothing ever happened with it.

Chaney and Carradine actually had story suggestions?

Oh, yes. We kicked it around at the Hollywood Stage *and* at Chaney's house in Toluca Lake. We had two or three sessions.

Rochelle Hudson, another oldtimer—how did you end up with her in Gallery of Horrors*?*

I don't remember how that happened. I was familiar with her work from the old days, of course. She'd come in from Arizona to do our picture. I don't know if she was looking to "come back" or if she was simply looking just to *do* something. I just remember her as being very sweet.

If the picture was made in five days and there are five stories, that tells me you did a story a day, right?

Pretty much.

So the sets would be built and a story done, and then new sets and the next story, and...

Well, there really weren't new sets, they just moved wild walls around. Like the inspector's Scotland Yard office in "King Vampire": They'd just bring them in flats and put them in the middle of the big castle set and then throw up a bookcase and find what props they could, and there was his "office." Believe me, it was "on the run"—it was *really* on the run. It was quite an experience.

You're making it sound like a lot of fun.

It *was*. Actually, in some weird, kinky, bizarre way, I enjoyed doing *that* more than doing a movie the traditional way, because it was really fly-by-the-seat-of-your-pants picturemaking.

How could you have John Carradine in your employ—and yet have Mitch Evans play Dracula in the picture?

That wasn't my decision.

I'd have loved to see Carradine as Dracula, instead of in "The Witches Clock."

Well, see, Dave Hewitt's heart wasn't really *in* horror films. Dave was doing it for one reason: Just to get it *done*. It wouldn't have made any difference if it had been a biker movie, or a sci-fi film, or a beach party thing. He would set the camera down, say *action* and that was *it*.

Well, you can pretty much tell by the camera set-ups that he didn't want to go the extra mile. Or even a quarter-mile!

[*Laughs*] Oh, *yeah*. I would take him to one side and I would say [*under his breath*], "Dave, I think it would be a better idea maybe if you would move the camera over *here*..." Austin McKinney would always be on my side in these matters. That's the only time Dave would kind of lose his cool, 'cause he was under such incredible pressure from these... "money people." I'm *calling* 'em "money people" but they really didn't *give* Dave very much, did they [*laughs*]? They wanted this delivered on x-y-z date, and they *got* it.

You reportedly play a second role—in "Monster Raid," as the decomposed living dead corpse of the murdered doctor.

Yeah, that was me. Ron Doyle [who played the live doctor in flashbacks] didn't want to mess up his pompadour [*laughs*]. I was substantially taller than he was, but I think it matched. I mean, a corpse is a corpse is a corpse, right? Actually, I thought the corpse makeup was effective when I originally saw it "big" [on the screen]. But something's happened to the color in that picture over the years, it's degenerated. The color all went away, it all became yucky and dark. You can't see *anything*. That really isn't the way Austin McKinney shot it. Austin was good enough to work on *The Terminator* [1984] with James Cameron [as process photography cinematographer]—Austin was a good cameraman, he didn't shoot junk.

Who did your corpse makeup?

I did. I got a bald cap and spirit-gummed all of that down. And I used a lot of nose putty and greasepaint, and some dental caps.

Dental caps?

I went to a dental supply house, and they had the plastic caps that you could fill with adhesive and mount right over a broken tooth, just for a temp job. I bought a bunch and applied them to the outside of my face, to my jaw, as though half of

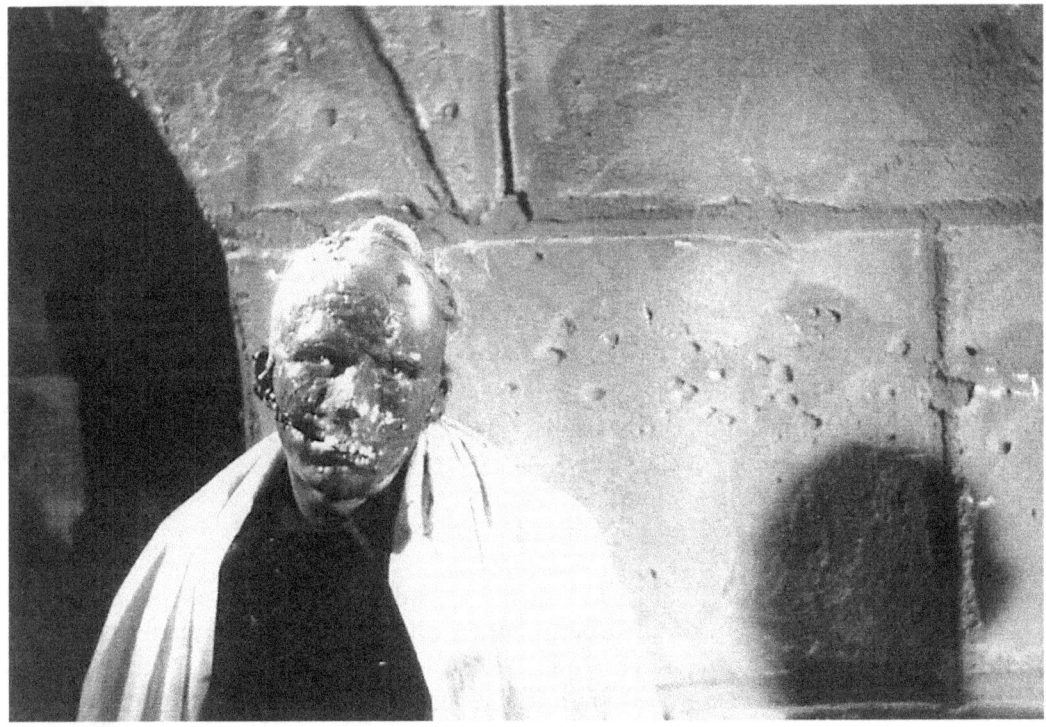

Jones created and applied his own horror makeup to play a walking corpse in one of the stories he had scripted.

the face was gone and the teeth were showing through. I also took a rubber band and put it around my head to make the nose look different and to make the ears look like they'd rotted off at the bottom.

Even though there's no twist at the end of that story—"Monster Raid" is the one story without a climactic twist—it's my favorite of the five.
    It was supposed to have a twist at the end: The corpse shoots up the wife [Hudson] with the life-restoring formula and, now that he has made *her* immortal, he takes her in his arms and says, "Now give your husband a great big *kiss*…" and then he kisses her. *That* would have been the "tag," and that would have been … satisfying, at least. In a *disgusting* way, but it would have worked!

Why was that not shot?
    I wasn't on the set when this happened, I was hacking and slashing away at some typewriter that was archaic even then, but Dave told me that Rochelle Hudson said she didn't want to be on-screen with the corpse.

There's a shot in the movie which is the corpse's p.o.v. approaching Hudson, and you can see the corpse's hands—
    Those were Dave Hewitt's hands. There was no makeup or anything on 'em,

they were just "fuzzed out." Doing it that way placated her. That same day, I put on the corpse makeup and we did several shots. Then, later, on a Saturday morning, I ended up putting that ferschlugginer makeup on *again*, to do the scene where Vic McGee opens my casket and helps me get up out of it. As I was lying in that casket on the tomb set, one of the special effects guys (at least that's what they *called* them) said, "Oh, let's make this better..." And he took a whole big huge bag of Fuller's earth and poured it all in the casket as I was lying in it—and then closed the lid!

What effect was he hoping for? How did he think it would add to the scene?
I ... don't ... know ... why ... they ... did ... that [*laughs*]. Maybe they were trying to kill me, maybe they didn't like me. Maybe they hated the film! I was in there *dying*, breathing that dust—it was horrible. And it was hot. I could hardly wait for Vic McGee to open it so I could come up. It was pretty awful. That was a Saturday morning number, with nobody around but Austin and a couple of other people. I think that scene was m.o.s. [filmed without sound].

Was every night a late night, working past midnight?
[*Wearily*] Ev-er-y ... night, yes. It was a very cooperative group.

Throughout the picture, there are blood-red cartoon transitions between scenes—dripping blood, a bat, a heart, things like that. Your idea?
Dave and I talked about that and I storyboarded that stuff out for him. I thought that, since the picture had very little else going for it, maybe some lively opticals would give it a little more feel of "budget," or "production," or call it what you will. By the way, I didn't write any of those ponderous, diabolically long intros that Carradine delivered.

I know. I've talked to Gary Heacock, and he takes the blame for those.
They're interminable, aren't they?

Were you there the day Carradine shot the intros?
Yes, I was. Carradine stood in front of a blue cyc.

Did he have cue cards, or was he able to remember all that crazy stuff?
No, John remembered all that crazy stuff. He'd read something once and he'd *have* it. Carradine was pretty amazing, he just remembered *every*thing. He was one of the best studies I had ever seen.

Heacock told me the reason he wrote those long, looong intros was because the picture had come up short time-wise.
No, the picture didn't run short—they would have *known* that. The problem was, they didn't have enough money to do another episode, as originally planned. That's what *really* happened.

Was the extra episode written?

I believe that a good portion of it was. It was kind of a gross story—I don't remember all of it, but Forry Ackerman was going to play a wicked king whose kingdom was plagued with pestilence and rats. The tag was that, since the rats were eating the people, somehow at the end, rats were fed to Forry alive. That was a special role tailor-made for Forry, and I remember he was very disappointed when it didn't happen. Carroll Borland was going to be in that as well, as the queen.

Did you come up with the title Dr. Terror's Gallery of Horrors*?*

No. And I do not recall who *did*.

Where did you see the movie for the first time?

I think I saw it in Lewisham, in England. It's a suburb of London ... a place you don't want to *go* [*laughs*]. It's one of the few sections of London where you really don't want to spend a lot of time. There's just something very uncomfortable about it, it kind of feels like you're at "Hobbs End" [the creepy London district in *Five Million Years to Earth* (1968)] or something!

The audience reaction?

I don't know, because I left before it was over.

How far into it did you get?

Oh, probably 20 minutes. And thought to myself, "I left Hampstead and took the underground *all* the way to Lewisham ... to see *this*??" [*Laughs*]

You probably had seen "dailies," and had a pretty good idea what it would look like ... no?

Actually, I had already seen an assembly—the only things that were missing from it were the opening and closing credits and the stock footage. They put that assembly together *so* quickly, it defies logic in today's picturemaking world. I don't understand movies at all any more, incidentally. I think you actually have a lot of directors who are less competent than Dave Hewitt and they're making these monster big hits, and they're all done with trickery and foolery and no content. I mean, when you think about it, a lot of them have less content than *Dr. Terror's Gallery of Horrors* [*laughs*]!

You're not going to get any argument out of me about that!

It's all form over content. Some wise man once said, "Art, like magic, is hoax redeemed by awe." Well, I always kind of agreed with him. I don't understand the movies at all today.

Why don't you get a screenplay credit on the movie?

I didn't *want* it. In fact, I was really angry when I finally saw a print that had titles applied to it and saw that my name was there [credited with "Original Stories"]. I'd asked them to use one of my a.k.a.s, and they didn't. I don't think it was done with any malicious intent, I think it was just something that skittled by.

Producer-director David L. Hewitt and Jones display a copy of Jones' 'zine *Monster Mania*.

Did it do well at the box office?
    I know that it made money before it even *went* to the box office. They laid it off to TV, they'd pre-sold it. When you laid a picture off to television in those days, *that* would primarily *more* than cover your production costs.

What was the best and the worst story?
    Oh, gosh. [*Pause*] You really know how to nail a guy down [*laughs*]! I don't think there *is* a best. I'm really not terribly fond of this movie—although I have fond memories of it. But as a piece of cinema, I would say, out of all the films that I've been involved in, it's probably the one that I like the *least*, aesthetically. I think

"The Witches Clock" and the Jack the Ripper story which became "King Vampire" would have been good, but the way they eventually came out wasn't the way they were written. Dave Hewitt had a problem with showing blood in the movie and he had a problem about ... well, about anything at *all* that might be [considered objectionable]. There wasn't even a ratings system at that time, and yet he was very concerned about that kind of stuff. I even had to convince him that in "King Vampire," when I'm dead on the ground, after being beaten by the mob, that there ought to be some Max Factor Technicolor Red [phony blood] used. I went and got some and put it on.

So you did try to talk him into showing more blood and so on.

Yes. I kept saying, "Well, gosh, I just got through working on a movie where blah blah blah happened...," and he'd say [*firmly*], "I don't *like* those kind of films." And *I'd* say, "Then ... why are you *making* one??" He and I would get into these little confrontations. But they were short-lived and we were always friendly.

You haven't given me the impression that David Hewitt wrote much of anything. Why does he get a screenplay credit?

I guess when you're running the whole show and the guy who did the work is 7000 miles away, you can do any damn thing you like [*laughs*]! For the screenplay, he used his pseudonym "David Prentiss," which a lot of people thought was me: "Russ Jones hiding behind the pseudonym 'David Prentiss.'" Well ... no. *No.* As I said, I didn't want my name on it at *all*. It was fun, but I knew it wasn't gonna look good on the résumé!

Dr. Terror's Gallery of Horrors (American General, 1967)

A Dorad Corp. and Borealis Enterprises, Inc. Co-Production; 82 minutes; Associate Producer: Gary R. Heacock; Produced by David L. Hewitt & Ray Dorn; Directed by David L. Hewitt; Screenplay: David Prentiss [David L. Hewitt], Gary R. Heacock & (uncredited) Russ Jones; Original Stories: Russ Jones; Photography: Austin McKinney (Totalvision and Pathé Color); Art Director: Ray Dorn; Editor: Tim Hinkle; Lighting Director: John McNichols; Sound Recording: Jay Hathaway; Set Construction: A-1 Studio Service; Makeup: Jean Lister [Jean Hewitt]; Music & Sound Effects: Commercial Sound Recorders; Rerecording: United Pictures Sound Studios; Script Supervisor: Jean Hewitt; Also known as *The Blood Suckers, Gallery of Horror* and *Return from the Past*

John Carradine (*Host*). "**The Witches Clock**": John Carradine (*Tristram Halbin*), Roger Gentry (*Bob Farrell*), Karen Joy (*Julie Farrell*), Vic McGee (*Dr. Finchley*). "**King Vampire**": Roy Doyle (*Brenner*), Margaret Moore (*Mrs. O'Shea*), Ron Brogan (*Insp. Marsh*), Roger Gentry (*Mob Leader*), Russ Jones (*Suspect With Blood on Glove*). "**Monster Raid**": Rochelle Hudson (*Helen Spalding*), Ron Doyle (*Dr. Charles Spalding*), Roger Gentry (*Dr. James Sevard*), Vic McGee (*Desmond*), Russ Jones (*Charles' Corpse*). "**Spark of Life**": Lon Chaney, Jr. (*Dr. Mendell*), Ron Doyle (*Dr. Cushing*), Joey

Benson (*Dr. Sedgewick*), Vic McGee (*Amos Duncan*). "**Count Dracula**": Roger Gentry (*Jonathan Harker*), Mitch Evans (*Count Alucard [Count Dracula]*), Karen Joy (*Medina*), Vic McGee (*The Burgermeister*), Gray Daniels (*The Coachman*), Gary R. Heacock (*Hans*)

Richard Kiel *on* Eegah

> *As we were pulling away [from the movie theater] in Arch Hall's car, I heard this voice: "Eegah! Eeeegah!" I turned around in my seat, and there was this little black boy, about ten or eleven, running after the car, yelling, "Don't forget me, Eegah! Eegah, don't forget me!" And I never* have*!*

Mention the name Richard Kiel to the average cinephile and you'll probably find that many believe that the towering actor first burst upon the movieland scene as Jaws, the steel-toothed menace in two of Roger Moore's James Bond films of the 1970s. But by the time he jumped on the Bondwagon, Kiel had in fact already served a long Hollywood apprenticeship, guesting on scores of TV series and acting in a succession of exploitation movies. Science fiction and horror films were of course a natural for this 7'2", 330 lb. native of Detroit, Michigan, whose imposing size made him the ideal choice for the title role in the 1962 Fairway-International release *Eegah*; 21-year-old Kiel starred as a caveman who has survived into our modern times—his "Primitive Passions Turned On" (ad line) by the teenage brunette (Marilyn Manning) who infringes on his stamping grounds in the California desert. Kiel talks about the film, its writer-producer-director Arch Hall, Sr., and how he finally got his 17EEE foot in the door in Hollywood, in this Eegah-ly awaited interview.

How did you first get acquainted with Arch Hall, Sr.?

There was a guy I met who was about seven feet tall, Buck Maffei. In the very first TV show that I ever did, an episode of *Klondike* [1960], I played a barnstorming fighter going through Alaska, and Buck had a little part at the end of it. Buck was an actor who didn't do a whole lot of stuff, but he was a kindly guy. He had met Arch Hall, Sr., who was getting ready to make a movie.

Eegah?

No, *Striganza* was the name of the movie. It was going to take place on the island of Striganza, where there's this guy who has achieved eternal youth by drinking the blood of the female virgins he has sacrificed—it was one of those typical C-minus movie plots [*laughs*]. Buck was interviewed for the part of the guy, but he wasn't quite right for it. Buck was quite overweight—he weighed maybe close to 400 pounds. Arch Hall wanted somebody humongous but not that heavy. So, in a moment of benevolence, Buck suggested that *I* go out and see Arch Hall. Buck told me about him and then he either took me out there to introduce me or he told me how to get there, I don't remember now. I *do* remember Arch Hall telling me about this movie, about this character ... and I remember thinking it was a little strange. But at that point in time, I was eager to do *any*thing to get my career started. I feigned enthusiasm ... but maybe I made some comments about the sacrificing-of-virgins idea that gave Arch the impression that it wasn't too appealing to me. I think Arch sensed my disapproval.

Where did you meet Hall?

He owned an arcade of offices on the corner of Olive Avenue and Lincoln Street in Burbank, with a parking area behind it. A two-story thing, apartments [on top] and then, down below, offices, one after another. Arch had apparently saved his money, and he now owned quite a bit of real estate. He had been a successful radio guy. He and his wife Addelyn Hall did a popular radio show called *What's Buzzin', Cousin*—they starred in it, and I think they produced and wrote it too. And [in the '30s and '40s] Arch had been in numerous films, a lot of Westerns and things. In fact, they made a movie *about* Arch's life [1961's *The Last Time I Saw Archie*, with Robert Mitchum as Hall] which *I* thought was interesting. Arch had a lot of chutzpah, he was sort of well-known for that, and the movie played that up. Like, when Arch was in the service during the War, they had him in the entertainment division, Arch having been a radio actor and so on. The entertainment people had different uniforms, *unique* uniforms, so people didn't know who they were when they were roaming around. Arch found that by running around with a clipboard and a pencil, people were terrified that he was somebody with power, somebody who could get them into trouble. He would come in and be very domineering, and get airplanes to take him to see old friends in different parts of the country [*laughs*]—really, he was quite a character! *The Last Time I Saw Archie* was about Arch Hall, written by a guy he knew [William Bowers, also a character in the movie, played by Jack Webb], but without getting Arch's permission. Arch later sued 'em and they paid him a settlement.

Was there actually a script for Striganza?

I think there was. Anyway, I was out there at the little arcade talking to Arch about *Striganza* and I happened to notice a sign in a window, FOR RENT. I asked, "What's that FOR RENT there?" and he said, "Oh, it's a little office. I rent them pretty cheap." I asked, "*How* cheap?" and he said, "Thirty-five a month. Including water."

[Laughs] Oh, man—you couldn't get the water *for 35 a month these days!*

So I said, "Well, let me take a look at it." It was just an office, but it had a washroom. No shower or anything, just a wash basin and a toilet. But 35 a month for a starving actor trying to break in ... I thought I could manage that. I figured, "I could stick a bed in here, and do sponge baths in the sink, and survive for 35 a month..." So I rented it from him.

You were still single at the time?
Yeah. And I know it's hard to believe, but there were months when I was having problems coming up with the $35. *And* the money for the electricity and the phone. Well, actually, no, I didn't *have* a phone, I went down to the drug store-diner on the corner and used the pay phone in there. If you ever see *Eegah* again, you'll see in a part near the end, where the police are coming to chase me, an old '51 Ford parked on the street. That old crashed-up '51 Ford with the mashed-in grill was *mine*. The car was so bad that the driver's door didn't open, you had to go in and out the passenger side and slide over. The seat was all broken-down so I had a piece of plywood so that I wouldn't be sitting on the floor [*laughs*]. And it had a cracked block, and I kept getting water in the oil. But I found that by changing the oil about three times a week, I could keep this thing going. I used to go to a gas station and buy used oil—people would change their oil, the gas station would keep the old oil, and I would go in there and buy it, for like a buck, and stick it in this thing. Then I found that Stop Leak kind of helped a little bit, and I'd have to keep putting *that* in there. In the beginning, it was really bleak!

It's starting to sound like a story out of the Depression!
The guy who had the drug store-diner, his name was Phil Stopeck—he would let me charge things so that, when things were tough, when I was in between jobs, I'd be able to eat. It was the kind of drug store where the bottles of stuff on the shelves were like half-empty from evaporation [*laughs*], he'd bought them at an auction or something. And he had out-of-date toys and sundries, all sorts of different things that he got dirt cheap. The food there was just barely edible. But that's where I went because Phil Stopeck would let me charge things, and then when I would do a show, I would pay my bill. I had the same sort of accommodation at the corner gas station. And, because I was *in* Burbank and near the film business, I met people in the gas station and in the diner who were involved in TV and movies, and I got a few parts out of that. But it just seemed like every time I would do a show, I would have to take all the money I would earn and pay everybody *back*!

You know, one of the reasons I wrote a book [*Making It Big in the Movies—The Autobiography of Richard "Jaws" Kiel*, 2002] was to discourage people who think you just go out to Hollywood and become a movie star. It's not that easy.

I loved your book from start to finish—but especially the first part where you were struggling. That *was more interesting to me.*
Yeah, and all the innovative things I had to do in order to be able to get into the studios—getting to know the gate guards and so on. A lot of real determination, I think, was the key. My father used to say, "The harder I work, the luckier I get." In other words, luck doesn't come by itself, luck is usually the result of a lot of dedication, inspiration, preparation and hard work.

Anyway, I remember getting behind a little bit in my rent, and Arch Hall immediately saying, "Instead of *Striganza*, now I've got this idea for a movie about a caveman. I'm gonna give him a name like *Eeeeegah*..." [*Laughs*] He starts telling me the story idea, and he begins developing the script. And he says, "Don't worry about the rent. When we make the movie, we'll settle up..." But in the meantime, I had told my younger sister, my *only* sister Georgann about *Striganza* and a little bit about the plot, and she was like *fascinated* with this thing. It just seemed like for *years* Georgann, every time I would see her, would ask, "When are you gonna do *Striganza*? When are you gonna do *Striganza*?" I must've heard that question a hundred times [*laughs*]! I *learned* from that to never talk about possible future things, with *anybody*, because these things don't always happen. Like a lot of actors, I finally ended up making a rule to not talk about something [that's in the planning stage]. Because in the movie business, many, many things that are talked about never happen.

So Striganza *was never made—which I guess was for the best, because it didn't sound like you were very anxious to do it anyway.*
There were some types of films that I just didn't do. There was a thing I was offered called *House on Bare Mountain* [1962] which was like a nudie-cutie thing. Carrying around naked ladies wasn't something that I wanted to do. I wanted to be an *actor*. I realized I was never gonna play Shakespeare roles, but I wanted to do something *more* than just do *that* [nudies]. My friend Bill Engesser, who was an inch taller than me, ended up doing *House on Bare Mountain*. He did it under the name "Hugh Cannon"—I guess a play on words for like "Huge Cannon," kind of a phallic symbol name or something [*laughs*]!

Incidentally, the whole reason that *Eegah* came about was that [in 1959] Arch Hall had made a movie called *The Choppers* with Tom Brown, an actor who'd been around for a long time playing juvenile roles and then ended up a leading man. There were a couple other experienced character actors in it, and then the Choppers, a gang of teenage car strippers, was played by Arch's son Arch Hall, Jr., and *his* friends. It was a little black-and-white movie that Arch Sr. couldn't get anybody to distribute. And he had spent quite a bit of money on it, I think more money than he spent on *Eegah*, which was in color. Arch couldn't get anything out of it, couldn't get it distributed, and I guess somebody suggested to him that if he were to now make a color film, then he could package the two of 'em together and distribute them himself, as a double feature. At that time, in the drive-ins, they had a lot of double features. So he made *Eegah*.

A good bit of Eegah *was shot in the Palm Springs–Palm Desert area.*
Yeah, we went out to places that he knew well—he had a home out in Palm Desert, he and his wife Addelyn. Arch Jr. had a dune buggy out there, and [starring in] *Eegah* was kind of an opportunity for him to hop up his dune buggy a little bit and use *that*, and to get to perform some songs. I think that Arch Sr. and Addelyn thought Arch Jr. could be [the next] Ricky Nelson. Ricky Nelson got started on *Ozzie & Harriet* [the popular TV series], and in the very, very beginning,

Ricky Nelson wasn't very good on those TV shows, if you remember them. Or maybe they're before your time?

Yeah, I'm afraid they are.
Ricky Nelson was very, very immobile. The first few songs that he did, he was so shy and so like a stone. He barely moved—it was like the deer in the headlights [*laughs*]. And yet, because of the power of television, because it went into so many jillion homes, he became very popular with the teenagers. I think that Arch Sr. and Addelyn thought they could do the same thing with *their* son, using *movies*. Unfortunately, movies—especially C-minus, D-plus movies!—don't have that audience of millions that a TV show, a big hit TV show, has. But Arch Jr. was a nice young man and he was very talented musically, with his guitar and his friends. Some of the people involved [in Arch Jr.'s band] went on to do big things in the record business.

Eegah *was a very low-budget picture. What were some of the things you guys did to save bucks?*
Well, for one thing, Arch Sr. found that he could buy what they call "short ends" [as his raw film stock]. On a big movie like (say) *Silver Streak* [1976], when there's just enough film in the magazine on the top of the camera to do one more take, they usually take it out and then load the camera with a full roll of film. A lot of times, that little bit film of unexposed film that *was* in there, which is perfectly good, is kept by workers who then sell it to independent film producers, especially college-type kids who need to buy their raw stock for almost nothing. That whole movie *Eegah* was made from short ends. They had to have a guy whose job was to constantly be reloading the magazine with these short ends.

I had a friend named Ronnie Kinchela; his brother, who went by the name of Roger Christian, used to be an announcer on a big rock 'n' roll station in L.A. Ronnie was dying to be in the film, and he *was* [acting under the name "Ron Shane"]: At the end, he was the detective and his friend Bill Rice was the uniformed cop who shoot and kill me. Ronnie also worked on the film behind the scenes, doing grunt-type stuff. One day we were out in the middle of the desert in the hot sun, it's like 110, and we see this little speck out in the distance coming running towards the location. This little speck gets closer and closer, it's Ronnie Kinchela and he's yelling something, and then finally you could hear, "*The film's no good, stop shooting! The film's no good, stop shooting!* The film's no good, stop shooting! The film's no good, stop shooting!*" Oh, my God! Arch Hall got on the phone and talked to the lab, and he found out that the short ends we'd been using were out-of-date. If you keep short ends too long, they'll go bad. Well, somebody had sold us some that were waaay beyond the date, and they were turning a different color! The scenes had like an orange cast or a yellow cast. But Arch found that they could probably color-correct it to the point where it'd be good-enough, and so we continued shooting.

Once the problem was brought to his attention, but he learned they could color-correct it, he continued to use short ends?
Yeah. Then also, they hired a guy to do the sound, a guy who was a radio

"Love Breaks the Time Barrier" (ad line)—and Richard Kiel broke into starring roles—with the caveman horror-action-romance-comedy *Eegah*.

announcer at a little tiny station in a park in Burbank—it was like one of those thousand-watter stations. I remember that a Japanese gas station owner did commercials on it, probably for ten bucks apiece, and the reason I remember was that his whole family did a singing jingle, the Japanese family that owned this gas station: "Frying A, Frying A Gasorine." This announcer's name was Bob Davis—he's also *in* the film. Anyway, Bob Davis sort of conned his way into being the sound man by saying that he *was* a sound man—he just wanted to work on the movie. But he had the stuff hooked up wrong, and so for about the first week or ten days of shooting, nothing got recorded.

And therefore had to be dubbed later.
Right. Most of the [early shooting] was with me and they had to dub it all, and I guess Arch Hall figured that as long as all my stuff had to be dubbed, he might as well do it himself. So it was actually Arch Hall being Eegah, the voice, "wistinchabla," "washtao" and all that stuff.

Eegah's "dialogue," if you want to call it that, sounds almost American Indian.
Arch Hall was from South Dakota, he grew up there. Deadwood, Cedar Rapids, in that area. He was "into" the Indian stuff.

So pretty much everything that comes out of your mouth in that movie is really Arch Hall?
Not "pretty much everything," *everything.*

The sound guy who bollixed things up, he was also in the movie, you said. Playing...?
He and Addelyn Hall play the drunk and the woman at the motel. Some of Ad Hall's friends were the ladies at the Shadow Mountain Country Club [in Palm Desert]. At the motel, Phil Stopeck, the diner-drug store guy who let me charge things, is the guy coming down the stairs when Eegah's going up. It was like a family affair.

You're telling me this guy Bob Davis did the sound—but in the credits, it says Sam Kopetzky.
Sam worked on it for sure, but this Bob Davis was the guy handling the sound in the beginning, up until the point where they found that the sound wasn't being recorded.

[Laughs] That'd be a good time to get rid of him!
Bob Davis wasn't familiar enough with the equipment, but he was trying to do it, to brave it out, to fake it. I can understand that. At one point, I was told by my agent, "If you're ever asked if you can ride a horse, tell 'em, 'Of course.' 'Cause usually all you do is just get off and get on." So I took it one step further when I was offered an episode of *The Rifleman*, I said, "Oh, I was practically *born* on a horse." Then when I saw the script, I was terrified: I had to gallop down this big hill and rein up, along with my partner Kevin Hagen, in front of the Rifleman and his son. The mistake is sometimes taking on more than what you really can do. Sometimes it works out—it worked out for me on that *Rifleman* episode. Sometimes it doesn't, and I think that's what happened to Bob Davis. But he was a nice guy, and he did a good job in his little acting role as the drunk.

How unpleasant was it for you, shooting out in the desert?
I was pretty bare except for that loincloth, and so it wasn't so bad, especially in the shade. I was looking at the pressbook just the other day, and according to the pressbook, "Temperatures ranged between 122 and 125." I don't *think* so [*laughs*]!

And was it cold at night?
In Palm Springs, night is a lovely time, good temperatures. Even when we shot in Burbank, it was never cold.

Now, where exactly were you shooting?
The sand dunes and the cliffs, when I'm chasing the dune buggy, that was just as you entered Palm Springs, the north end of Palm Springs, not too far from where the aerial tram is today. The actual opening of the cave, up in the top of the hill, when Eegah is carrying the girl [Marilyn Manning], was shot—without permission—on some famous actor's property, I think it was one of the Marx Brothers. We also used the cave in Bronson Canyon in Hollywood.

A soundstage cave (made out of soot-blackened cloth!) became the desert lair of Eegah (Kiel) in the low-budget production.

Why two caves?
 Well, the one in Bronson Canyon was accessible, you could go inside of it and film inside of it. The other one, the one in Palm Springs, wasn't a big-enough cave, and also it wasn't accessible, it was way up the side of the mountain. Somebody doubled me in those shots, because it was kind of a dodgy thing to get up there.

Was that the only time you were doubled in the movie?
 Yeah. Then the interior of the cave was shot on a soundstage. The cave walls were fabric which was darkened with soot or lampblack. It would make you all dirty and black.

What do you recall about Marilyn Manning, who played Roxy?
 You have to understand that Marilyn Manning was the receptionist-nurse of a chiropractor who had rented an office in Arch's arcade. (As I recall, the chiropractor was Tommy Sands' brother.) I guess Arch saw her in there and had coffee with her at the diner-drug store or something, and... There's been some speculation as to whether they were romantically involved. I don't know. But I *do* know that he was very fond of her. My guess was that she was about 25—at least, that's how old she *looks* to me. She was a mature-looking young lady, very pretty. But Arch

Hall, Jr., was like 16. So [casting them as boyfriend-girlfriend] just didn't jive, it didn't work.

What also *doesn't work are all the scenes where he sings songs to her about "Vicki," about "Valerie"—every name in the book but hers!*

Yeah, that *especially* didn't work! There's a scene early on where she drives up in her sports car to the gas station and Arch Jr. is the attendant, and the dialogue goes something like, "Roxy!" "Tom!" Do you remember the [Stan Freberg] comedy record that starts off, "John...," "Marsha!" "John...," "Marsha...," "John?" "Ooh... Marsha...," "*John!*" It was very funny, a big hit on the radio. Well, to *me*, the acting in *Eegah* was like that, it was like the acting in a high school play where people are waaay over the top, too loud. In movies, you don't need to reach the last row, but all the acting in *Eegah* was like trying to reach the last row in a high school play. And it's *funny*! The dialogue, the whole situation with the father and the daughter [Hall Sr. and Manning] in Eegah's cave, is *so* bizarre, where he's instructing her and she's afraid. Her acting, again, is really loud and over the top ... and his is, too! Remember, he was a radio actor. Well, this was a chance to me to *look* at that and say, "This is *not* how to do it." I learned from these bad movies that, no matter what the director says, do what you know works. Don't do what you know *doesn't* work. I was learning as I earned: *This* doesn't work. *That* doesn't work. *Don't* project, don't try to reach the people in the back row in a movie. When your head is filling the screen, you can talk very quietly, and they have microphones that pick it up.

Marilyn Manning may not have been the world's greatest actress but she looked nice in the picture, and I'm sure that's all Arch Hall cared about. Senior and *Junior!*

[*Laughs*] Oh, yeah. And I'm sure that all the young guys who went to see *Eegah* really liked her a lot. When you're a 12-, 14-year-old boy, going with a bunch of kids to a drive-in movie, you can identify with somebody [like Manning] who's a little bit older. (*I* had a crush on Debbie Reynolds when she was doing movies like *Susan Slept Here*, y'know!) At that time, that bikini she wore was quite a sexy thing. She was very attractive and very nice.

Eegah, it's so bad in places that it's campy. I think that a few of us actors who were in it recognized that it was going to have to be campy to be entertaining, and we gave it some humor. Like when I'm in the country club and I go by the chef who's carving the roast and I take a big bite of it. Or the scene where Eegah busts into the ladies room. Or the scene in downtown Palm Springs where Eegah sees the female mannequin behind the plate glass, and there's that pantomime where he's blocked by the glass from touching her. Those things were not in the script. Originally it was gonna be a deadly serious movie: *Eegah—The Name Written in Blood*. But we gave it some humor. In fact, one of the catchlines, one I think they used in TV commercials, was "The Lovesick Giant"! I think it's more of a comedy than it is a dramatic film.

Specifically, whose idea was the humor in Eegah*?*

I think there were several people who added some humor. Some of it was a little broad, like Bob Davis playing the drunk in the scene with Addelyn Hall. But it worked, it was funny.

And the humorous scenes that involve you, like trying to get at the mannequin?

A lot of those things were my ideas. It's kind of like in the Bond films: If you took away all the humor from Jaws and made him a guy who just kills people with his teeth, after a while you'd get tired of that. I think that Alfred Hitchcock originated the idea that, when you have intense drama in movies, it's good to break away to something light, humorous, cheerful. And then go *back* to the killer tryin' to kill ya. *That*, I feel, made *Eegah* a more entertaining movie. And I think I was able to use some of that in *The Spy Who Loved Me* [1977], and then even more so in *Moonraker* [1979]. The James Bond diehards didn't like me in *Moonraker*, but the people who bought the tickets did. That's really the name of the game: You're an entertainer, you scare people, you make people laugh, you make people cry ... and, mostly, you get people to buy tickets! That's the bottom line.

Where did you stay when you were shooting down in the Palm Springs–Palm Desert area? At Hall's place?

No, in a little old motel just on the way out of Palm Desert, on the road to Indio. Next to it there was a big date orchard, and we shot some scenes of me walking through there. (I don't remember if they're in the movie or not; I think maybe a little bit of it.) Right at that motel where we stayed, we shot the scenes with the dog barking at me by the swimming pool and Bob Davis as the drunk. The Shadow Mountain Country Club was nearby and we shot scenes there, the scenes where I go through the kitchen. At that time, Palm Desert wasn't much of anything, except for the Shadow Mountain Club, which was *the* big thing; now there are a jillion golf courses out there. At that time, there was a Motel Six in Palm Springs that was actually six dollars a night. It was up against the red rocks, the Taquitz Canyon and all that, it had a lovely pool, and six bucks a night. They had pay phones in the rooms in the original Motel Sixes, and black-and-white TVs that you had to feed with quarters. But *still*, what a bargain!

Was any of Eegah *shot in the Halls' Palm Desert house?*

Not that I know of.

For Eegah, *Arch Hall used a pseudonym for writing, producing and directing, and he's got a different pseudonym for acting in it. Why didn't he want his name on the movie?*

Because it starred his son.

And he didn't want two Arch Halls in the credits?

Yeah.

I think it's funny: I grow up reading that Hall made Eegah *in order to showcase his son, then I see the movie again for the first time in years and I see that Hall Sr. gave himself as much or more screen time than the kid. Jr. is hardly in the middle third at all.*

Meet the Parents? Kiel introduces cave prisoner Marilyn Manning to "the folks."

That's right. In the earlier movie *The Choppers*, Arch Sr. [had only a small part], and he did not direct it. It had some seasoned character actors, and it was done with a full I.A.T.S.E. crew. Arch decided to make *Eegah* "on the cuff," so to speak, and play a role along with all his family and friends—and people who were renting offices from him [*laughs*]!

How did Sr. and Jr. get along? It's kind of a unique thing for a father to be making low-budget pictures in order for his son to become a movie star. What was their relationship like?

I think his son appreciated it, and he did the best he could to become a hit singer. It was probably pretty disappointing for him that it didn't work out that way. I think it's probably a chapter in his life that he looks at as being a thing of the past. People have to understand that he was maybe 16 when he did *Eegah*. It takes a while to get used to everything and to learn how to act. *I* had the advantage of being unusual and being able to get roles and learn as I earned, and go to acting coaches for specific roles, and learn different things that helped me. But Arch Hall, Jr., just kind of got thrown into the cake mix [*laughs*]. I don't know what he does now. I'd like to see him.

Would you agree with me that the story of Eegah *is kinda like* King Kong?
Yeah, it's the giant who wants the girl.

And follows her back to civilization.

Right. After Marilyn Manning shaves me, I even do the sniffing-her-clothes routine, like King Kong does with Fay Wray.

The club you carry around throughout the picture—was it real? Was it heavy?

The club *was* real, but it wasn't that heavy—it was a big piece of manzanita. A piece of manzanita that, just naturally, was a club.

I see you pick Marilyn Manning up effortlessly in Eegah, *and the first part of your book is full of anecdotes about having jobs moving refrigerators and things like that. But most of the producers I've interviewed tell me that whenever they hire a really big guy to play a monster, physically the guy is always a disaster.*

At *that* time, I could do all of that very easily, I was extremely strong in the upper body. And there's also a "technique" to doing things like that. I don't care *how* small somebody is, if somebody just lies there, playing dead, if they're just dead weight, they become very, very difficult to deal with. A girl can pretend to faint and go limp, but she doesn't have to be dead weight. When you're carrying somebody, if they hold on a little and allow themselves to become a part of your body, it becomes very easy.

Actually, except for The Phantom Planet *[1961], you haven't played that many costumed monsters in movies, have you?*

I was Bigfoot in one of the *National Geographic Specials* [1969]. It was big bucks for, like, one day, and I ended up working a lot of overtime, so I made a pile of money. But I swore at that time I would *never* ever do anything like that again, it was just so miserable. I still have patches of missing hair on my legs where they just glued this stuff right onto me, and then they were in such a hurry to cut the overtime and get out of there after working like 27 hours in a row that they just ripped it off, and pulled out the hair on my legs by the roots. Roles like being inside of a Darth Vader suit, or Chewbacca, or whatever—you perspire so much, you lose so much weight, and it's just so miserable. There were people who did that, and they *enjoyed* doing it, and that's great. But that wasn't for me.

On Eegah, *you had a cameraman, Vilis Lapenieks, who went on to do more mainstream things.*

Vilis was good, he was a hard-working guy and he did a great job. There were some nicely filmed things, like when Eegah is running along the top of this huge cliff throwing rocks down. Another [cinematographer] who worked for Arch Hall, he did that horrible thing *The Nasty Rabbit* [1964] for Arch, was Vilmos Zsigmond, who went on to receive Academy Awards and Academy Award nominations for some huge films [*Close Encounters of the Third Kind, The Deer Hunter, The River*]. At the time he was working for Arch, he was fresh over from Europe, willing to do anything and everything and going by [the name of] "Ziggy."

Are you missing a front tooth in Eegah?

No, I have a wide gap, kind of like David Letterman had. I've since had tooth bonding, to fill it in.

According to Kiel (seen here with Marilyn Manning), *Eegah* provided some invaluable acting lessons—in what *not* to do!

Any idea how long it took to make Eegah? *And how much it cost?*

It was probably something like four, five weeks. A couple weeks here and a week there. I did my *Twilight Zone* episode "To Serve Man" right in the middle of filming *Eegah*. The budget ... the figure I remember was like $27,000 in cash, which would cover meals and rentals and hotels, and paying the people. Arch was able to get the lab work done "on the cuff" until he could get money coming in from the distribution.

Was the whole thing filmed in the Palm Springs–Palm Desert area?

No, there were the scenes at Bronson Canyon that I mentioned. And remember the scene at the end, where Eegah is shot and falls into the pool? That was at some house out by Burbank Airport somewhere. The titles were shot in the alleyway behind Arch's office arcade in Burbank—there was a big hedge where they put the mummy heads and all that stuff. The scenes with the helicopter were filmed up in some canyons near Burbank Airport. It was the middle of summer [1961], really, really, really hot weather, and Arch had hired what was probably the cheapest helicopter you could get, one of those little Bell helicopters. It didn't want to get off the ground with both Arch and me in it.

The sand dunes north of Palm Springs provided the backdrop for the Eegah-vs.-dune buggy chase sequence.

With Arch and you and the pilot.

Right. It just didn't have enough lift, with that heat—Arch was a pretty hefty guy too. So they had to take turns hauling the camera, the cameraman, Arch and then myself up to the location where they were going to film me looking up at the helicopter. I don't like helicopters—they killed people in that one film with Vic Morrow [*Twilight Zone—The Movie*, 1983]. Years later I did another low-budget film called *Flash and the Firecat* [1975], and that was *not* a pleasant experience. I was a detective in a helicopter chasing bank robbers, a young couple in a dune buggy, and the mud was coming off of the wheels of the dune buggy and hitting the windscreen of the helicopter. And the pilot was this former Vietnam helicopter pilot who was a little wacko, and we were chopping branches off of trees as we were chasing them up and down the sand dunes of Pismo Beach. It was just crazy, and I was lucky that I survived that. *Flash and the Firecat* was a similar kind of situation [similar to *Eegah*], man-and-wife producers making a picture starring *two* of their sons. But it was just a miserable, miserable movie to work on, I guess because times had changed for me and it was kind of like going back to *Eegah* days after being in other things that were first-class.

Arch Hall, Sr., told the authors of The 50 Worst Films of All Time *that some of you guys almost got sunstroke, working out in the desert, but that everybody had a lot of fun.*

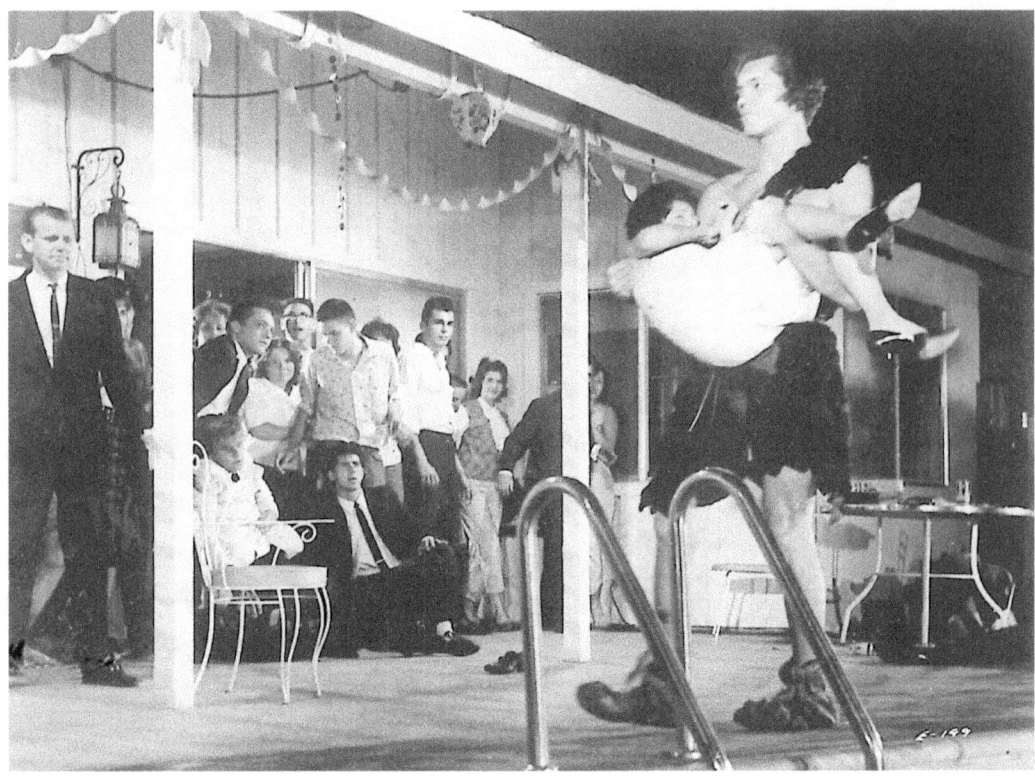

The *King Kong*–like plot of *Eegah* ends with Kiel (here seen carrying Marilyn Manning) plunging—well, not off the Empire State Building, but into a Burbank swimming pool.

Yeah. It was a group of people, most of us new in the business, all trying to do the best we could with what we had to work with, and just going along with the whole thing.

Did Arch Hall deduct the back rent you owed him from your salary?
Yeah, I think we settled up. Also, I moved out of that ground floor office in Arch's arcade to the second story, into a full-fledged apartment. That was part of the deal for doing the movie.

What do you remember about promoting Eegah*?*
That the difference between promoting that movie on the road and doing the James Bond promotions was like Heaven and Hell [*laughs*]! But I still enjoyed it. We went on the road to promote *Eegah*, Arch, Arch Jr. and me. Arch had bought a new Cadillac Calais Coupe—it *sounded* nice, Calais, but he ordered it without power windows, without power seats, without air conditioning. He *did* finally have an air conditioner installed, because we were going to be traveling through the South—he got one of those "hang-on," under-the-dash air conditioners. We left Burbank and our first stop, for lunch, was McDonald's in Barstow. I kinda knew *then* where we were going in terms of the kind of tour this was going to be!

Eegah was, like, a horribly done movie in terms of quality, *but*—it did huge, huge business on the drive-in theater circuit, along with *The Choppers*. We kicked it off in a three- or four-state area: We went into Columbus, Ohio, Dayton, Ohio, Cincinnati, Ohio, Louisville, Kentucky, Lexington, Kentucky, Charleston, West Virginia, Huntington, West Virginia…

You got to all those places in Arch Hall's car, from California?
Yeah, towing a little trailer, a small U-Haul rental thing to carry additional luggage (because there were three of us) and Arch Jr.'s guitar and amplifier equipment.

And on this long trip you took with the Halls, what you saw between them was the normal father-son relationship?
They got along very well.

Did you or Junior help with the driving?
No.

Arch Hall did the whole thing?
Yeah. And at each drive-in, during the intermission, Arch Jr. would get up on top of the snack bar, where he could do that, and they would have lights on him and he would be "singing"—lip-synching to the songs from the movie. Then I would be running around dressed in the caveman fur skin with my big club, scaring the heck out of the teenage girls. It would be advertised that we were going to be there at each of these drive-ins, and the places would fill up. I remember I had an ingrown toenail that was sort of infected, and at one of these places, this kid came up and stomped me on the foot—"*See*? He's not *real*!" It was all I could do to not hit him with the club [*laughs*]! And I gotta tell you about this one young kid in Bluefield, West Virginia, which was like a coal mining town—Appalachia. (Movie tickets were still selling for 50 cents in Bluefield while everywhere else they were a dollar and a half.) As we were pulling away in Arch's car with the little trailer in the back, I heard this voice: "Eegah! *Eeeegah!*" I turned around in my seat, and there was this little black boy, about ten or eleven, running after the car, yelling, "Don't forget me, Eegah! Eegah, don't forget me!" And I never *have* [*laughs*]! This "kid" is now in his fifties, probably a grandfather, and I *didn't* forget him!

One night when we were in St. Louis, we went out for a little ride, for Arch to show his son where he went to college. Well, I guess St. Louis had really changed since he was a young man—for one thing, there were a lot of racial problems. When we went through a park, we got pulled over by a police car, a black-and-white station wagon with a dog in the back, and the cops asked us, "What in the *world* are you doing in this park at night?!" Arch Hall said, "Well, I used to come here with girls…," and the cop said, "You better get the hell *out* of here, because this is *not* a safe place to be." I also remember staying at a nice old hotel there. Other than that, the only hotel that I remember was in Huntington, West Virginia, downtown, an old, elegant hotel. They had their old china, with their name on it, and they served country ham and red-eye gravy. Oh, and I remember being in a small restaurant somewhere, and on the menu were lamb fries. I'm sure Arch Hall knew what they were, he'd been around for a long time even *then*, but when I asked him what they were, he said, "Ask the waitress." When the waitress came over, I said, "Excuse me. What are lamb fries?" She kinda got red-faced ... and she said they were lamb testicles! Then she asked, "Do you *want* some?" "No thanks!!" [*Laughs*]

Sounds like Arch Hall may have set you up for that one!

Yeah, right! I also remember doing a thing where we went to a little league game, me in my caveman outfit hitting a few balls with my club, to spread the word that Eegah was in town. I think this was in West Virginia, near Huntington. Going to this little league game was something that the local theater owner thought would be a good idea. Back in that part of the country, little league was a big deal—they actually had really nice little league fields with two-story bleachers and dugouts and announcing booths and all that kind of stuff, it was really first-class. So it was a good idea. After that, we went to some little beer bar that somebody had recommended, a place where they made hamburgers and stuff. We're in there, and I'm dressed up in my caveman outfit having a cheeseburger. And this policeman has a great idea: He thinks that we can get a big photo spread in the newspaper if we'll just do what he suggests, which is putting me in the police car and driving to the police station, and (while en route) he says over the radio that he's got a culprit in custody, a guy who's extremely large and hostile, and he needs assistance. Well, when we pull into the alley in the back of the police station and all these cops come rushing out with their guns, I realize this is *not* a very good idea [*laughs*]! I could have been shot and killed! And of course the newspaper doesn't show up! So nothing happened with that, except it was a big joke for all the policemen. Then they take me into some drunk tank-solitary confinement sort of a thing where there's this crazy guy who they had locked up. They open it up and now suddenly there I am with my club and my caveman suit in front of this guy, the town drunk. The poor guy, I scared the hell out of him—it was just like the scene with Bob Davis in the movie! But it was kind of sad—you just don't *do* that, it was really super-mean. *They* thought that was funny.

[Laughs] I'm afraid I do too!

Well, it was sad to me 'cause I realized, y'know, this guy is like out of his mind and he's having enough trouble with delirium tremens and stuff without having some giant caveman with a club, dressed in furs, appearing suddenly in his cell!

Box office–wise, you say, Eegah *was a hit.*

The combination of *Eegah* and *The Choppers* did big business all over America and Canada. It made Arch so much money that he was able to make about a half a dozen *more* films, films that had much bigger budgets. Films like *Wild Guitar* [1962], also starring his son. Then they made *The Nasty Rabbit*, which was even worse than *Eegah*, 'cause it didn't really have a very good story. I think it was financed by the lead, Mischa Terr.

You think he bankrolled that one?

I would think so. He was so bad, I can't imagine somebody *casting* him [*laughs*]! After that, Arch still had enough money to make a movie called *Deadwood '76* [1965], a big, widescreen Western in color. It was based on Billy the Kid. Arch had some decent actors in it, wonderful music, it had a good theme song that was sung by a good singer, it had beautiful scenes like the wagon trains at sunset, *all* that kind of stuff. It was technically well done, but it failed to entertain the audience. Also, it came out at a time when they didn't *have* drive-in Westerns any more. At that point, the only Westerns being made were big, big, *big* Westerns. *Deadwood '76* just didn't make the grade. You could get away with making a movie about a caveman, starring a teenager [Hall Jr.] who hadn't really matured as an actor, you could get away with *Wild Guitar* or *The Choppers*—but this Western that he made really just died. I think he lost all of the money that he had made with *Eegah* and with some of the other movies that had done fairly well. He sort of parlayed [the profits from those pictures] into this sheer junk movie *Deadwood '76*. It was kind of a sad thing. But [the Halls] still had this bunch of films that they had made, that they could continue to sell to TV and make a few bucks here and there. I think that Mrs. Hall, even after Arch died, was able to keep a little income coming in from them.

Were you in any of the Halls' subsequent pictures?

Only in a little tiny scene as a ranch foreman in *The Nasty Rabbit*.

So that was my relationship with Arch Hall, a little bit of background about how I got started with him and what it was like doing *Eegah*. And, look, I don't disregard *Eegah*, I don't put it down. I put it in the category of one of the steps that I took in my career. I'm not ashamed of it. It was great practice to play this character who didn't really have any lines in English. It was all pantomime. It was great practice for playing Jaws in the James Bond films later on. And I learned something important from Arch Hall: On our tour, he would walk us all into a newspaper office in Cincinnati or Dayton or Columbus or wherever, or into TV stations. We didn't have an appointment, we weren't invited, we didn't have any p.r. company or big movie machine behind us. We just walked in and he'd say, "Here are Richard Kiel and Arch Hall, Jr., the stars of the movie *Eegah*, and they're available to do interviews." And, by golly, these newspapers and TV stations and radio stations would interview us! By getting the people to come out to the movies [*Eegah* and *The Choppers*] in these states, it kicked the movies off really well, and the word got around that this was a viable package. So it showed me how you could promote a movie.

Just by barging into newspaper and TV offices.

Newspapers and TV stations needed stories, and if you were a walk-in story, they would interview you. Later on, when I went to Chicago to promote another movie, *The Human Duplicators* [1965], I had enough chutzpah from having *done* that with Arch Hall, to not be afraid to go into the major Chicago newspapers and try to get on the major Chicago TV programs. All four Chicago newspapers—Chicago had major four newspapers at that time—did a story on me. Which is something that would *not* normally happen. If one of the Chicago papers broke a big feature story, it'd be doubtful that any of the other three would follow it the next day.

Because they'd been scooped.
Right, the others would chuck their stories. Well, as it turned out, they were *all* trying to be the first one, and the very next day, there was a feature story on me in all four Chicago newspapers.

On you and Human Duplicators.
Yeah. One was a wonderful story by a gal who was related to Dear Abby and Ann Landers, her name was Ann Marsters. It included a nice photograph of me that she had a photographer take while she was interviewing me, and the caption was RICHARD KIEL, BIG AND BRIGHT! That was really quite an interview for *me*—particularly after starring in movies like *Eegah* and *The Human Duplicators* [*laughs*]. And then I got on the TV show ... are you familiar with Jack Brickhouse? He was a big-time sports announcer in Chicago, and he had a TV interview show, *Brickhouse and* ... I forget, somebody else. I was on that for the whole hour.

If it was a sports show, why were you on there?
Uhhhh ... good question [*laughs*]! I don't know! I guess just because of my size. Anyway, the whole trip promoting *The Human Duplicators* was sooo successful, going the newspaper and TV route and popping in for ten minutes at *this* theater and ten minutes at *that* theater, half an hour at *this* theater. *Human Duplicators* was in like 27 theaters in Chicago, it was a big hit in Chicago, and then because of *that*, they asked me to do Toronto, Canada. So what I learned about marketing movies from Arch Hall, I was able to use with *The Human Duplicators*. And I used those techniques myself, later on, with *The L.A. Times* and *The L.A. Herald-Examiner* and *The Valley Times*. Just promoting my*self*. I remember, at *The L.A. Times* I didn't get quite the reception that you would in Cincinnati [*laughs*]. I was rebuffed by secretaries, and sort of hanging my head as I walked out the door, when a guy in suspenders walked over and said, "My name is Charles Champlin and I'm a writer here. I'd like to do a feature story on you. If you'll come into my office and sit down..." The guy eventually ended up being the Entertainment Editor of the Calendar Section, he kind of followed my career, and when I did *The Spy Who Loved Me*, he did a nice review on it. But the main point was that I *did* get stories in the *Examiner* and the *Times* and the *Valley Times*.

And, in addition to the exposure, I'm sure you also learned how to "handle" interviewers.
Yes, I sure did. But there was something else I learned, too: You could go to Chicago and be really lucky and blessed, get into all four of the newspapers, be on the *Brickhouse and Whatever* show—but when you got back to Los Angeles, you were still the same guy who left! What you need to do is to do publicity where the jobs are, where people are doing the hiring, where the decisions are made. All of the promotional stuff that you do in Boston and Detroit and all that, it's good if you're selling a book, or if you're on the road selling a movie. But it doesn't help you get jobs.

Having experience with interviewers *did* help out when I did *The Spy Who Loved Me* and I was at the Royal Premiere. The press were there waiting to do their interviews but Roger Moore and Barbara Bach were late, and the director Lewis Gilbert was late. And the press had already interviewed [producer] "Cubby" Broccoli dozens of time. So, since *I* was there, they started to hit on *me* with all these questions. The press can be very nasty—at press conferences like that, there are always one or two people who are very rude and adversarial. It's like during a Presidential press conference, there's always the person who asks the loaded question trying to embarrass the President or make him look bad. But I'd had enough experience doing press conferences and interviews that I was able to deal with it. I remember, at the Royal Premiere, this interviewer from one of the British tabloids asking, "Mr. Kiel, have you seen all the James Bond movies?" I said, "Well, I believe so. Most of them, if not all of them." "So, you've seen allll the James Bond movies. Now, let me ask you a question: Who do you think makes the best James Bond?" Here I am, working with Roger Moore and we're getting along really, really well; and of course I'd grown up on the Sean Connery movies and, like a lot of people, I liked Sean Connery as Bond very much. But if I say Connery, it's gonna be splashed in the headline, RICHARD KIEL PREFERS CONNERY TO MOORE, and I'm gonna make Roger Moore mad. And if I say Roger Moore, then I'm gonna make all the Sean Connery fans angry with me.

And you'll look like a suck-up to Moore.
Yeah. Then, all of a sudden, it was like God gave me the right answer: I said, "Well, I kinda go for George Lazenby myself." [*Laughs*] The whooole cadre of press, there were maybe 40 of them, all laughed like *you* just did. And they were not only laughing at what I said, they were kind of laughing at the guy getting zinged, the guy who asked the loaded question. (Which really pissed him off!) Mr. Broccoli was there, and I guess he determined, "Hey, here's a guy who can hold his own with the press and has the right answers." So he sent me out with various Bond girls, we got to go to different places, I got to bring my wife and my family, and it was a huge success. And I think that was part of the reason that they decided to keep the character of Jaws alive and to bring me back for another film [*Moonraker*], because I was good at promoting the films around the world.

And if you trace it all back, this is all thanks to Arch Hall.
Exactly.

I guess this is a good time for me to get my *rude, adversarial question out of the way:* Eegah *is often called one of the 10 or 50 (or whatever) worst films of all time. (A), is it one of the worst films of all time, and (B) is it even* your *worst film?*
No, it's not *my* worst film. I would say that a movie that cost many, many, many times as much as *Eegah*, maybe 100 times as much, or *200* times as much, starring Jackie Gleason, Carol Channing, Groucho Marx, Arnold Stang and Mickey Rooney, would be my worst movie.

Kiel sinks his (cobalt steel) teeth into his signature role: "Jaws" in the James Bond adventure *The Spy Who Loved Me* with Roger Moore.

Which would be Skidoo *[1968].*

Which would be *Skidoo*. That movie never went to video; *Eegah*'s on video. People might laugh at *Eegah* but it's still making money. *Skidoo*, try to get it on video in America. You can't! Then there was another movie I made for Paramount, starring Alan Arkin, called *Deadhead Miles* [1972].

Which didn't get released at all, *did it?*

No. Both of these movies had really bad plots, the stories didn't make any sense. They just didn't play. So there are a couple of multi-million dollar disasters compared to a $27,000 success [*Eegah*]. I admire people who at least make an effort. Arch Hall made a few of these real low-budget movies and then he tried to go *bigger* time [with *Deadwood '76*]. That blew all the money, but I admire the fact that Arch got out there and tried and did some things to entertain people.

What was Hall Sr. like in his later years?

Toward the end, the mid- or late '70s, he had either divorced his wife or they were estranged, and he had gone around the world and learned a lot about life and become a whole different guy. He was more sensitive, and wanted to do things that were of a higher caliber. He was living on Lido Island, in a modest house with his little dog Pooh Bear, still writing and doing his songs. He did some children's songs. Some of the songs he did were quite good. Some were quite philosophical. He was working on projects, things that were more "historic." He would have been a good guy to do things for Disney, where he'd have had the money to do them right.

My wife Diane and I went a couple of times to his place out there. He was very charming, very nice to be around, and he appreciated people coming out to see him. I actually co-wrote a movie script with him, *The South Shall Rise Again*—it was from his idea. I had that big friend Bill Engesser and we would have played brothers, one on one side of the [Civil War] and one on the other.

Arch Hall had the ability to charm people—to make you *enjoy* stopping at McDonald's in Barstow [*laughs*]. Arch Hall and I remained friends, because he *was* what he *was*: He was quite a character.

And how 'bout Junior? How often did you see Junior after Eegah*?*
I was at Junior's wedding to his first wife. Junior ended up flying for the Flying Tigers squadron, flying cargo planes during Vietnam and all that stuff. I don't know what Junior's doing now but I would imagine that he's either an airline pilot or retired.

He'd be a natural for the all the "nostalgic" celebrity autograph shows these days.
It must be kind of difficult for him, and embarrassing, to be the subject of [a movie spoofed on] *Mystery Science Theater*. I don't make any bones about it, I'm a three-time loser on *Mystery Science Theater*, I think I hold the record: *The Phantom Planet*, *The Human Duplicators* and *Eegah*. But making those movies was good practice, and you learned things. Hey, people can laugh at *Eegah*, it doesn't bother *me*, 'cause I went on to do [bigger, better] things.

But movies on the level of Eegah—*that was as far as Junior got.*
I'm sure there were a lot of young ladies (who are now *older* ladies) who liked *him* in those movies. He was also in a movie called *The Sadist* [1963] and he played a very good villain in it—it was loosely based on the Starkweather killings.* Arch Jr. was a good musician and singer, and I think that, had he had a different kind of an opportunity, he could have *been* a new-kid-on-the-block singer who might have made it big.

Ray Dennis Steckler, who's got a tiny part in Eegah *and worked on it behind-the-scenes, once wrote an article where he claimed that he visited Arch Hall the day before he died, and that Hall said that you and he were talking about doing an* Eegah *sequel.*
How do you say in a nice way that Ray Steckler was full of hot air? Arch Hall and I did write that screenplay *The South Shall Rise Again*, and we got Kenny Rogers to do a demo of songs for the proposed movie. But we never discussed the possibility of doing a sequel to *Eegah*. Arch did share with me his pas-

---

*In 1957–58, Nebraska teenagers Charles Starkweather and Caril Fugate went on a grisly murder spree that horrified the country.

sion for two characters in history that he would like to see movies or mini-series done about, Pocahontas and Cassius Marcellus Clay [the eighteenth-century Kentucky antislavery leader]. Arch got *me* interested in Clay, and over the years after Arch died, I did casual research on Clay until the time came when I had lots of time to write and I made several trips to Kentucky to go to museums and libraries. It seemed to me that Arch Hall's interests in his mature years were more "esoteric" than in the past, and I don't see a sequel to *Eegah* fitting into those new desires. I believe that, when he made *Deadwood '76*, he was reaching for a higher level than before; and right before he died, he had more of an interest to contribute something worthwhile to humanity. And I believe that he *did* contribute as he got me so interested in this man Clay's amazing story that I have written a novel, three screenplays and a miniseries based upon Cassius Clay. Currently the co-writer of the Harrison Ford movie *Witness* [1985] has been engaged to rewrite and polish my novel. That is scheduled to be accomplished by January 15 of next year [2003].

So ... what accounts for Eegah's *lasting popularity?*

I believe that *Eegah* is one of the better-known "Worst Films of All Time" as it was entertaining enough to be seen by a lot of people at drive-in theaters across America and Canada and to be worth poking fun at. Even though the acting, the film quality, the sound quality, all *that* might qualify it as being one of the worst films of all time, it's become kind of like a little cult movie. As I mentioned earlier, I guess that I am one of the few actors to be a three-time loser on *Mystery Science Theater*, and if they were to comment on my more obscure films I would probably be a *five*-time loser. I'm sure that if you were to look at *The Nasty Rabbit*, that you would agree that this film would deserve the honor more than *Eegah*. Another film I did, *Las Vegas Hillbillys* [1966], should also be somewhere near the top of the list of "worst films" of all time. But, as Henry Ford said, "Nothing ventured, nothing gained." It's easy to be a Monday morning quarterback but one only really learns how to play the game by getting in there and taking a few hits and learning from those experiences. *I* learned from all of these experiences, and it eventually paid off for me in a big way.

Eegah (Fairway-International, 1962)

90 minutes; Associate Producer/Editor: Don Schneider; Original Story, Produced & Directed by Nicholas Merriwether [Arch Hall, Sr.]; Screenplay: Bob Wehling; Photography: Vilis Lapeneicks [Lapenieks] (Eastman Color); Music Score: Henry Price; Recording Engineer: Sam Kopetzky; Production Manager: H. Duane Weaver

Arch Hall, Jr. (*Tom Nelson*), Marilyn Manning (*Roxy Miller*), Richard Kiel (*Eegah*), William Watters [Arch Hall, Sr.] (*Robert I. Miller/Voice of Eegah*), Clay Stearns, Addalyn Pollitt [Addelyn Hall] (*Woman with George*), Bob Davis (*George, Drunk at Motel*), William Lloyd, Deke Lussier (*Band Member*), Ray Steckler (*Mr. Fishman*), Ron Shane (*Detective*), Bill Rice (*Policeman*), Phil Stopeck (*Scared Man on Motel Staircase*), Joan Kinchela, Yvonne Rice (*Women at Poolside*)

Kay Linaker on Tod Browning and James Whale

> *Tod Browning was a "whole" human being. He was a well person. ... And I'm very, very sorry for the other guy.*

She may never have been a household name, but Kay Linaker *was* a busy Hollywood actress in the 1930s and '40s, the author of one of the most popular cult films of the 1950s (1958's *The Blob*), nowadays the oldest person in the New Hampshire educational system—and, as this interview amply proves, a valuable, voluble witness to film history.

Born in Pine Bluff, Arkansas, Linaker was educated at a private school in Connecticut and later attended New York University. While living in New York, she became interested in the stage and began attending the American Academy of Dramatic Arts. Her work on Broadway brought her to the attention of screen scouts and she was signed for her first movie roles.

In Hollywood, Linaker made the acquaintance of the two most famous directors of the Golden Age of the Horror Film, one socially, the other professionally. She was a neighbor and personal friend to Tod Browning (*London After Midnight*, *Dracula*, *Freaks* et al.) during World War II, and acted under the direction of James Whale (*Frankenstein*, *The Old Dark House*, *The Invisible Man*, *Bride of Frankenstein*) in his final features *Green Hell* (1940) and *They Dare Not Love* (1941). She sheds a fascinating new light on both these men in the twilight of their film careers in this revealing interview.

You never acted in a Tod Browning movie. How did you get to know him?

I bought a house in the Malibu Colony, not long before the start of World War II. I was living there with my mother, who was then probably pushing 50—a fantastically beautiful woman. I took her for walks, we went up and down the beach. I didn't know anybody there at all. On the second or third day that we lived there, we were taking our walk and we came to this kind of plump, blondish man who was

Tod Browning and James Whale—what were these mysterious figureheads of 1930s fantastic cinema really like, and why did their careers come to such abrupt and early ends? For the first time ever, Kay Linaker provides the answers to these questions.

standing with his hands on his hips, looking out at the area back behind his house. As my mother and I approached, this man turned around and looked at us and said, "Ohhh ... so *you're* the new ones." I said, "Yes," and my mother said, "This is my daughter, who just bought the place. We are going to be very happy in 56 [56 Malibu Road]." He said, "Well, my name is Tod Browning. And if you'll wait just a minute, I'll go in the house and get my wife Alice, because she always likes to meet my new friends." So he went in the house and he brought Alice out. Alice was small, blond, absolutely charming. She and my mother became fast friends right at that moment. I sort of stood by and watched this happen. Next thing I knew, Mrs. Browning said, "Oh, *please* come in and have a cup of tea."

We went in and we had a cup of tea, and Tod came along. He sat with us and chatted, and then finally he said, "I've *got* to go out and look again and make up my mind." I asked, "What are you making up your mind about?" He said, "I'm going to plant a garden in the back lot. I don't want a tennis court; we *can't* put in a pool because of the water level. So I'm going to just put in a garden." I asked, "What kind of a garden?" and he said, "A *practical* garden. Vegetables." I asked, "May I go out with you?"

We went out and we stood and we looked at it, and he said, "You know, I see a waving field of grain." I said, "Well, I don't know that wheat will do well so close to the ocean." He asked, "What do *you* know about farming?" I told him about my childhood and about my father's farm, and about how my father read the bulletins from the Agriculture Department—everything that was new, he tried. I think he was the first person in Arkansas to plant soybeans. I was telling Tod about this, and he was fascinated, and finally he asked, "What do you think your father would have thought of for here?" I said, "I *think* he would have tried corn." Tod said, "It's a wonderful idea. I'll plant corn. And, you know, if this is a success, I can sell my vegetables to the store"—there was a little store in Malibu, owned by a remarkable gent named Mr. Jones. With that, my mother and Mrs. Browning came out, and they were informed. Tod looked at Alice and asked, "Would you like a few flowers?" and she said, yes, *that* would be nice.

I have to ask ... how much did a Malibu oceanfront home cost in those days?
   Mine was 32,000.

I bet it would sell for twice *as much today!*
   [*Laughs*] I think probably it would be around two million. It had a living room, a dining room, five bedrooms and four baths. And a double garage.

Was Tod Browning's house any nicer than yours?
   Oh, yes! It was more a Tudor house, and mine was like just a beach house.

Planting corn, per your suggestion—is that what Browning did?
   Yes. As you turned into the road at Malibu, the very first garden was Tod Browning's. So as you came into Malibu, the first thing you saw was corn. Right up to his property line, he put in vegetables and whatnot.
   About a year later, along came December the seventh—I was standing making pancakes when the radio announced that the Japanese had bombed Pearl Harbor. What followed, as I'm sure you can imagine, were some very, very interesting times. At that point there were, *at* Malibu, only 11 permanent families, and we had to do *every*thing [homeland defense-related], we all wore three or four hats. It was very interesting finding yourself in the position of farmer-minute man-gas rationer-air raid warden-*every*thing. My mother was chief air raid warden; her district went from Thelma Todd's to the Ventura County Line, from the tide line back to the crest of the Santa Monica Mountains. And if you can imagine how frightening it was when there was a blackout! Your job, when it was your turn to do it, was to stand out on the highway with a blue-covered flashlight, a very small flashlight, waving it up and down to stop the traffic. You always wondered if the first truck was going to *see* you.

So stopping the first *car or truck was scary.*
   Well, it *always* was a truck—you see, gas rationing had started. Once you stopped a truck, you had them turn their headlights off, then you went and stood behind it and waved down the *next* one and the *next* one, until the "all clear" came. But, yes, it was the *first* one that was scary.

There were so few people there in the Colony that everybody had to do a little of everything.
   That's exactly right—and you get to know people pretty well under these circumstances. Now, not everybody there was from the motion picture industry. We had one gentleman who was a corset salesman, and there was a man there who wrote stories for magazines, his name was H. Venor Dixon. He had been a dancer until he read one of his sister's magazines and said, "Hell, *I* could write something better than *that*!" and she said, "Well, go ahead and *do* it." So Mr. Dixon did it, and he mentioned to Tod what he was doing, and Tod said, "Well, why don't you talk to my agent?" He did, and began selling stuff like crazy. *And* he worked in the things that we were doing.

Tod Browning was riding high as one of MGM's top directors when he directed the melodramatic *The Show* **(1926) with John Gilbert (right). (Photofest)**

Did Browning serve on Malibu's gas rationing board?

No. Warner Baxter was on the ration board, and he asked Tod to go on with him, but Tod said, "No. Get Katie. Katie'll be fine on the ration board." So I agreed to be on the ration board. But what Tod *did* do was figure out how some people there in Malibu could *get around* gas rationing. Up in the hills behind Malibu, behind the Malibu Ranch, was a settlement of Italians who had come over to America, and they were tailors. They found that they couldn't afford to live down in Los Angeles, so they came up [to the Malibu area] where it got cheap. They would buy a little piece of land and build a little tiny house, and then they commuted into the manufacturing district, the tailoring district in Los Angeles. It was a nice 45-minute ride, they used to just drive in individually in their little cheap cars, their very old Fords and very old Chevys. But when we got to the point of gas rationing and gas tickets, there was nothing in the rules that said, "When you live 45 miles from your work, you can get special tickets and extra gas"—there was nothing about that in the book.

It didn't matter how far you lived from work, everybody got the same amount of gas for their car.

Oh, yes! And you didn't get *much*! Finally Tod came up with an idea: "Why don't you get these people to buy 15, 20 dollar cars?" which you could *do* at that time. "Then we can give them tickets for *those* cars, even if they don't run." So that's what we did, we followed Tod's idea: We told them to buy cars that were really no good, that they could pick up for $20. They would bring them home (usually *tow* them home [*laughs*]), because the cars had to be *on* the property. Once they were on the property, we could give them the basic gas ration card for each car. And so that's how Tod made it possible for them to get to work in their own cars. That whole hillside was littered with these old wrecks [*laughs*], but that was how we got through *that* part of it.

How did the gas rationing affect people like you and Browning?
We pooled on *every*thing, to save on gasoline. For instance, there weren't Laundromats in Malibu, so we made a deal with a laundry in Santa Monica that they would do our laundry if we got it in by a certain time in the morning. Then we took turns, one person collecting all the laundry—

From all the different families in Malibu.
—and driving it into Santa Monica early in the morning, and waiting 'til the whole thing was done, and then bringing it home to the Colony and dropping it off at all the different houses. That was to save on gasoline. On *another* day, someone did the marketing for everyone. One person went to the big market in Santa Monica with the lists and the money and the ration tickets from everybody in the Colony. Market day was a long, drawn-out thing, 'cause you had 11 lists. The only way that you could do it was if you took one person's list when you got there and did allll the marketing for that person, and put it in the car, and then came back and started all over again.

Eleven times.
Eleven times. Everybody took a turn, and Tod took *his* turn.

The store where you did the marketing—was that also in Santa Monica?
Uh-huh.

Why didn't you go to Mr. Jones' store?
Because it was too *damned* expensive [*laughs*]!

And your mother was the chief air raid warden for Malibu.
Yes, she was, and *as* the chief air raid warden, she was responsible for alerting the Army post for anything that came over. We had a switchboard in our house, in case things began to happen. One day I was on the beach, sitting on the bulkhead, when a screenwriter who lived around there, Charles Belden [*Mystery of the Wax Museum*, 1933], came down the beach. This was a gent who sometimes ... drank a little bit too much. He came running down the beach, he was long-legged, long-armed, he had on shorts, he had binoculars around his neck, and I was the first per-

Browning (right) supervises the filming of *Freaks*' (1932) classic banquet scene. (Photofest)

son he saw. He came up to me, breathless, and he said, "Look out there. And if you don't see what *I* see, take me to Mount Sinai to dry out!" I looked, and I saw it: A submarine conning tower that had a rising sun painted on it. We could just see the top of it. I said, "You're *not* goin' to Mount Sinai," I ran in the house and had my mother take a look. Immediately she called, and very, very shortly afterwards, I mean *very* shortly afterwards, like ten minutes, over our house came a torpedo bomber, beautifully camouflaged.

By camouflaged, you mean it was painted sky-blue?

Yes, it was painted so that you didn't see it, but on its belly, the torpedo was bright orange. It looked like a robin redbreast.

So you could see the torpedo but not the plane carrying it.

That's right. That torpedo bomber came so close to our chimney, the vibration from the plane going over was so strong that the top ridge of our chimney jiggled right off, the bricks fell down. We kept watching, and after a while we didn't see the plane any more and we didn't see the submarine any more. Of course, they never told us what happened. But three days later, flotsam and jetsam began coming up from south of the Colony, where the tide took it. So it took it a while to get up, but we now knew that the submarine had been hit.

We had all kinds of experiences. Another thing that we had to do was man the fire watchtower on a 24-hour basis [watching for Japanese planes]. We rotated. Tod was of course one of the watchers, he would climb the fire watchtower and do his eight-hour stint. All by himself. I did it too. We *all* did it. We *had* to. We would take up a thermos of coffee, and the binoculars were left in the tower.

How high up was this watchtower?

It was on the top of a ridge, and there were about 25 steps up to the top. You climbed up the outside stairway and walked in this little room that was ... oh, it couldn't have been more than eight by ten. You sat there, and on the walls were the silhouettes of all of the enemy planes, and the silhouettes of *our* planes. And there was a telephone. Whenever anything flew by, you called and gave the code identification and you gave *your* identification.

And how often did anything fly over?

Not much came over. When it was your turn, you went up and you sat for eight hours. Believe me, it's a long time!

What were the bathroom arrangements there?

There ... *were* ... none. But [*laughs*], it was something that we all had to do. Then we had to have a first aid class. Living up near the police station was a retired Army doctor, and he agreed to teach us. I remember he once said, "The thing that's bad about the world now is that the medical profession doesn't acknowledge the really important use of a cow dung poultice." Fortunately, that was not in what we had to learn for first aid [*laughs*]! He taught us first aid, down in the police station—everybody from the Colony went. Everybody except Warner Baxter's wife Wini [silent film actress Winifred Bryson], who was not well, and so she was excused. But everybody else had to go to the first aid class.

Because...?

Because there were so few of us that we figured, if anything *happened* [an enemy attack], we would have to go out through our area and take care of our own. Tod and Alice came to the class, of course. And then Alice decided we needed some money to get equipment for our first aid station, and she decided we would have a sale, an auction of movie stars' little gadgets. Their pocketbooks, and their cigarette cases, and things like that, which would be donated. Alice made up a list of people and we made calls, and we got astonishing, astonishing donations. We got things like mink stoles and all that sort of thing, because it was Mrs. Tod Browning who was having this sale. We held the auction at the police station, and some of the stars who had *made* donations were there. (I remember that Joan Crawford was there—such a nice and gracious lady.) Well, you never saw such a mob of people as we had. The auction went on from nine o'clock in the morning 'til five-thirty in the afternoon. And all the time that we were there, Tod was there as a runner, along with

What a drag: Lionel Barrymore (right) and Tod Browning consult between takes on 1936's *The Devil-Doll*. (Photofest)

everybody else in the Colony. We took in over $3000, and that allowed us to buy the drugs and the gauze and everything that we needed for our first aid station.

Did you get the impression that Browning was fairly well-to-do?
 Oh, yes. *Oh*, yes! He didn't have anything to worry about. But I don't think it

mattered to him whether he had a lot of money, or whether he had just enough so that he never had to worry.

Did the Brownings ever mention why they never had any children?
That was something that was very, very sad to them. They wanted children badly. But Alice never could have one.

So it was Alice's "problem"...?
Uh-huh. Alice ... she was not too well. That's the reason that they came down to Malibu.

Alice told you all of this?
She didn't tell me, she told my mother.

She told your mother that it was because of her medical condition that she and Tod never had any kids.
That's right.

Were any other directors living there in Malibu, that you can recall?
Remember Charlie Ruggles, the actor? His brother Wesley Ruggles was a director, he was married to a lovely young French actress [Marcelle Rogez] and they were Tod's nearest neighbors. They were kind of friendly, in a casual way. (Wesley Ruggles suffered from an "enlarged ego," according to Tod!) But the thing is that, when we were living at Malibu, nobody was a star or a director or anything. We were just *people*. Warner Baxter lived there year-round, Warner had a very big house. His wife Wini was a darling lady, but she was very ill, so they didn't have too much company. Well, *no*body had too much company, 'cause you couldn't get gasoline to go back and forth [*laughs*]! These were interesting times.

Did Browning ever reminisce about his films?
You never talked about that with him 'cause you knew he didn't *want* to talk about it. Tod had had a fight with Louis B. Mayer [head of MGM], and Louis B. punished him. Mayer would not release Tod from his MGM contract, there was no way he could get released. But he wouldn't give Tod *any*thing to do. Mayer would send one lousy script after another out to Tod.

For Browning to comment upon, or to rewrite, or...?
No, to see if Tod would *direct* 'em! Tod would turn them down, of course. And Mayer would call Tod in to MGM, and Tod would have to drive in to the studio and wait around. When his appointment with Mayer supposedly was for one o'clock, suddenly "things would happen" and Louis B. wouldn't be able to see him until *three*. Tod never did get out of his MGM contract—that's why he didn't do anything more after his enormous success. At one point, he was getting ready to go to the Directors Guild and file a complaint against Mayer, and the reason he *didn't* go was because he realized that, if he did, it would cause great ructions. And he didn't want to be the person who did that.

Did he ever mention what his fight with Mayer was about?
He never talked about it.

Other than the fact that there was a fight.
Other than the fact that he would always refer to Mayer as a son of a bitch. Tod was tight-mouthed in everything except his marriage and his garden and what he did during the War. He was very open about everything like that. But, you see, Tod would not return dirt with dirt. Consequently, whatever happened [between Browning and Mayer], he just clammed up. That was true of most people. In the time that I was in California, the people did not gossip about one another—at least, not *my* friends. If something untoward happened, they didn't talk about it.

I don't think I'd have minded getting an MGM paycheck every week for sitting around my oceanfront Malibu home. But Browning didn't think that was a sweet deal?
Oh, no. *No*! Because that meant that he couldn't do what he enjoyed *doing* most. Next to gardening!

He was still in good shape physically when you knew him?
Oh, yeah, he was in fine shape, *very* fine shape, and he had friends all up and down the beach. Actually, though, he was kind of a loner. He was perfectly satisfied with Alice's company. But when he was called upon to do work during the War, he was right there. Never any arguments at all.

Why did you move out of Malibu?
We decided that it would be a good idea to put up a breakwater, a wall, and we found out that a pile-driven one would cost us $150 a foot. So we all agreed that we would do this. The man came and he started the pile-driving, and each of us paid him as he finished our property. Most of the lots were 40 feet wide, some were 45, some were 50, some (like Warner Baxter's) were 110. Everybody paid as we went along. Now, the corset salesman was on the road, and we hadn't been able to get to him. When the pile driver people got to *his* place, they just left it open and went to the *next* place, figuring they would come back later and do it. Well, the corset salesman did come back, and he said, "*I'm* not gonna pay for this. If *you* want this done, *you'll* have to pay for it." We all got very angry, and we behaved in a childlike fashion: We refused to put in the couple of bucks it would have cost each of us to take care of it. We were going to *show* him, by God! Well, the people with the pile driver left, and they were not gone three months when we had the storm to end all storms. The ocean came in through this one place, the break in the wall on the corset salesman's property ... backed up on the ebb of the tide ... and took down one after another of these pile-driven bulkheads. We were left with nothing. Then when the storm got worse, *all* of our foundations were full of water, and all our grass was killed by the salt water. So we all learned from that, that when somebody refuses to do something for the good, what you do is just...

Bite the bullet and take care of it.
Exactly. What several of us did as a result of this was to sell our property, and I was one of the ones who sold.

After you left, did you keep in touch with the Brownings, or was it a clean break?
  I moved into Westwood and then I went on the road with a show. Somehow you don't write to people when you're on the road. So, yes, we lost touch, but I liked Tod Browning. I liked his wonderful sense of humor. And the way he *adored* his wife, and would do anything at *all* for her. Ours was a very warm and wonderful friendship.

Which brings us to James Whale.
  Poor, tragic Whale.

Was Green Hell *your first contact with him?*
  Yes. At that time, his star was in the descendent. Until I met him on *Green Hell*, I had never really heard very much about him. The only thing anybody knew about him at that point was, he was a quiet man. And everybody did kind of know that he was of the bisexual persuasion. But one thing you *must* understand: At that time in California, nobody made anything *of* that. If they were bisexual ... so? So that was their particular way of life. As long as your experience with them was healthy and normal, nobody made any fuss about it. Nobody ever *talked* about it.
  I went over to Universal to see Whale about *Green Hell*. We chatted in his office for a few minutes, and he said, "How do you feel about playing a whore?" I said, "If it's a good part, it's fine." He laughed. Then he said, "Fine. Go up to wardrobe." And, before I left, he added, "By the way, to save you reading the whole script, I will just tell you that you are 'picked up' by George Sanders [in a South American bar], and later you go on a safari with Sanders and the rest of the group. It's going to be a tiring, wearing experience." I said, "...Yes?" He said, "We are doing it on a soundstage. We are bringing in all of the trees and bushes and whatnot, and planting them, and watering them. So it will be a really humid, hot set." I said, "Well ... everything has its price." He laughed again, and off I went to wardrobe.

How many outfits did you have in the picture?
  I only had two outfits: I had the outfit I wore in the scene where Sanders "picks me up," and then I wore jodhpurs and a pith helmet for the jungle scenes. That was the outfit I wore *most* of the time.

What was the first thing you shot?
  My first scene, which is the only thing of me that is now left in *Green Hell*. The bar "pick-up" scene, in which I have no dialogue. The atmosphere on the set at the time was already ... really negative. The picture was just starting, but George Sanders had already managed to make himself totally unpopular with everybody. So we got the first scene done, and you could feel the negative tension every time Sanders moved in. You see, Sanders had played his first decent part in *Lloyd's of London* [1936], in which he played a bastard. He did *so* well with that that he decided he would *be* the bastard. And he *was*—he *majored* in bastardry [*laughs*]! No matter *who*, he would find something nasty to say about him. This particular day on *Green Hell*, he managed to sort of alienate *every*body, everybody from the board boy right straight on up.

Gloria Stuart, James Whale (left) and two assistants indulge in a silly posed publicity shot for *The Old Dark House* **(1932). (Photofest)**

And Whale's reaction to this?

Mr. Whale said nothing. He was just very quiet. But he had a kind of a frown. You could see that the very thought of George Sanders was upsetting to him. And you could also see that Mr. Sanders *enjoyed* that. Sanders enjoyed sort of ... *making* people hate him.

What about some of the other actors, like Douglas Fairbanks, Jr., and Vincent Price—how did you find them?

Because I was the only woman in the cast who was there—the other women in that bar scene were extras—everybody was particularly nice and "nurturing" to me. They were very, very nice and I formed very pleasant relationships with allll of the gentlemen on the picture.

Allll of them except Sanders.

Well, *no*body had a relationship with Sanders. Nobody spoke to him. And it really irked him that he would come on the set and make remarks and nobody responded. So then he would go back in his little canvas dressing tent, or he would sit on the sidelines and read. Or he would walk around making remarks to people, not waiting for them to answer—which they wouldn't do anyway. That man could not say anything kind or pleasant. He made a whole *career* out of it, on screen *and* off.

Anyway, we finished that day's work ... there were a couple more days in the bar there ... and then we went straight into the first jungle sequences. And it was really *hell*. It was *so* humid. It all was mud. And it stunk, people got sick from the smell. But you got *used* to it—do you know what I mean? Your senses become sort of *bored* with sending messages constantly: "It smells bad, it smells bad, it smells bad...," and so everybody became used to it. But when we went to lunch, it was unbelievable to step outside and it smelled so *good*! The jungle set was on the largest soundstage at Universal, the whole jungle was built in there. What they did was bring in set pieces as we proceeded into the jungle.

And was the set as hot as Whale had promised you it would be?

Ohhhhh, yes! They couldn't do anything about it because, remember, this was before air conditioning. We only had fans, fans that were up high—suction fans pulling the hot air and the stinky air up and out. But the moisture that they had in this mud was too much for the fans, they just couldn't handle it. And besides, of course, they had to turn all of the fans *off* when we began to shoot. It didn't take long for that place to become really miserable.

At that point, things began to be a little tough. Mr. Whale became kind of ... kind of *tense*. Everybody was aware that he was unhappy. He wandered throughout the making of that film—he didn't sit down in the director's chair too much, he was ambling. And he found it just exceedingly difficult to *talk* with the actors. He didn't want to look at them when he was talking about how he saw the action, the movement in the upcoming scene. So we [the actors] sort of sat around, and everybody got nicely acquainted. It was a nice, warm feeling, and we had a very pleasant time. But, as I say, when it came time to work, it was becoming increasingly difficult, because Mr. Whale was becoming *angry*, and he was making side remarks. For instance, if (say) Douglas Fairbanks, Jr., was doing a scene, Whale would sort of mumble under his breath during rehearsal. *Not* to anybody in particular. But you knew that you were not pleasing him. No matter what, you knew you were not pleasing him. And this was a great *joy* to George Sanders. Sanders would walk around and make remarks *about* Whale, nasty remarks, *just* [loud enough] so that Whale could hear if he was listening. Things became increasingly tense.

Green Hell was made at a time when King George VI was getting ready to make a speech to the world—it had to have been his announcement of England's declaration of war on Germany [September 1939]. One day, it came over the radio that King George was going to make his speech to the world. Because he stuttered, everybody was very interested in how he was going to sound.

In order for us to hear the speech, what they arranged was that there would be radios all over the soundstage. Just before King George was to go on the air, like ten minutes before, the work on the picture shut down, and everybody moved to the radios. We actors moved to a part of the soundstage that had not been dressed [as jungle]. On the edge of the jungle set, where we had all our little canvas dressing tents, we had a semi-circle of canvas chairs where we were going to sit and listen to the speech.

That was when I think Mr. Sanders gave his most convincing performance. He came and stood and said to all of us sitting in the chairs around the radio, "You are not going to be such asses as to pay attention to this fool, *are* you?" Remember, the "fool" to whom he was referring was the king of some of these people—there were some Britishers on that set. When Sanders made that remark, Vinnie said, "Well, if you don't want to hear it, why don't you just step outside?"

Well, that set things off. Sanders began talking about the King and what an ass he was, and laying bets what the King was going to say. People *tried* to avoid him—*every*body tried to avoid him. But he absolutely kept on and on. All of a sudden, the radio announcer introduced "His Majesty." With that, Sanders kind of drew himself up and said, "And *now*, I will interpret..." At that point, Fairbanks came forward and stood nose-to-nose with him, and said, "*You* will keep your mouth shut, or I will beat the *hell* out of you." Sanders kind of stepped back, and put that typical Sanders smirk on, and said [*with a nervous laugh*], "Oh, well, now reeeally..." Fairbanks said, "I mean it ... with *everything in my soul*." At which point, Vinnie got up and moved in, and said, "If you disrupt *my* listening, *I* will *hold* you." At that moment, the King began to speak and everybody sort of froze. Fairbanks and Vinnie and Sanders held their poses—believe me—through the entire speech. They stood through that entire speech, and Fairbanks was nose-to-nose with Sanders. By the time the speech was over, everybody was sort of breathing deeply. Finally Sanders said, "You're *not*—" At that point, James Whale, who'd been sort of "in the background" as this all happened, interrupted and said, "No one gave you permission to *speak*." And that was the last positive that I heard James Whale say!

Did Whale stay "tense" throughout the picture?
Actually, the further we got into the jungle, and the more the script became almost a parody, the more he seemed to start to enjoy it. Finally James Whale was having fun. It didn't dawn on him that this was a horrible, horrible picture. But he seemed to have difficulty in making decisions. When the script girl would say, for instance, "The only thing we have left to do today is the two-shot of Doug Fairbanks and one of the porters," he would say, "No, no. No, we have some more to do." And we would sit and *wait* while he made up his mind what shot he was going to call. It was almost as though he was "on" something. You know that strange thing that happens to people when they've just taken a drug? When the pleasure and the remoteness seems to come over them? *That* was what we had with Mr. Whale. It was a strange situation, because when we had started the picture, everybody thought that it would be a good experience. After all, Douglas Fairbanks, Jr., didn't *have* to do *any*thing. Vinnie Price was at the height of his early career. The guy who played the doctor, Alan Hale, was very, very successful. Everybody went into this with a very positive attitude.

About how long were you on Green Hell?
About four weeks.

What was your character like? Was she flirty, was she scared, was she...?
 I was a *nice* whore [*laughs*].

Did Whale give you much direction in the jungle scenes?
 No, not really. Anything you wanted to do was fine.

How was your character killed?
 I was shot with a poisoned arrow. When they stuck it on me, it was kind of in the hollow of my neck.

Did you have any sort of death scene or last words?
 No, no, no. By the time they got to me, I was dead [*laughs*].

Did you have any contact with Joan Bennett, who came into the picture after your character was killed?
 Joan Bennett was a very pleasant human being, *very*, very nice. She was really a delight. Now, of course, she was almost blind, you know. Oh, her eyes were *so* bad that she rehearsed with these thick glasses on. Whereas the rest of us had our marks on the floor in regular masking tape, they had to use whiter tape for her. And she had to know where people were, because she only saw a blur. But she was very sweet. All the things that her sister Constance wasn't, *she was*. She was just such a nice person.

Final thoughts on the movie itself?
 With just hyping up [the campy parts] a little tiny bit, it could have been a blockbuster—because *then* it would have been a take-off. As it is ... well, have *you* seen this abortion [*laughs*]?

What do you recall about acting in Whale's final feature, They Dare Not Love*?*
 My experience with Mr. Whale on *They Dare Not Love* was entirely different. I don't know why in Heaven's name he ever agreed to do the picture. I don't know why he agreed to *any* of the casting.

George Brent, Martha Scott, Paul Lukas and you.
 He had nasty things to say about *every*body. He was just in such a desperate state.

So, the same way he mumbled under his breath about (say) Fairbanks' performance in Green Hell, *he also made his little comments here?*
 Oh, they weren't little any more! And his language was absolutely amazing.

Four-letter words, you mean.
 Oh, yes!

What were these people like?
 Martha Scott had a beauty all its own. She had a freshness and a warmth and

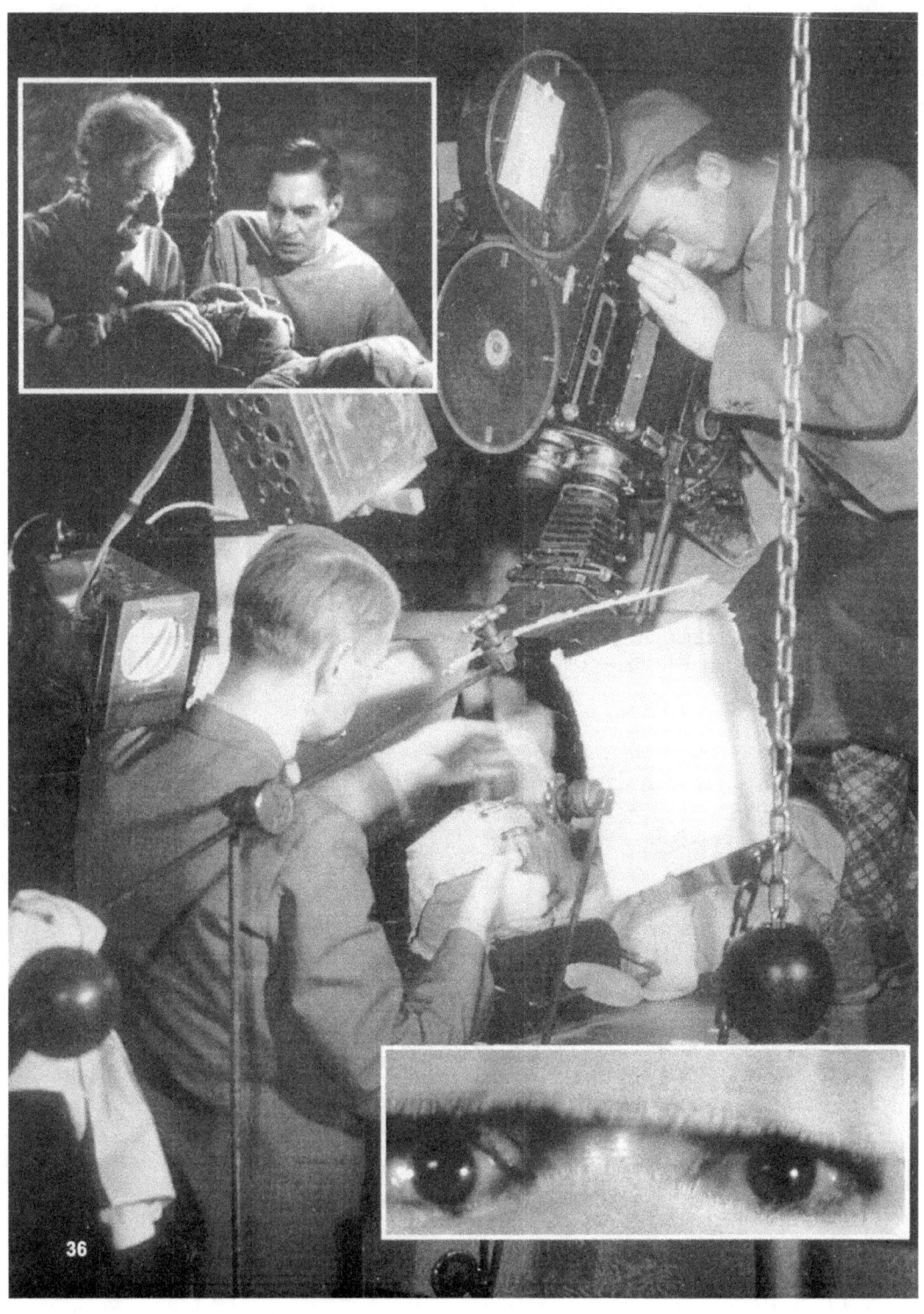

The filming of a classic shot: It is Ernest Thesiger who removes Elsa Lanchester's bandages in *Bride of Frankenstein* (top inset), but director James Whale performed the service on set, unveiling the bride's eyes for an unforgettable image (bottom inset). (Photofest)

a thoroughly *good*, wholesome, almost fairy-story quality about her. It was the wonderful quality that she had in the play that "made" her, *Our Town*. A lovely, delightful human being. George Brent was one of the *really* nice guys. He could talk about the ridiculous things that he had done in his life, and be very honest about it, almost as though he was talking about somebody else. He was a thoroughly charming, nice guy. And Paul Lukas was a delightful gentleman. He was pleasant, he was charming, he was a talented actor and he knew what he was doing.

The first day that we all worked together, we were doing a scene on a pier where I meet George Brent and Paul Lukas. As far as I was concerned, I was havin' a good time. It was a very good part, and it was a part where I had, if I'm not mistaken, 22 costume changes. A great deal of the romance that I had with George Brent was done in [short] scenes—in a speedboat, at the races, dancing in a nightclub, all that sort of thing. A lot of them were process, and there was not a lot of dialogue. It was almost silent picture acting. One thing that Harry Cohn insisted on: I was playing the richest girl in the world and I had to have the kind of clothes that the richest girl in the world would wear. I don't know whether [costume designer] Edith Head got credit on that picture, but she got double pay for designing the costumes. Edith was a delightful person and we were good friends, and she made me some beautiful, beautiful clothes. Harry Cohn insisted that I go to his office and model each piece as they finished it. Harry also made arrangements for a jeweler to come on the set every morning with the jewelry I was to wear, and I was bonded for a million dollars. You never saw anything like the jewelry I wore in that. Just un-be-liev-a-ble stuff. The experience of that film was delightful ... *until* James Whale ... I swear to you ... had a breakdown.

Were you there that day?

Yes, I was. One day, Martha and I were doing the nice little scene where I meet her for the first time—she was playing a young lady who has come to the United States and she was impoverished and she was working in a dress shop. We had done probably a week's worth of work by this time. About halfway through the first blocking, all of a sudden James Whale said, "Not only do I have the two worst actresses in Hollywood ... but I've got the two *ugliest* fuckin' broads that ever *were*."

Well ... we just ... stopped. *Ev-er-y*-thing ... stopped. And when he had total silence, he began to rave and rant, again [attacking] the two of us, Martha and I. Finally, she and I looked at one another, and with one voice we said, "Excuse me, please." We left, and we went in the set dressing room, where we looked at one another and we said, "*What* is the *matter* with him?" That was just the first of the outbursts.

The next day, Martha brought her husband Carleton Alsop on the set. Rather, her husband *came* on the set. I think he was a business manager or something like that, a very, very nice guy. An average-sized gent, a very quiet man. He came on the set, and sat down, and everything went along (*we* thought) very smoothly. All of a sudden, Whale had to do another set-up with the two of *us*. Well, the minute that we were called, we went over and stood waiting for him to tell us where he wanted us and whatnot. And all of a sudden, he started again.

Again along the lines of "They can't act," "They're ugly" and so on?

Oh, yes. He lost it to such a degree that he screamed and yelled. And when he really got wound up, Martha's husband got out of his chair, and walked over to him, and said, "I want you ... to shut your mouth. I want you to keep it shut ... until I come back from talking to Harry Cohn."

And Whale's reaction?

It was as though somebody had poured cold water over Whale. He just sat down. As long as it took Alsop to run up to Cohn's office, get Cohn and bring him back—that's how long Whale sat. Almost in a daze.

Once he sat down in a daze, what did everyone else do?

*Every*body just sat in a daze. Nobody said boo. By the time Alsop brought Cohn onto the set, Whale had started pacing. Cohn came on with Alsop and walked over and very, very quietly said to Whale, "You're through. Get off the set." And *that* was the end of our first director. And ... from that point on, Mr. Whale just ... waited to die.

The "official line" in the Hollywood trades was that Whale left the picture because he'd come down with the flu.

Whenever anybody was having problems with Cohn or Louis Mayer, they didn't dare say that there were problems. If they did, they'd find themselves barred from the lot and all kinds of stuff. So that was the cover-up: The person who was having problems was "ill." Whale didn't have the flu but he *was* reeeally sick.

That was when director Charles Vidor came in to finish the picture?

We had *two* other directors. How the picture was ever finished, I don't know. Whale had set this *feeling*, and now nobody was comfortable. We all had a hunch that this picture would never be released. And it then became particularly difficult for George and Paul, because the second director didn't like *men* [*laughs*]! George and Paul couldn't do *any*thing that pleased him. And he let them know that. You can imagine how uncomfortable and unhappy we all were. This director was a refugee from Germany, he spoke pretty good English, but he only lasted a week. Then we got Charles Vidor.

Finally the picture was ended, and we felt that it was not going to be released for a long time. I never saw it. I think Cohn was [fed up with] it by that time, and hated it so much, and it had cost him so much money. And originally this was intended to be a real *big* picture, the picture that was going to be better than anything that Columbia had done up to that point. It was also going to show that [Columbia's number one director] Frank Capra didn't have to do it in order to make it a big picture.

What had been the collective feeling toward Whale throughout his days on the picture?

Nobody on that picture developed a hate for Whale. Everybody was *sorry* for him. Everybody thought that he should be taken *off* the picture, yes, we all agreed *that*—but there was no hate. If he had suddenly come down with TB, we would have felt the same way. We *knew* he was sick. When he did what he did in front of Alsop, at that point, he was really, really "out of it." He would have been very comfortable in a padded cell.

Did he again give the impression that he was "on" something, as he did during the latter days of Green Hell*?*
No, not so much. You see, after a while on *Green Hell*, he thought it was just fine. *Every*thing was fine. He loved everything that was going on. *That* was why we thought he was "on" something. We thought he was on a happy pill.

Any final comments about your experiences with James Whale?
The only thing I can say is that, at the time that James Whale was having problems, I wish that psychiatric drugs had been further developed. The drugs that we have now for psychiatric problems. In his early life, I understood from little things that people said, he had been a very pleasant human being. Before he got sick, he was a fellow who could do a fine job, as his films indicate. But then there came the breaking point. After that, he was just ... not a whole person. He was a "part" individual functioning on ... not even two and a half cylinders. Somehow or other, it just ... *bothered* me to see somebody in such bad shape. I wish he had had an easier end.

You knew both Whale and Tod Browning right at the very ends of their movie directing careers. Can you compare and contrast them just a bit?
Well, Tod Browning was a "whole" human being. He was a very, very happy man—in his marriage, in his place in society, and what he did. He was *not* miserable. Just don't talk about the film business to him, and Tod was fine. He was a gracious, warm, old-fashioned "country guy." He was a well person.

And I'm very, very sorry for the other guy.

Teala Loring

> *My mother and father were going to see [White Zombie] and I wanted to go. My dad said, "No, she can't go. She'll never let us have any sleep." So I finally talked my mother into taking me—and Daddy was right, I was scared to death. For a week, they had to take me in bed with 'em!*

Teala Loring's stint in the motion picture business began and ended in the 1940s, before the later (and longer) Hollywood careers of her actress-sisters Debra Paget and Lisa Gaye. But despite the shorter run, Loring packed a number of memorable movies onto her acting résumé, from small parts in the classics *Holiday Inn* (1942) and *Double Indemnity* (1944) to co-starring roles in low-budget horror thrillers.

Born on October 6, 1922, in Denver, Colorado, Loring (real name: Marcia Griffin) got her professional start as a toddler, appearing in vaudeville with her mother. Sisters Debra and Lisa and even brother Frank Griffin would all develop an interest in acting, but it was their eldest sister who led the pack, landing a Paramount contract in the early '40s and later toplining a succession of B features—among them PRC's *Bluebeard* (1944) with John Carradine and Monogram's *Return of the Ape Man* (1944) with Carradine and Bela Lugosi.

What did your parents do for a living when you were a kid?

My mother was in show business, but my dad wasn't. He always said that somebody had to make a living, keep food on the table and a roof over our heads [*laughs*]! When I was born, I think he was a coal miner then. Then he worked on the railroad—he worked up in Berthoud Pass, way up high there, about 10,000 feet. I remember him telling me that, when they had to go out and work the switch for the trains going through, they would have to completely wrap their faces up because they couldn't breathe that air up there, it would be like 50 below zero.

And your mom was in show biz.

Mother was a singer and a comedienne—there was still vaudeville. I started working with my mother. I didn't *do* much—a cute little three-year-old doesn't *have* to do very much! I could do tap and toe. So I danced, working with Mother. We traveled around—Colorado, Wyoming, Montana. We came out here [to California] when I was four: One girl who was in the Our Gang comedies was kind of outgrowing them, getting a little bit too big for the part. They brought me out and I tested for it. But they wanted me to be trained for six months—she had six months to go yet on her contract, I guess. My mother got homesick and we went home to Denver, so that was the end of that. Probably just as well! We lived in Denver until I was about 17, and then we finally all moved out to California.

A lot of the articles written about Debra in the 1950s say that your mother pushed all of you into show biz.
No, no, she didn't. Mother was not a stage mother. I worked, and I thoroughly enjoyed it. When we came out here, Debbie, Lisa and Frank all wanted to go into [acting]. So Mother put them into a school. I don't know if you remember Queenie Smith. She had been the first American-born prima ballerina at the Metropolitan Opera, and she was a good actress too. She had a school in Hollywood, the Queenie Smith School—she taught ballet, and then they had other people in there who taught tap. The kids all took lessons from them. *Plus,* she taught dramatics. Debbie and Frank and Lisa did plays and things, and they just thoroughly enjoyed it. They also went to a "professional school," Hollywood Professional, which isn't there any more—they finally closed it down four or five years ago. They didn't have gym and things like that there, but they had their basic classes—math, history, English and so on. The kids went from about nine in the morning until one in the afternoon. Schools like that were for children who wanted to be in the theater.

And you were already too old for this?
Oh, yes, I was already under contract to Paramount.

How did you get your foot in the door there?
An agent had seen me work at a theater, the Orpheum Theater. It was a movie theater, but they had stage shows between the movies. The agent saw me dancing there. I wasn't really doing much acting at that time—I was *interested* in it, but I had never *done* anything. Paramount signed me up to a regular stock contract. They had 9000 of us there [*laughs*]. Well, at least 50 of us! They would train you, they had wonderful coaches. You'd go in and have dramatic classes and all. So the kids, Debbie and Frank and Lisa, all wanted to be a part of it too. Mother never shoved anybody into anything. She told 'em, "The first time I tell you to go practice, and you don't, I won't work with you any more, I won't try and help you." She felt that they had to *want* it enough that they would get in and really work for it. She was definitely not a stage mother.

You were "Judith Gibson" at Paramount. Where did that come from?
They didn't like my real name, Marcia. Gibson was my mother's maiden name … and I don't know *who* dreamed up "Judith," that was somebody at Paramount, I guess.

You changed your name to Teala Loring a few years later.

Glamorous Teala Loring dressed up major pictures in small roles and small pictures in major ones.

I had been wanting to change it for quite a while, because there was a girl under contract there, a singer, and her name was *Julie* Gibson. We would get each other's calls and fan mail and checks. And that was her *real* name, so she was not about to be changing *her* name! But I had "Judith Gibson" for about a year and a half, two years. One day at Paramount, somebody called me into the office as I was getting ready to do a Technicolor short there. It was Irwin Allen, who was a producer at Paramount, just starting out—he was directing Technicolor shorts. He asked, "What do you think of 'Teala'?" I said, "I don't know who she is." [*Laughs*] He said, "Well, that's *you* if you like the name!" He said Teala was an old Irish name that hadn't been used in many, many years. But he couldn't think of a last name to go with it. He said, "You think about it," so I went home and talked to Mother. Mother said, "'Teala' is Irish, and 'Loring' is English," and that's how we came up with the name Teala Loring. I always liked it. I never *did* like Judith Gibson.

Well, what do your friends call you?

In church and places like that, "Teala" is kind of hard, people can't pick it up, they call me Sheila and other things. So at church, or anything like that, I use Marcia. My husband has never called me anything but Teala. My son-in-law once asked me, "Should I introduce you as Marcia or Teala?" I said, "Oh, just introduce me, I don't care *what* you call me. Just don't call me late for dinner!" When it comes time to bury me, I don't know *what* they'll bury me under [*laughs*]!

What was your very first movie?

I think it was *Bombs Over Burma* [1942]. I was under contract to Paramount, and I did that on a loanout [to PRC].

Describe for me a day at Paramount when you weren't *in a picture—what would you come in and do?*

We had a wonderful coach there, Bill [William D.] Russell, a fine dramatic coach who later became a director. And we'd have dramatic lessons. You'd come in with another contract player and do different scenes. One of my classmates was that tall, handsome blond fellow who later went over to Hawaii to do the TV series *Hawaii Five-O*, Richard Denning—I'd work with him.

Would you see the various stars around the lot?
Yes, you'd see them going to and fro, and in the commissary at lunchtime.

Why did you leave Paramount?
After about two years, I knew I wasn't accomplishing anything. And while I *was* making a lot of money, I knew that [when Paramount loaned her out], they probably got four or five times what I was earning. When it came time to renew the contract, Mother and I and the agent decided I was not going to stick around there under contract any more.

Return of the Ape Man *and* Bluebeard—*were you still under contract to Paramount then?*
Yes, those were loan-outs.

Again getting back to Debra, some of the articles I read said that your mother would be on the sets of Debra's movies. Was your mother on the sets of your movies?
No, because I was older. Debbie started when she was just 14.

Return of the Ape Man—*what memories of that one?*
Well [*laughs*], it was kind of a funny picture to make. I was always kind of shy. My mother always told me, "Nobody likes pushy kids," and never to be pushy. So, as far as really getting to know any of the people, I didn't. If they talked to me, I answered back, and that was about the extent of it. But it was kind of fun to make. They had a young boy, probably 22, 23, who doubled Frank Moran, the actor who was playing the Ape Man. We talked, we had a lot of fun laughing and joking together, me and this stuntman. I was a little bit worried when Frank Moran had to pick me up and swing me over his shoulder. There was one scene where he did, and I thought sure he was gonna drop me! But most of the time it was the young stuntman. Frank Moran was nice but kind of quiet—he didn't have a lot to talk about! He was like me, he just kind of sat back and waited for somebody to say something to him, I think [*laughs*]!

An older actor named George Zucco was originally signed to play the Ape Man but he was replaced by Moran. Did you ever get to see Zucco in action?
No. I knew that he was supposed to have been on there, and that he had actually done some of the wardrobe tests and things. But I never did see him. They said he wasn't well, but *I* always figured maybe he didn't think the part was quite up to his standards!

Instead of having a stuntwoman for you, *I notice that they just replaced you with a dummy sometimes.*

Wallflowers on the set of *Return of the Ape Man*, Loring and Frank Moran share a cute moment between takes.

Yes, and half the time it looks like the wig is falling off! That had to have the dummy in the scene where the young stuntman went hand over hand across the rope over the street with the dummy slung over his shoulder. The stuntman had said, "She doesn't weigh very much, but I can't do it with her over my shoulder," so they made up that dummy.

Had you even heard of Bela Lugosi before you did this movie?
[*Emphatically*] Oh, yes, yes, I knew who Bela Lugosi was back to when I was a child. I *llloved* horror movies when I was growing up, and one of the first ones I ever saw was called *White Zombie* [1932]. My mother and father were going to see it, and I wanted to go. They'd heard it was a pretty scary movie, so my dad said, "No, she can't go. She'll never let us have any sleep." So I finally talked my mother into taking me—and Daddy was right, I was scared to death. For a week, they had to take me in bed with 'em! Daddy said, "See?! I *told* you we shouldn't take her to see it!" I was maybe nine.

All of us were raised up on movies—Westerns and horror movies, whatever was playing. They were *clean* movies, they weren't anything that you couldn't take your

Loring was scared to death for a week after seeing *White Zombie* with Bela Lugosi—then found herself co-starring with him (and Frank Moran) in *Return of the Ape Man*.

children to. Not like nowadays. Today, before you can take 'em in to see something, you have to make sure it's okay for 'em.

What was Bela Lugosi like?

He was quiet ... and I think he was quite a drinking man! He just quietly sat back with his little cup of whatever he drank. You'd never know he was drinking, except that you could smell it. But he was a nice person.

What memories of the fire scene in Return of the Ape Man?

It was kind of hot and kind of scary. I was glad when it was over, and we didn't have to do it again. It was a little bit frightening.

Did you ever meet Sam Katzman, who produced Return of the Ape Man?

I met him quite often, on interviews and things. He was a down-to-earth guy. And I met his wife, she was always coming around on the set. She had a terrible name, Hortense [*laughs*]—the guys were always making fun of her name. Not to her face but, still, I didn't think it was very nice. It *was* a strange name, Hortense! They were both very nice people.

Six years after Return of the Ape Man, *your leading man "Michael Ames" reappeared in Hollywood with a new name [Tod Andrews], pretending he was making his film debut. I don't think he wanted people knowing he had been in movies like that!*

[*Laughs*] Oh, quite possibly! But while we were making the movie, I saw no sign [that he was unhappy]. Like me, I think he was just glad to be working!

Incidentally, the way they wrote *Return of the Ape Man*, I was supposed to play a piano in one scene—but I *couldn't* play the piano. But John Carradine could, he played beautifully. So they just had *him* do it instead. I had that happen to me in a couple of movies. When I did *Delinquent Daughters* [1944], I didn't drive, and I kept *telling* 'em, "I don't know how to drive a car." (I had to drive a car in a getaway scene, after my boyfriend robbed a bank.) I kept saying, "But I *really* can't, I don't know how to drive a car." They said, "That's just silly. *Every*body knows how to drive a car." So when it comes time for me to drive the car, I said, "I told you, I don't know how to drive." I didn't even know how to *start* the car! They said, "Well, why didn't you tell us?" and I said, "I've been tellin' you since before the movie started, and you wouldn't *listen* to me!" [*Laughs*] So they put a rope on the front of it and *towed* me out!

Did you enjoy working as fast as you had to work on these B pictures?

Well, I didn't know anything different. That's how I started out, with [B pictures], so that was all I knew! It's not like I had started out with a DeMille epic and worked for six months, and then gone into one of these fast pictures!

What's your favorite movie, of the ones you were in?

Oh, I don't know. I enjoyed doing *all* of them…

Well, if you had all your movies on a shelf and I walked into your house and I asked you to show me one … which one would you show me?

I liked the Bowery Boys picture *Bowery Bombshell* [1946]—I liked that as well as anything.

So it wouldn't be Return of the Ape Man *then?*

[*Laughs*] No! I would show it to you, but it wouldn't be my first choice!

Bluebeard *was a popular B picture you made around that same time—but a much smaller part.*

I enjoyed doing that. I played like a female detective, a member of the French Sûreté—the French police department. The only thing I didn't like was that John Carradine, who played Bluebeard, was supposed to kill me … and, after he killed me, they wanted me to get into a coffin. Well…! I asked them, "Do I really have to get in the coffin?" and they said, "Of *course* you do. We have to have a funeral scene." I think it was probably the last scene I had to do on the picture. I was so worried the night before, knowing it was the first thing we had to shoot in the morning, I said, "Mother, I don't want to *do* this…!" She said, "You just go 'head. You just hold your breath and you do it and you'll be just fine." So I *did*, but I wasn't too happy about it! To this day, when I see people doing a scene in a coffin, I think, "I sympathize with you!" It was kind of an eerie feeling.

You were still living at home at the time when you made these movies?
Yes. We had a little house in Hollywood.

What recollections of the Bluebeard *cast?*
Very nice. Jean Parker played my sister on that, and she was nice. She was a quiet person, not pushy or outgoing or anything. When we worked together, we spoke, but that was about it! Nils Asther was also very nice, and so was John Carradine. He didn't talk a whole lot, but he was very pleasant, he'd always give you a nice "Good morning!" and "How are you doing?" and "How do you feel?" It just felt kinda comfortable working with him.

The director of Bluebeard *was something who's since become rather well-known—*
Ulmer. Edgar Ulmer. Yeah, I liked him, he was really neat to work with. He just kind of let you go ahead and see what your interpretation would be.

The Bowery Boys—how were they to work with?
[*Laughs*] Crazy! Very nice but very crazy. Especially Huntz Hall, he was the craziest of them all.

Crazy in a nice way?
Oh, yes. He wanted to take every girl out, and if you didn't say yes, he didn't *like* you very well. He asked me a few times and I said no. But he was fun to work with.

And no problems with him after you said no?
No. He just didn't really talk to you very much after that!

And Leo Gorcey?
He was nice. Leo's father Bernard Gorcey was also in *Bowery Bombshell*, he was the little guy who owned the sweet shop, and also Bernard's other son, Leo's brother, Dave Gorcey. I thought, "[Leo and David] *had* to have a different mother!" because that young boy Dave Gorcey was so nice-looking compared to the father and his brother Leo. He *definitely* had to have a different mother [*laughs*]!

Why did you leave the business?
I got married in 1950, and had two children. After that, I didn't have any children for seven years—but then I had four more, one right after another [*laughs*]. My husband [Gene Pickler] worked at the studios, he was in construction, building the sets and tearing 'em down. We're still married—we just had our fifty-first wedding anniversary.

And you left the business because...?
I didn't especially want to work. Also, my grandmother—my mother's mother—

had been very ill, dying of cancer. We had a nurse taking care of her during the day, and then I would go over and my grandfather and I would take care of her at night. They thought she would die within two or three months, but she lasted six or seven months. We took care of her like that, so there was just no working for me during those months. She died in February 1950. After that ... I don't know ... the parts weren't coming along, and then I started going with my husband and we got married in June of '50. And I just didn't really have any desire to go back to work any more. I'd enjoy it thoroughly. Our first child was born in May of '51—

And then you had plenty to do after that.
 Oh, yes, that kept me busy. And then in '52 our second child was born. Then I didn't have any 'til '59, and then from then on I was *very* busy [*laughs*].

Did you ever hold a nine-to-five job after the actress days?
 No. Never did.

Where do you stand now? Six kids and how many grandkids?
 I have 15 grandchildren, and five great-grandchildren. And another one due in December [2001]!

Looking back on your career, how do you feel about what you did?
 Oh, I enjoyed it. It was nothing that will go down in history as wonderful, not like *The Ten Commandments* [1956] and some of those things that Debbie did. But I enjoyed doing 'em. I'm not ashamed of 'em.

Robert Nichols

> *We were all young actors [in* The Thing from Another World*] and we all got along really well, and had a lot of fun doing it. The way the film was "created," the dialogue and everything, it was great fun to do.*

One of the earliest and best entries in the 1950s' sci-fi cycle, director Howard Hawks' *The Thing from Another World* is a marvelous bridge between the horror flicks of the previous two decades and the then-newborn SF movie genre. A chilly, no-frills story taking place in the shadow of the North Pole, it is set into motion when a UFO crashes in the vicinity of a government experimental station; military men and scientists rushing to the scene discover a spaceship—and its occupant—frozen in ice. The alien is brought back to the station in an ice block, but is accidentally thawed and set free, a hulking killer (James Arness) composed of green vegetable matter and seeking human blood.

Playing the main military roles in this RKO production was a quartet of up-and-coming young actors whose characters establish a very "Hawksian" kind of screen camaraderie via wisecracking, fast-clip dialogue: Kenneth Tobey, Dewey Martin, James Young—and Robert Nichols, a native of Oakland, California, and a newlywed stage veteran when he joined the cast of *The Thing*. A prominent role in the popular chiller didn't lead to stardom for Nichols, or for any of the *other Thing* players, but it did pave the way for dozens of additional film assignments (in Hollywood *and* England) and much TV work. Here he recalls "Mr. Hawks," *The Thing* and the secrets of its success.

How did you get your start in the acting world?

My start was as an entertainer in the Army, during World War II. I did the lead in a G.I. production of *Babes in Arms* at Ford Meade, Maryland; and then at Fort Bliss, Texas, I did a *lot* of stuff; and then in Japan, right when the War was over, I was with Special Services and I was emceeing and doing comedy and so on. After I got out of the Army, I went to the Royal Academy of Dramatic Art in London—I was trying to be a classical actor. Very little has *come* of that [*laughs*]! While

I was there, I auditioned as a song and dance man at the Players Theater, which is Victorian music hall, and I was hired and worked there for a year—I worked there part-time while I was going to school. Then I met Howard Hawks, who was casting *I Was a Male War Bride* [1949] in London, to be shot in Germany. He cast me in the film.

How did you happen to meet him?

An agent. It was very funny, because of course I'd never done a film, I didn't know a damn thing about filming. I was going to be [*haughtily*] a Classical Actor. This was 1948, I guess, and there weren't many American actors living in London. In fact, I think probably less than ten. I walked into the office, and Mr. Hawks said, "You're an American, aren't you?" I said [*with surprise*], "Y-y-yes. How do you *know*?" He said, "I can tell by the way you walked into the office." Then he asked, "Are you any *good*?" [*laughs*], and I said, "Well, why don't you come to the Players and take a look at me." He said, "You're fine, you're in the film." I didn't *do* anything in *Male War Bride*, I did four tiny little bits. But my first scene in front of a camera, ever, was a scene with Cary Grant and Ann Sheridan. Actually, it was a pretty good little scene, it was the scene where Ann Sheridan's motorcycle breaks down, and I was the mechanic. And [*laughs*] … I was scared to death! I didn't know what I was doing. But Cary came over and said, "You look a little nervous," and I said, "Y-y-yeah…!" He asked, "Why?" and I said, "I've never *done* this before." He said, "Well, there's nothing to it. If you don't get it right, we'll shoot it again. And if you *do* get it right, we'll shoot it again! We're gonna be on this scene for a couple of days." Well, *I* didn't know *that*, I thought you had to shoot and away you went!

Then Cary said, "If there's anything you don't understand about what we're doing, just come on over and ask me. I've been in the business quite a while, I've gotten pretty good at it!" Well, I stuck to him for the next four *weeks*, I hardly ever left his side. He was *so* patient and *so* pleasant, and he really gave me my education in film acting—he taught me how to hit marks and how to overlap and how to match action and how to "cheat the camera" and all those little things that you have to pick up. Annie Sheridan was just the most wonderful, darling, gorgeous lady who ever was. And Hawks was … well, Hawks was a very cool man. I did four films for him, and he was not a *warm* personality. But Hawks was fine with me. He gave me one piece of direction, he said, "Bobby … do you realize that right now, your eyebrows are going up 15 feet at Radio City Music Hall?" I knew what he meant [*laughs*], 'cause I've always had a tendency to be a fairly exuberant actor.

You went to Germany to shoot those scenes?

Oh, yeah! That was in Heidelberg—I was there for, oh, a month, five, six weeks.

At that point in your life, did you see yourself staying in England and making your living there for the rest of your days?

No, not really, but I expected to stay there for a *few* more years. But Mr. Hawks said, "If you come out to Hollywood, I'll put you in my next film," and Annie Sheridan said, "Here's my phone number. Give me a call if you get out there." And I'd

Polar disorder: William Self, Robert Nichols and Kenneth Tobey prepare to meet the threat of *The Thing*.

also made very good friends with Marion Marshall and Randy Stuart [other actresses in the movie].

After *Male War Bride*, I went back to England and started back at the Players Theater again when the Home Office called me and said, "You've been working without a work permit." I said, "Work permit? What's *that*?" Well, *I* knew what it was—I knew perfectly well I'd been working without a work permit. They said,

"Well, you can't *do* that," and they added, "You'll have to leave the country in two weeks." So [*laughs*]—I was *deported*!

And that's when you moved back to the U.S.?

That's right, I moved back home to California. I got in touch with Annie Sheridan and she had a party for me, introduced me to a lot of people. Then I got an agent, and I started to work as the general understudy to all the parts in *The Drunkard*, which was a show that ran in Los Angeles for 25 years. I understudied every part in that show, and then did song and dance stuff in the olio.

Did you also touch base with Hawks?

Yes. Mr. Hawks, when we were in Germany, told me to get in touch with him if I came out to Hollywood, and *that* was very easy to do. In fact, I liked to ride, so I used to go up to his house in Bel-Air and exercise his horses. It wasn't a big, regular thing, but I'd go up there on occasion and take a horse around. Then I got into a production of *She Stoops to Conquer*, playing Tony Lumpkin, in a small theater in Hollywood, and John Huston's wife Ricki Soma was one of the leads in it. Huston came to see the show and he put me in *The Red Badge of Courage* [1951], which was my first film in Hollywood. And then *The Thing* came up, and Mr. Hawks put me in *The Thing*.

When you were offered The Thing, *you jumped at it, I would think.*

Oh, *yeah*—I was thrilled! I didn't have to read or anything. I just went into Mr. Hawks' office, I was sent in by my agent, and Mr. Hawks said, "Oh, Bobby, we got a good part for you" and "It's gonna be fun working with you" and so on. It was a wonderful thing to have happen, a real break, because it was a pretty good part and it was 19 weeks of work, so I really got a chance to find out what the *business* was all about. And acting in Hollywood *is* a business. One likes to *think* of it as an art, but it's *not*, it *is* definitely a business. You have to know how to get parts, how to *go* for 'em, what to take and all the rest of it. I stayed there for ten years.

Let's get something out of the way right at the get-go here, the requisite question "Who directed The Thing?" *What light can you shed?*

Chris Nyby had been Hawks' editor on *Red River* [1948] and other Hawks pictures, and I think Mr. Hawks wanted to give him a start as a director. Also I think that, because *The Thing* was essentially a B film and all of us were unknown, beginning actors, I think that Mr. Hawks didn't want to have his name associated with this B picture. I think that's the reason why [he didn't take the credit]. Also, I think he wanted to help Chris. Chris did become a very competent director—I worked with him later, I've forgotten in what. As you undoubtedly have heard, Hawks directed every frame of *The Thing*. Chris sat in ... he was *there* all the way through ... he was certainly a presence. But Hawks did the directing.

And how did you enjoy working under Hawks' direction?

Hawks had a technique in *The Thing* that was very rare—I've never worked this way again. We had no script. Well, there *was* a script, but we didn't pay any attention *to* it—or, if we did, it was very, very little [*laughs*]! We would arrive on the set early in the morning and sit around "in conference"—we weren't even in costume or makeup yet. Mr. Hawks would say, "Well, here's what's gonna happen in *this* scene. Now, Ken [Tobey], you say *this* and Dewey [Martin], you say *that*, and Billy [Self], you say *this*..." Lorrie Sherwood, who was Mr. Hawks' secretary, would be taking down all the dialogue. Then he'd say, "Okay. Let's hear it," and we'd run it. After we ran it, Hawks would then say, "Now, after *this* line, you say *that*" and so on. We made up the scenes, it was more or less improvised. You can tell, on seeing the film, that that was the way it was done.

Mr. Hawks would put [the scene] on its feet in the set, and stage it. Then our stand-ins took over on the set, they would walk the scene while it was being lit, as *we* [the actors] got costumes and makeup and stuff. This was usually around, oh, ten o'clock in the morning. Then we would sit around and run the dialogue some more, and Mr. Hawks would change a little bit here and a little bit there and "polish" it. Finally, around 11 in the morning, we would do a master shot—well, usually, oh, five or six master shots. We would break for lunch, then shoot all the different angles in the afternoon.

Here's another thing that Hawks constantly did (and he used *me* this way a lot): He would take an actor aside and he would say, "Look, after so-and-so says this line, I want you to throw *this* line in *real fast*," and he would give you a new line. Then they'd start to shoot the scene, and suddenly out of left field here would be a line that nobody had ever heard before. And there would be an "adjustment" to it—we were all pretty sharp actors. *That* would be the take that Hawks would be going for.

Did things like this ever cause a problem, or were you all seasoned enough to deal with unexpected dialogue?

It probably did cause a problem now and then, but he liked to do that. Hawks was a master with the very fast, overlapping dialogue. As he told us, when we were working on it, "If *we* slow down, and the audience catches up with us, we're *lost!*" [*Laughs*] "We have to stay ahead of 'em, all the way."

One other thing that Hawks pulled was just incredible. Remember the lab scene when [the disembodied hand of the Thing] came to life on the table? The hand was just a plastic, rubbery thing. As usual, we all gathered around the table and the hand, we rehearsed all morning on that scene and then did a take or two. After that, we broke for lunch. Well, we gathered around the table after lunch, we continued shooting ... and suddenly, that damn hand came to life! I mean, it started moving! Well, we were just ab-so-lute-ly flabbergasted and shocked, because ... how the hell could it *do* that? We'd been *playing* with it all morning! Well, what happened is this: We had a midget on the picture, Billy Curtis—in the scene where the Thing shrinks as it's being electrocuted, he was the last of the Things. Well, Billy was around quite a lot. So, during the lunch break, a hole in the table had been cut, and also a hole in the hand, and Billy Curtis was under the table with his hand inside the fake hand, and on the cue, he started moving it. Well, I'll tell you, it was eerie—it was *really* eerie! Hawks *loved* doing things like that.

Director Howard Hawks (with glasses) surrounded by the *Thing* cast, including John Dierkes (right foreground) and Nichols (blurry background, hands clasped). (Photograph courtesy Bob Burns)

That was with the camera rolling?
　Oh, *yeah*! That's the take you *see* in the picture.

Do you have any recollection who came up with your classic line from The Thing, *"I saw Gary Cooper in* Sergeant York"?
　Mr. Hawks. Of course, he directed *Sergeant York* [1941].

You mentioned that you found Hawks "cool." Did he eventually "warm up" around you, or—that's just the way he was?
　No, that's the way he was, that was Mr. Hawks, you didn't expect a great deal of warmth. He had *cold* blue eyes, he looked like a general with his cropped, crew-cut hair, and he always had real style in his clothes. He was a gent-le-man, he really was. I was very uncomfortable with Mr. Hawks. At first I thought he didn't like me, but when he used me in four films, I realized he probably *did*.

But it was hard to tell.
　Yeah! He was just not a warm person. In fact, it's so funny, his only direction

to me in *The Thing*, for alllll that film, was, "Bob ... you're *not* on a stage now..." And I knew what he meant [*laughs*]—I knew I was going a little bit too far.

You mentioned The Thing's *cast of "unknown, beginning actors." Would it have "worked" as well any other way?*

No. I think that, due to the fact that we were all unfamiliar, the movie somehow was more believable.

You all may have been unknowns, but all good actors, top to bottom.

All good people, yes. Dewey Martin had quite a career after *The Thing*, and Robert Cornthwaite was a masterful actor, a beautiful actor. I expected Bob to have a much, much bigger career than he did—I don't understand why he didn't. He's one of my best friends in the world, I just had lunch with him a couple of weeks ago. Wonderful fellow, consummate artist and charming guy. Also a very talented writer. I directed him a couple of times, in the theater. We have remained close friends for ... well ... 50-something years now.

Kenneth Tobey, the star of The Thing, *was also in* I Was a Male War Bride. *Did you encounter him on that picture?*

No, Ken only worked in the States. In fact, except for Jim Young [Lt. Eddie Dykes], *nobody* from *The Thing* did I meet beforehand. Jim Young and I had done a couple of shows together at a little theater called New Horizons, and were actually pretty darn good friends. Ken Tobey was a nice guy, but ... he had his problems. Hawks got very, very aggravated with Ken. There was a rivalry between Ken and Dewey Martin, and Dewey sort of took over as Hawks' favorite actor. Then, of course, Hawks used Dewey in two films after that, in starring roles [and never used Tobey again]. But I liked Ken, he's a nice guy, and I thought he was a very good actor.

How did that present a problem for the production, the fact that there was a competition between Tobey and Dewey Martin?

It didn't present a problem, there was just ... a certain edginess when they were around [*laughs*]. Ken has ... Ken *had* a rather abrasive personality. Dewey had been a pilot in the War. And Hawks took to Dewey as we progressed on the film, and kind of "turned off" Ken, although Ken was the lead. It *wasn't* an uncomfortable situation, although we were aware of what was going on. Dewey, who I quite liked, was a very, very ambitious young actor—like lots of actors are—and he played up to Hawks. And Hawks was impressed with the fact that he'd been a pilot. It just was a developing interest. It was uncomfortable for Ken. And [*laughs*]—and Ken was having his own problems with [co-star] Doug Spencer as well, which I'll tell you about later! Good, talented actor, though, Ken ... I got along fine with him. In fact, there was not a person in that company that I didn't enjoy being with. Generally, things were quite easy—Hawks would not *allow* tension on the set. There was no yelling, no shouting, everything was organized. Hawks ran a very serene ship.

I believe Dewey Martin has completely dropped out of acting. Did he seem to enjoy himself during the time he was an actor?

I haven't talked with Dewey in a number of years, but I think he was very disappointed with the way his career went. He had such a lot of success to begin with, around the time of *The Thing*, and then he did *The Big Sky* [1952] and he did *Land of the Pharaohs* [1955] for Hawks. His career really peaked. But it only lasted, what? four or five years, and then it was over. I think that was very disappointing to Dewey. I don't mean this in a negative way, but there was a lot of ego there. Which there *has* to be with actors—there's nothing wrong with that. I think he was terribly disappointed in how his career went.

As long as you're on a roll, what about the other members of the cast? Starting with Douglas Spencer?

Well [*laughs*], Doug was an interesting character. Doug and I were very good friends, we lived about a block from each other up in Laurel Canyon and so I saw a lot of Doug. And Doug really wasn't an actor. He had been Ray Milland's stand-in for years, and then he *became* an actor in his middle age. He and Ken didn't like each other *at all*—which in a way helped in the film [*laughs*]! They did not get along well. But I think Doug did a damn good job in the film, he did the part the way it needed to be done.

Tobey told me he thought Douglas Spencer was an upstager.

Well, *Ken* thought so [*laughs*]! They got on each other's nerves. I felt that neither one was to blame ... or that *both* were. But there was a lot at stake: Ken was building a career, Doug was building a career. They both wanted to make points at the time.

John Dierkes [Dr. Chapman]—one of my best friends, he remained a close friend for many, many years. He was a very bright man, so warm and avuncular, a joy to be with ... but, again, not an actor. I kept suggesting to John that he take an acting lesson [*laughs*], and he thought I was a fool! But he and Cynthia, his wife, and me and *my* wife Jennifer lived near each other and we saw them an *awful* lot, and loved them dearly. Paul Frees [playing Vorhees, one of the scientists] ... oh, *such* a good actor, and that beautiful voice. And a fun person to *be* with. *That* was the great thing about that cast: We all got along *so* darn well, a lot of friendships started there. It was a good bunch of people.

What about George Fenneman [Dr. Redding], who was later Groucho Marx's announcer on You Bet Your Life?

He was Chris Nyby's next-door neighbor. Has anybody talked to you about George Fenneman's "famous" scene in *The Thing*? George was a top radio and television announcer, and he had this one scientific scene, talking about some gobbledygook. They started rehearsing it, and it seemed okay, and then they started to shoot it. And George ... simply ... went ... up. They got up to something like 22, 24 takes, and he hadn't gotten through it. Finally Hawks said, "Well, I guess we better do this tomorrow...!" (That sort of thing never bothered Hawks, he never got angry or upset.) They broke for the day, and [*laughs*] poor George had to live that whole night with this nightmare speech! I think they'd gotten up to 24 takes, it was an *awful* lot. The next day, on the set, he got it the first take, of course. But that first day, George was just going out of his mind, he was so frustrated. Something like that is really embarrassing.

Among the actors [playing the other scientists], Eduard Franz was, of course, a wonderful actor. And also Norbert Schiller. But most of those actors were in *their* group, and *we* were in *our* group.

The actors playing scientists would hang out with each other, whereas you actors playing military men—

Would hang out with the *other* actors playing military men! I'm sure it was the age difference, and the difference in backgrounds. Norbert, Eduard, the actors like that, they were Europeans, and they were that much older than we were.

When I watch the movie, I do think that I sense a feeling of camaraderie among you guys that seems real.

Oh, I think there *was*. Jim Young and I were friends to begin with, and Billy Self [Corp. Barnes] was just a great guy. We were all young actors and we all got along really well, and had a lot of fun doing it. The way the film was "created," the dialogue and everything, it was *great* fun to do.

Being friendly with Young and Self—did that translate into TV work for you later, when both became behind-the-scenes mucky-mucks?

[*Laughs*] *No!* After I got back from England, I got in touch with Jim, because I liked him, because we were friends. But when he was producing [the soap opera] *General Hospital* ... I think he felt embarrassed about the fact that I was now an out-of-work actor! And Billy ... I dunno, I also never connected with him [work-wise]. We're still friends, I see him once in a while. I do a lot of writing, and he's taken an interest in that.

Margaret Sheridan, the female lead?

Margaret Sheridan was a darling lady. Sort of a road company Ann Sheridan, and I just can't say anything better than that. Maggie was a very self-assured, confident young woman. She was not an actress—I think she was an airline stewardess before *The Thing*. But she had that look that Hawks loved, that kind of tawny, "nice cheekbones" look. She was fun, she was a *honey*, and she got along swell with *all* of us.

And James Arness—what memories?

We first met each other at the audition for *Red Badge of Courage*. We were all lined up in a row, and I made the mistake of standing next to Jim. I looked like a damn midget, and he looked like a giant [*laughs*]! We cancelled each other out, although I *did* get a part in the film.

Nichols (seated left) listens intently as *Thing* co-star Douglas Spencer exhorts the world at large to "keep watching the skies!"

And he did not.
    No. We remained friends over the years, and then I did a couple of *Gunsmoke*s. It was always great to see Jim. He's a nice man. A *very* nice man.

Where did you shoot first?
    At RKO. We shot at RKO for weeks and weeks and weeks. The really interesting scene was the one in the barracks, when we set the Thing on fire. I was the one who shot the Very pistol that put him on fire. Once the barracks started to burn and the Thing [now played by stuntman Tom Steele] was on fire, *we* were substituted by our stunt doubles. It was staged in such a way that we were in the barracks to begin with, while the shot was starting, then [once the fire broke out] *we* got off the set and the stunt doubles came in and replaced us. Now I'm not sure this was a continuous action, or whether they stopped the action and substituted stuntmen for actors.

That does make sense [replacing the actors in mid-shot]—that way they wouldn't have to light up and put out the stuntman more than once. So your memory is that perhaps the stunt doubles came in and took over while the cameras rolled?

I think so, but I'm not 100 percent certain. Dick Crockett was my double, incidentally.

Was there more than one camera for the fire scene?
I don't know, but my guess would be that there were two or three. Anyway, after RKO we went down to the Ice House in downtown Los Angeles and shot all of the stuff in the passages, all the scenes after it started to get cold in the experimental station. That way, they could get our breath [to show].

Identical sets built at the Ice House to the sets built at RKO, that you'd been acting on already?
Yeah.

The Ice House—unpleasantly cold?
It was pretty damn cold. And of course outside it was warm. You'd put on those big parkas and stuff outside and be burning up, and then you'd go into the Ice House ... and freeze [*laughs*]! I have worked under more pleasant conditions.

We finished all of the interiors and then we went up to Cut Bank, Montana, where they had built exterior sets. But this was the first year in 40 years that it did not snow, which spoiled everything. Cut Bank is one of the coldest places in the United States, and that year it was too *cold* to snow—it was something like 40 degrees below. And *if* they had gotten the snow, it was too cold for the cameras to operate. We sat around up there in Cut Bank for a couple of weeks, and then Mr. Hawks took us back to California. We were off for a few weeks, and then we shot the scene of the discovery of the saucer out in the Valley, out at Calabasas, with fake snow and fake ice.

Up in Cut Bank, all you were waiting to do was the saucer scene, correct?
No, there would have been more than that. They had built the exterior sets [for the Arctic station] and, if there *had* been good snow, they would have shot the scenes of the people coming in and out of the place. They eventually went up to Alaska and shot those exteriors with doubles, without *us*.

Did you see the exterior sets up in Cut Bank?
No. We hardly went out of the hotel!

How did you fill the time in Cut Bank?
Well, you try to stay sober until the afternoon [*laughs*]. You read, and pass time. Jim Young and I were roommates, and we got along fine, but ... it was no fun. As I mentioned, we were on the film for 19 weeks, but six of those weeks we weren't shooting because of the problem with no snow in Cut Bank.

What's easy to forget about The Thing *is the fact that it's funny as often as it's scary—if not* more *often.*
Oh, yeah! Well, that was Hawks. You look at *Bringing Up Baby* [1938] and *His*

Girl Friday [1940] and *Ball of Fire* [1941] and all of those, those are funny, funny films. It was so odd that he was such a stern man because he must have had a great sense of humor. But he certainly never showed it!

When you saw The Thing *for the first time, what were your impressions?*
I first saw it at some theater in Los Angeles, in a preview. I thought it was *great*. Russ Harlan, of course, did the photography—he was on *lots* of Howard Hawks pictures. A brilliant cinematographer. And down-to-earth and funny, very amusing, easy to get along with. He and Bill Neff the gaffer, they, and *all* of Hawks' crew, were just easy ... quiet. As I mentioned already, there was never any yelling on the set, there was never any tension. Everything was just as easygoing as you could imagine a film set to be.

Did you ever see the 1982 remake of The Thing?
No. I was—[*laughs*]—I was warned against it!

*One of your subsequent Hawks movies had a comedic science fiction plot—*Monkey Business *[1952].*
I really didn't do anything in it. I had one little scene, again as a mechanic, and that was kind of fun because Marilyn Monroe was in it and she was a darling.

Hold That Line *[1952] was another sci-fi comedy. Were the Bowery Boys "characters," or just a pain in the ass to work with?*
Oh, no, they were fine. Well, *Huntz* [Hall] was a good actor—Huntz was really *quite* a good actor. Gorcey was just exactly like he is on film. Sort of a bad version of Mickey Rooney!

You mentioned wanting to be a classical actor during your Royal Academy days. What type of roles did you hope to play in Hollywood?
I just wanted to make a living. When I went into the business, I was a very ordinary-looking, rather chunky young man. With a lot of energy, but ... not an awful lot to recommend me as far as being physically prepossessing. Even being *ugly* would have made it easier [*laughs*]! And I figured, if I could just make a *living*, I would be content. Of course, it doesn't work *out* that way: Once you start making a living, you start wanting to do better work.

At some point in the late '50s or early '60s, you moved back to England and began working there again.
It was in 1960 or '61 and I was *thoroughly* fed up with the kind of work I was doing. I had a part in *Giant* [1956] that was good, there were occasionally some good roles, but for the most part I was pretty much an elderly juvenile. And I felt that I needed to make a complete change from what I was doing. My wife Jennifer and I, we sold our house in the Valley and went over to England with our kids—my daughter Christie, who was about eight, and my son David, who was about six. This time I didn't have a problem getting a work permit, my wife being English—she was born in England, she's Alan Napier's daughter.

Nichols has little memory of his other SF role: Helping Rex Reason (left) build the Interociter in Universal's *This Island Earth*, starring Jeff Morrow (on view screen).

You worked in occasional films, and also on the stage.

That's right, I started working in the theater in London—I did the girl's father in *Bye Bye Birdie*, I did Bratt in *How to Succeed in Business Without Really Trying* and several other parts. And a *lot* of good film work. We were there for five years. But then I came *back* [to the U.S.] ... we felt it was time to come home. I realized that, much as I loved living in England, that I would always be a foreigner. And my wife is more American than *I* am [*laughs*], so *she* wanted to get back too! And we felt that the kids would eventually be living here, and so they should be exposed to American schools and what have you. So we went back to Hollywood and it was a major mistake, because all the work that I had done in London, in the theater and in films, meant ab-so-lute-ly nothing. I began doing more work in the theater [in Hollywood] than anything, and also directing in the theater. Then, when my kids grew up, when my daughter got married and my son was going to UCLA on a volleyball scholarship, my wife and I decided to go to New York and see what would happen. And it was a *wonderful* move. I started working almost immediately, and my wife got into wardrobe supervision and she became the top wardrobe supervisor in New York, she did *Tootsie* [1982] and *Saturday Night Fever* [1977] and lots of films. It was a good move ... a *very* good move. I only did theater—I can say that

Nichols in his last stage role to date, as the grandfather in *Ragtime*.

You still working?

I had an interview just last week [March 2002] in Los Angeles, I still have an agent working there, and I didn't get it. Oh! *this* was a little hair-raising: While I was doing *Ragtime* in Los Angeles, my agent sent me out on an interview for a part in something, I don't know what, a line or two. The casting director, who was all of 22 years old, said to me, "Have you ever been in any films?" I said, "Yes, I've done over 60 films. And over a hundred television films." She said, "Well, is there anything that *I* might have seen?" and I said, "Well, I would *hope* so. I did four films for Howard Hawks." She said, "*Who*??"

And I thought, "Oh, the hell with

my film career came to a grinding halt in 1973 [*laughs*]! I did some good stuff in New York and a *lot* of regional theater.

This interview would have happened a lot sooner if I could only have found *you—you've been "on the road" a lot* lately.

The last ten years I've been *mainly* on the road. I went out for a year with Mickey Rooney in *A Funny Thing Happened on the Way to the Forum*, for my sins. (He's hell to work with!) Then I played opposite Mitzi Gaynor in *Anything Goes* for almost a year, that was just delightful; and I spent two years in *Ragtime*, playing the grandfather, which was lots of fun. I did it Los Angeles and Chicago. It's been an interesting career.

Robert Nichols today.

it…" I just don't want to *know* those kind of people. I mean, Hawks was *so* brilliant, and had such a great eye for films, and could do *any*thing, comedy or action or what have you. A casting director not knowing who that man was is just … it's just *insulting*.

You meet somebody for the first time and he shows a lot of interest in your movie acting career and he asks, "Let me borrow one of your movies." Which one do you give him?

I would say *Giant*. I think it was the best film I ever did, and I liked my part in it. I played Pinky, Jane Withers' husband—she and I were the best friends and next-door neighbors of Rock Hudson and Liz Taylor. I was all the way through that film. I can't say that I did anything particularly *brilliant* in it [*laughs*], but it was a damn good film.

How often do you watch a movie of yours?

Hardly ever. There are one or two that I might be interested in seeing.

Is The Thing *one of 'em?*

I *have* a copy of *The Thing*, actually. And I will probably watch it again … in another year or two!

Ted Post on Bela Lugosi

> *The Lions Club wanted to honor Bela at a luncheon ...*
> *and they had him get up and make a speech. Off the cuff.*
> *Well ... he knocked everybody for a loop. He was so brilliant,*
> *so funny, so satirical, so insightful ... everybody was*
> *in tears with laughter. I never forgot that.*

Inextricably linked with the character of Count Dracula, Bela Lugosi played the role just twice in feature films on the silver screen (*Dracula* [1931] and *Abbott and Costello Meet Frankenstein* [1948]). But he portrayed the venerable vampire first, and far most frequently, on the stage, beginning with the star-making 1927 Broadway production. This was followed by tours and also by small-scale presentations in summer stock theaters, vaudeville houses—even Army camps.

Lugosi may have had his final stateside "turn" as the Count in 1948, in a production of *Dracula* at Connecticut's Norwich Summer Theatre; the 65-year-old actor headed a cast which included Richard Kiley as Jonathan Harker and Simon Oakland as Van Helsing. (Also in attendance: A nurse with smelling salts, a lobby skeleton and black-hooded ghouls ushering nervous patrons to their seats!) Supervising the production, and now here to paint a word-picture of Lugosi as he limned one of his final vampire portrayals: the show's director Ted Post.

Born March 31, 1918, Post cut his show business teeth on the stage in his native New York, directing children's programs at community centers. After making a name for himself via years of outstanding theater work, Post segued into the adventurous arena of early television. He has since directed countless segments of top TV series (*Gunsmoke, Perry Mason, Twilight Zone, Columbo*, many more) and feature films ranging from Clint Eastwood's *Hang 'em High* and *Magnum Force* to *Beneath the Planet of the Apes* and *Go Tell the Spartans*. Returning to his theater roots, Post recently directed the 2001-02 Festival of the Arts at Bel-Air's University of Judaism.

How many years had you been directing for the stage when Dracula *came along?*

I started thinking seriously about becoming involved in the theater in 1938 or '39. My friend Alan Manson and I were ushering at the Loew's Pitkin Theater in Brooklyn on weekends, to make money for our schoolbooks and so on. Alan would get up on the stage at midnight, after the audience had left, and he would do monologues, soliloquies from Shakespeare. Not yet being involved in theater, or even *thinking* of ever becoming part of it, I was kind of stunned by his comfort, his ease, his way of doing something that seemed to convey so clearly the character, whether it was Hamlet or Richard III or Henry. He was beyond belief, I was kind of stunned that he had this kind of ability. I said to him, "Are you an actor?"—I'd just met him—and he said yeah. I asked, "Where do you act?" He said, "When I can get a job, in summer stock." I said, "Wall Street? Stock in Wall Street?" [*Laughs*] He said, "No, no, no. Summer stock is theater activity during the summer in various different towns. For eight, ten, twelve weeks, they do one play a week. Usually I'm involved with one of those companies."

And that was the point at which you began to get interested.

I'll tell you how interested I was: While I was ushering, I would get so fascinated with what I was looking at on the movie screen, sometimes I'd forget to take the people down to their seats. I'd stop in the aisles and get caught up with what was going on on-screen!

I later joined the Hebrew Educational Society in Brownsville, a group looking to fill a part called "Dr. Karlsen" in [the play] *Professor Mamlock*. I read and I got the role. Not that I was that good—I was awful!—but they needed someone. After I'd done some acting, I decided I wanted to really learn a lot about the world of show biz and I went to Tamara Daykarhanova, who was formerly an actress with the Moscow Art Theater. She'd come to the States with the Moscow Art Theater, she and Stanislavsky, she decided to stay and she formed an actors' workshop. I read for her and she said, "My God, you have to learn quite a bit." [*Laughs*] But she said I had *some* kind of charisma, and she said she'd take a chance on me. So I got an acting scholarship and I worked on learning what the *actors'* problems were, so I could understand the actors' language.

My first professional summer theater experience was at Cedarhurst, Long Island, where I directed ten plays in ten weeks starting with *Claudia*. In 1946, after I came back from the Army, I had my second summer job, which was in Clinton, New Jersey. I had Olive Deering and Annie Jackson and Beatrice Blau—very wonderful people—in this particular acting group. The results were unbelievable, the reviews were unbelievable. That's how my career began, because of the quality work that I did in a very short time, in four, five days. Sometimes in two, three days!

In '47 I directed at Yardley, Pennsylvania, and then Herb Kneeter, who was the producer at the Norwich Summer Theatre, called me up and asked me whether I'd come in and direct in '48. The first thing we did there was *The Glass Menagerie*. I had as my star Susan Peters, who was once under contract to Metro, but who was now in a wheelchair, permanently paralyzed from the waist down, because she had shot herself accidentally a few years earlier. We got great reviews.

When Bela Lugosi came in to do Dracula, *where did you meet him for the first time?*

He came to the theater, he and his wife Lillian, and I met him and we sat down and talked. There seemed to be a strain there, and his wife was more talkative than he, evidently trying to be very helpful and to "un-strain" him, because he was tense.

Before I go into that, let me say this: My initial feeling about meeting Lugosi was that I was going to get even with him, because when I first saw the film *Dracula*, he scared me so badly that for many years I had to sleep with the light on! I kept hearing him say "I am ... *Drac*-u-la," and his walking toward me awakened all those dark feelings. I explained this to him, I told him he had scared the hell out of me [in *Dracula*], and he said, "I did?" I said, "Yes, you did! It was a very frightening performance. And now I wish to make sure that, when we do it in this theater, that you have the same effect on people coming to this theater to see the show. Let's make it happen." He said, "We will, we will..."

Telling him how much Dracula *scared you—did that help "un-strain" him and break the ice?*

Yes, it did, it broke the ice a little bit with him. He laughed, and he said, "I was that good, was I?" I said, "You were *better* than 'that good.'" In the movie theater showing *Dracula*, I saw other people reacting with great fear. They made sounds [*Post gasps and moans*], and they'd turn their heads away or put their faces in their hands and not look. And I was one of them [*laughs*]! Seeing *Dracula* turned me off horror films until I got back from the War.

Now you began rehearsing the play, with Lugosi and the rest of the players?

Yes, for a few days in the daytime, because at nighttime we had another show going.

The process was that you'd do a play at night, and rehearse the next week's play in the daytime...?

That's exactly what summer stock was about. It took about five days to get shows on their feet. I found Bela to be always interested ... always listening to what I was saying ... always telling me that he understood my suggestions and direction. But then, after he said he understood, never *ever* doing what I hoped that he understood.

What was your direction?

To pick up tempo and pick up pace a little bit. He was sort of slow, and I assumed it was because he was rehearsing something that had been "needlepointed" into his career, and that he wasn't going to fully demonstrate what he was going to do until opening night. He just walked through it in rehearsals, kind of casually.

Before we go any further—who picked the plays for the Norwich Summer Theatre, and what was your reaction when it was decided to make Dracula *one of the plays?*

Herb Kneeter could have picked them—we worked *with* Kneeter on picking some of the plays. As for the choice of *Dracula* ... well, first of all, it made me nervous a little bit just to deal with the guy [Lugosi] who scared the hell out of me. But I met him and, it turns out, I loved him. He was a very nice man, very quiet man. He told me, "Listen, I played leading roles in theater in Europe. *I was a leading man.* To come to Hollywood and get stuck in this one part [Count Dracula] has been the bane of my existence." He said he wanted to change and do other kinds of roles. And on one occasion he did: In *Ninotchka* [1939] with Greta Garbo, he played a Russian commissar and he did that beautifully. He played a strong commissar, a believer in what he had to do, which was fall in line with the Communist beliefs, etc. He was a *very* good actor, a highly intelligent actor, and he proved it by just that one role with Greta Garbo which he did brilliantly, I thought it was wonderful. We had little chats like that. Not too many—just little ones.

When he talked to you about his Hollywood typecasting, was he matter-of-fact about it, or unhappy, or worked up, or...?

He was *not* happy about it, but he was ... ironic. Ironically biting about it. He had a bite to his humor. One other thing I remember, and which startled the hell out of me, was when the Lions Club in (I think) Norwich wanted to honor Bela at a luncheon. Someone from the Lions Club asked me to ask Bela whether he would like to be honored, would he like to sit with them and have a meal with them and take a nice, healthy slap on the back. Bela said yes to me, so I called the people back and I said, yes, he'll have lunch. They asked, "You coming too?" "If you want me, yeah." So we sat at the head table, on the stage, kind-of, and they had him get up and make a speech. Off the cuff.

Well ... he knocked *every*body for a loop. He was *so* brilliant, *so* funny, *so* satirical, *so* insightful. He spoke so beautifully, and in such a funny, comical, ironic way, that everybody was in tears with laughter. I never forgot that. I didn't realize that he had this kind of insight or this kind of information or this kind of knowledge, and the ability to present it a very funny, satirical, ironic light.

What was he speaking about? His career? The world at large?

He had a full, rich knowledge of current events and history, and the film and theatrical profession, and he spoke about his career and about Hollywood. I wish I'd had a recording machine and been able to capture that speech. He got such huge applause at the end, they wouldn't let him go—and we had to go back to rehearsal! The applause was so prolonged I had a hard time getting him back to rehearsal.

How many people were at that luncheon?

Oh, it was packed.

Once Dracula *opened, did he pick up the pace the way you kept asking him to?*

On opening night, before the curtain went up, I asked him again to pick up the tempo a bit, I said, "It will help make the moments a little more exciting, a little more vibrant, just by doing that." He said, "I'll do it, Ted." And then he did it *slower.* I went backstage after the first act and I told him, "Bela, please, it's gotten slower." He said, "I thought I *picked up* the tempo." I said, "No, Bela, it went slower.

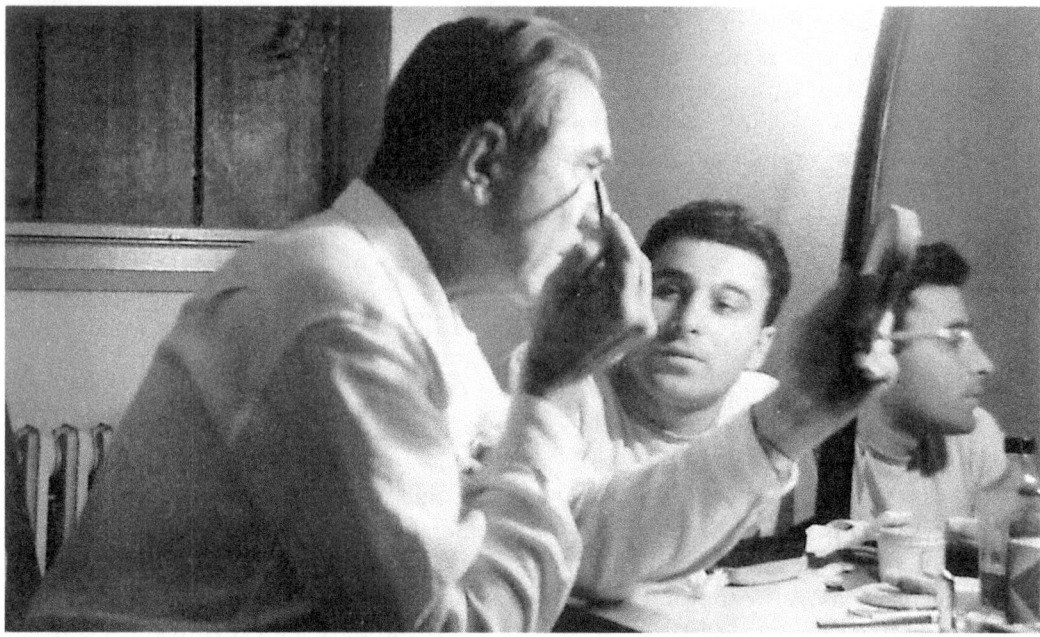

Ted Post (watching Bela Lugosi apply his Dracula makeup) first saw the actor in the 1931 movie *Dracula*—which scared him so badly, he began sleeping with the lights on.

And what's happening is, the scenes are flattening out. They're becoming less interesting by doing it with that slow pace." He said, "I'll pick it up in the second act." So he went back on stage, and it was *even slower*, the second act. Afterwards, I went back again to his dressing room—and his wife was there, putting a needle into his arm.

Which you assumed was...

I thought it was heroin. So he was taking a lot of drugs, and I didn't know it. I opened the door, into his dressing room, and there she was, his wife, doing that. He was not shocked by my entrance, and neither was she. I guess they assumed that everybody knew this about them. I said, "I'll come back later"—but I didn't. I didn't talk to him again that night, after seeing that. After seeing what I saw, I knew I was wasting my breath. I knew that any direction given to him would fall on deaf ears.

Years later, Peter Lorre played one of the leading roles in an episode of *Rawhide* that I was directing ["Incident of the Slavemaster," 1960]. One day he came over to me and said he wasn't feeling well, that he had a huge headache and didn't feel as if he could do the scene.

I said, "I'll jump to another scene while you rest up a bit, and we'll see whether you feel better." He said, "No, no. I'll tell you what I'll do ... give me a few minutes, and I'll be all right." "Okay," I said, "take whatever you need." He came back about ten to fifteen minutes later and said, "I feel better."

Then, the next day, the same thing happened again. So I got suspicious. And when he said, "I'll be back in ten minutes," I followed him. He had drugs—he took a shot of heroin, or coke, or whatever it was he used. Then he vomited. I was watching him. Then I rushed back to work, and a few minutes later he came back and he said, "I feel better now" and he did the scene! He was another great talent—as probably Bela was, a terrific talent.

You mentioned earlier that your career got off to a good start because of your quality work in these quickly done shows. What was the secret of your success with them?
Knowing what I had to do in order to communicate my ideas to the actors, to get what I needed. I never let anything happen on the stage that was unmotivated. It was all clearly spelled out. One thought ignited another, and it looked real, and there was energy and there was rhythm and there was timing—all those things that you don't see in summer theater. Usually you see very ragged performances. I never allowed that. I always motivated and justified it for them. That's how I built my reputation, through summer theater. A *lot* of summer theater.

Did you ever do that for Lugosi—give him motivation and justification to pick up the tempo?
If I'm remembering right, I gave him a direction which said, "You're on a deadline. You can't wait for the sun to rise, you've got to accomplish *all* your mission within these few hours. I think you should be consciously aware of that so that, as a *result* of that, there'll be more energy injected into the scene and into the character. That will make the scene vibrate a little more, in a more theatrical, interesting way." He said he understood me—but he didn't do it...

And the other actors?
When I told Dick Kiley or Si Oakland or [leading lady] Shirley O'Hara, they picked up tempo. Period. There was no hemming and hawing about that. With Bela, he *thought* he did it. But he was so heavily in drugs that he wasn't able to evaluate for himself that he was *not* picking up tempo.

What are some of your memories of Kiley and Oakland?
Richard Kiley was my discovery. I was directing *The Corn Is Green* for Equity Library in New York and he came late, after all the parts were taken. When he came in and asked, "Anything available?" I said, "Nothing. What do you do?" He said, "I can sing and I can act." Then he sang a few bars, and he stunned me. I said, "I'll put you in the chorus." I worked with him in the chorus, and he seemed like somebody worth knowing and worth dealing with. Later I asked him, "Would you like to join me in summer repertory at Norwich Summer Theatre, as my leading man?" And that's when Richard Kiley became my leading man—he did ten weeks worth of work there, and he brought his wife and children.
Si Oakland was another one who I loved very much. I saw him in something somewhere, he read for me and I said, "My God, I want you to be part of it." So he became part of my summer resident company there, with Shirley O'Hara. Shirley was a dark-haired, beautiful girl, and a very wonderful actress to boot. She was a girl who always looked younger than her age. She may have been 40 [in *Dracula*],

The Count never drank ... wine, but the cigar was omnipresent when Lugosi played the role! Bela in a legit *Dracula* production.

but she looked 25. Shirley was also a critic, a writer for *The Nation*. Very bright. Anyway, I had a great, wonderful little company there.

How did these other actors get along with Lugosi?
There were no conflicts at all. Except occasionally you may have heard a mumble, someone saying, "I wish he'd pick up his cue." They wished Bela would move a little faster, in other words. I would hear that. And, had he done that, it would have helped the show quite a bit. But he was not at that moment capable of doing that … or even capable of *knowing* that he was not capable of doing it. He assumed he *was* capable of doing it. Which tells me he was a bit heavily into things [drugs] that prevented him from really recognizing that he was not fulfilling the concept of pace.

So your fondest memory of him is from the Lions Club luncheon.
He *loved* that, he loved the idea that he would attend an affair like that and be their principal speaker. It was a different Bela Lugosi that afternoon, a Bela Lugosi I did not see in the theater, while we were working together. In the theater, I saw a very serious guy who came to work and looked at what it was that you were trying to do with the particular show, or a particular scene, etc. And I gathered that he was analyzing his co-workers, to see whether they (or I) were up to snuff, whether you knew what you were talking about or didn't know what you were talking about. He never said anything actually negative to me. He seemed to assume that what I was doing [would] work, and there was never any kind of a question that he asked me.

Where did Lugosi stay while he was working there with you?
I don't know which particular place he stayed at. *We* stayed at Mrs. Caulfield's—she had a home where she rented out rooms. I know Bela wasn't there—he and I would have been a little more intimate, socially, if he had. He was at some other place that Herb Kneeter arranged for him.

In one Lugosi biography, the author claims that Bela stayed in a hotel—and got some local publicity by having a coffin brought up to his room and sleeping in it.
Nothing like that *ever* happened. I would have heard of that. And Kneeter would have had a fit.

And his wife, Lillian?
He was very jealous of Lillian, I think. She was very worried about forming *any* kind of a relationship with a man. She was not a very giving person—the reason being, she was a little bit frightened of *him*, thinking that, if she gave you a little more attention than she should have, that he would be suspicious that perhaps there was something else going on. I had a strange feeling that she kept away from other men in his presence.

How popular was your production of Dracula*?*
We didn't have packed houses. We usually had a half a house, something like that.

Was that about average for a play at Norwich?

It was dependent on the play and the people, etc., and the interest the public had in that particular play. Sometimes we'd have a packed house, sometimes we'd have a half a house. It depended on what they wanted to see at that time. With *Dracula*, about a half a house, or three-quarters. But sometimes even less than a half.

And what were your feelings about it after it ended its run? Did you feel it was successful "artistically," or—

No, I did not. I did not feel that I had what I wanted from Bela. Bela to me was basically the problem. Not Richard Kiley or Si Oakland or any of the other members of the cast. Si was brilliant in *Dracula*. Si was *always* brilliant. Si and Richard were my pride and joy—and so was Shirley O'Hara. They were all terrific performers. And they had a lot of pressure to do a lot of work in five days—to put on a two-act play or a three-act play in five days, with a lot of "sides" to it. I envied them, I envied them that they had the kind of brains that could *do* that! But Richard Kiley, after the seventh week at Norwich that summer, suddenly found himself spouting lines from the *first* week [*laughs*]! He got lost and carried away, and he didn't even know he was saying lines from other weeks! He said to me, "I think I'm overworked," and I told him to take a week off, to get his brains settled!

Jonathan Harker is a pretty thankless role. Was Kiley able to do anything *with it?*

Yes. Richard Kiley was a very imaginative actor. He was somebody who would take a role and make choices that would bring more life to the character, give it more vibrancy and more energy. He'd come up with thoughts and ideas that would make it unique. Richard and Si liked to give "twists" to the character that would lend another aspect to it, an aspect that was not thought of by the playwright.

The actor who played Van Helsing in the 1931 Dracula *movie was just as slow-tempoed as Lugosi was. Did Oakland make something out of it?*

Always. The vitality came from my resident company. We pumped up the energy with the Oaklands, with the Kileys, with the O'Haras and a few others who were there. I had them move as though there was always the threat of something, like the Sword of Damocles was over the heads of everyone and they had to do something about it. It gave it a rhythmical thrust of urgency.

How long were you at the Norwich Summer Theatre?

I went there from '48 up to '50. But in '50, I got into a hassle with Kneeter. I was directing Eve Arden in some play, I finished with her and then I got into a hassle with Kneeter. He did some really terrible things, and I felt that he was hurting not only the theater, he was hurting practically everybody *involved* with the theater. So I quit. I took my wife and child back with me to New York.

Your lasting impressions of Bela Lugosi? When you think back on him today, what's the first thing that enters your mind?

I think of him as a man who should have had better opportunities, who should

```
┌─────────────────────────────────────────────────────┐
│      NORWICH SUMMER THEATRE                          │
│           MASONIC TEMPLE                             │
│   CONNECTICUT'S MOST BEAUTIFUL AIR-COOLED THEATRE    │
│   Eves 8:30    376 — Tel. Norwich — 623   Sat. Mat. 2:30 │
│   TONIGHT AND FOR ENTIRE WEEK, H. L. KNEETER Presents│
│          THE GREAT MASTER OF HORROR                  │
│          BELA LUGOSI in "DRACULA"                    │
│              SPINE   CHILLING                        │
│   ┌───────────────────────────────────────────────┐  │
│   │ NEW PRICE POLICY!  BARGAIN SAT. MAT. 2:30     │  │
│   │ ENTIRE  BALCONY  ............. $1.00 and tax  │  │
│   │ ENTIRE  ORCHESTRA and LOGE .... $1.50 and tax │  │
│   │ FREE REFRESHMENTS WILL BE SERVED BY THE CAST AFTER │ │
│   │     THE MATINEE.  EVERYBODY WELCOME!          │  │
│   └───────────────────────────────────────────────┘  │
│          BEGINNING MONDAY, AUGUST 9th                │
│   Janet Blair-Francis Lederer in 'For Love or Money' │
│          Direct From One Year on Broadway            │
│   Mail or Phone Reservations Accepted at Box Office or on Sale at │
│                  MARA'S DRUG STORE                   │
└─────────────────────────────────────────────────────┘
```

An August 6, 1948, newspaper ad for the Post-directed stage production of *Dracula*, perhaps Lugosi's final U.S. appearance as the Count. Notice that Francis Lederer, the first actor to succeed Lugosi as Dracula in an American movie (*The Return of Dracula*, 1958), *also* succeeded him at the Norwich Summer Theatre.

have been allowed [by Hollywood] to play the kinds of roles he played before he came to America. He was a Hungarian leading man. He should have been given more opportunities to play *other* kinds of roles. But that was something he had a tough time convincing the Hollywood moguls to do—and which they did *not* do. He was not in any way encouraged by the people he worked for in Hollywood. They didn't give him any opportunities, except maybe the wonderful director who did *Ninotchka*, Ernst Lubitsch. Lubitsch was the one who gave him the opportunity to do something else besides an ogre. So Bela found himself doing horror pictures, even doing some of the Frankenstein pictures—he found himself doing all these particular studies which were rooted in the same thing that built his reputation, which was Dracula.

For some reason, people seemed to cotton to that type of character. To this day! Horror pictures are big, big commercial box office hits, they make millions and millions of dollars. It stuns me to find that audiences throughout the country, and even the world for that matter, dig this type of material. They understand it and they like it. I can understand it when it's done brilliantly. I like when things are done with a great deal of subtlety. But when you have a guy coming at you with a chainsaw ... that's not so subtle [*laughs*]!

Lugosi had a very subtle way of playing his character. One thing he did do, which I liked very much about him, even though he was slow: He did Dracula as a romantic. A man in love. *That's* what made it palatable. *That's* what made him viable. Sometimes Dracula would make a remark and suddenly you saw another side to the man, you felt like the man really wanted to be human again, but it was a hopeless dream. He could never be human again. Bela gave it that kind of a twist, you could tell that he wished he could come back to life again and be normal and *live* a life of love and all of the other things that were denied him as a corpse.

All in all, in an odd sort of way, [working with Lugosi] was a rich and multi-colored experience, and one that I treasure.

William Self

> *We had a clichéd statement in our [TV series] development meetings, we'd say, "There are some shows that you can sell and can't make, and there are others you can make and can't sell." Science fiction gets you very close to the ones you can sell but can't make.*

Most frightening scene in a 1950s SF movie? Among several worthy nominees, one sequence does stand out as the chilliest: The movie is Howard Hawks' *The Thing from Another World* (1951), the setting is a North Pole government experimental station, and the scene features a young Air Force corporal with his back to the block of ice in which a newly arrived alien visitor is encased. The audience—but not the serviceman—knows that the ice is melting. Dimitri Tiomkin's theremin score turns ultra-ominous as a long shadow slowly begins to move up the corporal's back...

The actor menaced by the Thing in this unforgettable scene was Dayton-born William Self, here appearing in his best film role as Barnes, one of five corpsmen (Kenneth Tobey, James Young, Dewey Martin and Robert Nichols were the others) engaged in a top-of-the-world struggle for survival with the extra-terrestrial terror (James Arness). Self soon moved up through the Hollywood ranks: He started working in television production the year after *The Thing*'s release, and became the executive vice-president of 20th Century-Fox Television in the 1960s. His list of small-screen credits includes the classics *Peyton Place*, *M*A*S*H* and *Batman* and the Irwin Allen series *Voyage to the Bottom of the Sea*, *Lost in Space* and *The Time Tunnel*.

How did you land your first movie role?

I graduated from the University of Chicago in 1943 and worked in Chicago at an advertising agency for a brief period. Then I decided to try to be an actor ... and I came out here saying I *was* an actor. The first movie I got into, Bill Wellman shot a test of me and put me in a picture called *The Story of G.I. Joe* [1945] with Robert Mitchum and Burgess Meredith. That was the beginning. Then, somewhere along the line, I worked for Howard Hawks for the first time in *Red River* [1948], and eventually I was in four Hawks pictures—*Red River*, *I Was a Male War Bride*

[1949] and *The Thing* [1951]. I was also in *The Big Sky* [1952] but I was cut out of that.

I found a book that said you taught tennis to the sons of Howard Hawks.
No, but I did teach tennis around Hollywood to quite a few people. Charlie Chaplin I played with a great deal ... Tracy and Hepburn ... I was one of the guys who, on Sundays, went to Jack Warner's house, right at the edge of Beverly Hills, and played with those people. A lot of my jobs were as a result of tennis, but not *Red River* and not my association with Hawks. That was purely a professional meeting. My agent at that time got me a meeting with Hawks for *Red River*. Hawks said "Fine" and I never knew whether I had the job or not—I never got a copy of the script, weeks went by, I didn't know where I stood. But eventually they called me and said, "Okay, you can fly to Arizona and start your role in *Red River*." That was the first time I worked for Hawks, and he obviously liked me—he hired me three times additionally. I never understood, honestly, *why*, but there was a story that I believe is true: Someone once asked Hawks, in an interview, "Who is your favorite actor?" He said, "I don't know. It's either Cary Grant or Bill Self." [*Laughs*] Whether that's a totally true story or not, I don't know—I like to believe it. And, many years later, a little incident happened when he and Paul Helmick were casting some new picture. Helmick was his assistant director-production manager-closest ally. In this casting meeting, Hawks said to Helmick, "You know who'd be good in this part? Bill Self." And Helmick said, "Mr. Hawks, Bill Self is president of 20th Century-Fox Television." Hawks said, "*I* didn't know that...!" [*Laughs*] He'd obviously just lost track of me, and didn't know what I was doing. But he remembered me, and apparently he liked me.

What was he like to work for? What kind of director was he?
He was certainly one of the best directors I ever worked for, and I worked for Bill Wellman and Billy Wilder and Charlie Chaplin. But he was unique. He was a very reserved person, very soft-spoken—he was always "Mr. Hawks" to all of us lowly actors. And he would always take a certain amount of time to answer your questions. If you'd ask him something, he would *think* about it, deliberately, right in front of you, and then finally give you an answer. I think he was terrific, and I enjoyed working with him an awful lot.

Looking over Hawks' list of credits, it seems so unlike him to make a monster movie. Any clue what drew him to The Thing?
The story that I heard was that Hawks envisioned it as a big-budget picture, and he was going to do it with major stars. But RKO would not approve the budget, at which point Hawks said, "Okay, I'll make it with all unknowns. And I won't put my name on it as director"—because he didn't wanna cut his salary and he didn't want to be associated with what was looked upon initially as kind of a B movie. So that's how that all came about, according to what I *heard*—I don't know if it's true or not. What had intrigued him to do it in the first place, I don't really know.

But you do remember a rumor that he wanted to do it as a big picture with big stars.

Yes. Hawks never told me that, but that was the story that was around—I think pretty much between the members of the cast, who were a little surprised that they got the *jobs* they did.

In your opinion, would The Thing *have been better, as good or worse with major stars in it?*

Oh, I think it would have been worse. Part of the appeal of the picture is that we were almost real people to a lot of audiences. Had Cary Grant been in charge, it wouldn't have worked. This was like a whole bunch of regular guys and a girl you'd never seen before, having this adventure. I think it was enhanced by that. I also think that it was enhanced by being in black-and-white. The remake [*The Thing* with Kurt Russell, 1982] was in color, and I thought it was not nearly as good as the original.

And not just because it was in color—it just wasn't a good movie.

No, no. In the first place, the violence in the original *Thing* was almost all off-screen. Close to the *only* violent action was the monster at the door [having the door slammed on its arm], and the monster chasing *me* down the hall. But that really wasn't violence, because he never caught me [*laughs*]. None of the original cast was killed in the movie. Those people who *were* killed, you didn't even know who they were.

They were just names. We never saw actors in those roles.

I think it was the absence of blood and violence that made it unique and very scary.

There isn't even a castlist at the beginning of the movie.

That's true, none of us got any billing up front. I think the whole thing was designed to "sneak up on you," in a way.

The combination of lengthy takes and overlapping dialogue sounds like a recipe for disaster to me. How were the actors able to cope?

We all were encouraged to overlap the dialogue. We had rehearsals before each scene, and maybe in some cases we were told, "Wait a minute—I don't *want* it overlapped *there*." But we were sort of encouraged to make it sound as much like a normal conversation as possible. And Hawks was not a stickler for saying the words exactly as written. I know in my hysterical scene, after I came flying down the hall to tell everybody the Thing was loose, I'm not sure I said the exact right words out of the script. I *have* worked with directors who don't change a word. Hawks was *not* that. If you said it, if it seemed natural, if it made the point, he let it stand. You had to say what was *meant* to be said, but you didn't have to do it word by word. That was true of him every time I worked with him. We all knew that was what Hawks wanted, and so we all just kind of pitched in and did it. Not being *absolutely* held to the script permitted us to have some flexibility in what we said. It was a deliberate style, it was no accident.

It's a requirement, I have to ask this question: Who directed The Thing?

The controversy of who directed *The Thing* is interesting. Chris Nyby [who gets screen credit as director] generally ran the rehearsal, and Hawks stood on the sidelines with his arms folded and watched and listened. Then Chris would go over to Howard and they would have their private conversation, and Chris would come back and talk to *us*. A lot of things would stand, but about others things he would say, "Well, let's try this" or "Let's try that" or "Why don't you come in *here* instead of *there*?" Hawks was directing the picture from the sidelines. In my hysterical scene, I was overboard the first time I did it. Hawks said, "Look, Bill, you're too 'high' when you begin, you have no place to go. You gotta tone it down and we'll 'build'…" That was one of the few times that I felt Hawks really directed me. The other times, it would be Hawks talking to Nyby talking to the cast.

When Howard Hawks was alive, Nyby would talk about The Thing *very humbly—"Hawks let me direct a shot here and there." Then, after Hawks passed away, Nyby took more and more of the credit.*

I didn't see any of that. I felt that Hawks was always pretty generous to Chris: When Hawks was asked who directed it, he said, "Chris Nyby directed *The Thing*." Chris was a very nice man. He may have taken a little more credit than he deserves [*laughs*], but it would surprise me if he really claimed he directed the picture independently of Hawks.

Hawks made The Thing *for Winchester Pictures, his own independent company.*

Ed Lasker was part of the Lasker family that was very big in advertising. Hawks needed a financial partner, especially at the development stage of projects, and he formed Winchester Pictures in association with Ed Lasker. Lasker was basically some of the money, maybe *all* of the money, behind that operation. I don't think he had any creative input.

Margaret Sheridan, who gets top billing, had been under personal contract to Hawks since 1945, but this was her first movie.

She was a girl that, I think, Hawks really believed might become [the next] Lauren Bacall. She was *going* to go into a Hawks movie [*Red River*], but then she got pregnant and lost that opportunity. After that, her career never went anywhere to speak of. She was extremely nice, a very pretty girl—but a very inexperienced actress. I don't mean she wasn't good in *The Thing*, I thought she *was*. But it wasn't like dealing with, say, Katharine Hepburn or somebody [*laughs*]!

Robert Nichols called her "one of the guys."

She was very democratic, she just bummed around with us and sat with us and ate with us. There was nothing aloof about her.

Kenneth Tobey had only had small parts in movies prior to The Thing. *Was he "ready for prime time"?*

Ken was a very good actor, and I think he *was* "ready for prime time." Some-

Self (kneeling right) and Dewey Martin prepare to give *The Thing* a warm welcome.

thing later came between Hawks and Tobey, and I never knew what it was. We all felt that Ken was going to go from *The Thing* into *The Big Sky*—and, as you know, that didn't happen. What that was all about, I don't know. I felt Ken was very believable, a *very* good actor. And Bob Cornthwaite [Dr. Carrington] was phenomenal. He had a great memory, and he had a great ability to say those impossible lines! He just rattled them off, without any apparent problems. I think the whole cast *liked* each other. I didn't think there was anybody in the cast who didn't get along.

Ken Tobey told me that Douglas Spencer ["Scotty"] was an upstager, and he didn't care for that.

Doug Spencer came up through the ranks—he had been a stand-in for Ray Milland at Paramount for many years. I don't know whether he thought he was more important than the rest of the cast or not, I don't want to say that he *did*, but he *wasn't* as much a part of "the gang." He certainly was an old veteran compared to most of us, having been a stand-in for years.

James Young, another one of the leads, later became a TV producer just as you did.
  He, too, was a nice guy, and I'm sorry that he died a few years ago.

Dewey Martin seems to be something a recluse these days.
  I don't know why. I have had absolutely no contact with Dewey Martin. Years ago, someone had a *Thing* reunion at one of the local theaters out here, and he invited me and a few of the guys. Tried to get Dewey, but ... no luck.

When the TV series Voyage to the Bottom of the Sea *was coming together at Fox, while you were an executive there, Martin was reportedly a candidate to play Capt. Crane.*
  I don't recall. I was *at* Fox at that time and I was very much involved with *Voyage to the Bottom of the Sea*, but I don't honestly—35, 40 years later!—remember the details.

The impression I get from other Thing *veterans is that James Arness was a little embarrassed by his role, and didn't pal around with the rest of the cast.*
  No, he didn't. But, you know, with all that makeup on, I think it was a little hard to "sit around the campfire" [*laughs*]. He was really not "part of the cast," in our opinion. He was [more like] a highly paid stuntman. (I'm being a little facetious.) But I honestly think his makeup was a factor.

The Thing is barely in the movie—maybe two minutes of screen time in the whole picture—and half of the time, like when he's fighting the sled dogs or running around on fire, it's not even James Arness!
  That's correct, Jim was *not* around very much. They obviously had doubles for the fire sequence, the dog sequence and everything else. When the Thing came through that door, *that* was Arness, and walking down the hallway about to be electrocuted, *that* was Arness. But a great deal of the time, he was not there.

For the fire scene, were any of the cast involved?
  Yes and no. We were all involved setting it up, but we were all doubled—or greatly doubled—when the fire started.

The scene of you in the room with the giant ice block, and the shadow falling on you—I think it's the best scene in the movie.
  That was a scene that was very hard for me to do—the whole hysterical bit, after I see the Thing. Hawks was very, very patient with me, I must say. And I think it turned out okay.

Do you agree with me that that scene where the Thing's shadow falls on you...
  That was terrific, I thought.

Who came up behind you in that shot? I'm sure they didn't put James Arness in costume and makeup so that he could cast a shadow on you—so who was that?
  I honestly don't remember. Someone once asked me if I was really scared. I said no, I was afraid of Howard Hawks [*laughs*]!

A great deal of The Thing *was shot at the California Consumers Ice House.*
　　We went to the Ice House because Hawks wanted—absolutely the right thing to want—our breath to start showing. You couldn't do that on a soundstage. So they built the whole complex in the Ice House. Actually, most of the time, we weren't cold at all—they kept the heat up in the Ice House for most of the picture. But, for the scenes after the Thing turns off the generator, *then* the Ice House got cold, of course. *Those* were not pleasant days, but we weren't freezing or anything.

So you're saying a lot of the film was shot at the Ice House with the place not cold, your breath not showing?
　　Absolutely. All the early scenes, before the Thing turns off the generator, were shot in that same location, the Ice House, except that it wasn't functioning as an ice house. The Ice House was our principal location.

After the Ice House, the cast and crew went up to Cut Bank, Montana, to shoot snow scenes—and it didn't snow. Did you shoot anything in Cut Bank?
　　My memory is that we didn't shoot a thing. Cut Bank was picked because it's supposed to be the coldest spot in the United States and the first area to get snow. Neither happened [*laughs*]!

What was the town's reaction to being invaded by Hollywood?
　　It was very interesting. I happened to sit next to Mr. Hawks when we were flying in on a Constellation, and as we approached the little runway in Cut Bank, I said to him, "Oh, look at all the townspeople out there to greet us." He said, "They're not out to greet us, they're out to see us *crash*. This size plane has never landed at this airport before!" [*Laughs*] We got into Cut Bank and sat around and shot pool and whatever you do in a small town when there's nothing to do, and when it didn't snow, we came home. The story we heard was that the studio insisted we come back. I think Hawks would have sat it out and waited for snow, for the realism of the setting, but we *did* come back.

Kenneth Tobey told me that, while you were all up in Cut Bank killing time, the most entertaining person there was Paul Frees.
　　I knew Paul very, very well and he was a very entertaining guy. Most of his life he made his living as the Man of a Thousand Voices—he did a lot of voiceover work in cartoons and everything. He was very amusing because he could do all these different impersonations and so forth. I would say that he probably *was* our most entertaining off-the-set actor.
　　Incidentally, one day I was sitting in the lobby of the hotel in Cut Bank and Hawks came up to me and asked, "Do you bowl?" I said, "Yeah, I can bowl. I'm not a *good* bowler, but I can bowl." He said, "Let's go bowling." This was an absolute shock to me—Mr. Hawks, who I respected greatly, came up to me, a small-time actor, and said, "Let's go bowling." So we did, we bowled for *hours*. We went back to the hotel and he thanked me. That's when I asked one of the crew guys, "What was *that* all about?" and he said, "You don't *know?* His father died today." I guess Hawks just wanted to be distracted.

Thing "director" Christian Nyby (center), Self and Kenneth Tobey prepare to screen the 1982 Kurt Russell–starring remake. (Photograph courtesy Ed Magnus)

What had Hawks been hoping to shoot in Cut Bank?

He was going to shoot the flying saucer scene, he was going to shoot the exteriors using *us* going from the plane into the compound, he was going to shoot all the exteriors *around* the compound. With real snow and Eskimo dogs. But, of course, that didn't work. One amusing story that's supposed to be true was that the Eskimo dogs we had with us in Cut Bank were not brought back to Hollywood—Hollywood "stunt dogs" were hired for the North Pole scenes that were actually shot on the RKO Ranch in the San Fernando Valley, in the heat. And those Hollywood dogs wouldn't put their feet on the cold snow! At the RKO Ranch they had a great deal of artificial snow, which was okay with the dogs, but they then also had ice machines to make the more realistic snow. These dogs were Eskimo by birth but not by habitat [*laughs*], they were Hollywood dogs, and they didn't *like* that cold stuff. We had a bunch of uncooperative Eskimo dogs once we got back here! Whether that's entirely true or not, I don't really remember, but I do know we had *some* problems with the dogs.

At Cut Bank, was the compound already built and the "flying saucer" buried in ice in anticipation of shooting?

The compound was built. I really wasn't that involved with the production staff so I don't really know whether the flying saucer thing had actually been laid out or not. But there *was* a compound there.

So all the long shots of the Air Force guys trudging around the compound through the snow—

We were being doubled in all those shots—getting off the plane, coming into the compound and so on. That was all shot with doubles after the cast had returned to Hollywood.

From the cold of Cut Bank, you went to the RKO Ranch to shoot the flying saucer scene.

Where, obviously, it was not cold. And we had all the winter coats and equipment on us and everything else, so it was very, very uncomfortable. We were more uncomfortable there than we were in the Ice House! They did have some problems—we would be sweating, and the dogs wouldn't want to perform on the artificial snow, and whatever. I remember that *not* being a totally easy [shoot]. And when the flying saucer blew up, the camera followed the cloud of smoke up to the sky and the camera tilted up beyond [the top of the sky backdrop]. That's in the picture.

What memories of shooting of the final scenes, where the Thing is electrocuted?

We were all wondering how they were going to do it [shrink the Thing down to nothingness]. They used people of various sizes, a shorter double for James Arness and then a midget. I was fascinated watching them do it.

By the way, one day when we were about to finish the picture, Hawks decided to pull a gag on the makeup man, a guy named Lee Greenway. Lee had gotten lazy—he knew what he needed [for work every day], and he didn't bring anything else. Hawks called me and Lee Greenway in, and several other people, Nyby, obviously, and people like that, and he said, "We're gonna shoot an alternate ending to the picture. I want to be able to make a choice between the scene where Doug Spencer is saying 'Keep watching the skies…' [the last shot of the movie] and another ending. I want to shoot a new ending where they leave Bill Self behind up at the compound for a month or so—he's ordered to stay there in case anything comes up. And then they come back and find Bill there and he reports to them about what has happened." Hawks turned to Greenway: "I want a beard on Bill Self, to show the passage of time. Just let me know when you're ready." Well, a little while later, I went lookin' for Greenway, and I couldn't find him *any*where. I asked somebody, "Where's Lee Greenway?"

At this point, you think it's on the level.

Oh, absolutely—I wasn't in on the gag. And I was panicking, because there was Mr. Hawks sitting there waiting for me to show up with a beard, and Lee hadn't even started on me. I finally found Lee Greenway: He was in the Ice House storeroom where they kept the dead dogs and, because he didn't have any artificial hair with him, he was shaving the belly of one of these dogs to get the hair to put on me [*laughs*]! I said, "Lee, you're *not* gonna put that dead dog's hair on my face!" About that time, Hawks came along and said, "Okay, forget it...," and I found out he just wanted to teach Lee a little lesson!

You had actual dead dogs there?
Yes, for the scene where they find that the dog in the cabinet has been drained of its blood. And, I guess, for the sequence where the Thing and the dogs fight. So, yes, there was a *supply* of dead dogs there, several of them. And they had hair on 'em that almost became my beard [*laughs*]!

I'm sure you're not going to be able to answer this, but—where does a motion picture studio go for dead dogs?
Well, I *don't* know that. Hopefully these dogs died of natural causes [*laughs*]!

Do you happen to recall seeing the movie for the first time?
We were all invited by Hawks and the production company to see the movie—I've forgotten where the theater was. I was very pleased with it. In the first place, it was the biggest part I had ever played at that time in my life, and therefore it was a step-up in my career. *And* I thought it was a very good movie. *Time* magazine picked it as one of the ten best movies of the year that year.

George Clooney is talking about remaking The Thing *for TV, perhaps as a mini-series.*
They certainly would have to stretch the material to do a mini-series. One of the secrets of the success of *The Thing*, I think, is that it was a relatively short film, only 87 minutes.

You mentioned earlier that you were cut out of Hawks' The Big Sky.
On the interview, before I got the job, I asked him, "What's the part?" and he said, "We're gonna do the same thing we did in *Red River*." He said that, instead of playing a wounded cowboy, which is what I played in *Red River*, I was going to be a wounded Frenchman who comes down the river in a canoe! We did it. Then later, when I saw Hawks, he said, "Bill, too many people [seeing *The Big Sky*] remembered the scene from *Red River*. And you're out." I never saw the footage, so I don't know whether that was the real reason, or whether it wasn't any good. But, anyway, I was out.

Did you see much of Howard Hawks after you stopped acting in his pictures in the early 1950s?
I went down to see him just before he died. He was given an Honorary Oscar in 1975, and I sent him a wire saying CONGRATULATIONS MR. HAWKS. Well, he called me up and he said, "I only heard from two people. I heard from you and Betty Bacall." And then he invited my wife Peggy and me to come down to Palm Springs and have lunch with him, which we did. We had a lovely time with him, at his house. He was sitting in the living room with his leg up on a cushion of some kind—he'd either broken or sprained it riding his motorcycle! There was a housekeeper there who served us lunch, and he had his dog with him. And I once read that he later

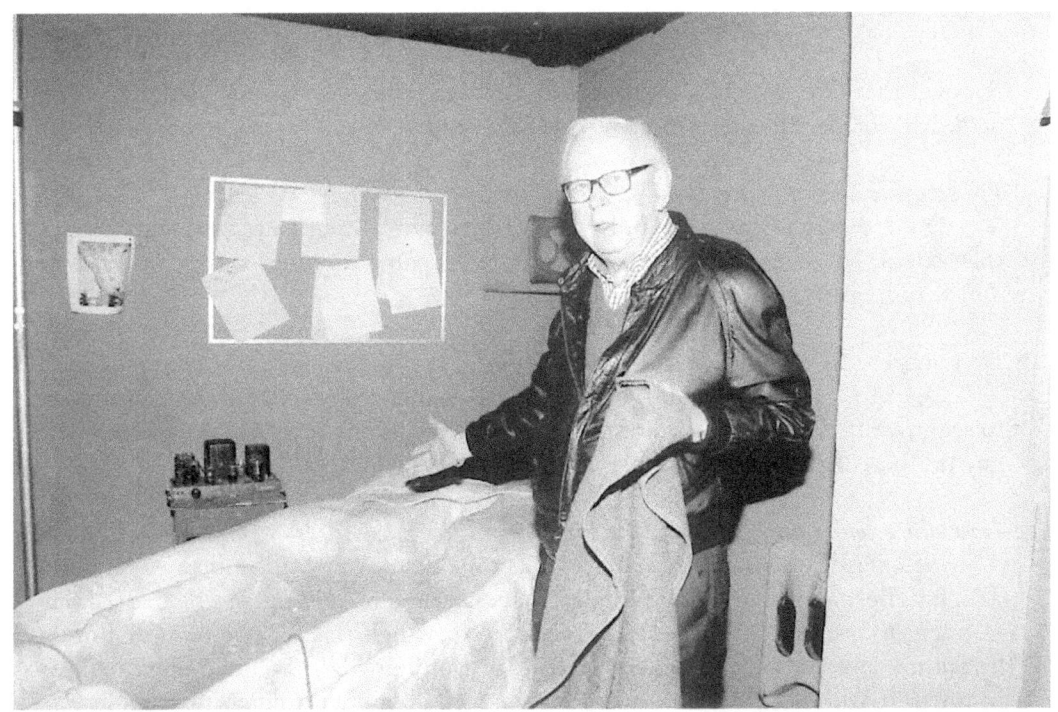

The Thing was the theme of Monster Kid Extraordinaire Bob Burns' elaborate 2002 Halloween show at his Burbank home. *Top:* Special guest Self poses on the set with electric blanket and half-melted ice block. *Bottom:* Self and Burns are menaced by the Thing (Jake Garber) himself. (Photographs courtesy Kathryn Indiek)

fell over that dog, which is what caused his final injury. Very shortly after that, he died. I liked Mr. Hawks, and he obviously liked me.

I'm happy to hear that you had that time with him at the end.
Yes, I was too. It was the only kind of "personal" thing I ever did with him to that extent. I'd never gone to his house, he never came to mine ... this was kind of a nice ending to our relationship.

Do you ever watch your old pictures today?
Once in a while I do—once in a while I turn on something and am surprised to see myself. What's very interesting is me is that I don't feel any *connection* to the guy up there. It brings back a few memories, and that's about it!

How did a young actor become a TV producer?
1952 was the last time I acted. At that time, I knew a producer named Bernard Tabakin. Bernie was going into a new business called television, and he had a commitment to produce a series called *China Smith*, which was for syndication. Bernie Tabakin knew me socially, and he said, "Bill, you know all the unemployed actors in town." I said, "Yes. I'm *one* of 'em!" [*Laughs*] He said, "I can't go through agents the normal way, I can't pay over scale." It was incredibly low-budget, I think it was $17,500 or something per episode—or was it 12.5? Anyway, Bernie said to me, "Will you help me cast that show? I will pay you $125 a week, as my assistant." I said, "You know I'm an actor, and if I get an acting job, I will have to take it." He said, "Oh, I understand that." Well, I have never acted a day since! I went to work for Bernie, worked on that show, and got a little experience.

You came on before any *of the episodes were shot?*
Yes. And I was on the series during the shooting of it. It had that *incredibly* low budget, and we shot 13 half-hour episodes in a total of 21 days.

Wow!
And Dan Duryea, who was terrific, starred in it. In *those* days, the Screen Actors Guild did not require you to wrap up a complete episode before you went on to something else. So if there was a bar scene in all 13 episodes, we would shoot all 13 episodes' bar scenes while we were in that set. That was one reason that we were able to do 'em so quickly. And Dan, to his credit, had to know the dialogue for 13 episodes, 'cause he didn't know which episode we were going to be doing first [*laughs*]! Also, we never changed his wardrobe, he wore a white suit all the way through, which everybody thought was a terrific theatrical gimmick. But it was an absolute necessity, 'cause we didn't know what episode he was in! By leaving him in a white suit all the time, we didn't have to worry about that. I remember one episode was about four minutes short, so we found some stock footage of a Chinese parade and just put it in there, and that brought it up to length. The most boring TV episode, probably, ever made [*laughs*]!

You soon had a more prestigious early TV credit in the Schlitz Playhouse of Stars.

John Gibbs [the producer of *Schlitz Playhouse of Stars*] was a combination agent and producer for the Robert Montgomery show [*Robert Montgomery Presents*] out of New York. I don't really know for a fact how he got the job as producer of the *Schlitz Playhouse of Stars* but my understanding is that Gibbs was in Milwaukee for whatever reason and met the Uihlein family, the owners of Schlitz, and the decision to go with Gibbs as the new producer of the show was made soon afterwards. *Schlitz Playhouse of Stars* was being done live out of New York, but now under Gibbs it was going to be done out here [in Hollywood], on film. My dad worked at Schlitz in Milwaukee, he was the advertising manager at that time, and my dad said to Gibbs, "My son is in the television business. Look him up and he can maybe help you get started."

Gibbs came out here, I did not know the man, and said he wanted to do the *Schlitz Playhouse of Stars* on film—this was in 1952. And, since he'd never done a film show, he felt the best thing to do would be to sublet the deal—he was talking to people like Hal Roach, Jr., and those kinds of production companies to do the *Schlitz Playhouse of Stars*. I said to Mr. Gibbs, "Y'know, if you *do* that, one year from now, *they'll* have the show and you will not. Why don't you set up your own production company? I can help you, because I know a lot of people behind the scenes..." Of course I didn't know as much as I *thought* I did, but he said, "Okay, let's see if we can do that." We started a company called Meridian Productions—Gibbs came up with the name, and he was the principal owner. I was at that time called the associate producer, though there *was* no producer on that show, and I helped Gibbs set up that company. Well, I basically set it up *for* him. He went back to New York, and I suddenly was making the *Schlitz Playhouse of Stars*, our show, *on* film, from scratch. I actually produced 208 episodes over the next four years—we did 52 half-hour shows a year. I was suddenly a producer. Eventually I had producer credit, and went on from there.

Part of what's made that show famous is the great casts.

During the course of doing those shows, which we did from '52 to '56, I used any and all actors who would do television, including Ronald Reagan and James Dean and Eddie O'Brien and Charles Bickford and Walter Brennan and all those people who were willing to do television in those days. I met an awful lot of agents, naturally, hiring all these people, and I got to know a lot of other production people. Howard Hawks actually helped me set up the company. I went to Hawks and said, "I've got this challenge, I've got to set up a television production company." He told me, "Well, don't overlook the top movie people. They can go as fast as they have to go." And so I hired, for those first episodes, Russ Harlan, who had done *Red River*, as photographer, and George Amy, who had won the Academy Award for *Air Force* [1943] and some other Hawks pictures, as editor. Those people all came to work for me, and Meridian Productions suddenly had a very distinguished production crew.

So each episode cost a little more than the average China Smith, *I'd assume!*

[*Laughs*] My impression is that those shows were done for around 27,500, something like that. Based on those four years of experience, when that show ended for me, the William Morris Agency came to me. They had dealt with me a great deal, they were about to package *The Frank Sinatra Show* [1957-58], and they wanted me to produce it. I met Frank, and eventually I produced *The Frank Sinatra Show* for Sinatra's company and ABC. And when that ... failed [*laughs*], Bill Dozier hired me to go to CBS in the development area. And the first project I developed was *The Twilight Zone*.

What was your background with William Dozier at that point?
I knew Bill Dozier as a big name. He'd been head of Universal Pictures, he'd been head of RKO Pictures, and then he went over eventually to become head of the West Coast for CBS. I don't think I had ever met him during that period. When the Sinatra show closed, I wrote Dozier a letter and said that I was looking for a job at a network. I had no network experience other than producing shows *for* the networks. He responded and we had an interview, and he hired me for CBS. I went there as a Program Executive—kind of a vague title [*laughs*]—and I was primarily in the development field, looking for new programs and making pilots.

And your first assignment was Twilight Zone.
That was the very first assignment. I did not create in any sense of the word *Twilight Zone*: CBS had a deal with Rod Serling to do a pilot called *Twilight Zone* and it was assigned to me. That was really my first "science fiction experience."

Working with Rod Serling—what kind of memories?
Terrific. But [*laughs*], we got off to a very bad start! Serling had written a script called "The Happy Place" for the pilot, and I had read it. "The Happy Place" dealt with an old folks' home where the people thought they were going on a picnic, and they actually were going to be put to death by gas—it was a euthanasia story! Dozier set up a meeting for me and Serling, I had never met Serling. Serling came into my office at CBS, at Beverly and Fairfax in Hollywood, and he asked, "How'd you like the script?" I said I hated it.

He was, obviously, kind of shocked. "My God," he said, "everybody else loves it! Including your boss Bill Dozier and *his* boss Hubbell Robinson [New York head of CBS programming]. You *hate* it?" I said, "Well, I hate it because, Rod, you're going into a commercial thing. It's not *Playhouse 90*. You're gonna have to have an advertiser, and I don't think the Buick people, or any *other* advertiser, will want to sponsor a show where, in the first episode, you kill nice old people."

What was his reaction?
He left the room in a huff. He went to Dozier, who later called me and said, "My God, what *happened*? Serling wants you off the project." I said, "Well, I'm sorry to hear that. 'Cause I admire him, I think he's a tremendous talent, I'd love to work on the show. But I had to tell him what I thought." Dozier said, "Well ... stay away from him. Don't try to contact him. I'll see if I can put it back together. But ... Rod really wants you off the show." A couple of days later, and I honestly *do* think it was

only a couple of days, Serling came to see me, unannounced. He came into my office and threw a new script on my desk and said, "You're right, and I've written another story." And *that* became the pilot—it was called "Where Is Everybody?" Earl Holliman starred in it, the director Robert Stevens did a terrific job, and that was the show that "sold" it. And Serling and I became great friends. We played penny ante together, he and I and his wife Carol and my wife Peggy. Also in that group were Angela Lansbury and her husband Peter Shaw, who was an agent with William Morris. Serling and I had a terrific relationship. He was incredible. He could write a half-hour script in a couple of days. He dictated all his scripts into a machine, some secretary would transcribe it, and that was it. And, really, if *he* wrote the script, you could almost shoot it.

Did he really come to think that you were right about "The Happy Place," or did he write another script to keep the peace?

He never confirmed or not, too much, what he felt [about that]. But I think he agreed when he really thought about it.

On a show like Twilight Zone, *what were your responsibilities?*

My biggest contribution was not doing the wrong script. Creatively, it was 99 percent Rod Serling. He came up with the stories, he wrote a great number of the scripts, he rewrote the ones he *didn't* write. But he needed some guidance on what director to hire, or what film editor to hire, and so on. A lot of the *Twilight Zone* crew, almost the *entire* crew for the run of that series, came from Meridian and the *Schlitz Playhouse of Stars*. The cameraman George Clemens was from Meridian, the assistant director Eddie Denault was from Meridian, the production manager Ralph Nelson was from Meridian. Generally speaking, all the way down to the gaffer who worked with George Clemens, they had all worked on *Schlitz*. I gave Rod all those names, *that* was my contribution. But I really did not ... I don't think *any* of us, [producer] Buck Houghton or *any* of us, "created" it. It was all Serling.

Incidentally, after the pilot sold, Serling wanted me to join Cayuga Productions and produce the series. But I had only been with CBS a short period of time and I was reluctant to go with a production company headed by one guy—Serling. If anything went wrong, that was the end of my job! I thought I'd better stay with CBS, which I did.

You mentioned a moment ago that your "biggest contribution was not doing the wrong script."

[*Laughs*] Yeah, I always felt that was my only really *creative* contribution to the show.

Does that mean that every episode's script crossed your desk?

No, because once I made the pilot, then it moved into a different area, the area of "ongoing series." I don't remember how conscientious I was, I *may* have read most of the scripts, but it wasn't my job any more.

How about the selection of directors for Twilight Zone, *did you have much input there?*

That also became someone else's job—the actual choices would have been [made by] Rod and Buck Houghton. But most of the directors who worked on the show *were* people I knew or had worked with—for instance, I knew John Brahm very well. And Bob Florey. Bob Florey was a very interesting director. He was a Frenchman who in the early days of Hollywood was Rudolph Valentino's publicist, he traveled in Europe with Valentino. Anyway, he eventually drifted into television directing, and directed a lot of *Loretta Young Show*s and the *Schlitz Playhouse of Stars* and later, when I went to Fox, he directed a lot of *Adventures in Paradise*. He was very stylish, and won an Emmy for directing in television for one show. And he was ideally suited for *Twilight Zone*, I think—he had kind of a "cockeyed camera look" to his shows, which were very distinctive. Of course, he directed movies like *Murders in the Rue Morgue* [1932] and *The Beast With Five Fingers* [1947], and actually wrote the original screenplay for *Frankenstein* [1931]. So *Twilight Zone* material would be right up his alley.

How did Buck Houghton get involved on Twilight Zone? *Through you?*

Buck Houghton was a very capable young producer assistant at RKO when I first came out here. When I started the *Schlitz Playhouse of Stars* and reached a point where I could afford a story editor, I hired Buck Houghton to do that. Then, when I was at CBS and Rod offered me the job of continuing to produce *Twilight Zone*, I didn't feel I could *do* that—I had recently joined CBS and I didn't feel I could dump 'em. I suggested Buck Houghton as a possible producer, because he was very knowledgeable about *making* a television show and Rod Serling was very knowledgeable about *writing* a television show. I thought it was a good combination, and that turned out to be true.

Was there ever any hesitation at all about having Rod Serling narrate and on-camera-host Twilight Zone?

Before we decided on Rod, there was a lot of effort to find the right narrator. We actually went to Orson Welles and we went to Westbrook Van Voorhis, the voice of the "March of Time" films. But they all sounded a little pompous, like they were talking down to this audience that might not understand what the show was about—which a lot of people *didn't* [*laughs*]!

Did they screen-test?

I honestly don't remember that they were screen-tested, but I think they *did* do a track. In other words, they did in a sense audition for it, but I don't have a memory of seeing them on-camera. Meanwhile, Rod kept saying, "Y'know, I'd like to narrate this...," and we—"we" being CBS—kept saying, "Well, we're lookin' for somebody." And then we finally settled on Rod, which was a lucky decision. Rod brought to it a kind of an "everyman quality."

If you had selected Welles or Van Voorhis, would they have also been on-camera?

Yes, we were looking for an on-camera host.

How many CBS-TV pilots did you produce?

I made four pilots, and two of 'em sold and two of 'em did not. *Twilight Zone* sold; *Hotel de Paree* with Earl Holliman sold. But the other two didn't. One was an anthology series—Tony Randall and Maureen O'Hara did the pilot, and *that* didn't sell, surprisingly. And we did a Sidney Kingsley thing called *World in White*, and that didn't sell either. I stayed on at CBS and *Twilight Zone* was one of the shows that I was "the CBS executive" on. There were others, *Gunsmoke* and *Have Gun Will Travel* and some of the *Playhouse 90*s and so on. They didn't give us any credit on those shows.

You were also involved in a half-hour show called World of Giants, *with Marshall Thompson as a miniaturized government agent. What memories of that?*

World of Giants...? Oh, yes, that *was* a show that I was involved in. I'd completely forgot about it! It was a Ziv show as I remember. I honestly blacked out on that one.

So has the rest of the world!

It was an assignment, and I wasn't creatively very involved. If you hadn't reminded me, I would have forgotten about it. *World of Giants* was a victim of not having enough money to do that concept. The license fee for making the show was inadequate.

Educate me—what exactly is "the license fee"?

A network would agree to pay a production company so-much for a show, regardless of what it really cost to make. Obviously the network always tried to pay them *about* what it would cost to make. But many, many times, the production company could *not* do it for the license fee. The justification for the production company still *doing* the show was that they then owned the syndication rights, so in subsequent years they would get their money back and make a profit.

We had enormous problems with Ziv on *World of Giants* in that they really didn't have enough money to do the show right. It was not well done and, as I remember, it failed. It was "short-lived," as we say. I don't have any other memories of it specifically, other than that we just didn't have enough money. The producer was Otto Lang, who had been a movie director and producer, and then later another guy, a producer named William Alland, was involved. They both were capable guys in that field, but in those days in television, it was just an impossible concept.

A few years later, when you were at Fox and Irwin Allen's Land of the Giants *was first proposed, was* World of Giants *in the back of your head—*World of Giants *and all the problems you had with it?*

I'm sure it was, but probably *not* in a negative way. I felt that the failure of *World of Giants* was very much due to the fact that we didn't have enough money to make it. That and the fact that we didn't have the right... [*Pause*] I don't want to be *too* critical of those *World of Giants* guys, but I didn't feel they were creatively as knowledgeable as Irwin Allen. I felt that if *any*body in the world could handle a show as

Marshall Thompson stands outside a giant attaché case—one of the (too) many props that spelled budgetary trouble for TV's *World of Giants*.

tough as *Land of the Giants*, it was Irwin Allen. He storyboarded everything, he was meticulous in his research and he had a large staff. And I thought that he, maybe, could pull it off. So I didn't oppose trying to do *Land of the Giants*, even though I knew the problems. But on *Land of the Giants*, those problems *were* there. Even though we had a much bigger budget, it still was probably not adequate to do the necessary sets and the props.

Okay, we're getting ahead of ourselves. Why did you leave CBS and go to Fox?
I had produced the *Twilight Zone* pilot, and it was bought by a man named Peter Leveythes, who died just last month [January 2002]. He was with the advertising agency that bought *Twilight Zone*, and was very impressed with it, and knew

Close quarters! Six-inch *World of Giants* spy Thompson learns the folly of hiding in a slot machine.

that I had produced it. So then when Peter left the agency and went over to 20th Century-Fox as president of the television division, I believe I was the first person he hired to come over. I went over as an executive producer with a rather ill-defined job—at the moment, Martin Manulis was still head of production for television, and yet Martin did not have anything to do with hiring me, Peter did! So it was kind of an awkward "bridge" there. Eventually Martin Manulis left Fox and Roy Huggins came in, and when *he* left after about a year, I became head of television. I went to Fox December 1, 1959.

Where your job completely flip-flopped. You went from a job at a network getting production companies to supply you with series, to a job at a production company supplying series to the networks.

Right, I've done both of those. It's easier to buy 'em than to sell 'em, I found out [*laughs*]!

And at Fox you started working with Irwin Allen, who cooked up a number of SF series there.

There was great skepticism in the industry [about Allen's proposed SF series], and *I* was one of the skeptics because of *World of Giants*. I knew that science fiction was expensive, and time-consuming, and difficult. And here was Irwin Allen saying, "Let's do *Voyage to the Bottom of the Sea*." Irwin came in with the concept to do *Voyage to the Bottom of the Sea,* and I actually went with Irwin to the William Morris Agency, who represented him, to a man named Sammy Wiseborg, to discuss this project. Sammy said, "You can't do it. There's no way you can sell it, there's no way you can produce it. Irwin, forget it." They thought *Voyage to the Bottom of the Sea* was too expensive and that they couldn't get a decent license fee, and that it would be too complicated to do one a week—they were very negative, and they didn't want Irwin to do it. Irwin got upset about that. His feeling was, "You're my agent, you should be on *my* side. You're saying all the things the *network* can say, but *you* shouldn't be saying 'em!"

When Irwin and I left the office, Irwin was upset that his own agent wouldn't support this project, and convinced that he *could* do it on a weekly basis. And he said, "I'm leaving William Morris"—and he left 'em [*laughs*]! He went with an agency called General Artists Corp., and they were receptive to doing *Voyage*. They were not as big as William Morris, but they were much more concentrated in television than William Morris was. They were the agent on the show when we sold it to ABC. The show actually sold very quickly, as I remember; ABC looked at it and they said, "Let's do it."

You showed it to ABC in New York.

Yes. In those days, we all trekked to New York to show our pilots to the network or the advertiser involved. I remember that Mike Dann, the head of programming for CBS in New York, used to say, "Isn't it amazing how great shows on the West Coast turn to shit by the time they get to New York?" [*Laughs*] *That* did not happen, however, with *Voyage*. It was well received, and we did it. *Voyage* ended up making a lot of money.

Was the guy at William Morris at least half *right, did* Voyage *turn out to be a tremendous amount of work?*

It *was* a lot of work, and very complicated. But Irwin *did* it. Irwin was so incredibly organized, and laid it out in such detail. They'd have a storyboard on every scene. I think that was the key to making it work. I don't know if I know of anybody else who could have done the number of science fiction shows that Irwin did at one time. And keep it all going.

Was he able to do Voyage *for the license fee?*

My impression is that, while it was not done *exactly* for the license fee, it was not incredibly *over* the license fee. Incidentally, I once got in trouble, because in some interview I gave when Fox had eight or nine shows a week on the air, I said, "If we sell one more show, we'll go broke!" That comment was picked up by the financial analyst, and came up at a stockholders meeting in New York run by Darryl Zanuck. I was on the panel. Someone said, "Mr. Zanuck, what did Mr. Self mean when he said, 'If we sell one more show, we'll go broke'?" And Zanuck, of course, panicked, he had *no* idea what I meant. And he said, "Well, Mr. Self is here. Let him answer that."

So I answered it, I said, "I mean that we *all* make an investment over and above the license fee on these shows, and that's a cash flow problem. But it's worth it, because over the years to come we will make a major profit"—that was my thumping-around reply [*laughs*]! But that was literally true: When we had eight or nine or ten shows a week on the air, we did have an enormous outflow of cash. Which of course later, in many cases, like *M*A*S*H* and so forth, well paid off.

When a company like Fox is making that many TV series, doesn't that take up practically all the space at the studio? For as many years as a series is on the air, soundstages are permanently devoted to the Voyage *sub, or to the Batcave, or to the* Lost in Space *planet, or to what*ever*—correct?*

Yes, those sets stayed up for as long as the show was on the air. We not only used many of the stages at Fox on Pico Boulevard, we used stages at Fox Western Avenue, which was the original William Fox studio going back to Tom Mix's day. There were quite a few stages there. And then we leased at Desilu Culver additional stages—we leased I think almost *all* of Desilu Culver. I remember that the Batcave was out there. So, yes, we were all over town.

The Voyage *pilot was in color, and I'm told that Irwin Allen fought very hard for color for the series right from the get-go. But Season One ended up black-and-white.*

There were very few color shows on in 1964, and color would have increased the budget on *Voyage*—I've forgotten how much, maybe six or seven thousand dollars. So we just decided not to do it.

What memories of the Voyage *casting process?*

Irwin had made a feature film *Voyage to the Bottom of the Sea* [in 1961] and there was some talk of whether we should try to get some of those people, including Robert Sterling [Capt. Crane in the movie]. But I think we couldn't afford Bob Sterling on the television show. Those feature people were given some consideration, but we just didn't have that kind of a budget. So we had to go with David Hedison and so forth. That was easier to pull off.

Was Walter Pidgeon, star of the big-screen Voyage, *ever considered for even a minute?*

I don't think so. He would have been too old for the part. We got Richard Basehart as the admiral.

Hedison told me that Basehart was part-owner of Voyage.

No, I don't think that's true. Richard Basehart, as I remember, had a profit participation, which is very different than being a part-owner. Basehart was a freelance star by television standards, and we had to negotiate a deal with him, and in the case of an actor like him, he would have a profit participation.

Lost in Space—*how did that come about?*

Lost in Space almost didn't make it. We did that one for CBS, and Jim Aubrey was president of CBS at that time. Aubrey had a lot of reservations about developing it. And he was the powerhouse at CBS. He was called King James the First ... and he was also called "The Smiling Cobra" [*laughs*]! He had quite a reputation as a very tough decision-maker.

We developed *Lost in Space* as a pilot script, and then as a pilot. Again I went with Irwin Allen to New York to screen the pilot, and there was great concern on our part about what Jim Aubrey's reaction would be. And our concern turned out to be justified. When we screened it with Aubrey, I think on a Friday, we could tell this show was not his cup of tea. He said, "Well, Irwin, you've done a terrific job, it's a spectacular show in many ways. But *I* think it may be a little juvenile. I'd like the weekend to think about it." So we said okay, and Irwin and I went back to the hotel and sweated it out. Monday morning I called CBS and asked for Jim Aubrey, and the telephone operator said, "He doesn't work here any more." I said, "No, no. There must be another Jim Aubrey. I mean Jim Aubrey the *president*." She said, "No, Mr. Aubrey does not work here any more." The new head of CBS was a man named Jack Schneider. So Irwin Allen and I hiked over to CBS, and Aubrey's name wasn't even on the building any more! He'd been fired over the weekend. Rumor had it that his firing was the result of an incident at a Jackie Gleason party in Florida, but I have no idea what that was all about.

Did you know this Jack Schneider?

No. Jack Schneider had been, I believe, a station manager in Philadelphia and he was unknown to most of us in television production—we would normally not have dealt with a Jack Schneider. Schneider's first job when he took over, and he took over over that weekend, was to contact all the people who had pilots pending for the fall schedule. This was right at the pilot season, the poor guy didn't have much time to make up his mind! His office called and asked Irwin and me to come over and meet with him, which we did. He promised to run the *Lost in Space* pilot as soon as he could and get back to us as soon as he could. And fortunately he felt different than Jim, he said, "Let's put it on." So it was *that close* to not ever making it.

How much say did you have in the casting of these Irwin Allen series?

I would say I was the final word. I would not even worry about who he was casting in the lesser roles, but in the star roles I would be very concerned about who we were using, because it was a Fox show, and Fox distribution, and Fox owned it. So I would say that I would be very surprised if any Fox show got on the air that had anybody in it I didn't want [*laughs*]!

There's a CBS memo that mentions the possibility of Eddie Albert and Maureen O'Hara as the stars of Lost in Space—*does that ring any bells?*

No, it does not. When you develop a series, *any* series, you suddenly find that some people are saying, "Well, why don't we get Marlon Brando?" [*laughs*]—a lot of impossible names come up in the early days of casting. Then you finally get around to being practical about it. It's very possible [they were under actual consideration] but I can't conceive of Maureen O'Hara ever really being interested from *her* side!

One of the Hollywood trade papers called the Lost in Space *pilot the most expensive pilot ever made.*

I don't doubt that it came close [*laughs*]. We were into all those special effects.

What impressions of Guy Williams and the rest of the Lost in Space *cast?*

They were all terrific. In the first place ... I don't mean this in any demeaning way ... but most of them were glad to have a job. I think they were all thrilled to be *in* the show, and they were very cooperative, and no real problem.

Jonathan Harris was a last-minute addition to the cast, as the cowardly Dr. Smith.

Yes, he was. A lot of people felt that he was too much of a comedy character. But he became almost the star of the show in some ways. So that was fortunate.

I keep hearing that Red Skelton was connected in some way with Lost in Space—*what's the deal on that?*

When we took the concept to CBS to do *Lost in Space*, there was a guy at CBS named Guy Della Cioppa. He was an executive at CBS, and he was also an executive in the Red Skelton company. And the Red Skelton Company, by virtue of Red's long affiliation with CBS, had a blank pilot commitment at CBS. It was worked out that *Lost in Space* became that commitment, and Red Skelton's company actually owned part of *Lost in Space* along with Irwin Allen.

Did you ever have to deal with Red Skelton Lost in Space–*wise?*

I have no personal knowledge of him *ever* having been involved, creatively or otherwise. He just had the company headed up by Guy Della Cioppa, who was the one we dealt with.

Why were Lost in Space *and* Voyage to the Bottom of the Sea *canceled—was it simply a question of ratings?*

As I recall. I would think that they ran out of gas.

A one-eyed giant menaces the Space Family Robinson (aboard "The Chariot," lower left) in *Lost in Space*'s pricey pilot episode.

Were Allen's shows respected by Hollywood insiders and media at the time, or were they regarded as "kid shows"? Considering how popular they were, they certainly didn't get much coverage from, say, TV Guide *and places like that.*

Were they *respected*? Well, maybe "respected" is ... [*laughs*] ... maybe "respected" is the wrong word! I think they were *admired* by most people who knew the problems of making a science fiction show on a television budget. But why the critics weren't more impressed with them, I don't really know. I suspect they didn't know how difficult they were.

Another Irwin Allen sci-fi series from that era, Time Tunnel...?
Time Tunnel was also a very, very expensive concept. *Lost in Space* and *Voyage to the Bottom of the Sea* had "the basic set"—you were on a submarine, or you were on a planet. On *Time Tunnel*, the two guys [stars James Darren and Robert Colbert] were consistent, but it was almost like an anthology. There had to be new sets every week.

I remember it using clips from a lot of old Fox features—that must *have helped!*
Yes, it did. But the two guys would end up on board the *Titanic*, or in King Arthur's Court, or wherever, so as I said, it was very expensive. And as a result, it was not a commercial success for Fox. We were glad to do it and all that kind of stuff, but I would be surprised if *Time Tunnel* ever showed a profit. It was a fringe show for us. It was also an enormous drain on Irwin, as I remember—he was doing all these shows at once. It wasn't really proving right for Fox *or* the network.

After its cancellation, Time Tunnel *did get a lot of play in foreign countries, and ran in dozens of U.S. markets. But with all that, you still don't believe it made a profit?*
I really don't remember. How long a show has to stay on the air in order to go into syndication and become successful—the rule of thumb has been generally three years. But I would say that that would vary very much. *Peyton Place* was unique in that it was a continuing story, and it really never did well in syndication (even though we had hundreds of episodes) because it required such a commitment from the audience. Once it went into syndication, we weren't able to *get* that commitment. So it isn't just a matter of how many episodes you have.

Larry Stewart, casting director on the Irwin Allen series, recalled that there was some concern about casting a black actor—Don Marshall—as one of the Land of the Giants *stars. He said there were fears that could alienate some affiliate stations in the South.*
We did not have trouble getting Don Marshall cast in *Land of the Giants*—because he really wasn't the lead. Had he been the lead, like Diahann Carroll was on *Julia* [the 1968-71 TV series], that might have come up. But I don't think it came up with Don Marshall.

Stewart also says that Sam Elliott and Barbara Hershey were contenders for starring roles in Land of the Giants.
I don't remember that. I had used Barbara Hershey in a show called *The Monroes* [1966-67] and I think that was her first television series—I *knew* Barbara. When you're casting a series and you're dealing with casting directors, they may throw out a lot of ideas, and if some of 'em don't strike you right, you just don't even remember 'em [*laughs*]. So Larry probably would know more than I about whether these people were considered.

We've already talked about some of the challenges involved with Land of the Giants...

Yes, and the fact that that one *really* took me back to that other science fiction thing [*World of Giants*]. It just was an impossible concept. If there was a pencil on the desk, it had to be ten feet long. Or a chair that they were gonna climb up had to be 20 feet tall. The sets were incredible to build, we were always struggling to make the show. Also, it also never really caught on to the extent that *Voyage to the Bottom of the Sea* or *Lost in Space* did. I think we were all glad to get out of it when that was done. It was a difficult show.

Despite all these production-related hardships, did you enjoy working in science fiction?

Yes, I did. But we had a clichéd statement in our development meetings, we'd say, "There are some shows that you can sell and can't make, and there are others you can make and can't sell." Science fiction gets you very close to the ones you can sell but can't make. You just have to be very, very careful in that. All of those Irwin Allen shows were *very* difficult to do for the license fee.

Irwin Allen—your lasting impressions of the man?

I greatly admired Irwin Allen, he was a terrific guy. He was knowledgeable, he was hard-working, he knew his job. And he was a very honorable guy. I remember the legal department called me once and said, "We've got a problem with Irwin Allen's contract. *He's* signed it and *we've* signed it, and it contains an error, *very* much in Irwin Allen's favor. What can we do about it?" I said, "Well ... what's the problem?" and they told me, and I called Irwin and I said, "Irwin, the contract is signed and we acknowledge that, but ... it's not what we really talked about." I reviewed what we talked about, and he said, "You're right. You're absolutely right. Have 'em fix the contract." I had great respect for the guy.

How involved were you in the early days of Batman*?*

I have lots of memories of *Batman*, I was very much involved in it. I had some discussions with ABC about a nighttime comic strip, and they did some research on what *were* the popular comic strips. The most popular was I think *Little Orphan Annie*, which wasn't available, and the next one was maybe *Dick Tracy*, which wasn't available, and so forth—and finally *Batman*. I didn't know much about *Batman*, and I was in New York for these discussions, so I went to a newsstand and I asked the guy, "Have you got any *Batman* comic books?" He said he did. I said, "Well, put 'em in a plain paper bag. I do *not* want to walk into the Plaza Hotel carrying *Batman* comic books!" I took 'em back and I read 'em, and felt they had a lot of potential.

A man named Doug Cramer was in development at ABC, and I told him that *I* felt we had to do a show that would appeal to adults as well as children. And that, for *that* reason, we should get a name author to write the pilot. He said, "That's great. Who?" And I said, "Well, I have one thought, which is Eric Ambler." He asked me, "Can you get Eric Ambler?" and I said, "I have an entrée to Eric Ambler." So I came back to Hollywood and I called up my former employer Bill Dozier—I had met Eric Ambler at Dozier's house socially. "Bill," I said, "we're thinking of doing *Batman*, and you could produce it, and I'd like to try to get Eric Ambler." He said,

Years after *World of Giants* left the airwaves, the similar *Land of the Giants* was also plagued by the same type of production woes. *Top to bottom:* Don Matheson, Deanna Lund, Kurt Kasznar, Gary Conway, Stefan Arngrim.

"I don't think you have a chance, but let's try." So I had lunch with Bill Dozier and Eric Ambler at the old Romanoffs and told Eric Ambler what I had in mind. He was very gracious ... and laughed at me ... and he said, "Bill, I am *not* going to write *Batman*." That ended *that* dream! But Dozier was very enthusiastic by now, and he had some other thoughts, and so we went in another direction. Bill brought in Lorenzo Semple, Jr., who wrote the *Batman* pilot.

Some fans have speculated that the very successful theatrical reissue of the 1940s Batman *serials was the inspiration for the TV series.*

The TV series was certainly not based in any way on the 1940s serials. *Batman* came about the same way that [the TV series] *Peyton Place* did, as I remember. We were in a meeting with I believe Ed Sherrick, who was vice-president in charge of programs for ABC out of New York, the top program guy, and Doug Cramer. On *Peyton Place and* on *Batman*, I kinda remember that we said, "What is *not* on the air?" because that would be a chance to come through with something that was unique. We realized that there was no nighttime serial in prime time—hence *Peyton Place* was developed. And there was no nighttime comic strip in prime time. So that's really what was the inspiration for both those shows: We looked around and said, "What's not there?" and then we tried to supply it.

Were you also involved in the casting of Batman?

Yes I was. And every so often I'll meet somebody who says, "Do you remember me?" I say, "I'm sorry, I don't." And he'll say, "You interviewed me for Batman." So apparently we interviewed a lot of people! The casting of that was very difficult. We already had a commitment from ABC on the series, because we said, "We can't afford to make the pilot, with building the Batmobile and the Batcave and all the wardrobe and so on, unless we *know* we're gonna make some episodes." So we had a commitment from them to make, I think, 13 episodes. But we still had to make a pilot for sales purposes—for *their* sales purposes. When we finally decided on Adam West and the boy, Burt Ward [as Batman and Robin], we made the pilot. And after we made the pilot, we did what they call an ASI test. In those days, every show made had an ASI test—there was a company on Sunset Boulevard that did that, and *everybody* tested every new show there. It had a screening room where we'd get an audience together, and each seat had a knob on it so that each person could react to the show scene by scene. When they like something about the show, they turn the knob to the right, and when they *don't* like something about the show, they turn it to the left—they respond to the action on the screen as it happens. Afterwards, a composite record would be prepared and, like a seismograph, it would show ups and downs. On a comedy show, you really should get a score in the 90s. If you get into the 80s and 90s, you have a chance at having a hit.

And how did Batman *do?*

Well, we tested *Batman*, and it was annoying the audience—the score was 50. Or below. We had a meeting afterwards, a dinner meeting. Ed Sherrick from ABC had flown out [for the screening] but his flight was delayed. Later that evening he

Holy initiative! Deciding that what America needed was "a nighttime comic strip," Self and ABC-TV collaborated on the creation (and the serio-comic tone) of the *Batman* TV series with (*right–left*) Adam West and Burt Ward.

came into the Beachcombers where we were having dinner and said, "What'd we score?" I said, "Fifty," or whatever the score was. He laughed, and he said, "Come on, come on—what did we score?" I said, "Fifty." He said, "…You're kidding." I said no. It was a disaster.

Did ABC want "out" of their commitment at that point?

Yes, in fact, they did. But we analyzed it and thought about it, and finally decided the audience didn't know what we were trying to do. In the original version, those animated POWs and BAMs, and other things like that, were *not* in the show. We decided we had to say to the audience, "We're *kidding* all this. We're having fun. It's a comic strip." And we re-did the whole post-production on it, and it aired on ABC—

And became a big hit.

And I remember vividly, the night that *Batman* premiered, I got a phone call at home. Which surprised me, because I had a private number. A young man said, "Mr. Self, are you involved with *Batman*?" I said yes. He said, "I'm at the University of Stanford and I've just looked at it with my friends, and we have one question: Is it supposed to be funny?" [*Laughs*] And I said, "Yeah, it's supposed to be funny." He said, "That's what I *said*! And we loved it!" So, once again, we had to tell 'em what we were doing. And from then on, it was a big hit.

Was there any hesitation about making Batman *a two-part, two-night-a-week series?*

There was a lot of discussion about that, pros and cons. The "pros" were, obviously, if you make a good Monday night show, you've insured yourself a good Wednesday. But ... vice versa is the danger [*laughs*]! But that was basically the network's decision, that was not Fox's decision.

Did Adam West and Burt Ward really not get along, as so many have claimed?

I don't remember that. I wasn't in a position to be on the set that much—I was sitting in my office, making bad decisions [*laughs*]. But that was not my impression.

Whose idea was it to feature a lot of "name" actors as the villains?

It was Dozier who came up with that, because he knew a lot of those people and he could attract them. Once the show became a hit, it was not hard to get 'em—people were calling us up saying, "I'd *like* to do *Batman*." Initially, it was tough to get the first couple people to do it, but then everybody had a ball. Cesar Romero [the Joker] and Burgess Meredith [the Penguin] and all of 'em, I think they all loved it. There was nothing else quite like *Batman* on the air, it was unique, and it was successful. So they wanted to be in it.

Why did William Dozier take on the job of narrating Batman*?*

As I understand it, Dozier did it for a very good reason. Well, first of all, he was very good at it, or we wouldn't have approved his doing it. But he also wanted to keep up his membership in the Actors Guild, because of the medical plan. Bill had done other narration and stuff over the years, and was a member of the Actors Guild, and he did *Batman* 'cause it qualified him for continuing.

Did you have any input on the 1966 Batman *movie?*

No, not really. [Fox vice-president in charge of production] Dick Zanuck obviously saw the success of *Batman* and he decided to do a movie. He dealt directly with Dozier on the movie, I was not involved at all.

Why was Batgirl [Yvonne Craig] brought onto Batman*?*

I just think we were being opportunistic. We thought that would help it.

Do you remember how The Green Hornet *came about?*

With the success of *Batman*, we obviously looked around for another possible show of a similar nature, and came up with *The Green Hornet*, and negotiated for those rights. It was Dozier who found Kato—Bruce Lee. I had to approve him, and Dozier brought him to my office. I'd never heard of him. He went through his ... "hand maneuvers" for me [*laughs*], they all looked very threatening, and I thought he was fine! So that was Dozier's contribution—one of many—to *The Green Hornet*, bringing in Bruce Lee.

Why was The Green Hornet *so short-lived while* Batman *was such a smash?*

I don't know now—I may have had a guess if you'd asked me closer to that time.

But, you're right, it just never took off. I was surprised it didn't do better. Maybe the public was getting tired of that kind of a show, maybe it was up against too much opposition.

The last sci-fi series made at Fox while you were there—Planet of the Apes.

The man at CBS who wanted to do *Planet of the Apes* as a series was Bob Wood. He was president of CBS network at that time and he not only wanted to do a television series, he wanted to buy the movies. For obvious reasons—it wouldn't make sense to be promoting a series and not have the movies to exhibit later, or concurrently, whatever they decided. So Bob was the spearhead of that.

I recall being told that Fred Silverman, another CBS exec, did not like the series.

I don't really remember Freddie's position at that time, but Bob was Freddie's boss, so that would account for [the series] going forward. The man who was most concerned about it was Bill Paley—Bill Paley wasn't convinced it would work. That was the period of the "family hour," and [the key to getting] *Planet of the Apes* to "work," in all of our judgments, really would be the violence that you could put in it, the conflict between the apes and the humans. That's what the movies were about. Paley was very concerned that, in order to get it into the family hour, we'd have to lose some of that—and would we lose too much? I'd hired a writer-producer named Tony Wilson, whose father had been a famous writer-producer at MGM, Carey Wilson. Tony was very talented. He and I flew to New York for a meeting with Bill Paley about the project. That meeting was also attended by Bob Wood and I believe Freddie Silverman. We tried to address Mr. Paley's concerns, we told him some of the storylines we were doing and how we hoped to handle it. And at the end of that meeting, Paley said, "Well, okay. If that's what you believe, then I'll go along with you," and he put his stamp of approval on doing it. A little digression: I thought Bill Paley was terrific. More than once he made that speech to someone: "I don't agree with you but if you believe in it that strongly, let's try it." That was his attitude on *Planet of the Apes* and that was the approval we needed. We came back and made the show ... and never solved the problem that haunted us from the beginning. If things got too violent, then we couldn't use it in that episode. And so [*laughs*], it became more of a conversation piece rather than an action piece. And that didn't work.

Why did you leave Fox?

I was there 15 years—I went to Fox December 1, 1959, and I left Dec. 31, 1974. I would not have left for another television job, but I wanted to try my hand at features, and Fox was not very active in that field at that time. A man named Mike Frankovich, who had been head of worldwide production for Columbia Pictures, had gone independent and had his own company and was going to do movies. He approached me and said, "Why don't we join forces? We'll try to do both movies *and* television, and we'll both be involved in both." So we formed a partnership, Frankovich-Self, and we produced two features, John Wayne's picture *The Shootist* and a Charlie Bronson picture called *From Noon Till Three* [both 1976].

Looking back today, Self is most proud *not* of his acting career, but his years as one of the deans of the Hollywood production chiefs.

During those two years, I realized that I was used to doing *much* more in the way of activity—projects and successes and failures and everything. To do one movie a year, *maybe*, was *not* what I thought it was going to be. So about that time, CBS was looking for a head of the West Coast, and I went back to CBS in that job.

Are you retired now?

Yes and no. If you mean am I earning any money, then, yes, I'm retired [*laughs*]. But I still keep my hand in a little bit, I still have a production company with Glenn Close. We've done three *Hallmark Hall of Fame*s but I don't know that we'll do any more. I think I'm mostly retired, to be truthful.

Compared to other series you did, like Peyton Place *and* M*A*S*H *and other classics, how do the sci-fi shows stack up in your affections?*

Well, they have a very unique position in my career. If I want to impress people, I talk about *M*A*S*H* or *Twilight Zone*. Or *The Shootist*, the movie with John Wayne. But I always have a great affection for *Batman* and those kind of ... [*laughs*] ... off-the-wall series! And of course *Twilight Zone* was really the foundation of my getting going in a big way. I had been producing a relatively successful show in *Schlitz*, but *Twilight Zone* became an enormous hit, and that was a great help to me.

There are "remakes" of Lost in Space *and* Time Tunnel *currently on the horizon [in early 2002]. Your gut feeling—what are their chances?*

I wish 'em well. But I must tell you something: I know that if I had walked into a network a few years ago and said, "I want to do a remake of *The Fugitive*," "I want to do *Batman* over," "I want to do *Lost in Space*," they'd say, "Poor Bill Self. He's living in the past!" [*Laughs*] I'm surprised, in a way [by Hollywood's remake-mania]. But as far as the *Lost in Space* and *Time Tunnel* remakes go—listen, I hope it works.

I hear through the grapevine that you're working on your autobiography...?

It would be wrong to say it's an autobiography. I've been very fortunate: Spencer Tracy and Fred Astaire and Katharine Hepburn and all these people have been very, very good friends of mine, and other people who I've known, whether it's Charlie Chaplin or [tennis champ] Bill Tilden, you name it. And the book is really my impressions of them and of Hollywood rather than, "I was born on such-and-such a date" and that kind of thing. It's incidents in relationship to some of these people.

What do you look back upon with more pride, your acting career or your producing career?

My producing career, because I was more successful as a producer than I was as an actor. I loved being an actor, but it scared the hell out of me at *all* times [*laughs*]. It's a fondly remembered part of my life, but obviously my producing career was a little more successful.

Natalie Trundy

> *At lunchtime, we [ape actors] would all traipse to La Scala. You should have seen us going into this restaurant, with Kim Hunter and Roddy McDowall in all the ape makeup! Sitting in the restaurant, eating veal piccata, salads and everything else.*

Missing from too many recent discussions of Tim Burton's new *Planet of the Apes* [2001] and the original 1968–73 movie series that inspired it is any mention of Arthur P. Jacobs, the public relations man–turned–20th Century–Fox producer who shepherded the first five films into production and spawned the entire phenomenon. Who better to help rectify this situation than actress Natalie Trundy, who was not only Mrs. Jacobs during this "hairstoric" era but played in all four sequels to the original *Planet of the Apes*: 1970's *Beneath the Planet of the Apes* (as the subway-dwelling mutant Albina), 1971's *Escape from the Planet of the Apes* (as a human animal expert), 1972's *Conquest of the Planet of the Apes* and 1973's *Battle for the Planet of the Apes* (as Lisa, chimpanzee mate of Roddy McDowall).

Boston-born Trundy showed an affinity for the camera from an early age and was modeling by her ninth year. She won her first acting job (as Red Riding Hood on live TV) at age 11, moving on to commercials, more live TV, Broadway and summer stock. One of her summer performances was caught by Samuel Taylor, who was searching for an actress for his upcoming film *The Monte Carlo Story* (1957). Fourteen-year-old Trundy and her mother were whisked off to the title city, where she worked with stars Marlene Dietrich and Vittorio De Sica—and encountered Arthur Jacobs for the first time. They met a second time years later, married in 1968 and lived in the Hollywood fast lane until Jacobs' early death in 1973. Trundy is today the president of Jacobs' company (APJAC Productions) but devotes more of her time to church work and her pets.

According to your publicity, you were a teenager when you first encountered Arthur P. Jacobs.

I met him when I was 14 years old, when I was making my first film, *The Monte Carlo Story* with Marlene Dietrich. He was not yet a producer, he was still in pub-

A veteran of four of the five original *Planet of the Apes* movies, Natalie Trundy began her career as a child model.

lic relations, and he represented Dietrich, the principality of Monaco, Prince Rainier and Grace Kelly. Right in the middle of the street where we were filming, he said to my mother, "When she grows up, I'm gonna marry her." And he did! I was his only wife. I'm sure he had many girlfriends, but I was the only wife.

Were you right there when he said that?
　No, no, he said it to my mother, away from me. I'm looking at this man, more than twice my age, and I asked my mother, "Who's that old man?" As far as I was concerned, he was just an old man [*laughs*]! He was 30-something years old, for crying out loud, and I was like 14 and a half, not even 15 yet! I was just a little girl, and he was considerably older, needless to say. Anyway, we met again a number of years later, and ended up married and happy.

In between your first two meetings with Jacobs, you did a lot of TV, including Thriller *and* The Twilight Zone.
　For *Thriller*, I was in the first episode ["The Twisted Image"]. To tell you the truth, I don't remember how I got the part. I obviously must have auditioned for it. It was a [*Fatal Attraction*-type] part, hounding Leslie Nielsen. I knew Leslie personally as well, he lived up the street from me. I was still young, I couldn't drive yet, so he used to pick me up in the morning and take me to Universal! It was directed by Arthur Hiller, who has now been nominated for many awards. And *Twilight Zone* was fun. It was a little on the weird side, to say the least [*laughs*], but it was a fun show. I met Rod Serling—he was a very nice person. He actually interviewed me when I was up for the part.

How did you happen to meet up with Arthur Jacobs the second time?
　I was living with a girlfriend of mine in London, Vanessa Mitchell, and her little son. We shared a flat together. We were so poor—like church mice. Vanessa and I used to go in to her little son to get pennies to take the tube [subway] into London! We all lived in the same flat, in one big bed! Oh, God! Well, Vanessa went to the opening of the Playboy Club in London and there Arthur was, sitting there, very morose. Arthur was living in London at this time, working on the filming of *Doctor Dolittle* [1967]. Here she was with her boyfriend, and she saw him and recognized him and started chatting with him. She said, "You'll never guess who's living with me. Natalie Trundy." He perked up—and he rang me the next day and invited me out to dinner. I refused. Then he sent me this great big thing of flowers that took up the whole living room of our poor flat! So I agreed to go to lunch with him. He sent his chauffeur to collect me … and it went from there.

And you got married in London in 1968. Who was at your wedding?
　Mort Abrahams [co-producer of the *Apes* movies] … Carol Channing … Peter O'Toole … Petula Clark … Leslie Bricusse and his wife Evie [actress Yvonne Romain] … there were so many people, I can't even remember. Sammy Davis took a lot of pictures. And of course Vanessa and my parents, and my sister and aunt and uncle.

Were you dating him in 1967 when he was making the first Planet of the Apes? *Did you visit the sets of that movie?*
　How 'bout Page, Arizona? Oh, God in Heaven! It was 120 degrees! That's where they shot the opening parts of the movie. The reason Arthur couldn't go was that

Years before playing the chimpanzee Lisa in two of the *Apes* movies, Trundy came as Zira to a 1967 Halloween party. Doctor Dolittle (left) is her future husband Arthur P. Jacobs.

he already had a bad heart at the time. So, guess what, *I* had to go. I called him and I said, "You know, Arthur P., I'm gonna dump you now!" Page, Arizona, even at nighttime, it's 100 degrees. It was awful. We had fans, there was no air conditioning.

Were you staying in a hotel?

If you want to call it a hotel, yes. You don't even want to know about it [*laughs*]! Then when we made *Tom Sawyer* [1973], that was in Missouri, and that was as bad [hot]. I had to stay there for *that* whole thing. Then we went to Natchez, Mississippi, for *Huckleberry Finn* [1974] and I said, "Holy Christ in Heaven, here I go again!"

What kind of movies did Jacobs especially like *to make?*

He once said, "I will never in my lifetime make a film that cannot be seen by the whole family." He owned the rights to *Midnight Cowboy* [1969] and he gave them away. He *gave them away*. He said, "I will not have my name on it." He gave them to [producer] Jerry Hellman, and that movie made millions of bucks. But he said, "I will not have my name on it."

What was your reaction when you first heard he'd be making Planet of the Apes?

I thought it was sensational. Science fiction, you know!

I've read, and been told, that early on, there was apprehension that people would find it funny.

Really, a lot of it *was* funny, but a lot of it was very serious. If you think about it, it was also, in a way, very political. By the way, and this is a true story: During the filming, at lunchtime, the gorillas would eat with the gorillas ... the chimpanzees would eat with the chimpanzees ... and the other ones would eat together too. One group here, one group there! Except for the stars, of course.

This was on the first movie?

This was on *all* of them!

These Apes *movies must have been such large-scale, time-consuming projects. Were they just five movies that he made while you knew him, or was this the "Planet of the Apes era" in your lives?*

It was. Completely!

Trundy laughingly chalks up her appearances in her husband Jacobs' movies to plain-and-simple "Hollywood nepotism."

Whose idea was it for you to start appearing in the Planet of the—

[*Interrupting*] Mine [*laughs*]! Nobody else's! I wanted to be in it ... I wanted to be part of it. I was in all except the first one.

So we can chalk your four roles up to nepotism—or is that too strong a word?

No, no, no, no! *Not* too strong a word!

Linda Harrison ["Nova"] was the girlfriend, and later the wife, of Richard Zanuck, so that's the way she got her part too.

That's right.

So you just said to your husband, "You're making a Planet of the Apes *sequel [Beneath], I'd like to be in it"—was it as simple as that?*

I said, "I *wanna* be in it!" [*laughs*]—and I *was*. All of them, from then on! I really did 'em for *fun*, if you want to know the truth.

While making her *Apes* saga debut as the mutant Albina in *Beneath*, Trundy chatted on set with her producer husband.

For Beneath, *would you have preferred playing an ape, or the role that you did play?*
　　Oh, I liked playing Albina. It was fun, and I didn't have to wear ape makeup.

For at least one scene, your makeup had to be an ordeal.
　　Those radiation burns had to be painted on my face every single day. It really wasn't an unpleasant process, but taking it *off* was a killer. My makeup man had to

take it off with a hair dryer, set on COLD. And he had to use acetone to get it off my face. It was so painful I would cry. Day after day after day, that was not terrific!

At one point, you also had to wear a mask of your own face over all that makeup.
Fortunately I don't have claustrophobia, but imagine people who do. I mean, they couldn't work, it'd be impossible. We all wore appliances, they weren't just masks. The extras wore ape masks, etc., etc., but the stars who played apes wore appliances and, as Albina, I wore appliances. For the original *Planet of the Apes*, before Maurice Evans took the part of Dr. Zaius, Edward G. Robinson was supposed to do it. But he couldn't take the heat and he couldn't take the makeup—his heart was sort of on the weak side. So they got Maurice Evans. *He* was a dear friend of ours, too.

Kim Hunter told me that Sal Mineo, who was in Escape *with the two of you, was another person who had trouble with his ape makeup.*
Yes, he did, he was claustrophobic. He and I weren't close during the makeup process, we were all allocated to different makeup rooms, but I do remember that he did have trouble with it. His character didn't last too long in the picture, he got killed right away—and I think he was very happy about it, to tell you the truth [*laughs*]! Incidentally, I got along with Kim Hunter wonderfully—what a nice lady. A *real* lady. A wonderful woman.

Did Jacobs ever appear in any of his own movies?
No. But always, in all of his movies, some character had the name of Arthur. For instance, in *Escape from the Planet of the Apes*, the one where I played the psychologist, psychiatrist, whatever, with Bradford Dillman, the character who was like the zookeeper, *his* name was Arthur. He always got an Arthur in somewhere!

When I was a kid going to see the Apes *movies, to me they were just family entertainment and makeup and action and a lot of fun. But now that I'm older, I recognize some of the political and social undercurrents. Whose idea was it to slip all of that stuff into the movies?*
Oh, the writers. And Arthur.

Was he a political person? Did he have time *to be?*
No, he didn't have time to do *any*thing. He worked 29 hours a day, ten days a week. And I think that's what killed him. He was only 51 when he died.

Richard Zanuck admits that he was also unaware of the undercurrents at the time.
I don't think anybody was so aware of it at the time, necessarily. But when you think, years later, about all of the things that happened here and there and everywhere, it was very pursuant. Pursuant to what's happening ... even *today*! To tell you the truth, I didn't "see" it at first either. But it's come to me now. Even [series star] Roddy McDowall and I discussed it at one point.

Just out of curiosity, being the wife of the producer, did you get preferential treatment on any of the Apes *sets?*

Absolutely not. Don't think I wouldn't have accepted it, for your information [*laughs*], but I didn't! I worked as hard as everybody else!

You talked about your husband's workaholic lifestyle. Did that leave time for any home life?

Well ... not too much.

How did you deal with that? Did you resent it?

No. I loved him so much ... we just had a good life together. He wanted children—he didn't marry me to be an actress, he wanted children. When I had my sixth miscarriage, we were living in London then. I was in the bathroom and I started to bleed, and I said, "Arthur, please call the doctor." The doctor came *with* a specialist, an Ob/Gyn, and they said, "Mr. Jacobs ... she just lost another baby." All he did was sit on the end of the bed and cry. It was a little baby boy. I was five months pregnant. Well, at least I've got two children now [by her second husband], God bless 'em.

Where did you live during those years?

We lived at 713 North Beverly Drive. We also had a flat in New York, in the Sherry Netherlands Hotel, on the twenty-first floor, and a house in London.

Not a bad lifestyle!

We went round and round and round.

Did you do much entertaining at your house in Hollywood?

Yes, we did lots of it. And in London as well. We used to have massive parties.

Did this jet set lifestyle agree with you?

Oh, it did, I loved it! *Loved* it.

Drop a few names—who were your best friends and most frequent guests during those years?

Well, Michael Caine and his wife ... Gregory Peck and his wife ... and people like Quincy Jones from the music end. And Roddy McDowall always. Arthur and Roddy loved to play Monopoly. We used to show movies every Saturday night—we had a projection room in our house. There were certain people who were sort-of "regulars," and Roddy was always one of them, because Arthur and he adored each other. After the other guests would leave, I'd already be half-asleep, it'd be around midnight, Arthur and Roddy would sit on the floor and start playing Monopoly. And Monopoly can go on forever. Finally around three or four o'clock in the morning, I'd say, "Good night, guys. I'm going to bed." So all our dogs toodled upstairs with me. I came down about eight o'clock in the morning and they were still sitting on the floor playing Monopoly. I said, "I think it's coffee time, guys," and they said, "No, we're not finished yet!" [*Laughs*] They did it all the time—not every single week, but a lot.

Just the two of them?
Paul Dehn [the British writer of the *Apes* sequels], who stayed with us when he was here in America, sometimes played too. One weekend Groucho Marx was there—he was *so* old by then! He said, "Can I play?" and Arthur said, "No. Just sit there and smoke your cigar!" [*Laughs*]

What was it that you and your husband liked about Roddy McDowall?
He was a very sweet, caring person, and very intelligent. And I adored him. But the two of us listened to very different types of music. He enjoyed classical, while I always listened to rock 'n' roll. When we were together in an *Apes* movie, we had an agreement that whoever reached the makeup department first would win the right to pick the music we would listen to. I would have the Beatles in my machine and he'd have classical music in his. It was a good-natured race between us to see who would get to choose the music for the day. I didn't always make it first. I *like* classical music, but at two o'clock in the morning, when you're trying to stay vaguely awake, it can put you right to sleep [*laughs*]!

At two o'clock in the morning, would you be having your makeup taken off at the end of a work day, or put on at the beginning of one?
At two o'clock in the morning, it was the beginning. It took four hours to put the appliances on. Before they put the bottom part of the face on, the mouth, Roddy and I used to order our breakfasts. Here we were ordering breakfasts at, like, four-thirty or five in the morning. But [the commissary] didn't serve makeup men any breakfast. So this is what I used to do: I would order 20 hard-boiled eggs, ten orders of French toast, ten steaks, lots of toast, orange juice freshly squeezed and coffee. (The coffee they'd make in the makeup room was lousy!) Finally the guy in the commissary looked at me and he said, "Miss Trundy! How can you consume all this food and stay so slim?" I said, "Easily!" [*Laughs*]

Who were *the makeup men?*
My favorite makeup man was Jack Barron. He was exclusive to me. Roddy's makeup man was Joe DiBella. And of course John Chambers and Dan Striepeke, who were like the supervising makeup men, would come around.

And these were all nice, patient guys?
Oh, they were wonderful. We used to joke and I'd start to laugh, and poor Jack said to me, "Would you stop laughing, for Christ's sake? You're gonna ruin all my stuff!" I told him, "I can't help it!!"

Being on the set of an Apes *movie must have been a trip.*
You get used to it. By the way, there was one day when we were shooting *Escape* in Beverly Hills and we put one of our little dogs, Katherine, in the movie. She was

As "Stevie" Branton in *Escape from the Planet of the Apes*, Trundy bonded with Zira (Kim Hunter), "a wonderful woman."

named after the character in Arthur's *Goodbye Mr. Chips* [1969] played by Petula Clark. A little Yorkshire terrier, with orange ribbons in her hair. We had the dog groomer there, brushing her hair, so she could look pretty as she quickly went through the lobby of the Beverly Wilshire Hotel!

At lunchtime, we would all traipse to La Scala—the owner was a dear friend of ours. You should have seen us going into this restaurant, with Kim Hunter and Roddy in all the ape makeup [*laughs*]! Sitting in the restaurant, eating veal piccata, salads and everything else. And when we got back to the set, the makeup man looked at us and said, "Boy, you must have enjoyed it 'cause you look like disasters!"—you know, from the chin down! And walking through the streets of Beverly Hills to the restaurant, people stopped and stared. "Are we really seeing this? Is this for real?" Some people even bumped into each other!

Any other anecdotes about Escape*?*

I went into a cage with a tiger. I had no fear. I will tell you something: If they don't sense fear, they don't hurt you. The one thing the trainer said to me was, "The only thing they can't stand, it *does* drive them crazy, is if you are on your period.

They smell it." It's the truth. But I used to go in with them and play. They never put a fang out to me, they never put a claw out to me. They were so sweet. There was a tiger and a baby lion.

Bradford Dillman, your leading man—did he also go in the cage?
No. He looked and he said, "I don't think so." [*Laughs*] He asked me, "How can you *do* that?" and I said, "I have no fear toward them, and therefore they have no fear toward me." That's how it works. And, believe me, these guys were not declawed or anything like that!

Your husband gets a lot of credit for the Apes *movies—deservedly—as well as some others. I often think Paul Dehn gets short-changed. Do you agree with me?*
I certainly would. He was a love. He was so quiet—sometimes you'd walk into a room and think he'd be snoozing. But he wasn't. He was English. A very sweet, quiet man. He's passed away, he's no longer around.

Was his enthusiasm for the Planet of the Apes *movies on "high" all throughout the series?*
Oh, yes!

Was there ever any concern on anybody's part about the fact that you were showing up in all these Apes *movies in different roles?*
No, I don't think so, because they changed me around. In *Beneath* I was all covered up and in *Escape* they dyed my blonde hair strawberry blond. Then I was an ape in the last two.

So what was your major complaint about the ape makeup?
Those big brown contact lenses they put in my eyes. One night Arthur and I were at a dinner party at the home of Walter Grauman, the director. (The lenses, of course, were out by then.) Suddenly I turned to Arthur and I said, "I can't see anything ... take me home!" I was crying, in the middle of dinner. So he took me home and he called his doctor Charlie Kivowitz, and Charlie said, "Put her in the bathroom, let her sit on the toilet and put wet compresses on her eyes 'til I get the ophthalmologist." They came and looked at me in my bathroom—and by now it was like 11 o'clock at night. And Arthur was told that I could not wear those lenses again. So from then on, for the rest of the movie, I had to work with my eyelids kinda "down," so the camera didn't see my blue eyes. An ape has to have brown eyes! So I just kept 'em closed, like I was sleeping.

There was lots of action in the last two Apes *movies. Would you come and watch the shooting even if you weren't in that scene?*
I was around for some of it, but usually I only was around when I was required to be—I always had other things to do. I would sometimes show up on the set, even when I wasn't shooting, because we had several dogs and they had to come to the studio every day. At one point, we had ten dogs. We had three Great Danes, we had a border collie—you know what border collies are? They're the ones that can herd

Trundy visits John Chambers and the Oscar he won for the original *Planet of the Apes*.

a whole flock of sheep, or cattle, or everything else—one dog can do it! They're shepherding dogs, and they run sideways—it's indigenous to the breed. Then we had the little guys, Yorkshire terriers and poodles. And there were days when everybody had to go to the studio!

They all had to go to the studio because…?
 'Cause Arthur *wanted* them there [*laughs*]—Arthur would never leave them at

home! Arthur's secretaries used to scream at them all the time—all the secretaries except poor Sylvia, 'cause she'd been with him for 20 years. The other girls said [*with agitation*], "We can't *take* this!" He had five secretaries, and it would be poor Sylvia who had to take them out for their walks! Ten at a time! The big Danes didn't have to be on a leash, they were very well-trained, but the little guys that would scoot *any*where, they *had* to be on a leash. *Then*—it was funny—the border collie, Sunday, proceeded to give us ten puppies—and so *they* had to come along too! We had this chap who worked for us, Handy Andy, and we had an APJAC van, so we'd all pile in and we'd go to the studio. All of the dogs that we ever had were named after movies. We had Becky, we had Tom Sawyer, we had Huckleberry Finn…

Did your husband's love for dogs rub off on you?
I've had animals all my life. I love them.

Where were you when you heard that Jacobs had died?
I was in the South, in Mississippi, making Arthur's *Huckleberry Finn*. He couldn't go because of the humidity—he'd already had one heart attack, *he* couldn't stay there. But he used to call me every morning, ten o'clock my time in Mississippi, seven o'clock here in Los Angeles. He was an early riser.

One morning I was trying to teach Southern belles how to waltz when Bobby Greenhut, the associate producer, came and he said, "Phone call." I assumed it was my husband. I went to the office, to the phone, and it was Andy. I said, "Where's Arthur?" and he said, "Arthur's *dead*." My legs went to rubber, I collapsed. I didn't faint, but I went down on the floor. Greenhut came in and he said, "What's wrong?" and I said, "Arthur's passed away."

Where did he die?
He was found in his bed. When Andy came that morning to pick him up to take him to the studio, the housekeeper said, "Mr. Jacobs didn't wake up." So Andy went up and found that he was gone. He was lying on top of the bed in his pajamas and dressing gown, with the dogs all around him, like they were trying to keep him warm. That's how I found out. And then they couldn't get me out of Natchez, Mississippi! They only had two mail planes a day there! So what they did was get the governor's Lear Jet, bring it down. I had to ride to the plane with a policeman, on the back of a motorcycle—there were only two cops in Natchez. I arrived in Los Angeles in jeans and a T-shirt. And Charlie Kivowitz met me at the airport and he said, "Let's go into the VIP Room, I'll give you a shot of Valium." I said, "No, no, no, I don't *want* a shot of Valium. I just want you to take me to my husband"—Arthur had already been brought to a mortician. Charlie hemmed and hawed and I said, "Charlie, I have a hundred dollar bill in my pocket. If you don't take me, I'll take a cab." So he did take me to the mortician's place, and the mortician came out and he said to me, "Your husband isn't quite ready yet." I said, "I don't give a flying fuck. I want to see my husband. I don't care if he's 'ready' or not. Just leave me alone with him." And I went in and I sat and talked to him for about an hour. Just holding on to him. And … it was okay. Do you think I cared whether he was 'ready' or

not, from a mortician?? Do you think I need a shot of Valium from the doctor?? I don't *think* so!

Then I got back to my house—I had asked for *nobody* to be there. Well, the house was *full* of people. About the only one good person was Gene Kelly—he manned the phones. He said, "Sweetheart, just go in the other room, leave all these people alone." And then there was another person who everybody used to criticize. Her name was Rona Barrett. She lived across the street. She also manned the phones. People used to call her a bitch. She was *not* a bitch, she was just a columnist, for cryin' out loud, doin' her job. But, believe me, she was at my house and she started shooing people out—she said, "Get out. Out!" She came up to my boobs, she was so short [*laughs*], but she got them out of there! She said, "Mrs. Jacobs has to be alone now. Mr. Kelly and I will take care of everything." Which they did.

Did you retire from acting after he passed away?
I did a couple of TV shows, like *Quincy* and shows like that, but I sort of let it go. I did remarry at one point, and I have two beautiful children, 24 and 23.

Your second husband—are you still married to him?
No. Got rid of *him* [*laughs*]!

In more recent years, you made a humanitarian trip to India.
Not once—I've been there 12 times! I worked with Mother Teresa, and I slept in her convent. This is what she did: She had a walking stick, and we'd go up and down the streets and she'd keep poking people who were lying in the street. If they were alive, and not too ill, they'd go to the House of the Ill. If they were dead, they'd be taken to the House of the Dying, where she'd pray over them. Then we'd find the poor little babies—they're always girls, 'cause [in India] they only want *boys*, you know. The little girls they get rid of, which is really awful. They're all so adorable, they've got these big black eyes, and they're so small I could almost put them in the palm of my hand. And so we'd have to pick up the babies. I'd have a big knapsack and I'd put the babies in and we'd take them to [the orphanage]. I've adopted about 25 of them.

You adopted 25 babies? They lived with you?
No, no—I *pay* for them. I've got adopted children in India and China, about 40. I support them. Because the nuns cannot afford to support them, needless to say. What do you think I'd sleep in a convent for [*laughs*]? On the floor, with the other nuns and getting up at four in the morning. Mother Teresa used to come and poke *me* with her damn stick! I'd say, "I'm *up*, Mother!"

And today?
I volunteer at church, I spend a lot of time of there. I feed the homeless every Saturday afternoon and every Sunday afternoon, which is not pleasant. You see them … not just men, *women*. And the women bring their little children. I always try to keep a couple of cookies for the little guys. I do it from my heart. Do you know

In her post-movie career days, Trundy did humanitarian work alongside Mother Teresa.

what it's like, standing there in a line with these poor people. Forget the *men*, but, I mean, the women with their babies? It's so depressing, I come home and cry. I happen to be very Catholic and so I also go to Mass every day. And I'm not allowed into church without my dogs.

[Laughs] Really?
 Don't laugh so hard, it's the truth! The priests say to me, "If the dogs aren't here, you're not welcome!" [*Laughs*] I toodle into church with my two dogs and my walking stick.

Do they behave themselves in church?
 Oh, they're perfect. We sit in the front pew, and they're absolutely perfect. And when there's Communion, they have their tongues out like they're going to get Communion! If you ever saw a picture of it, you would drop dead. One of the priests said to me [*in an Irish brogue*], "Natalie, I'd like to bring them down some cookies, but people will think I'm giving them Communion." [*Laughs*] I said, "No, no, no. When Mass is over, we'll go next door to the rectory and have a cup of coffee, and then you can give 'em any cookies you want!"

Are you going to see the new Tim Burton Apes *movie? Are you looking forward to it?*

I *will* go to see it but I'm *not* looking forward to it. The first *Apes* belonged to my husband. And with all of this publicity about the new movie that's been coming out, *nobody* ever mentioned his name. If you'll permit me a closing comment, I want to say that the most important thing that I loved was being with him. He took me everywhere he went, even if it was just to New York for a day. *Every*where. He never left me behind. I loved it. Imagine if they had frequent flyer miles then!

Martin Varno on Night of the Blood Beast

> *The [*Night of the*] Blood Beast sneak preview was at a theater in or around L.A. On my left side was sitting Forry Ackerman, and on my right side was sitting Jerry Bixby. And their main job was to keep my hands held down so I wouldn't cut my throat.*

The sci-fi/horror movie fad was red-hot in the mid–1950s, with the number of releases rising every year, and then shooting into orbit after the Russian launch of Sputnik 1. In the two days of that historic October 4, 1957, event which inaugurated the Space Age, 43 films involving satellites and spaceships were announced for production. Roger Corman was one of the many moviemakers suddenly involved in the Hollywood space race, promptly producing *War of the Satellites* in late 1957 and, in partnership with his brother Gene, *Night of the Blood Beast* the following spring.

Brought aboard to write the *Blood Beast* script was Martin Varno, 21-year-old son of veteran actor Roland Varno. A sci-fi buff, Martin concocted the story of an astronaut (Michael Emmet) whose return from space is a middle-of-nowhere crash landing which he does not survive. His body is recovered by colleagues and brought to a nearby tracking station, where he mysteriously *returns* to life—or, more accurately, returns to *lives* (plural): A fluoroscope examination reveals that his body has become the "carrier" for a host of tiny alien creatures.

A non-union writer hired at a rock-bottom rate, Varno later engaged the Brothers Corman in a bloody, beastly Writers Guild arbitration battle—and now laughingly recalls the saga.

I was born in the Hollywood Hospital. I am told that three wise winos showed up in front of my mother's room, but one of them, Benny the Putz, had forgotten

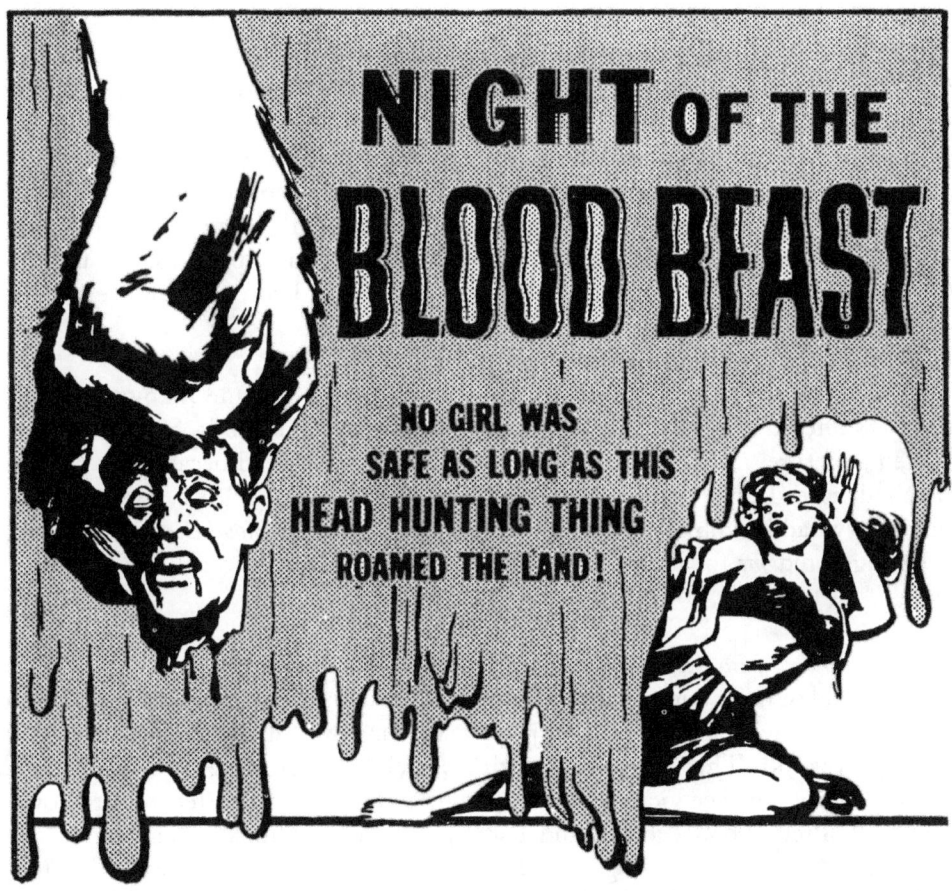

"NIGHT OF THE BLOOD BEAST": STARRING
Michael Emmet • Angela Greene • John Baer
AN AMERICAN-INTERNATIONAL PICTURE

Just two years out of his teens, Martin Varno penned the Roger Corman–produced space monster shocker *Night of the Blood Beast*.

to bring the frankincense, and they didn't want to come in and worship with just a *couple* of gifts when there were three of them. So they left a partially consumed pastrami sandwich and then beat it out of there. Of course, I can't tell you whether this is true or not, 'cause I was just a wee baby!

Your father was an actor so I assume you also grew up in Hollywood. Were you on the sets of any of your dad's pictures?
 Very few of them, because I was really pretty small. I was on the sets of one or two of them, and I can't tell you which ones. I wish I could.

A writer, is that what you wanted to be when you grew up?
 Actually, I wanted to be an actor. And discovered early on that I was not good at it.

When did you begin writing?

At an early age. The first job I ever had was writing for a publication called *The Canyon Crier*, which was started in the late '30s or the early '40s by a man by the name of Norman Rose. Norman hired me, my first writing job, for $5 a week, which was a lot of money in 1947. It was my job to write a weekly column on the kids in all of the mountain areas, from Malibu all the way to the other side of Griffith Park, which is a big, long area—lots of canyons in there. I'd write about, oh, "Little Joey Schmerdlapp has a Golden Retriever who just had nine puppies, and they are just so beautiful"—*that* sort of stuff. And, by golly, I made my $5 cash every week.

How did you get the job of writing Night of the Blood Beast?

One of my very best friends, an ex-roommate, was Jerome Bixby the writer. Jerry was offered *Night of the Blood Beast*, but wasn't able to do it. See, he had just written a picture, *It! The Terror from Beyond Space* [1958], and because of *that* one, somebody else (I don't remember who) jumped in and said, "Please, write *us* a picture." Jerry had just obligated himself to that person when *Blood Beast* came along, so he suggested *me* for it: He said, "Hey, I've got a friend who could do it just as well..."

Why were you so "into" science fiction at that time?

A friend of mine knew Forry Ackerman and had introduced me to him. I'd been reading some science fiction and I enjoyed it very much, and Forry invited me down to a regular weekly Thursday night meeting of a club known as LASFS, which stood for Los Angeles Science Fiction Society, in a little hotel on a side street toward downtown L.A. Pretty soon I joined and I was going every Thursday night and I was meeting some very interesting people. And also some of the standard sci-fi fans. Young ... usually extremely intelligent ... *totally* antisocial, they wouldn't know how to get a date with the opposite sex, no way, they could read a hundred books and they still wouldn't know! They were the kids that had their own special table in high school [*laughs*]. It was kind of sad and also wonderful, for those few who made it. I knew a lot of them, and they were incredible.

We had some startlingly good writers in those days: Jerry Bixby was one of them, and of course A. E. van Vogt was a wonderful character. I knew most of them well. In fact, at one point in time Ray Bradbury signed over to me for a six-month period all the radio rights to everything he'd ever written. I was just a kid, I must have been 21! I still have the letter somewhere—Forry negotiated this. I got together with [radio director] Anthony Ellis, who had been directing the wonderful CBS series *X Minus One*, and he was going to direct most of them. I wish I'd been able to do something with it, it might have made me a rich man [*laughs*]!

So Bixby lines you up for the Blood Beast *job, and now you're meeting Roger and Gene Corman...*

Their offices were at Sunset and LaBrea, at the old Chaplin Studios, which were at *that* time called Kling Studios. The Chaplin Studios still exist today, but as a recording studio [A&M Records]. It's a *beautiful*, wonderful old studio—some great stuff was filmed there, including many of the classics of Chaplin. Anyway, we had a meeting. Gene Corman had some sort of a weird idea for the picture and he threw that at me, and Roger threw things at me, and so did various other people. And they were gonna pay me a very small amount of money, maybe it was a few hundred dollars. So ... okay. I signed the contract with 'em, and went to work.

Did you know that the amount of money they were offering you was below union scale?
I didn't know it was below scale because I didn't know what scale *was*. I wasn't a member of the Writers Guild of America at that point.

I see in the credits that it's based on a story by Gene Corman.
Ha!

Did *Gene actually sit down and write something, or did he just tell you his ideas?*
He wrote nothing down. He had some rambling ideas but they didn't have very much to do with the movie that became *Night of the Blood Beast*.

Was the picture inspired by the real-life "space race" then getting underway?
Yes, of course it was. Definitely.

How long did it take you to write the script?
About six weeks.

Did you show what you were writing a little at a time to Roger and/or Gene?
Yeah, in some cases. Not all the time. I showed them big hunks of it, and didn't have any problems.

Did you get any uncredited help from family or friends during the writing process?
Yes, I did. From one of the top writers in Hollywood, as a matter of fact. A damn fine writer, and a man who taught me an awful lot about writing. A very, very dear friend who won an Academy Award for writing *The Defiant Ones* [1958], Harold Jacob Smith. Hal was a good friend of my father's, one of his very, very best, closest friends, and I had known him for a number of years. Unfortunately, because of Hal's political feelings, he'd been through some tough times. He was not one of the Hollywood Ten, but he *could* have probably been the Hollywood Eleventh [*laughs*]! Basically he was an idealist, he didn't hurt anybody—he wasn't sitting in a basement somewhere, making bombs to kill somebody. He wrote declarations of peace. And yet he'd been on a blacklist and nobody used him until Stanley Kramer [producer-director of *The Defiant Ones*], a good and courageous friend, said, "I don't give a god-damn, *I* will hire you. You're a fine writer!" and hired him. And, by God, Hal won an Academy Award for it, he and his partner Ned Young.

And Smith gave you some pointers?
I remember sitting at Hal's kitchen table—he was living on Laurel Canyon in a very, very nice home because he made a *lot* of good money on [*The Defiant Ones*].

I was shooting him lines and so on, and he said, "Look, why don't you do *this*?" "Why don't you do *that*?" Of course I'd listen to this guy. In the Blood Beast's speech at the end, there was something like, "Because you don't understand me, because you see my countenance as different than yours, you see me as an embodiment of evil." A lot of that was Hal. It was a good line, but they snipped it out. Jerry Bixby also gave me some good pointers. I saw Jerry an awful lot during this time, we were good friends, and talked together on the phone a lot.

The idea of a "pregnant" man was certainly pushing the envelope in 1958. Your idea?
   Yes, but I didn't think of it in terms of a "pregnant man." I was just thinking of the astronaut's body as a vehicle, to get the little alien critters (which in the movie looked like seahorses) to Earth. So it was my idea, yeah, but I didn't think of it as a "pregnant man."

I'm sure you knew as you wrote it that it was going to be low-budget. What guidelines were set down for you by the Cormans?
   None, because I gave them the impression that I knew pretty much what I was doing, and they sort of got the idea that I wasn't going to use 50,000 extras and things. *Naturally*, I wasn't going to write something like that, I knew they didn't have the money. I was very, very conscious of the money—I always *am*.

Conscious of how much money the producers have got to spend.
   Yeah. *Any*thing that I wrote, I was conscious of, "What can be done?" If you go overboard, you're just spinning your wheels and wasting your time, because they're going to turn to you and say, "*We* can't afford that!" I probably sat with the Cormans on a few occasions and asked, "Can we *afford* to do this? Do you think we can do *that*?" And they'd say, "Well, we can do *this*, but let's change the story so we don't have to do *that*. It would be a lot cheaper that way." "Cheap," don't forget, was the main word in their vocabulary, Gene and Roger. Actually, Gene didn't open his mouth, really, until Roger told him he could.

What was the title of your script?
   Creature from Galaxy 27. That was also the shooting title. It was my title, I made it up. It was released as *Night of the Blood Beast*, which was *not* my title, it was made up by either Roger or Gene.

What kind of research did you do? Medical? Aerospace?
   Lots of that. Lots of time spent in a library two blocks west of Vine, which was a wonderful place until some son of a bitch homeless jerk who decided that he didn't like books burned it down.

Did you visit the locations or the set as the picture was being shot?
   Yes. The exteriors of the "tracking station" facility were shot on Mount Lee, near the famous HOLLYWOOD sign, outside what *was* the first television station in Los Angeles. It is still a television station for emergencies—if there's a major

emergency in Los Angeles, it takes over every channel in L.A. It's up there at the top of the hill, high above Hollywood, and I got [permission to shoot there] simply by picking up a telephone and *asking* for it. Nobody else had ever *had* that idea—I guess everybody assumed that the city wouldn't *allow* it. Well, I thought to myself, why not call the city and *find out*? I called, and the city said sure, but there *was* a fee: In those days, there was an $8 fee per actor [*laughs*]. The crew could be any size. So that's all we had to pay, $8 times six actors. This television station is right over Hollywood, so you have a magnificent view. It's really a very beautiful structure. I was inside of it—we went inside a *couple* times, but we didn't do any shooting inside of it.

Incidentally, my father was in the first dramatic television show released in Los Angeles, just before I was born, and it was transmitted from up there. It was a murder mystery or something, in 1935 or '36. He said it was incredible: The actors had to wear white makeup, and then blue makeup over their lips. He said it was "wonderful," there were about like, oh, 40 television sets in Los Angeles at the time, each one about an inch and a half diameter. Another thing that was very interesting about that television station: That place had at one point during the Second World War an incredible AM transmission, military-government transmission of something like 2,000,000 watts! They used to send information and propaganda stuff to our allies around the world. A true story: On Sundays, they would get some of the Hollywood stars who were foreign-born to broadcast from there. For instance, Greer Garson might be up there and she'd be saying to her fellow English people, "Stiff upper lip, America's right behind you," things like that. Well, one day they had Errol Flynn up there. What a lot of Americans do not know is that Flynn was a wanted man—all of his life, there was a warrant for his arrest in Australia if he ever went back there, for forced sex with the daughter of a very, very big police magistrate in Sydney. That's why he never went back. One day on Mount Lee, they were beaming directly to Australia and Flynn was saying, "Mates, it's very important that you know that America is with you" and "The Battle of the Coral Sea was a fantastic thing because you were behind there as we came in" and "God bless you" and so on. "And, oh," he added, just as he was finishing up, "a special word to Police Magistrate Jones there. I just want to let you know that ... I will never come back to your country, you miserable cocksucker ... and, by the way, your daughter was *grrreat*!" [*Laughs*] And this was transmitting to Australia!

The first Blood Beast *footage shot was the exteriors at that TV station?*
Yes.

And all the stuff in the underbrush—same area?
That was down below, in Griffith Park—famous Bronson Canyon. As a matter of fact, that cave was a Bronson cave. And after that, the interiors were all done on a stage at Kling.

What was the budget?
The number 87,000 comes back to me, but I can't swear to that. I do know for a fact that it was under 100,000.

Were you also around during the shooting at Kling?

I would say that, for about three-quarters of the picture, I was on the set. I was there ostensibly to make any script changes or anything like that. And I did make a few.

The actors in the movie—would you care to rate the performances?

[*Laughs*] Oh, *must* I? They're pretty awful—just about everybody! John Baer had worked a little bit, he made a couple pictures before, he did *We're No Angels* [1955] with Bogart. He was a nice guy. Was *not* an actor. But he was "pretty" so the little girls got wet panties. Georgianna Carter just stood there looking perplexed most of the time, like somebody had reached over and inserted their finger into her ass. The only real honest-to-God actor there was Tyler McVey. Tyler was a wonderful actor, a consummate professional, and subsequently a friend of mine for a number of years. He had been a great radio actor—you heard his voice in classic radio in the '40s, *all* the time. A lovely man ... a *wonderful* man.

What about the Blood Beast, played by Ross Sturlin?

The monster suit had just been used in another picture about two weeks before [Roger Corman's *Teenage Cave Man*, 1958]—they changed it a little in order to reuse it here. Somebody said, "The nose looks too Jewish" [*laughs*], so they cut that down and it became a beak. And I think they sprayed it with something so it would look a little different. Poor Ross was *dying* inside of the thing—it was probably about 125 degrees in there [*laughs*]! Ross worked in a couple of the Cormans' pictures, and that's why all the monsters were fairly short [*laughs*]! Because Ross was a little guy!

There are a few scenes in Blood Beast *which make me think that someone involved in the movie was a big fan of* The Thing *[1951]. Had you seen* The Thing? *Was it an inspiration?*

Subconsciously, maybe. I loved some of the scenes in *The Thing* and I'm sure that crept in one way or another. But not overtly.

I'm thinking of the scene of the Blood Beast unexpectedly bursting into a room through a door, and then being driven out by fire; the corpse of Dr. Wyman hanging upside down (which is what the Thing did to its victims)...

Well, that's just what you *did* with corpses in those days [*laughs*].

Were you paid extra to stick around during production?

Oh, no, no. That's sort-of "the deal": You write a picture, you're always on the set. They might want dialogue changed, they might want a scene written real quick. That's just a courtesy. And I was very interested in how they were handling the picture, how they were putting it together.

And were you happy with the way they were putting it together?

No. They were changing things on me and not telling me about it. I could *tell*. Even at that young stage, my mind could put the scenes together. They were also

The monster from Corman's *Teenage Cave Man* (shot just a few weeks earlier) was slightly modified to become the Blood Beast (seen here doing battle with Michael Emmet).

writing dialogue and not telling me about it. I just wanted the courtesy! I got to the point where I called Forry, who was my agent, and said, "I am not working for these sons of bitches any more. I am sick and tired of the whole thing! *You're* my agent, why don't you do something about this?!" and blah blah blah.

So how did your dissatisfaction with them turn into Screen Writers Guild arbitration?
   When this whole thing started, I *wasn't* a member of the Writers Guild. I was, however, a member of the Masquers Club in Hollywood. The Masquers Club was the second oldest actors' elbow-bending and rollicking club in America, the Lambs being first. It was very near where I lived and very near where Kling Studio was, it was up on Sycamore. I'd come into the club at night when we were shooting, get a drink and see my friends, and they'd say, "Gee, your picture is being shot, why are you looking unhappy?" I'd say, "Well, because I'm working with some of the biggest assholes in Hollywood!" "Oh, tell us!"
   Now, some of these people at the Masquers were pretty damn big. Some of these people were *very* damn big. They were not only actors, they were producers and directors and writers and other people. That night, a very dear man by the name of Jay Jostyn happened to be there. Jay Jostyn was *Mr. District Attorney* in radio. That show was a big one—I mean, my God, what red-blooded American boy didn't

listen to *that* every week? Jay was a friend and I told him about the situation, and he really got pissed off that I was getting screwed by the Cormans. "Everybody knows in the business what pricks these people are. But one of the biggest problems is the fact that many, many people, especially people in my own union [the Screen Actors Guild], are getting work *constantly* from them. Even though the Cormans are screwing them [salary-wise] the actors are *not* gonna turn on 'em, because it's a steady income. The Cormans and others in Hollywood are not playing by the rules. We've had meetings where we've directly *talked* to the actors, saying, 'These people are screwing you, but we can't come and hold arbitrations against them unless you finger them.'" That was unfortunately true—it simply wasn't legal.

The Screen Actors Guild—well, no guild could go after the Cormans unless a member filed charges against them … correct?

Exactly. Jay said, "I realize we all need money to live but, gosh, you guys are being picked on by a guy who's becoming rich off of your sweat. He perpetrates it by saying, 'Well, yeah, but I'm gonna use you in the next picture,' and usually he *does*. The part may be something very small, and in some little picture, but you can always *count* on it, as long as you don't make waves, and you are valuable to him."

Then Jay said, "Even though you're not a member of the Writers Guild, I happen to know that the Writers Guild protects you. They represent you. *You* are a writer, and they represent you." I remember his exact words: As we were having our drinks there in the Masquers Bar, he said, "Marty, if I have to take you by the hand and stuff you in my car and drive you to the Writers Guild, I'm gonna *do* it. Damn it, you have to *call* them."

Which you did.

I *did* tell the Writers Guild what was going on, and they said, "Oh, *reeeally?* Well, yes, we think, gosh, we should make you a member, shouldn't we…?" In those days, I think it cost me $28 or $32 or something like that to join the Writers Guild of America West. Once I did, they said, "Welcome, brother!" holding their arms open, and then: "Now we'd like to talk to you about what's been going on with your picture…" I told them, and they said, "Let's arbitrate against the bastards. Will you sign papers against them?" and I said, "*Yeah.*" That's how the hearing came about.

Charging them with paying less than scale for a screenplay.

Right. Scale was in those days something like 1200 and change [for a script], and I had gotten something like 640, 680. The charges were based on money—the Writers Guild told Corman that he had to pay me scale.

I'm one of the few people who ever arbitrated against Roger Corman. Because so many people were so, "[*Gasp*] My God! I'm working! I'm working in a real movie! Roger's giving me a chance!" And, meanwhile, Roger's paying this guy hardly anything a week [*laughs*]! Roger *did* give a lot of people a chance: "I'll give you exposure. You just work for me and I will screw you over many times. But if you do it right, I'll keep hiring you, and at least you'll be able to pay the rent." Well, hey, that's better than nothing—*this* was the thinking of most people.

Did you ever go back to the set after that night at the Masquers Club with Jay Jostyn?
I don't think so, no.

So Roger was served the papers, and...
Yes, they sent him notice of arbitration. By that time, the picture was already made and they were in the cutting room. I remember hearing from somebody that Roger was served the papers in the cutting room, and he was throwing things around and yelling and screaming. *That* made me feel very good.

Who told you about him throwing stuff around?
It was somebody working on the set or around the set ... or it might have been one of the editors. Roger was reeeally incensed, really pissed off, and truly hated me, and declared, "He will never work for me again!" And of course I said, "*Yeeeeah*!!!" [*Laughs*] "Okay, it's a deal!"

Well, that made up for how unhappy you were during the making of the movie!
I became *so* damned unhappy at the way they were changing things around, things that they told me would *not* be changed. You don't *do* that with me. They did it ... not with sitting and talking to me rationally about it, they just *did* it. They were not serious, and they were screwing people even before we started. I mean, there were people who were unhappy because they got shat on a couple pictures *back*. And yet they were coming in and talking with Roger and Gene. The butt-kissing was thick and heavy!

Shouldn't the Cormans have tried to quietly pay you at that point and get you to drop it?
An offer *did* get to me: "Look, if you hang up on this thing, Roger and Gene will use you a *lot* in the future." I don't remember who told me that. One of the crew members. He said, "What are you *doing* this for? My God, you're throwing away a beautiful thing. You could be working for the next ten years!" Yeah, great ... turning out shit for Roger and Gene, at slave wages. Then, too, I got a phone call from [actor] Wally Campo, who was in several Corman pictures, and who was screwed right along with everybody. He called me at home, how he got my number I do not know, and he said, "You *bastard*. What you have *done* to Roger. Roger has been good to you, he *gave* you your *start*, your first picture—and you *did* this to him! This is going to *hurt* him." I said [*softly, seriously*], "God, I *hope* so...!"—and he hung up on me. I never spoke to the guy again. And Wally and I had been friends, more or less.

What can you recall about the arbitration?
As it ended up, I had two separate arbitrations with them. The first was for the money. In full Writers Guild Arbitration Court in Beverly Hills one night, with guys who were (basically) representing me sitting on the arbitration panel. There were several top writers on the committee that heard this thing! Right now, of course, I can't think of anyone's name, but *you'd* know the names—these were top, Academy Award-winning writers. I mean, if their *shadow* fell against me, I'd be so honored.

And they were saying to me, "Listen, Marty, don't worry about anything. We don't like to see our people *screwed*."

How did one arbitration hearing turn into two?
Well, I didn't know that [the Cormans] were also gonna try and screw me out of the *credit*: Little greasy Gene was gonna say it was *his* original story! At the first arbitration, they said, "Gene Corman wrote the original story," and I said, "He did *not!*" Well, [the Cormans] didn't realize that I had kept copious notes while I was writing the thing—I had been taught to date everything, it's something that I do to this very day. The arbitration board members asked me, "Do you have notes?" I told 'em that I had notes, *lots* of notes, and that I had put dates on *everything* … and they went, "Yaaaaaaaaay!" [*Laughs*] I gave those to them, and we had another big arbitration, and the Cormans were told, "No, you can't do this" [give Gene Corman story credit].

The two separate arbitrations, the money and the credit—they were on two different nights, obviously.
The hearing about the money took two nights, and then the hearing about the credit, which was two or three weeks later, just one night.

So you won on the credit. And on the money?
I also won on the money. But Roger refused to pay. The consequences of *that* were, he was told that from then on he couldn't use union writers. So, he used a bunch of *non*-union writers, for maybe a couple *years*. But eventually Roger wanted to use a Guild writer on something, and he couldn't, and it was really frustrating him, I understand from the inside. He finally said, "Okay, damn it, pay Varno the other 700 bucks," or whatever it was.

You had to wait for your money until the day came when he needed a union writer.
Exactly. At the time when this happened, I was out of the country. If I'd been around, I would have bitched about it and said, "Okay, add *another* thousand bucks to it for the discomfort that you caused me." We could have pushed it through, the Writers Guild would have backed me. But I was out of the country and they couldn't find me—I was in Mexico. I got home and there were all these messages for me, and one was from writer Bob Bloch, who said, "Marty, where *are* you? The Guild has some money for you." I ended up with something like seven, eight hundred bucks. I paid Ackerman, and there were back dues to the unions which I had to take care of, but I still ended up with what to *me* was a fortune at the time—that's a lot of years ago. And then Roger could use union writers. So that was the situation there.

You mentioned preventing Gene Corman from getting a story credit. But he does *get an on-screen story credit.*
What happened was that I got a phone call from a gentleman by the name of Kaye, who was with American International. At this point, the prints of *Blood Beast* had already been struck and sent out, and Kaye said, "Look, changing it is gonna

cost us *thousands* of dollars. It would mean recalling all the prints and redoing them." And I, like a softie, said, "Well ... *o-kay*." I should have just said, "Fuck it. I'm sorry, but you gotta do this." But ol' softie Marty said to him, "Look, it's not that important to me. *Leave* it that way."

Leave it "Screenplay by Martin Varno, Story by Gene Corman."
Yeah. And Mr. Kaye said [*rapturously*], "Oh, thank you—*thaaaank* you. *Thaaaank* you!" That was that. I didn't put it in writing, but it still (I guess) was considered legal, and they left it that way. So, yes, to this day the credits say, "Story by Gene Corman," but Gene Corman had nothing to do with it. It was not his original story at all, it was *my* original story.

Do you remember where you saw the picture for the first time?
Oh, do I ever! It was a real honest-to-God sneak preview. They talk about sneak previews today, but *those* aren't sneak previews—it's not a sneak preview when you publicize it six weeks in advance! Sneak previews are where there are a few people from the studio in the audience, and then a little man comes out with a microphone and says, "Folks, I realize that you're here tonight to see *Schnoopnoodle's Paradise*, but, guess what? we have a completely untried, interesting movie for you. And *Schnoopnoodle's Paradise* will be played afterwards. Anybody who wants their money back"—and of course nobody ever did—"can come and get it." *That's* a sneak preview.

The *Blood Beast* sneak preview was at a theater in or around L.A. On my left side was sitting Forry Ackerman, and on my right side was sitting Jerry Bixby. And their main job was to keep my hands held down so I wouldn't cut my *throat*. That's when I first saw it. Hey, at least people didn't start throwing things at the screen! It was not a bad *start*, I guess.

Were the Cormans there?
Yes, I remember we saw Roger and Gene just as we were walking in. They said [*nervously, awkwardly*], "Oh ... Marty ... Hiiii...," and I said [*flatly, coldly*], "Hi." Then we went and sat down in our seats. I had not been notified of the screening, and obviously the Corman brothers were *not* happy at my presence.

One of the things that helps Blood Beast *a little: I thought some of the photography was kind of interesting.*
That was John Nickolaus. He was a nice man, he did his job ... I'm sure that he added a lot more than [director] Bernie Kowalski did. We had some talented people around, some of whom I worked with before. The production manager, a guy by the name of Jack Bohrer, *we* worked on several pictures together; and the art director Dan Haller, *he* showed some imagination. I mean, they probably gave him a budget of $24.98—"Make a space rocket!" "Oh ... okay..."

How was the rocket made?
It had a wooden framework—plywood which had been taken to the mill and

sawed in circles for the "ribs" of the rocket. Then plastic sheet stapled around it. Then it was sprayed with some sort of metallic stuff. I thought that rocket was just awful! I also thought the blood cells [on a microscope slide] were awful. Also the little Blood Beast babies as seen through the fluoroscope, the critters that looked like seahorses. That surprised me, that that could be so terrible.

And your script—what do you think of that in 2002?
My God, I was a terrible writer in those days [*laughs*]! But, y'know, it was my first picture—what do you expect, I was 21 years old! I was not really expecting an Oscar. A Golden Globe, maybe, but not an Oscar [*laughs*]! Watching it recently, I noticed big differences between what happened in the movie and what actually *would* have happened in real life. If communication broke down between Cape Canaveral and that tracking station, there'd be an *army* of people descending on the place to determine why. And the people at the tracking station wouldn't have had Very pistols. If you happen to have a boat, Very pistols are wonderful for signaling over water. But anywhere *else*, they start forest fires [*laughs*]! But ... *that's* okay. A little artistic license there!

What was the "message" of the movie—if there was *one? I was never quite sure how the moviemakers wanted us, the audience, to regard the Blood Beast.*
Originally it was clearer ... *I* think. The idea was very simple: Just because something is ugly or "different" doesn't make it evil. That was *it*, it was so simple.

In your later movie career, you worked as a makeup man and as a sound editor.
Yes, I was a makeup man. Usually for special effects makeup. As a makeup artist, I'd do things like go to the coroner's office in downtown L.A. [for research]. I had a friend in the Medical Examiner's office and, for instance, I told him, "When you get somebody who's been shot right between the eyes, call me. I want to study him. See what it looks like." And one night, sure enough, he called me and he said, "We've got a customer for you." I was amaaazed at how little blood there was, how little trauma. And I used that knowledge in a picture where the bad guy, a biker, got shot right between the eyes. So ... there's value everywhere [*laughs*]! However, it didn't take me too long to realize I couldn't make a living doing this. Those days were hungry days.

As a sound editor, I worked under the table for some pretty big people, and then finally I was able to get into the union. My first legal job was at Universal, when they were doing dozens of television episodes a week—they were the biggest employer of sound effects editors in Hollywood. I love to cut sound, cutting sound is a very creative thing. The things that make me the proudest are, I have cut several pieces for Cousteau, and I've cut several *National Geographic*s. *These* people are great to work for, I'd do it for free if the union would let me. They give you the most help, they don't bug you, they don't look over your shoulder and say, "Okay, what have you cut *today*??" You do it, and they appreciate you.

The funny thing is that I worked for Roger on two other pictures, and he has no idea of that. I laid sound on two of his pictures, mainly 'cause I needed the money.

Martin Varno in the 1950s (left) and in the 2000s (right); now based in Denver, he's still writing.

It was lousy money, but it *was* money. The movies were pure crap, it was cars hurtling through outhouses and all kinds of "class" stuff like that. But it was also a lot of fun. Sound editors get their real big kicks with wonderful squashing sounds like that, you know!

If you could turn back the clock and not get involved with the Cormans, not have Blood Beast *on your résumé—would you do it, or would you bite the bullet and go through it all again for the experience?*

I think I would go through it all again for the experience. It taught me a lot, and it made me some good friends. And, hey, it was a first picture. How many 21-year-old kids get a chance to get a real movie made—even by a guy like Corman?

Night of the Blood Beast (AIP, 1958)

Balboa Productions; 65 minutes; First day of shooting: May 19, 1958 (shooting title, *The Creature from Galaxy 27*); Executive Producer: Roger Corman; Produced by Gene Corman; Directed by Bernard L. Kowalski; Screenplay: Martin Varno; Photography: John Nicholaus [Nickolaus], Jr.; Music: Alexander Laszlo; Art Director: Dan Haller; Production Manager: Jack Bohrer; Supervising Editor: Dick Currier; Editor: Jodie Copelan; Assistant Director: Robert White; Sound: Herman Lewis; Property Master: Karl Brainard; Title Design: Bill Martin; Makeup: Harry Thomas

Michael Emmet (*Major John Corcoran*), Angela Greene (*Dr. Julie Benson*), John Baer (*Dr. Steve Dunlap*), Ed Nelson (*Dave Randall*), Tyler McVey (*Dr. Alex Wyman/Voice of Alien*), Georgianna Carter (*Donna Bixby*), Ross Sturlin (*The Alien*)

Beverly Washburn

> *One of the [Thriller] prop guys stood up on a ladder, and on cue he started hitting me over the head with this cup on a fishing line. And he got* paid *to do that!*

Show biz was in the cards for Beverly Washburn right from the start: Born in Hollywood Presbyterian Hospital to a family with a vaudeville background, she was modeling as a tyke and making movies by age six. Disney fans remember her as the neighbor girl in the sentimental *Old Yeller* (1957), and TV fans as a regular on Loretta Young's small-screen series, but sci-fi and horror buffs have entirely different points of reference: She was the little girl visited by "the Unknown People" in *Superman and the Mole-Men* (1951), an *Enterprise* crew member who ages and dies in *Star Trek*'s "The Deadly Years," the hillbilly girl in the haunted house in *Thriller*'s "Parasite Mansion" and, most notoriously, the childlike psychotic Elizabeth in writer-director Jack Hill's demented *Spider Baby, or The Maddest Story Ever Told* (1964) with Lon Chaney, Jr.

Whose idea was it for you to start trying out for movie roles?

My aunts and uncles were in vaudeville, so there was that background. When somebody suggested to my mother that I do some modeling, she got me an agent and I *did* some children's modeling. That's how I got started. Then I just began the ol' audition thing.

The Killer That Stalked New York *was your first movie; was that your first audition?*

No. Actually, what happened is that my sister Audrey was working as an acrobat in a hospital in Long Beach, and I—

Working as an acrobat in a hospital...?

[*Laughs*] They were putting on a benefit show. I was about six years old and I tagged along, and I got up and sang. Well, Jock Mahoney was there—you remember him from [the TV series] *The Range Rider* and *Yancy Derringer*. He was about six-four and I was about two feet tall—I was always small! We talked, and I fell in love with him. He spoke with my mother, and my mother said I had an agent and all that. Jock thought I should be working.

Well, because I *did* have an agent, I went on all these auditions, but I never got anything. It was the old Catch-22 situation: They wouldn't give me anything 'cause I didn't have any credits ... but how do you get a credit unless they give you something? It was very hard to get started. At any rate, I had an agent and she sent me on this audition for *The Killer That Stalked New York*. When we got to Columbia, my mother sat in the lobby with me and they brought out the script for us to read. It said in the script, "There sits little Walda Kowalski with her long brown hair and her big brown eyes." I have blond hair and blue eyes. So my mother turned to me—she was always very supportive—and she said, "Honey, you're not gonna get this part because you're not what they're *looking* for. But just go in and do your best." As fate would

Beverly Washburn at the start of her career.

have it, we were sitting in the lobby and Jock Mahoney walked through—Jock was under contract there at the time. He remembered me from Long Beach, so he asked my mother, "What is she doing here?" My mother said I was auditioning for a part, but I wouldn't get it because they were looking for a brunette with big brown eyes. He said, "Just wait a minute," and he went in and talked with the producer. Well, he told the producer, "Oh, she's done *this* and she's done *that*"—of course, I hadn't done a *thing*! They kind of took me on his say-so, so my first part was a speaking role. Which are difficult to get. So I really feel that I would *not* have gotten that part if it hadn't been for Jock Mahoney putting in a good word for me. Once I had that speaking role under my belt, it was easier to go from there. And I *died* in that movie! I died in my first movie!

Did you ever act with Jock Mahoney in a movie or TV show?
No, I didn't. We stayed in touch over the years, but I never did work with him. Sally Field is his stepdaughter and I did work with Sally on [the TV series] *Gidget*. She's just a doll.

Were kid actors friendly to each other back in those days, or did the competition for roles make that tough?
We would see the same people at auditions over and over, and I think we were

all friendly. I made some *lifelong* friends in the business, like Sharon Baird, who was one of the original Mouseketeers. She was doing *The Mickey Mouse Club* when I was doing *Old Yeller*, and we've remained friends for all these years. And of course Tommy Kirk from *Old Yeller*, and then Paul Petersen and Tony Dow and Laurin Chapin and Cynthia Pepper and Annette Funicello—a lot of people I worked with as a teenager or as a child, and we've managed to stay in touch. Which I'm very grateful for.

Any recollection of Superman and the Mole-Men?
I was only seven or so. For *me* at that time, I was working with Superman. It was not until years later that I realized that I had worked with George Reeves—I mean, how cool is *that*? But when you're that little, you really have no concept. Like when I worked in *The Greatest Show on Earth* [1952], I was directed by Cecil B. DeMille; and then *Shane* [1953] I was directed by George Stevens; and *Here Comes the Groom* [1951] I was directed by Frank Capra. But when you're a child, you have no concept of that. As I became older and looked back over my career, I felt very blessed and very fortunate that I had those opportunities. But you don't think of that when you're a child.

What memories of the Mole-Men?
Well, you know, being on the set, it was just fun. I thought they were really cute. I knew that I was acting, that it wasn't for real, but seeing Superman was a thrill for me. Watching *Superman and the Mole-Men now* really gives me a chuckle, because they've come so far with makeup and costumes and all that kind of stuff. The Mole-Men were supposed to be covered in hair, but of course they were in those hairy suits which were so bad. You could practically see the zipper going up the back [*laughs*]!

You were in a number of science-fiction and fantasy TV series, starting I believe with Science Fiction Theatre.
Science Fiction Theatre ["The Strange People at Pecos"] was fun. I played a girl who people think is from another planet, because in one scene I get hit by a car and I get up and walk away and I have no pain. They had to construct this huuuuge cut down my arm for the scene after I get hit by the car. Being in makeup was fun, because back in those days they used Hershey's Chocolate Syrup for blood. I had this burning desire to lick it off [*laughs*]!

As a kid, did you ever have to do anything in a movie or TV show that scared you?
The only thing that was scary to me was an episode of *Fury* with Peter Graves. Fury was the name of a horse and Bobby Diamond played the little boy who owned it. Fury was kind of like Lassie, but in horse form [*laughs*]—he would do all these amazing things. I played a brat, and in one scene I slip and fall off this cliff. It was a fake cliff, built on a set, but it was about two stories high. I was probably about 12 or 13 at the time, and at that age, of course, you're not allowed to do any stunts. They had a little person who was an actual stuntwoman, dressed like me, with a wig and the same wardrobe. She was probably 35 or 40. On "action," she was supposed

Washburn played a youngster suspected of being part of a family of Martian spies (!) on TV's *Science Fiction Theatre* (with Arthur Franz and Doris Dowling).

to fall off the cliff. They had the crew on the bottom, out of camera range, holding a fireman's net to catch her. Well, they got her up on top of the cliff and she looked down and she said, "Uhn-uh. Not doin' it."

The director came over to me and he said, "The stunt person doesn't want to do it. Would *you* do it?" When I look back, I can't believe that they would do this to a child! They should never allow a child to do something like that! The director said, "If you would do this, it would really be fun. I have a daughter, and if *she* was here, *she* would love to do it"—he went on and on! I was *so* scared, but I didn't want to let on that I was scared because I thought they might be mad at me for holding up the production! And now *today*, looking back, I'm surprised that my *mother* didn't just say no. But she told me, "Honey, it's up to you. If you want to do it, do it, and if not, you don't have to." I was *so* afraid of letting them down that I said I would do it ... but I was so petrified! I mean, I scream on the merry-go-round [*laughs*].

So I went up there. They said, "Take your time. We're gonna roll the camera and we're gonna say 'action,' and you just take as long as you want. Just jump into the firemen's net, and we'll catch you." In retrospect, I would think that they could really get in trouble for doing that [*laughs*], because there's always a welfare worker on the set, and she's there to look out for the child and make sure everything is okay. You'd think that *she* would have said, "No, she's not allowed to do this"—but they let me do it! That was the scariest thing that ever happened to me, when I had to jump off a two-story cliff—I don't ever remember being quite that petrified again. It all went well. I landed in the firemen's net, and I'm still here. But it was pretty strange.

Did you also have teachers on the sets of these various movies and TV shows?
Yes. That's the law. They're called welfare workers, but they're actually certified teachers, sent from the Los Angeles Board of Education. When you're on a set, you're required to do three hours of schooling each day. And it *has* to be in at least 20-minute increments. In other words, you can be doing your math or whatever, and if they're ready for you on the set, they can't pull you out of school after five minutes, you have to have done at least 20 minutes of school and *then* they can pull you out. They don't do physical education or anything like that, it's just academic.

What happened if you made a movie or TV show in the summer when schools were closed?
They'd still have a welfare worker on the set, because you're only allowed to work so-many hours. It was always fun to work in the summer 'cause then you didn't have to do school. But summer was usually when the shows were on hiatus.

Kids who make a lot of movies and get most of their education that way—do they get a decent education, or are they short-changed a little?
Maybe a little bit. But some people were *very* smart, such as Jodie Foster and Brooke Shields and people like that who went on to college, Yale and so on. I regret that I didn't continue my education. I was an A student always, but when you're on the set, it's real easy, 'cause it's kind of like having a private tutor. I always went to public school [when not working].

Do you remember acting on One Step Beyond?
It was directed by John Newland, who also directed a lot of Loretta Young's TV shows. He was wonderful. It was an episode called "Premonition" and I played a lit-

tle ballerina. As I'm doing my pirouettes, I look up and envision this chandelier falling and crashing on me. I start screaming that the chandelier fell, and they call a doctor for me and they say that I imagined it. But I'm still screaming that the chandelier fell. (I screamed a lot when I worked as a child [*laughs*]!) Then Pamela Lincoln played me at a later age. And what happens is, years later, the chandelier actually *does* fall. That was a fun show to do. They wanted it to look like I was doing pirouettes, looking up, so what they did was screw this thing into the floor. I would just stand on it, and then they turned *it* so it looked like I was pirouetting around and around.

Like a Lazy Susan!
    Exactly! A Lazy Beverly, actually [*laughs*]! I love all the little tricks they used in these shows. My favorite one to tell is about *Thriller* ["Parasite Mansion"]. As I mentioned earlier, back in those days, they actually did use chocolate syrup for blood, because everything was in black-and-white. Remember the dinner table scene where I put my hand to my cheek and then pull it away, and now you see three claw marks and blood dripping down my cheek? What they did was take a little sponge and cut three ridges down it, and then they put Hershey's Chocolate Syrup down each ridge. They glued the sponge to my hand—I had my hand on the table, palm down, so you couldn't see it. Then on cue I screamed and reached up and grabbed my cheek. By the time I pulled my hand away, the syrup had transferred from the three ridges on the sponge, onto my face. It looked like claw marks!

After that, a metal cup starts flying around the room and hitting you.
    They tied one end of a line to the cup and they tied the *other* end to a pole, almost like a fishing pole. One of the prop guys stood up on a ladder with the pole, and on cue he started hitting me over the head with this cup on a fishing line. And he got *paid* to do that [*laughs*]!

Did you get to meet the host, Boris Karloff?
    Boris Karloff [didn't play a character] in that particular episode, but he *was* there one day to introduce all the guest stars. So we got to meet him, and I was just so thrilled. He was wonderful. But the one I *loved* working with was Jeanette Nolan. She was a sweet, dear lady, just the *nicest* lady, and such a brilliant character actress. I felt so honored to work with her. I was so sorry when she recently passed away—she was just wonderful.

She played a lot older than she was in that episode—and you were playing a lot younger.
    Years ago, I used to look younger than I really was. Now I could play my own grandmother, I think [*laughs*]! I guess being tiny was part of it.

Herschel Daugherty directed that Thriller.
    Herschel Daugherty was one of my favorites, I did *so* many shows for him. I worked for him many, many times, on *Wagon Train* and other episodic things. He was just wonderful. It got to the point where I wouldn't even have to audition if he was directing, he would just hire me.

House of Haunted Hillbillies: Washburn and Tommy Nolan contend with supernatural forces in the *Thriller* episode "Parasite Mansion." (Photograph courtesy John Antosiewicz)

Were you thrown together that many times coincidentally, or was he asking for you?
  He was asking for me, which was *really* a nice compliment. He was a dear man.

How did you first come in contact with the people making Spider Baby*?*
  You won't believe this, it's so bizarre. I was living in Hollywood, still living at

home with my mother. I lived on a street called Fuller Avenue in a big two-story white house, and down on the corner (which was Sunset Boulevard), there was a big grocery store called Ralph's. I was in there shopping one afternoon, and this guy was kinda like *lurking*, following me around. And he kept staring at me! Finally he came up to me and he said, "Excuse me. You're an actress, right?" I said yes. He said, "We're doing this project, and I really think you might be right for it. Would you come and audition?" I'm thinking, "This is bizarre!"—usually your agent calls you, but here I am in a grocery store! I thought, "This can't *be*!" [*Laughs*] I of course wondered if he was for real. Turns out he was a great guy, his name was Bart Patton and he was very involved in *Spider Baby*. He said, "I knew you were an actress, I've *seen* you before as a child. I didn't mean to be following you, but I wanted to talk to you." So he asked, "Do you have an agent?" and I told him who my agent was. When I asked him what the project was, he said it was a very low-budget picture. Of course, I didn't know at the time *howww* low-budget it would be—like $11 [*laughs*]! Anyway, he said, "It's gonna be with Lon Chaney, Jr." Well, that's all he had to say, because I was such a fan, I was *nuts* about Lon Chaney.

You were a fan of his monster movies? His Westerns?
Everything—I just loved Lon Chaney. And when I worked with him, he was everything I thought and *more*.

Anyway, when Bart asked me if I had an agent, then I figured he was legitimate—he didn't ask for my home phone number or anything. Sure enough, the next day my agent called and said I was to audition. I went over, and there were quite a few girls there auditioning. They would have us in two at a time to read, we'd read, and then they'd send us out and send one person home and then have two *other* people come in. This went on for two hours or more. Finally they came out and they said to me, "Okay, you can go." I automatically assumed that I didn't get the part. And I was really disappointed, because after looking at the script, I thought it would be fun to play that character.

Did you see the script for the first time that day?
Yes. And of course I thought it would be especially wonderful to work with Lon Chaney, Jr. I came home and my mom asked, "How'd you do?" I said, "Oh, I didn't get it. I'm really, really disappointed." That's one thing about being in the business: There *are* a lot of disappointments, and it's so easy to take everything personally and think that they don't like *you*. But sometimes you're just not physically what they're looking for, not the right type, or what*ever*. You have to kind of roll with the punches. Anyway, I was very, very disappointed, and so my mother said to me, "I've never seen you so down. Why don't we just go away for the weekend? Why don't we fly to San Francisco?" I thought that would be a good idea. So we made reservations and we flew up to San Francisco for the weekend. Well, my oldest sister Dorothy always would have a phone number on us and know where we were in case we had to be reached. And Dorothy was the second number that my agent had if he wanted to find me—back in those days, you didn't have answering machines. Anyway, my mother and I were in San Francisco and we got a call the next day from

Dorothy, who said, "Your agent called. You got the part." I was so shocked! I couldn't figure out why they told me I could go home. Well, I found out later that they had already decided on me [for the role of Elizabeth] and they didn't need to keep me there any longer, they just wanted to fill the other role [Virginia]. And for *that* role they hired Jill Banner, who was just terrific.

You met her that day?
   Yes. We read together—they teamed each of us up with different people. I would team up with *her*, then *she* would team up with somebody else, and then *I'd* team up with somebody else. They kept us there for quite some time, and when they came out and told me, "Okay, you can go," I just automatically assumed that "You can go" meant "You're *outta* here!" When my sister called, I was *so* thrilled, because I just really, really wanted that part, as bizarre as it was. I just thought it would be fun. And it really *was*.

Who was at the audition? Jack Hill?
   Yes, and his investors, and also Bart Patton, the guy who met me at the grocery store. Bart's wife at the time was Mary Mitchel, who also played in *Spider Baby*. They were all just wonderful, very nice, very professional.

At the beginning, was the movie called Cannibal Orgy?
   Yeah!

And that wasn't enough to scare you off right away?
   [*Laughs*] The key to my wanting to do it certainly was not the salary. It was just the opportunity to work with Lon Chaney, Jr. Plus, it was kind of a fun role—I had never played anything like that. Usually I was like the crying, whining person. It's so funny—I was at a *Star Trek* convention last year and this man came up to my table and he said, "I read on the Internet that you were going to be at this convention. Your name *kinda* sounded familiar, but I couldn't really place you. I was going crazy. So I looked you up, and *then* it came to me, I remembered. You were that little girl that was always *crying* and *whining*!" [*Laughs*] That was my claim to fame, I guess! So doing this part in *Spider Baby* was kind of a stretch and I just thought it would be really fun. And it was.

Do you happen to know how they lined up Lon Chaney to star?
   They had submitted the script to Lon Chaney and he loved it and he said yes, he would do it, but he held out for the salary that he required at the time. Well, this was a *very* low-budget movie, and they told him that they didn't have the money for him. He said, "Well, then I can't do it," he turned it down. At first they didn't know *what* to do, but then they decided that they would try to get John Carradine. Well, when they told Lon Chaney, "Never mind, we're gonna try to get John Carradine," he just wanted this part so badly that he decided to go for it and accept a lesser salary than he was accustomed to, just to do this part.

Beverly and Jill Banner as the homicidal sisters in writer-director Jack Hill's demented *Spider Baby*.

Once filming got underway, did you enjoy working with Chaney?

I *loved* working with him. He had nicknames for Jill Banner and for me. Don't ask me where these came from—and I don't know if you can put this in print! But he used to call *her* Cracker Ass and he called *me* Bubble Butt! Isn't that *special* [*laughs*]? I *hope* those were terms of endearment!

Jack Hill says that Chaney, who was quite a drinker, was able to keep his nose fairly clean during the making of the movie.

Yes. In his contract, it said that every afternoon he could go and have a couple of drinks, but that was *all*. And it never interfered with anything. There are different kinds of drinkers: Some people get loud and obnoxious, some people get mean, some people get sweet and silly. With Lon Chaney, I didn't really see *any* change. He just needed his drink. And he'd go have one, and then come back to work.

Did you ever get to tell him why you did the movie—because you were a fan?
Oh, yeah, I told him that, and he was very flattered. I'd describe him as a sweet, gentle soul. He was soft-spoken. I just think he was so wonderful as Bruno. He was the gentle giant type. And he sang the theme song—how cool is *that*?

What did you and Chaney talk about?
We didn't have a whole lot of time in between takes because ... well [*laughs*], because we had to make the movie in, like, an hour and a half! It was like, "*Do* the shot, and then get set for the *next* one." It was done *really* quickly, 13 days I think, with a really low budget. We were kind of in and out! But I was able to tell him how much I enjoyed his work and how thrilled I was to work with him. He was terrific.

The house in Spider Baby *is supposed to be out in the middle of nowhere, but I swear I can hear all kinds of "busy neighborhood" noise, faintly, in the background.*
It was a great old house but, yes, it was right off the freeway. They didn't have a big budget here, so they were dealing with kind of a small crew, and not the most expensive equipment. The house interiors were shot on a soundstage.

Talk about some of the other people in the cast.
Jill Banner and I were friends, and Sid Haig, and ... you know ... *every*body. Sid was just so bizarre! Such a character, and such a wonderful actor! It was hard not to laugh at some of his expressions, and when he was drooling and stuff. He had a great sense of humor ... and I *love* to laugh. So sometimes I had to contain myself and not laugh, because he was so off-the-wall. He was great. Mantan Moreland was great, too, just adorable. It was nice to work with that whole group. I don't think anybody had any idea that, yeeears later, *Spider Baby* would become a cult classic. I still get *fan mail* from it, which just *kills* me. I get letters from all over the world about *Spider Baby*, which is amazing to me, and I'm always so flattered. And some of the letters are just so cute when they'll say, like, it was their favorite movie. I think, "Huh?? Did you ever see *Gone With the Wind*?" [*Laughs*]

Jill Banner wasn't even really an actress at the time, from what I've read. Just somebody who went into the auditions hoping for a bit.
And she was wonderful in the movie, I think she really nailed that part. It was just so sad to learn that, several years later, she was killed in an automobile accident.

Did you have any "say" in your wardrobe or hair style?
They had a wardrobe person and she'd come up with things, and we could have

some input. But I never try to tell people how to do their jobs. If they would ask me, "Do you *want* to wear this?" or if they asked my opinion about something, that would be fine. But I've never been one to tell a wardrobe person or a hair person how to do their job, 'cause ... that's their job!

How did it feel to be in your early twenties and still getting these child-like roles? What were you hoping to progress to?

It's hard to say. I never really made a great transition into adult roles. I did a few things as an adult, but I guess I was not really fortunate in that respect, because as I got older, the parts were fewer and farther between. I guess that was another reason why I was so anxious to do *Spider Baby*, 'cause I hadn't worked in a while. As well as having the opportunity to work with Lon Chaney, Jr.

Would you have preferred Jill Banner's part?

I was happy with my part. *She* had that sexy-type quality about her, like in the scene where she's kind of seducing Quinn Redeker. Everybody thought she did a great job in that scene. I don't think I really would have been that believable—I've never really been the sexy type. No, the parts were cast the way they should have been. I liked my part, and I think she was wonderful in hers.

When I watch the movie, knowing Jill Banner is 17, the seduction scene does get a little too ... creepy.

[*Laughs*] I know—it's amazing, looking back! Some of the shows from years ago are really funny that way. I did an episode of *Wagon Train* with Lou Costello, "The Tobias Jones Story." Here I am, this little girl, traveling with this ... man [Costello's character]! And he was an alcoholic on *top* of that, and we're just traveling along! Today it would seem so inappropriate to have a little girl traveling alone with an older man, but they used to get away with it.

Did Jack Hill do much directing of actors?

Oh, yeah. I really enjoyed working with him. I worked with him again later in a movie called *Pit Stop* [1969]. That was a fun movie, too—that was with Brian Donlevy and Sid Haig. And Ellen Burstyn, only at the time her name was Ellen McRae. Years later, when she became famous, she changed her name to Ellen Burstyn. My brother George also starred in it, playing Ellen's husband.

Were the various Spider Baby *producers around?*

Oh, yeah. Everybody was always there and they were very hands-on.

When was the first time you saw the movie?

Right after we did it, we saw the final cut. It's a very campy, strange kind of a movie, a very bizarre movie. It seemed ... kinda hokey. But *fun*. Now, I think, people realize that it's meant to be very tongue-in-cheek and very campy. It *is* what it *is*, a fun movie that people can laugh at.

You were a brunette when you appeared on Star Trek.

People who remember me from *Old Yeller* and all those old shows know I always had very long, blond hair. In *Pit Stop*, I was cast opposite Dick Davalos, who also had blond hair. So I was asked if I would mind dyeing my hair dark brown, because they thought we would look better one blond and one brunette rather than both of us being blond. And being a woman, it would be easier for *me*. I said sure, that would be no problem. Well, they put this dye on my hair—this is a lot of years ago when they didn't have the chemicals they have now. What happened is, all my hair fell out—I had, like, *no* hair! So they cut it all off, because it was coming out in clumps anyway. My hair was now about an inch long, and I did *Pit Stop* with this very short, dark hair. Well, it was right after that that I did *Star Trek*.

I went on an audition for *Star Trek* and read for it. They asked me if I had any claustrophobic problems, because I would have to be in makeup for four and a half hours. [Washburn grows old and dies in the episode.] What they did was make a plaster cast of my face—I had to breathe through a straw while the plaster dried. Then from *that* they made my rubber mask that had all the wrinkles. At least I croaked in Capt. Kirk's [William Shatner] arms, so it wasn't a total loss. That was a really fun thing.

You've made at least one Star Trek *convention appearance.*

[*Laughs*] I was doing that convention when this guy comes up to my table and he sees all these pictures from *Star Trek*, when I had this very short, dark hair. I'm sitting there and he goes, "Oh, I remember *her*. She was that little girl in..." and he starts naming my movies. He goes on and on, and then he asks me, "So ... what's she doing *now*?" I say, "Well ... um ... that's *me*," and he gasps and then he goes, "*Get* outta town!" [*Laughs*]

Star Trek *fans aren't exactly noted for their social skills!*

By the way, when I did my *Star Trek*, it was the second season, and it wasn't even very popular at the time. Nobody had any idea that it would go on and on and still be popular 40 years later and be famous all over the world. I also made it onto the blooper reel, and some people seem to know me more from the blooper reel than the actual episode. On the blooper reel is an outtake from the scene where I come into a room and I say, "I don't feel very well." On the blooper reel, I come in and I pause and then I say, "I feel like hell, I can't remember my line!" [*Laughs*]

You were on two of Loretta Young's TV series, so I assume you two got along. What did you like about her?

Everything. She was the sweetest, loveliest person—*such* a lady, and so beautiful, and down-to-earth, and warm. I guess my two favorite people I've ever worked with in my life would have to be Loretta Young and Jack Benny. I worked with her many times on her show *Letter to Loretta* [a.k.a. *The Loretta Young Show*, 1953-61], and then when she had her series *The New Loretta Young Show* [1962-63], in which she played a widow with seven children, she had me as Vickie, one of her daughters. Unfortunately, the series didn't make it—we were opposite *Ben Casey*, which was all the rage, so our ratings were terrible. I think, like, nine people watched the show.

Loretta Young, the seven kids and who else?

[*Laughs*] I don't know! So it was cancelled, but we stayed in touch. She would do these incredibly warm, sweet things, just for no reason. For instance, she sent me this beautiful scarf. It wasn't a birthday or Christmas or anything, she just said she saw it and she thought of me. And then she sent me this little stained-glass dove, she said, "just to let you know that someone was watching over you." Then she sent me a little book on angels! These little presents kept coming, one at a time, just for no reason. That made it all the more special.

Washburn in a recent pose.

When we did *The New Loretta Young Show*, she was very hands-on—she was involved in the directing and the writing and the producing and the makeup and the hair and the wardrobe and *every*thing. When we would do the show, she would insist that we watch the dailies every day. Generally the studios won't allow the cast to see the dailies; dailies were for the producers and writers and director. But she insisted because, she said, "You learn from your mistakes that way. You can see what you did that you want to do again, or what you did that maybe you *don't* want to do again." It was an education! Every day, we would go into the projection room and watch the dailies from the day before, and she'd critique everybody. It was great.

The saddest thing for me is that I was supposed to go see her [not long before her death]. She was living in Palm Springs, and I spoke with her just about three weeks before she passed away. She was one of my all-time favorites.

I hear that you've written your autobiography.

Actually, my mother started it. It was *my* biography but from *her* point of view, so it was going to be called *The Trials and Tribulations of a Hollywood Mother*. It would have been from *her* perspective, a mother with a child in show business and all the things that *she* went through. She got letters to put in the book from Jack Benny and from Bing Crosby and from Bob Hope. Then she became ill, so she put it away in a drawer and never finished it. After my mom died, my sister Audrey said, "Why don't we pick up where Mom left off? As a tribute to Mom, we'll finish this book"—only it was now going to be from my *sister's* point of view, growing up with a child actress. It was to be called *Hollywood Child*. Then my *sister* got ill and passed away, so it fell by the wayside again. One day I was talking to my manager and telling him about it, and he said, "Well, send it to *me*." I did, and then *we* began working on it. Of course, we had to change everything—instead of a *bio*graphy, it's now an *auto*biography. Now my manager and I have decided to make it an audio book. It's still not totally finished, but we hope to have it out in 2001.

What keeps you busy nowadays?

I'm living in Las Vegas and I've been doing a lot of local TV spots, a lot of commercials. I did one just last week for a jewelry store, and in a few days I'm doing one for Sam's Town, a casino. And I'm trying to get this book out.

And doing occasional conventions.

That's right. I'm always very, very flattered when I get fan letters, it amazes me that people will write to me [*laughs*], and I like to do the shows because they're fun. It's like that old saying, "Once it's in your blood…" I've tried other jobs all my life, in between [acting assignments], everything from being a secretary to a receptionist to a waitress to a salesperson to a massage therapist and everything else. I've enjoyed them all, but what I really like to do best is *act*. That's what I feel is my element and what I *like* to do.

William Wellman, Jr.

> *When you wake up seeing three giggling black women, one with a candle lit, one trying to kiss you and one trying to hold you down, and there's no other light anywhere ... it's really strange! I thought I woke up in a nightmare.*

Any list of the 1950s' worst horror flicks would have to include *Macumba Love*, the Brazilian-made voodoo adventure starring Hollywood character actor Walter Reed as a "supernatural debunker" in Haiti, teenage *Playboy* Playmate June Wilkinson as his sexy half–English daughter and 22-year-old William Wellman, Jr., as Wilkinson's fiancé. Despite its many shortcomings, however, the picture is historic in exploitation annals, featuring ahead-of-their-time gory shocks and brief nudity and—more importantly—racking up multi-million dollar box office grosses which place it near or *at* the top of the list of the decade's most profitable B horror films. The shock-schlocker, out of legal distribution for decades, is long overdue for reissue and reevaluation (and perhaps more ridicule), as star Wellman explains in this exclusive interview.

Son of the legendary Hollywood director William Wellman (*Wings*, *The Public Enemy*, *A Star Is Born*, *Beau Geste*), Wellman Jr. was a relative newcomer to the screen in 1959 when director Douglas Fowley cast him, Reed, Wilkinson and Ziva Rodann in *Macumba Love*'s leads. Following its release—and *despite* its release!—Wellman went on to forge a lengthy career in feature films and TV (*Gunsmoke*, *Rawhide*, *V*, *Deep Space Nine*) and also as a producer, most notably *Wild Bill: Hollywood Maverick*, an award-winning 1996 documentary on the life and career of his famous father.

Were you in your dad's movies as a kid?

No. My brothers Mike and Tim were in movies when they were younger, but I didn't get in one until I was 19, a picture that ended up being called *Lafayette Escadrille* [1958]. That was my beginning.

Why did your younger brothers beat you into the business?

It just worked out that way. And yet *I* was the one who always went with my father on his sets and locations! In fact, at one time I chronicled 22 movies I was on the sets and locations of, from an infant on up. Some of these movies, if they were made during the summer vacation period when I wasn't in school, I could go the whole time. *Yellow Sky*, for instance, which was made in 1948 when I was 12. See, at 12, Dad could just leave me alone. I loved to just walk around and look at the sets and locations and talk to the wranglers and whatever. I thought the whole thing was absolutely fantastic. But an opportunity didn't come up for me to be in a film [until *Lafayette Escadrille*]. I never asked my father if I could be in a film — I don't think any of my siblings did either. That's just the way it was.

As a kid growing up, how did you see your future? In the picture business?
Well, actually, I never for a moment thought of anything other than being a professional baseball player. Starting at eight years of age. My father got me a mitt and started playing catch with me, and then I started playing organized baseball. In those days, there wasn't any little league — you had to play, like, in the Cub Scouts or something like that. I thought that was what I was gonna do all the way up until I was 18. But I wrecked my shoulder playing football, and it didn't heal very well and I couldn't throw very well any more. Also, Wes Parker, who later became a Golden Gloves player for the Dodgers, was at the same school I was at, a couple of years behind me. Everyone thought I was a pretty whiz bang baseball player, but Wes Parker was far better and more dedicated. He wouldn't do anything else but play baseball where I would do whatever was in season. For example, in the summers I would play golf and he was playing American Legion baseball. So I just thought, "Well, this isn't right for me. I've got to find something I want to do *all* the time." I didn't have the dedication for baseball that I thought I had, and so I went off to college. Then, after my freshman year, this situation came up with my father, where he called and asked me if I wanted to test for a part in *Lafayette Escadrille*.

Was that your first acting?
No, I always did plays in high school and college. But I never thought of it as a professional career. But once I got into it, I loved it right away. For 44 years now — November 2000 was my forty-fourth year in the business — there's not been one other business I've ever cared about. And I haven't *been* in any other business.

Another early film credit was, of course, Macumba Love.
How I got the role in *Macumba Love* is a funny story. I was dating June Wilkinson. She was living at the Hollywood Studio Club, a hotel in Hollywood — Marilyn Monroe and a lot of starlets stayed there when they first arrived in Hollywood. June had come over from England and I met her in an acting class, and now we were dating. At the Hollywood Studio Club, as you walked in the door, there was a big living room area. You walked up to a receptionist and announced yourself — you couldn't go up to the rooms where the girls lived — and you said who you were there for. They would call upstairs while you sat down in this living room and you waited 'til the girl came down. I'm sitting there, and there's already another guy sitting in the room, a guy who'd come in ahead of me. It was Douglas Fowley. He was

picking up a date, just like I was, and he was just sitting there waiting for *his* girl. I didn't *know* him but I certainly recognized him—he was in movies, my dad's *The High and the Mighty* [1954] for one, but I had never met him when he worked for my father. He was lookin' at me and I was lookin' at him, and after a while he asked me, "Are you an actor?" I said, "Well, as a matter of fact, I am." He said, "I'm going to do a film in South America and I was wondering if you'd come and read for one of the leads." I thought this guy was a little cracked [*laughs*]!

Then June came into the room, and he looked at June and he asked me, "Is *she* with *you*?" I said yeah. And he asked, "Would *both* of you come?" June asked, "What's going on here?" and he said, "I'm thinking of both of you for the young leads in my movie." *I was* thinking we shouldn't do it because he said, "Come up to my apartment"—and I thought, "Oh, *yeah*. We're gonna go read in this guy's *apartment*..." After June and I left, I asked her if she wanted to do it. I was against it. But she said, "Billy, we'll do it together. It'll be fun. We'll have fun doing it." June was always a lot of fun. She said, "It'll be a joke, it'll be a little adventure, we'll just go do it." So we went to the guy's apartment and we read—and he said, "I want you both to do this film. We're gonna go to Brazil and..." blah blah blah. And off we went.

Did you go to Fowley's apartment with June that very night?

No, no. We went a couple days later, in the afternoon. He had a pretty nice apartment, quite upper-class, in West L.A. We went up there, and there he was, and we read. And we both got the parts.

Did you ask your father's advice or anything?

Yeah, I had a meeting with my father. This was 1959 and I had an apartment in West L.A., not too far from my father's home in Brentwood. I came over there one day to see him, and I'm all excited—I've got the part, I've got the script, and I wanted him to read it. He was up in his bedroom, I remember—in his bedroom, he had a desk and an easy chair, and he liked to sit up there and read. Anyway, I went in and he was sitting there, and I was all excited because I had this job, my first starring role. Even though I had played some fairly decent roles, *this* was a lead. I said, "Douglas Fowley—" He said, "Douglas Fowley the *actor*? He's not a director!" I said, "Well, he's gonna direct *this*."

I asked my father, "Would you read the script? I'd like to know what you think." I gave him the script and he read it, and a few days later he called me and I came over and he said, "Bill, sit down. This is the worst script I have ever read in my life. Don't *do* this picture. Don't *talk* to anybody about this picture. Just throw it away and forget about it." I walked out of the room and I thought to myself, "Y'know, Dad's retired now, and he doesn't know what I can *do* with this role..." So, of course, I did it.

If we can cut to the end, the picture's shot and it's over with, and the first screening was in Jack Wrather's screening room in Beverly Hills, on Cannon Drive. That was sort of the "elite" screening room that people went to, and Fowley had set up a screening there that night. The Wrather screening room was not a great big one, as I remember—you could probably get 100 people in there, certainly not more than that. Maybe even less. And there was the group of us from the film; I think Ziva was there, and June, and Walter, and Douglas Fowley of course. And Wrather was there, and some studio people too. I took my father. And when we walked out of the theater, walking up Cannon Drive, I asked him, "What'd you think?" He said, "Bill ... that's the worst movie I've ever seen in my life. Don't *talk* to any of the people who were there tonight or who made the film. Don't ever *admit* that you were in this film..." [*Laughs*] And, at that point, I kinda knew, "Well ... it really *isn't* very good, is it??"

And then it goes and turns out to be a big moneymaker.

That was the funny part. My father made some remark like, "If this film ever makes a dime, then I haven't learned anything in all the years I've been in the business." That's pretty close to an exact quote, I think. "If this film ever makes a dime, then I haven't learned anything in all the years I've been in the business." So when the thing started making *millions*, he just could not believe it. Nor could I [*laughs*]!

Any chance of you remembering when Macumba Love *was shot?*

I believe we started filming in March of 1959. I know I was doing John Ford's *The Horse Soldiers* through the end of 1958—Thanksgiving, Christmas and into the first week of January. Then I went to Brazil in March or April of '59. June and I flew over together—*22 hours!* We started in L.A., had an overnight in Miami, and then on to São Paulo, Brazil. Alto-

Wellman today.

gether it was 22 hours air time: Six or seven hours in those days from L.A. to Miami, and then the rest of it was from Miami to Brazil, another 16. We stopped in Port of Spain, Trinidad, and Caracas, those were two stops along the way to São Paulo. At Caracas, we got out of the plane—we had a half an hour to kill, so we decided to go into the terminal and walk around a little bit. Well, the air field was full of insects—bugs. They were like beetles, and the air field was just *covered* with them. They were on the ground, they didn't fly, and you just crunched 'em as you walked. You couldn't *not* step on them, 'cause they were everywhere. So we crunched into the terminal and then we crunched back to the plane [*laughs*]!

Where were some of the places you shot in Brazil?

First we went to an island off the coast of São Paulo, Guaruja. It was a resort island for the wealthy. You had to take a ferry across. And you couldn't just *go* across, you had to get permission. Only the upper class could go there—you couldn't just be a tourist and go over, they wouldn't allow you in. My God, it was gorgeous, with beautiful beaches. The beach scene where I'm driving "the surrey with the fringe on top"—that was in Guaruja. Most of the beach scenes were shot there, but not all of them. There was a beach club in São Paulo where we shot some other beach scenes.

Wellman (seen here traipsing with Ziva Rodann) had a "glorious" time making *Macumba Love* in Brazil—never anticipating that the movie would later become the recipient of the dreaded "Oogie."

Where did you stay?

When we were in Guaruja, we stayed at a hotel there. They had very nice rooms with balconies. I roomed with Walter Reed. We were working on that island for a couple of weeks, then we went back to the mainland, to São Paulo, and worked in a studio. In São Paulo, we stayed at the El Commodoro.

What was the studio like?

It was a studio there in São Paulo that the government had spent a lot of money to build up, to try to entice people to come and shoot there. Evidently it was used for a while and then it was *not* used, so it was in decay again, and the government wasn't going to put any more money into that operation. It was a little bit of a shambles when we got there. There were a couple of soundstages, and all the stuff that you'd find at a studio. There was a little commissary and there were dressing rooms and there was (for a small studio) a *big* back lot—they had plenty of land. Brian Donlevy was doing a picture on another soundstage [*The Girl in Room 13*, 1961] while we were there. It was toward the end of his career, and he was not in very good shape. I used to go talk to him a little bit. No one else was there. They built some sets on the soundstage, but most of the stuff was practical locations.

Richard Cunha, who directed that Donlevy picture, told me the studio had a dirt floor.

Yeah, it did. The streets weren't paved either, you walked on dirt. The commissary had a cement floor to it, but I think the dressing rooms were also dirt.

And the jungle scenes? Where we they shot?

The jungles were right in the backyard—the back lot of the studio was the Brazilian jungles. So they shot a lot of those jungle sequences right there.

Do you remember how much you got paid?

I remember I was the richest I ever felt in my life while down there making that movie. I was making ... not a *big* salary, I was getting $600 a week. It was a lot to *me*. But the salary stayed here in the United States; the deal was, [the producers] had to post that money in to the Screen Actors Guild, who held it for us. We were on the picture for *such* a long time, several months, so a lot of salary went in there. But here's why I felt so rich: The Brazilian company picked up our per diem, and they gave us *much* too much. And since the government wouldn't let you take cash *out* of Brazil and back to the United States, we *had* to spend it. Well, I could not spend it all! I'd go out at night with two girlfriends there.

Separately, I hope!

Yeah! On Guaruja I met one of the gals, she was blond, and her name was Elizabeth. She didn't speak a word of English and I didn't speak any Portuguese, but I *had* taken Spanish in school. I could order from the menu, I could make myself understood, but we couldn't really have much of a conversation. We met on the beach and I saw her as much as I could—I was working all the time. But it was like Mexico with the duennas [chaperons], I couldn't really be alone with her. I would go over to their apartment—she lived in an apartment with her parents, who were very well-to-do. She was over there on a vacation from school, and we saw quite a bit of each other. Then when we went back to the mainland, I met *another* gal, a brunette, and I was dating *her* the rest of the time in São Paulo.

Another high-class chick?
  Oh, yeah, it was the same kind of thing. Now, *she* could speak English, so we could actually converse and all that. Because I had all that per diem money, I would take six, seven people to dinner every night. I was trying to spend the money anyway, and you could *take* six people to have a steak dinner at a nightclub and Chateaubriand and everything and see a show, and it'd cost you 20 bucks for the whole evening. Twenty bucks for *everything*, for me and all the people that I brought! I couldn't use up the money, because everything was so cheap! I was tippin' people, and buying *everything* I could think of. I bought jewelry, gold jewelry; I had suits made for me from the ground up; I bought snakeskin shoes—everything I could lay my hands on! A funny thing: After maybe three or four weeks, Ziva Rodann said to the Brazilian producer, "This is just beneath us, this small amount of money that we're getting for per diem…" So they gave us *more*! I said to her [*in a horrified voice*], "Ziva…!"

What was she *doing at night?*
  Ziva was dating a race driver, a South American race car driver, and he was taking her out just about every night. So she didn't *spend* any money! I was embarrassed to take any *more* money, I couldn't spend what they were giving me as it was! It was glorious. I was single, I had no responsibilities, and I thought I was doing *Gone With the Wind*. Everybody connected with the movie kept saying we were all wonderful, and … you know … we thought, "Well, I guess we *are*." But we were *horrible* [*laughs*]!

I assume June Wilkinson was no longer *your girlfriend by the time you got down there…*
  We weren't really *that* romantically involved. We were just friends, before the film and during the film. But it wasn't *that* kind of a thing, we weren't "an item." I was more entranced by Ziva, actually, as far as *that* goes.

Six years ago I interviewed Walter Reed, and three years ago I interviewed June Wilkinson … and neither of them had much nice to say about Ziva Rodann.
  Well, she had an attitude about her, but she didn't bother *me*. I don't know … I actually liked her. I thought she was quite attractive.

And Walter Reed?
  Walter Reed was a great guy. He *called* me last week! I guess he had seen *Wild Bill: Hollywood Maverick*, the documentary that I did on my father, and he called me to talk about old times. He's 85, and he doesn't know why he's still alive [*laughs*]!*

---

*Walter Reed died in August 2001, shortly after this interview was conducted.

He says he never did anything right—he drank too much, he smoked, he caroused, and he says he doesn't know why he's still alive! He had *two* heart attacks that I know of, but he's still feisty as heck. Did Walter tell you about drinking Pinga? It was Brazilian alcohol and ... oh, my God! It looked like vodka, with a worm in the bottom of the bottle. Walter was drinking this stuff—he said to me, "You don't want to drink the worm in the bottom, you just leave it down there." This was the strongest stuff ... I mean, you couldn't comb your hair once you took a swallow. It was just brutal stuff. I just drank it once, and I said, "Walter, you're *crazy!* This is like *moonshine!*" But he liked it, he used to drink it! He'd take a shot in the morning to get himself goin', to go to the set! Walter was so much fun. Like I said, Walter and I roomed together at the beginning of the shoot, to save costs. We roomed together on Guaruja, and then at the El Commodoro for a while. *They* [the producers] paid for our hotel rooms, that wasn't part of the per diem. But after a while, it was ridiculous, because we *had* so much money, and so I got a room by myself.

Were the producers, Steve Barclay and Mike Ripps, down there?
   Oh, yeah. Barclay was an American, a very good-looking guy—I think he'd been an actor. He was around a little bit, but not too much. Mike Ripps was a wild producer. Robert Altman should put him in the next Hollywood movie he makes about producers! This guy was really somethin'—dems and dese, he was loud, he was gonna conquer the world. He walked around with these ugly Hawaiian shirts and shorts, and I remember his legs were *white!* And the big cigar in his mouth. He was a character! He was from the South somewhere—I think he had a chain of theaters in the South, and he always put *his* movies in his theaters. I don't know if you remember pictures like *Poor White Trash* [1957], but that was one of his.

Why was Douglas Fowley, an actor, directing?
   I don't know *how* he talked his way in on this. And I don't think he really knew what the hell he was doing. It always seemed to me he was trying to emulate my father in how he talked and looked. But he didn't know much about directing. He was a great *talker*. But ... well, hey, look at the scenes. There's nothing unique about the creation of the scenes in there.

So the actors were on their own?
   Yeah. When my father would direct, if the scene didn't go the way he wanted, he wasn't going to give you a line reading, but he might just say something like, "You know, I think you need to just relax a little more..." That's as much as he would say. Fowley would go on and tell you stories for 15 minutes [*laughs*]! He loved to talk and tell long stories!

Stories connected to how he wanted you to do the scene?
   Well, yeah ... about the scene, about the weather, about past glories [*laughs*]. He was a great guy. There was *nobody* that wasn't a lot of fun, it was a wonderful group of people to be around—the Americans, at least. Some of the Brazilian actors were pretty nice people too, but we didn't have a lot to do with them. A *lot* of the

people you see in that film are real natives, out of the jungle. There are a lot of stories about *them*. [The filmmakers] just went in the jungle and rounded up a bunch of these people and brought 'em out and had 'em do dances and stuff. They were scary! Once they found a guy named Juvenil with a snake out in the jungle, they started putting the snake in every scene they could.

Did you come in contact with the snake?
No. This guy Juvenil, a native, had the snake, that was his pet. The snake was so big, it was *heavy*. He'd keep it draped around his shoulders, but he'd put it down on the ground every once in a while. You wouldn't walk on the set without keeping one eye on the snake. The snake was always trying to get away and go somewhere else. And it was big enough to do some damage. So we were always playing practical jokes—walking around and grabbing people by their ankles [*laughs*]. Their first thought was that the snake had 'em!

So everybody was afraid of the thing.
We actors all said to Fowley, "Hey, wait a minute. This snake is dangerous." And he said, "No, they don't bite. They're not poisonous and they don't bite." So we said, well, okay. Well, I saw Juvenil out there one time with a cigarette lighter, searing a wound. I walked over and looked at him close, and he had wounds *all over his body* from bites from this snake. It wasn't venomous—but that damn snake *would* bite! And of course it would crush you if it could. It was a boa constrictor.

You said before that you had a lot of stories about the natives. Please tell me a native story or two!
One night out in back of this studio, this dilapidated studio, they were shooting some stuff that I wasn't in. They were shooting the scene with the natives doing their dance around the spot where I was tied down, about to be sacrificed. They were shooting a lot of stuff where you couldn't see me, and so they told me that it might be an hour or two before they'd need me. I was tired, so I went in and I laid down in my dressing room and actually fell asleep. And while I was asleep, they lost power and the lights went out in the studio.

Well, three of the native women followed me up there. When I woke up, one of them had a candle because there were no lights; one of 'em was trying to kind of hold me down; and the third one was kissing me. That's the way they woke me up. And they were giggling while this was going on. When you wake up seeing three giggling black women, one with a candle lit, one trying to kiss you and one trying to hold you down, and there's no other light anywhere ... it's really strange! I thought I woke up in a nightmare. I came out of a sound sleep and leaped up, trying to figure out what the hell was going on here. I got past 'em and ran out of the dressing room, looking for the first light. And the only light I could see was the light of the arcs outside, down by the set, which was maybe a couple hundred yards away. They had their own generator, so they didn't lose power. So I ran out there. I didn't know where these native gals had gone...

God, that does sound just *like a nightmare.*

A little while later, they needed me in the scene, and Fowley wanted me to actually be tied up on the ground during this sacrificial scene. I was already lying on the ground when Fowley said to me, "I want to really tie you up, so we make it look real." I looked down at my feet, and right there, maybe 20 feet from my feet, were those three gals. In the whole group of all the natives that had been placed around, there they were, the three of 'em together, looking at me and giggling. And I said, "No, Doug, we're not gonna do that. You're not gonna tie me up. You can make it *look* like I'm tied, but I wanna be able to get free. You might have a power outage. I've had a couple of problems tonight." Some of those natives, you didn't know what they were up to. Forget about the three women, I'm talking about the rest of 'em. They were right out of

Despite scenes of voodoo rites, torture and deadly snakes, *Macumba Love* was more ridiculous than scary to 1960 audiences—who kept coming back for more.

the jungle—these were not civilized people, these were natives right out of the jungle. You have to understand that. The [filmmakers] went into the jungle and just rounded up a bunch of natives—probably some of them had not seen a lot of white people. And you just didn't want to get too near *any* of them. You didn't know anything about 'em, "where they were comin' from," and they had straaange looks on their faces when they looked at me and the rest of us. So I told Fowley, "No. You're not tyin' me up. If your generator goes out, I don't wanna be stuck here. I want to be able to fend for myself."

June Wilkinson had a brief nude scene in the water.
  Now *that* was ridiculous. Doug Fowley says, "We're gonna do this for the European version. I want you and June to swim out, and then a wave will come and it'll knock down June's suit. And Bill, *you'll* put the suit back up." Well, the waves are six inches [*laughs*]—there *were* no waves! So we're out there, and June is trying to fix the suit so it'll fall and trying to make it look [realistic]. She had a 44-inch bust—I mean, just absolutely incredible. She is so *big*, it's just a joke, you can't take that seriously. And then *I'm* trying to be gentlemanly and get the suit back up—but they're so huge, you can't get *around* them! We just sort of improvised it, and I looked like a jerk out there. I was embarrassed, and I *look* embarrassed!

Richard Cunha told me that, to compete with June Wilkinson, Ziva Rodann would "forget" to wear a bra.
  That's very theatrically stated ... but, yes, Ziva *did* do that, she did go without a bra. She had an absolutely gorgeous figure.

Why did it take months to shoot this thing?
  They were sending the sound and picture back to the United States to be processed, but I don't think they were sending it every day, they would wait (like) a week and send it. So it took a couple of weeks before they got any reports. One of the comments that came back was, "The sound is no good." So once they shot everything, they told us to take off for a couple of weeks while they got the loops together, and then we would come back and dub the whole picture. Ziva and I went to Rio—we stayed at the Trocadero Hotel on Copacabana Beach and we just had a wonderful time for two weeks 'til they called and said, "Okay, we're ready, come back." *Every line* in that movie is dubbed.

Walter Reed was offered a percentage. Were you?
  No. [*Pause*] And I don't think *he* was either. I can't believe it. Did he say he recouped anything?

He didn't take 'em up on the offer, he didn't want a percentage of a cockamamie movie like that. He just wanted his salary.
  Then that *could* be true. But it's just as well he *didn't* take the percentage because, even though the picture made a ton of money, he wouldn't have *gotten* any because of all the subsequent legal problems, I'll betcha. *Macumba Love* is the worst movie ever made *that made money*. That's my description of *Macumba Love*.

Brit bombshell June Wilkinson was just one of four, count 'em, four girlfriends 22-year-old Wellman had during the making of *Macumba Love*.

Did you start dating June Wilkinson again after you got home from Brazil?
    I don't think I've seen her since we got back from the location. Did she ever tell you the story, the *hysterical* story, about what happened the day we were leaving for home? She had been dating two guys down there: One was a young Brazilian race car driver whose name was Carlos, and the other guy was named Max Meth. (*Why* I remember his name, I don't know!) Max Meth was well into his sixties, as I remember, and he was an industrialist who had a patent on something that he had invented, that made mirrors clearer than anyone else could make them. He sold his "technology," so to speak, to various companies, and then he spent his time just going around the world and visiting all these companies. He ended up in São Paulo, Brazil, at the same time we were there shooting *Macumba Love* and he just fell in love with June. He would take her to lunch, and Carlos would take her out at night [*laughs*]. For the last several weeks, that was the way it went. So the day June and I were leaving, as we were waiting to go to the airport to fly back to the States, both of 'em came up and they said to June, "We have a proposition for you. We don't want you to leave. *We'll* continue to pay all your expenses *and* a salary if you'll stay here. Stay here and go to lunch with me"—this is Max Meth talking—"and Carlos will date you in the evening." [*Laughs*] The two guys had gotten together, and that's what they offered her. June was laughing, and of course she didn't do it, she went home.

Man, to see these two guys together…! Max looked even more elderly than his years, kind of short and squat, but a very nice guy. He looked very scientific. And Carlos was the perfect prototype for the young racing car driver—dark-skinned, Brazilian, handsome, with dark hair slicked straight back. Seeing the two of them together was so funny.

They walked up to her as a twosome and made that proposition?
Yes, at the hotel. The car was going to pick us up that morning and take us to the airport, and we were sitting there having coffee or something in the El Commodoro Hotel. They came in and made this proposition. I was right there.

They sat down at the table with June and you and made that offer?
Oh, yeah! I thought it was just absolutely hysterical. In fact, I said to June ('cause she really enjoyed their company, *both* of them), I said, "Hell, June, why don't you stay another week or two if you want, and have fun?" She said, "Oh, Billy, I don't want to do that. I want to get home, I want to get my career going."

Carlos, the race car driver—this was not the same race car driver Ziva Rodann was dating, was it?
No, Carlos was a different one. The race car driver Ziva was seeing was another really good-looking guy. Actually, I dated Ziva too. We were more of an item at the end of the shoot. We went to Rio together during the time they were getting the loops, and…

And you two were "a couple" at that point.
We were *kind of* a couple. I also had the two other girlfriends who I mentioned to you, at different times during the shoot.

What happened once you all got back to the U.S.?
Fowley started going to all the studios trying to get a distribution deal, and he was getting to be a laughingstock. Nobody would distribute the film, they thought it was so bad. The trade papers were making jokes about *Macumba Love, no* one was going to pick this movie up. So Fowley started traveling around the country with June Wilkinson, going on local television shows. He had been in a successful Western TV series, *Wyatt Earp,* so he had some "celebrity" about him and he could get on talk shows in different places. Eventually he got an independent theater owner in Phoenix, Arizona, to play the picture in one drive-in. People would drive in and see the movie at, like, seven o'clock and then they'd see the companion feature at, like, nine. And then they'd stay—they wouldn't leave. They'd stay and see *Macumba Love* again. They weren't leaving the drive-in! And so the theater owner kept the picture there for *weeks.* Well, the studios were getting all these reports from Phoenix, and they couldn't figure out how come this picture, this horrible picture, was getting all this interest. So United Artists bought the picture and put it out, and the picture did absolutely tremendous business. The last time I read a report on it, it had done $9,000,000. This picture cost $365,000. It was up to $9,000,000 domestic.

I thought my career was *over* [*laughs*]! But soon after that, my agent called me and had an appointment for me to go over and audition at Universal for a lead in a segment of *Laramie*. I went over there, and John Champion was the producer. I'll never forget: I walked into the office, and before I even had a chance to sit down he said, "Bill, I saw *Macumba Love* the other night..." Before my fanny hit the chair, I was up and starting out the door [*laughs*]. He said, "Wait a minute, wait a minute. Come back! Sit down!" And then he said, "*I* thought you looked like a young Montgomery Clift." Well, all of a sudden I thought to myself, "You know ... there's a lotta people in high positions that don't know *what* the hell they're doin'!" That he would think that, and that he would give me the lead in a segment of *Laramie*, from *Macumba Love*...! I was really scratchin' my head at *that*, I couldn't figure out how *that* happened!

You subsequently played the lead in a handful of other movies, too.

I've done 55 movies and 114 television shows. In order to write a piece for a little religious periodical called *Mustard Seed*, I just went and recounted to make sure I had my count right. Fifty-five features ... 13 leads. Thirteen and a *half* if you want to count a movie called *Tigers in the Sky* that went into production in 1971. Robert Fuller and I were the leads. It was *The Longest Day*, only with the Air Force, and it was the Vietnam War. This filmmaker had gotten all this tremendous footage from the government, and created a story that worked in all this footage. Anyway, after three weeks of shooting, we were called into a production meeting and they said they'd had a problem with the rest of the money coming through, and it would be there probably in another four or five days. They wanted to send us back to L.A. and then when they got the rest of the money, they'd give us a call and we'd come back. Well, the phone hasn't rung [*laughs*]. So that's 13 and a half leading roles I've had in movies.

In 1960, there was a riot at an Oakland theater showing Macumba Love.

Well, there you go—now you've got the idea. *That's* why people went to see that movie. It was wild. And then they did some things that seemed *really* ridiculous, but they worked: In the papers, they would show the poster for *Macumba Love* with the skeleton head and all the other wild-lookin' stuff, and it'd say, "The first 100 people will get shrunken heads from the West Indies." Well, they said MADE IN CHINA, these little heads that they gave out [*laughs*]! They were not very authentic-looking things, *very* small, with some ugly hair on 'em. And they also offered the first 50 people "Voodoo Love Potions"—they were little packets, similar to the packets of (say) Equal that you see at your table in restaurants today. These packets were a little larger and they were white, and they had VOODOO LOVE POTION written on them. But on the back it said SPRECKLES SUGAR, which is all it was. It was such a corny advertising gimmick, but it must have *worked*—people went and got the stupid Spreckles Sugar and the shrunken heads. They got a lot of people into the box office.

What were the "legal problems" with Macumba Love *that you mentioned a few minutes ago?*

The picture was so successful that the companies started to fight. You had Brinter International, the Brazilian company; you had Steve Barclay; you had Mike Ripps; and Fowley too. They were all fighting over the proceeds. Eventually it got into such strong legalities that the picture was pulled. It had really finished its full first run in the United States; I don't know *what* happened in Europe and South America. It had, just, maybe, one playdate on television, right after its initial run here in the States, and then it was pulled and it was never shown again. And it disappeared. Because of the legal problems, is the only thing I can think of.

I talked to Doug Fowley some years after that and he said, yeah, the whole thing was all a mess. So that was sort of the end of it. I tracked down [a print] not too long ago. I wanted to look at it, I hadn't seen it since the '60s and I'd told my kids all these stories about this movie and they'd never seen it. So I thought I'd try to get a print. Eventually I found out that MGM has the negatives and prints, but they're just holding onto them, they don't know what they want to do with them.

My sister Kitty was married to Jim Franciscus, the actor. During the time they were married, Jim would have these gatherings at his house—he was friends with George Peppard and a lot of other actors. And one night in the mid- to late '60s, he said, "Look, we're gonna have what I call 'Oogie Night.' Everyone will bring their worst film. It *has* to be a film that you have a lead in. We'll do it like once a month, somebody will bring their film, and it's gotta be bad. Then at the end of the year, we'll give a prize for the worst film." He took all of our names and put 'em in a hat and then we drew to see what order. Well, I got number two, and Jim got number one. So *he* brought a film called *I Passed for White* [1960], one of *his* first films. It was pretty bad ... but it wasn't awful. Since I was second, I brought a 16mm print of *Macumba Love* that I had borrowed from Doug Fowley. And that ended it [*laughs*]—no one ever wanted to bring another film because, after seeing *Macumba Love*, they knew they could not win the prize!

You've also been in a lot of sci-fi TV shows, It's Alive! *[1974],* The Puppet Masters *[1994]...*

The Puppet Masters is something I'd just as soon forget! I was hired to play this doctor-scientist guy, and most of what I did was action stuff. And they didn't use *any* of it—I mean, *none* of it. I ran around all over the place, doing action and being chased, and chas*ing*, a whole bunch of stuff that was never used. The only thing that's still in the movie is a scene in a hospital room with Donald Sutherland—he was in bed, and I was the doctor. And that's it, it's just a little tiny piece. I have always been impressed with Donald Sutherland, what a fabulous actor he is. He's a very nice person and he treats people well.

And It's Alive!*?*

I worked in four or six of Larry Cohen's films, and *It's Alive!* was probably the most successful. It was one of the first credits for Rick Baker ... *that* was his creation, that *It's Alive!* baby. Today Rick Baker is the best in the makeup business. He made that *It's Alive!* baby in his garage. They had various versions, and they also had a head that Rick could put on; they had giant furniture made so he would still

A fearsome-looking Wellman poses with the mutant baby star of the Larry Cohen shocker *It's Alive!*

look small. Larry was a very creative guy, very clever. I love that word for him, "clever." The picture was low-budget ... Larry would never get permits, never follow the rules, never do pre-production. He'd shoot *any*where ... until he got kicked out [*laughs*]. He never had permissions, so he was always compromising himself.

In *It's Alive!*, I play the next door neighbor and the baby kills me. So when Larry was doing the sequel *It Lives Again* [1978], of course I couldn't be in it 'cause I was dead. But by then I had started working as a producer—I worked as a producer on Tom Laughlin's *Billy Jack Goes to Washington* [1977]. Tom Laughlin is a guy who spends *more* time preparing before starting a picture than *any*body. So I go from him to Larry Cohen, who spends the *least* time preparing for a picture! Larry will write the script and on Friday he'll say, "Let's get a crew together and shoot Monday." *That's* pre-production. So I went to Larry and I said, "Look, I know you're gonna do a sequel to *It's Alive!* Why don't you let me be your producer? 'Cause you never get enough help on these films"—usually he didn't even *have* a producer, it was all *him*. There'd be nobody to help out, and he *needed* someone 'cause he was doing *every*thing. So I said, "Let me work for you and let's *have* a couple of weeks pre-production. You're gonna have fewer problems. And let's *keep the crew*"—in the past, the crews would always quit on him. He usually went through a couple of crews, 'cause he'd work 'em like crazy and he didn't want to feed 'em!

Did you get the couple weeks pre-production you asked for?

He gave me about five days [*laughs*], but I was able to set up a few things to make life a little easier. And I told him, "You give me the money to feed the crew, and it won't be your problem," but he said, "I don't wanna spend money feedin' the crew." I said, "Larry, you gotta do it. You work these guys 12, 14 hours and you don't feed 'em—you can't *do* that." So he gave me a certain amount of money each week … but it wasn't enough to carry us through the whole week. We were shooting in town so it was five-day weeks, and the money would usually last for four days. So on the fifth day, Friday, I would bring my wife Flossie in, and she fixed dinner for the company (it was a small crew) on Friday nights. Every Friday they were looking forward to Flossie arriving—whatever house we were shooting in, she'd go in the kitchen and fix something really nice. So we kept the crew throughout the whole picture, and I think that's the first time that ever happened to Larry Cohen!

Was the sequel as successful as It's Alive!*?*

It Lives Again did business, but not as much as the first. The original took the exploitation business by storm, it did tremendous business.

It was no Macumba Love*!*

[*Laughs*] I've worked in 55 features now, and *Macumba Love* was the most exciting of all of 'em. I was single, they were payin' so much money, I couldn't *spend* all the money. I was walking around just as happy as could be. And also thinking I'd gotten this "big break" … not realizing how bad the picture was gonna be! But I had a hell of a good time making that movie. It really was an experience.

Index

Page numbers in **boldface** indicate photographs.

Abbott and Costello Meet Frankenstein (1948) 258
Abrahams, Mort 304
The Abyss (1989) 111
Ackerman, Forrest J 188, 320, 325, 329
Adventures in Paradise (TV) 158, 284
Adventures of Captain Africa (1955) 140, 150–51, **151, 152,** 155
The Adventures of Ozzie & Harriet (TV) 195–96
Adventures of the Queen (1975) 173
Agar, John 81, 99
Ainsworth, Helen 86
Air Force (1943) 95, 281
Albert, Eddie **163,** 291
Alexander, Ruth 104, 105
All I Desire (1953) 117
All My Sons (stage) 18
Alland, William 77, 78, 79, 81, 285
Allen, Irwin 156, 157–58, 160–61, 162, 164, 166, 167, 168, 169, 170, 173, 236, 269, 285–86, 288–89, 290, 291, 292, 294
The Alligator People (1959) 73, 88–91, **90**
Alsop, Carleton 231, 232
Amateau, Rod 7, 8
Ambler, Eric 294, 296
Ames, Michael *see* Andrews, Tod
Amy, George 281
Anderson, James **43,** 48
Andrews, Dana 127

Andrews, Tige 35
Andrews, Tod 240
Andreyev, Leonid 37
Angeli, Pier 127–28
Ankers, Evelyn 25
Annenberg, Walter 33
Antosiewicz, John vii
Anything Goes (stage) 256
Archer, Anne 25
Arden, Eve 266
Argento, Dario 114, 136
Argosy (magazine) 104
Arizona Bound (1941) 99
Arkin, Alan 212
Arkoff, Samuel Z. 16, 24–25, 27
Arness, James 80, 243, 251–52, 269, 274, 277
Armgrin, Stefan **295**
Arnold, Jack 73, 74, 75–76, 77–78, 79–80, 81, 83, 117
Astaire, Fred 301
Asther, Nils 241
The Astounding B Monster (website) vii
The Atomic Submarine (1959) 94–113, **96, 100, 102, 104, 106, 107, 110,** 114, 123–25, **124**
Aubrey, Jim 29–30, 290
Autry, Gene 107

Bacall, Lauren 278
Baccaloni, Salvatore 88
Bach, Barbara 211
Backstage Wife (radio) 48
Badge of Evil (novel) 80–81
Baer, John 324
Bailey, David vii

Baird, Sharon 334
Bakalyan, Richard 35
Baker, Rick 362
Balanchine, George 36–37
Balin, Ina **169**
Ball, Suzan 117
Ball of Fire (1941) 254
Balter, Allan 160, 162
Band, Charles 111
Bang Bang (1967) 127
Banner, Jill 340, 341, **341,** 342, 343
Bannon, Jim 143, 144
Barclay, Steve 355, 362
Barker, Lex 10, **11,** 18
Barnett, Buddy vii
Barrett, Rona 315
Barron, Jack 310
Barry, Gene **87**
Barrymore, Lionel **222**
Basehart, Richard 156, 158, 160, 161, 162, **163,** 164, 165–67, **165,** 168, 172, 173, 174, 290
Batman (TV) 269, 294–98, **297,** 300
Batman (1966) 298
Battle for the Planet of the Apes (1973) 302
Battles of Chief Pontiac (1952) 1, 8–14, **11,** 15
Baumann, Marty vii
Baumuller, Dave vii
Bava, Lamberto 128
Bava, Mario 114, 128–29
Baxter, Anne 167
Baxter, Warner 218, 221, 223, 224
The Beast with Five Fingers (1947) 284

365

Beau Geste (1939) 347
Becker, Terry 167
The Beetle (unmade SF film) 95
Belden, Charles S. 219–20
Below the Border (1942) 99
Ben Casey (TV) 344
Beneath the Planet of the Apes (1970) 258, 302, 306–8, **307**, 312
Bennet, Spencer Gordon 101, 103–4, 124–25, 150–51
Bennett, Constance 229
Bennett, Joan 229
Benny, Jack 115, 177, 344, 345
Benson, Joey 183, **183**
Benson, Roy 57, 63, 65–66
Bentley, John 94
Berger, Senta 126
Berkeley, Martin 79
Berle, Milton 51
Bernds, Edward L. 120, 122
The Best of Everything (1959) 123, 137
Bickford, Charles 281
The Big Sky (1952) 250, 270, 273, 278
The Big Trees (1952) 14
Bikel, Theodore 56, 57
Billy Jack Goes to Washington (1977) 363
Bixby, Jerome 320, 322, 329
Black and Blue (1999) 50
The Black Cat (1989) 136
Blackenstein (1973) 152–54
Blaisdell, Paul **ii, 26, 28**
Blake, Angela **13**
Blake, Michael F. vii
Blau, Beatrice 259
The Blob (1958) 215
Bloch, Charles 136–37
Bloch, Robert 328
Block, Irving 95, 98, 99, 108, 111
The Blood Suckers see *Dr. Terror's Gallery of Horrors*
Bluebeard (1944) 234, 240–41
Boetticher, Budd 117
Bogart, Humphrey 98, 324
Bohrer, Jack 329
Bohus, Ted vii
Bojarski, Richard vii
The Bold and the Beautiful (TV) 168
Bombs Over Burma (1942) 236
Bonanza (TV) 93
Borland, Carroll 188
Bowers, William 193
Bowery Bombshell (1946) 240
Bradbury, Ray 320
Brahm, John 168, 284
The Brass Legend (1956) 7
Brennan, Walter 281
Brent, George 229, 231, 232

Brickhouse, Jack 210
Bricusse, Leslie 304
Bride of Frankenstein (1935) 215, **230**
Bride of the Gorilla (1951) 1, 2–7, **5**
Bringing Up Baby (1938) 253
Broccoli, Albert "Cubby" 19, 211
Broder, Bobby 7–8
Broder, Jack 1, 2, 3, 4, 6, 7, 8, 12
Brogan, Ron 180–81
Broidy, Steve 95, 98, 99, 103, 108, 111
Bronson, Charles 299
Brown, Hiram 37
Brown, Johnny Mack 143
Brown, Tom 195
Browning, Alice 216, 221, 223, 224, 225
Browning, Tod 215–25, **218, 220, 222,** 233
Bruhl, Heidi 114, 126
Brunas, John vii
Brunas, Mike vii
Bryson, Winifred 221
The Buccaneer (1938) 140
Buckman, Adam 156
Burch, Ruth 18
The Burning of Rome (1963) 126
Burns, Bob vii, **279**
Burr, Raymond 2, 3, 6, 7, 30
Burstyn, Ellen 343
Burton, Tim 302, 317
The Bushwhackers (1952) 1, 7–8, **8,** 15
Bye Bye Birdie (stage) 255
Byrd, Ralph 98

Cagney, James 3
Cahn, Edward L. 27, 97, 103, 104
Caine, Michael 309
Calvert, Steve **5**
Cameron, James 185
Campo, Wally 327
Cannon, Hugh *see* Engesser, Bill
Capra, Frank 232, 334
Carradine, John 175, 181, 182, 183–84, 185, 187, 234, 240, 241, 347
Carré, Bart 95, 97, 109
Carroll, Diahann 293
Carroll, Leo G. 77, **80**
Carter, Georgianna 324
Cassavetes, John 167
The Cat and the Canary (1927) 97
A Cat in the Brain (1990) 135
Challengers of the Unknown (comic book) 51
Chambers, John 310, **313**

Champion, John 361
Champlin, Charles 210
Chandler, Jeff 83, 117
Chaney, Lon, Jr. 1, 2, 3–4, **5**, 6, 7, 8, **8**, 10–12, **11**, 14–15, 140, 145–48, **147**, 149–50, 175, 181–83, **182, 183,** 184, 339, 340–42, 343
Chaney, Lon, Sr. 3, 14, 15, 146
Chaney, Patsy 147
Channing, Carol 211, 304
Chapin, Laurin 334
Chaplin, Charlie 270, 301
Chertok, Jack 143–44
Cheyenne (TV) 175
Chiller Theatre (magazine) vii
China Smith (TV) 280
Chiquita 23
The Choppers (1961) 195, 202, 207, 208, 209
Christian, Roger 196
Christie, Howard 82
Clark, Mark vii
Clark, Petula 304, 311
Clarke, Robert vii
Claudia (stage) 259
Clavell, James 89, 90
Clay, Cassius Marcellus 214
Clemens, George 283
Clement, Kevin vii
Cleopatra (1963) 125, 158
Clive, Colin **230**
Clooney, George 278
Close, Glenn 300
Close Encounters of the Third Kind (1977) 203
Cobb, Edmund 103
Cocchi, John vii
Cohen, Herman 1–15, **13, 14**
Cohen, Larry 362, 363–64
Cohn, Harry 8, 86–87, 231, 232
Colbert, Robert 293
Collier's (magazine) 88, 89
Columbo (TV) 258
Conan Doyle, Arthur 52
Connery, Sean 211
Connor, Allen 98
Connors, Mike 16–35, **18, 23, 26, 27, 28, 31, 34**
Conquest of the Planet of the Apes (1972) 302
Conrad, Robert 157
Conte, Richard 88
Conway, Gary **13, 295**
Conway, Tom 101, **107,** 108, 111
Cooper, Gary 248
Corday, Mara 74, 77, **80**
Corman, Gene 318, 320, 321, 322, 326, 327, 328, 329
Corman, Roger 16, 21, 22, 24, 26–27, 318, 320, 321, 322, 324, 326, 327, 328, 329, 330–31

The Corn Is Green (stage) 263
Cornthwaite, Robert 249, 273
Costello, Lou 343
Cozzi, Luigi 136
Craig, Yvonne 298
Crain, Jeanne 83
Cramer, Doug 294, 296
Crane, Richard **90**
Crawford, Broderick 146
Crawford, Joan 4, 16, 20, 21, 221
Creature from the Black Lagoon (1954) 75, 76, 79, 119
Creepy (comic book) 175–76, 177, 178
Crime of Passion (1957) 7
Crockett, Dick 253
Crosby, Bing 345
Cruel Swamp see *Swamp Women*
Cugat, Xavier 51, 117
Cult Movies (magazine) vii
Cunha, Richard E. 353, 358
Curtis, Billy 247
Curtis, Jack 51, 52, **53**, 54–55, 57, 59, 61–63, 64, 66, 67, 68, 70
Curtis, Liane vii
Curtis, Terry 51, 52–53, 54, 57, 61–63
Curtis, Tony 116
Czechoslovakia 1968 (1969) 91

Dallas (TV) 143
Damato, Glenn vii
Daniel Boone (unsold TV pilot) 24
Dann, Mike 288
Darren, James 293
Darro, Frankie 141
Daugherty, Herschel 337–38
Davalos, Richard 344
Davidson, Carson 57
Davis, Bette 40
Davis, Bob 197, 198, 201
Davis, Sammy, Jr. 304
Day the World Ended (1956) 16, 25–26, **26, 27**, 94, 101, 111
Daykarhanova, Tamara 259
Deadhead Miles (1972) 212
Deadman (comic book) 51
Deadwood '76 (1965) 209, 212, 214
Dean, James 49, 281
Deep Space Nine (TV) 347
The Deer Hunter (1978) 203
Deering, Olive 259
Defenders of the Earth (TV) 152
The Defiant Ones (1958) 321
Dehn, Paul 310, 312
de Laurentiis, Dino 16, 30
Delinquent Daughters (1944) 240

Dell, Myrna 15
Della Cioppa, Guy 291
Del Ruth, Roy 90–91
De Metz, Danielle 123
DeMille, Cecil B. 140, 334
Demonia (1990) 114, 132, 134, 135
Denault, Eddie 283
Denning, Richard 25–26, 237
The Desert Hawk (1944) 150
De Sica, Vittorio 302
Destination Tokyo (1943) 95
Deukmejian, George 34
The Devil-Doll (1936) **222**
Devil's Honey (1986) 129, **130**
Diamond, Bobby 334
DiBella, Joe 310
Dierkes, John **248**, 250
Dietrich, Marlene 302, 303
Dillman, Bradford 308, 312
The Divine Lady (1929) 101
Dixon, H. Venor 217
Dixon, Richard 9, 10, 12
Doctor Dolittle (1967) 304
Dr. Terror's Gallery of Horrors (1967) 175–91, **178, 182, 183, 186, 189**
Dr. Terror's House of Horrors (1965) 176
Donlevy, Brian 343, 353
The Doom Patrol (comic book) 51
Dorn, Ray 177
Double Indemnity (1944) 234
Douglas, Kirk 14
Douglas, Susan 36–50, **38, 39, 43, 47, 48, 50**
Dow, Tony 334
Dowling, Constance 74
Dowling, Doris **335**
Down Texas Way (1942) 99
Doyle, Maxine 98
Doyle, Ron 180, 181, **182, 183**, 185
Dozier, William 282, 294–96, 298
Dracula (1931) 215, 258, 260, 266
Dracula (stage) 258, 259, 260–68, **264**
Drake, Arnold 51–72, **53, 71**
Drake, Christopher 63
The Drunkard (stage) 246
Dubov, Paul **96**, 101, **104**
Due South (TV) 50
Dukesbery, Jack vii
Duryea, Dan 29, 280
Duvall, Robert 167

East of Sumatra (1953) 117
Eastwood, Clint 116
Eegah (1962) 192–214, **197, 199, 202, 204, 205, 206**

Eerie (comic book) 175–76
Ekberg, Anita 117
Elliott, Sam 293
Elliott, Wild Bill 143
Ellis, Anthony 320
Ellsworth, Richard 10
Emmet, Michael 318, **325**
The Enemy Below (1957) 156, 158, 173
Engesser, Bill 195, 213
English, Marla 27–28, 29, 104
Escape from the Planet of the Apes (1971) 302, 308, 310–12, **311**
Essex, Harry J. 74, 79
Evans, Maurice 308
Evans, Mitch 185

Fairbanks, Douglas, Jr. 227, 228, 229
Fairhurst, Lyn 63, 70
Fangoria (magazine) vii
The Fantasticks (stage) 68
Fante, John 88
The F.B.I. (TV) 180
Feist, Felix 14
Fenneman, George 250–51
Ferrer, Jose 46
Ferrer, Mel 39
Field, Sally 333
The 50 Worst Films of All Time (book) 205
50,000 B.C. (Before Clothing) (1963) 52
First Camera (TV) 93
Fitzgerald, Michael vii
Five (1951) 36, 39–48, **43, 47, 50**
Five Fingers (TV) 156, 157, 160
Flannery, Susan 168, **169**
Flash and the Firecat (1975) 205
Flesh and the Spur (1957) 24, 27–29, 99
The Flesh Eaters (1964) 51–72, **58, 60, 62, 64, 67, 69**
Flipper (TV) 74
Florey, Robert 284
The Fly (1958) 89, 90, 122, 156, 158, 167, 173
Flynn, Errol 323
Flynn, Joe 177
Follow the Sun (TV) 125–26
Foran, Dick **96**, 101, 105–7, **106**, 111, 125
Forbidden Journey (1950) 36, 46
Forbidden Trails (1941) 99
Ford, John 351
Four Times That Night (1972) 128
Fowley, Douglas 347, 348–50, 355, 356, 357, 358, 360, 362
Franciscus, James 362
The Frank Sinatra Show (TV) 282

368 INDEX

Frankenstein (1931) 215, 284
Frankham, David 122–23
Frankovich, Mike 299
Franz, Arthur **96**, 99–100, **100**, 105, **110**, 111, 125, **335**
Franz, Eduard 251
Freaks (1932) 215, **220**
Freberg, Stan 200
Freda, Riccardo 114, 126–27, 129
Frees, Paul 250, 275
French, Valerie **87**
Fresco, Robert M. 73–93, **92**
Frith, Christopher vii
From Noon Till Three (1976) 299
Fugate, Caril 213
Fulci, Camilla 129
Fulci, Lucio 114, 129, 130–31, 132, 134, 135–36
Full of Life (1956) 88
Fuller, Robert 361
Funicello, Annette 334
A Funny Thing Happened on the Way to the Forum (stage) 256
Fury (TV) 334–36

Gable, Clark 18
Gallery of Horrors see *Dr. Terror's Gallery of Horrors*
The Gangster Chronicles (1981) 154
Garber, Jake **279**
Garbo, Greta 261
Gardner, Ava 40
Garland, Beverly 21, **90**
Gaye, Lisa 234, 235
Gaynor, Mitzi 256
General Hospital (TV) 114, 251
Gentry, Roger 177, 180, 181
George VI 227, 228
Gettinger, Peter 97
Ghost Town Law (1942) 99
G.I. Joe (TV) 152
Giallo (TV) 136
Giant (1956) 254, 257
Gibbs, John 281
Gibson, Judith see Loring, Teala
Gibson, Julie 236
Gideon (1999) 35
Gidget (TV) 333
Gilbert, John **218**
Gilbert, Lewis 211
Gilligan's Island (TV) 117
Gingold, Mike vii
The Girl in Lover's Lane (1959) 120
The Girl in Room 13 (1961) 353
The Glass Menagerie (stage) 259
Gleason, Jackie 211, 290
Go Tell the Spartans (1978) 258
Goddard, Mark 162

Goetz, William 115
Goff, Ivan 20
Goodbye Mr. Chips (1969) 311
Goodwin, Archie 177–78
Gorcey, Bernard 241
Gorcey, David 241
Gorcey, Leo 241, 254
Gordon, Alex 24, 27, 94–113, **112**, 123–24
Gordon, Bert I. 97
Gordon, Richard vii, 95, 97, 99, 111
Grahame, Gloria 20
Grand Illusion (1937) 74
Granger, Farley 19
Grant, Cary 244, 270
Grauman, Walter 312
Graves, Peter 334
The Greatest Show on Earth (1952) 334
The Greatest Story Ever Told (1965) 160
Green Hell (1940) 215, 225–29, 233
The Green Hornet (TV) 298–99
Greenhut, Robert 314
Greenway, Lee 277–78
Gries, Tom 7
Griffin, Frank 234, 235
The Guiding Light (radio) 48, 49
The Guiding Light (TV) 49
The Gunman from Bodie (1941) 99
Gunman's Walk (1958) 120
Gunsmoke (TV) 88, 252, 258, 285, 347
Gunther, John 91

Hagen, Kevin 198
Hagen, Uta 171
Haig, Sid 342, 343
Hale, Alan 228
Hall, Arch, Jr. 195–96, 199–200, 201–2, 206, 207, 208, 209, 213
Hall, Arch, Sr. 192–94, 195, 196, 197, 198, 199, 200, 201–2, 203, 204, 205, 206, 207, 208, 209, 211, 212–14
Hall, Huntz 241, 254
Hall, Jon 140
Haller, Dan 329
Halsey, Brett 101, 105, 111–12, 114–39, **116**, **118**, **124**, **130**, **131**, **132**, **133**, **138**
Halsey, William F. "Bull" 114, 117, 120–21
Hammerstein, Oscar, II 56
Hampton, Orville H. 89, 90, 94, 95, 103, 108, 109
Hand, Leonard 114, 120, 121
Hang 'Em High (1968) 258

Harlan, Russell 254, 281
Harman, Estelle 18
Harris, Harry 168–69
Harris, Jonathan 291
Harrison, Linda vii, 306
Hart, John 140–55, **141**, **142**, **144**, **147**, **151**, **152**
Hart, Judith 97
Harvey, Ken 54, 56–57, 61, 63
Harvey, Phil **84**
Hatton, Raymond 25, 99
Have Gun Will Travel (TV) 285
Hawaii Five-O (TV) 237
Hawkeye and the Last of the Mohicans (TV) 145–50, **147**, 155
Hawks, Howard 243, 244, 246–47, 248–49, **248**, 250, 251, 253–54, 256–57, 269–71, 272, 273, 274, 275, 276, 277, 278–80, 281
Hayward, Susan 121
He Who Gets Slapped (stage) 37, **38**
Heacock, Gary R. 177, 187
Head, Edith 231
Heard, John 25
Hedison, David 156–74, **159**, **163**, **165**, **169**, **171**, 289
Heflin, Van 120
Heft, Richard vii
Hellman, Jerry 305
Helmick, Paul 270
Hepburn, Katharine 37, 270, 301
Here Comes the Groom (1951) 334
Hershey, Barbara 293
Heston, Charlton 35
L'Heure de la Verite (1965) 127
Hewitt, David L. 175, 176, 177, 179, 180, 181, 183, 185, 186–87, 188, **189**, 190
Hewitt, Jean 179
The High and the Mighty (1954) 349
High Low (TV) 53–54
High Noon (1952) 7
High School Hellcats (1958) 119–20
Hill, Craig 19
Hill, Jack 332, 340, 341, 343
Hiller, Arthur 304
Hilliard, John 101
His Girl Friday (1940) 253–54
Hitchcock, Alfred 201
Hold That Line (1952) 254
Holiday Inn (1942) 234
Holliday, Judy 88
Holliman, Earl 283, 285
Hope, Bob 345
Hopper, Jerry 169

INDEX

Horn, Leonard 168–69
The Horse Soldiers (1959) 351
Horton, Edward Everett 177
Hotel de Paree (TV) 285
Houghton, Buck 283, 284
House of Wax (1953) 35
House on Bare Mountain (1962) 195
How to Succeed in Business Without Really Trying (stage) 255
Howard, John 75
Hoy, Renate 114, 120
Hoy, Robert 117, 118–19, **118**
Huckleberry Finn (1974) 305, 314
Hudson, Rochelle 175, 184, 186
Hudson, Rock 116, 257
Huggins, Roy 288
Hughes, Howard 18
The Human Duplicators (1965) 209–10, 213
Hunter, Kim 308, 311, **311**
Hunter, Tab 120
Huston, John 246
Huston, Virginia 21

I Passed for White (1960) 362
I Want to Live! (1958) 121
I Was a Male War Bride (1949) 244, 245, 249, 270
I Was a Teenage Frankenstein (1957) **13**
Indiek, Kathryn vii
Indusi, Joe vii
The Innocent Hoodlum (unmade film) 17
Invasion of the Animal People see *Terror in the Midnight Sun*
The Invisible Man (1933) 215
Ireland, John 7, 8, 15
It Came from Outer Space (1953) 76
It Lives Again (1978) 363–64
It! The Terror from Beyond Space (1958) 320
It's Alive! (1974) 362–63, **363**, 364

Jack and Jenny (1964) 126
Jack Armstrong (1947) 140, 141, **142**, 143, **144**, 148–49, 155
The Jack Benny Program (radio) 115
Jackson, Anne 259
Jackson, Selmer 102
Jacobs, Arthur P. 302–6, **305**, 307, 308, 309–10, 311, 312, 313–15, 317
Jaffe, Rona 137
Jaguar (1956) 16, 22–24, **23**, 29
James, Claire **144**

Janti, Azemat **87**
Jergens, Adele 25, **27**
Jet Attack (1958) 99
John Gunther's High Road (TV) 91
Johns, Wilbur 17–18
Johnson, Russell 116–17
Jolley, Norman 83
Jones, Buck 99
Jones, Quincy 309
Jones, Russ 175–91, **178**, **186**, **189**
Jory, Victor 167
Jostyn, Jay 325–26, 327
Julia (TV) 293

Kane, Joe vii
Kanter, Hal 73
Karatnytsky, Christine vii
Karloff, Boris 337
Kasznar, Kurt **295**
Katzman, David 143
Katzman, Leonard 143
Katzman, Sam 16, 29, 141–43, 150, 239
Kaufman, Joe 20, 21
Kelly, Gene 315
Kelly, Grace 303
Kelly, Jack 117
Keys, Anthony Nelson 176
Kiel, Richard 192–214, **197**, **199**, **202**, **204**, **205**, **206**, **212**
Kiley, Richard 258, 263, 266
The Killer That Stalked New York (1950) 332–33
The Killer Who Wouldn't Die (1976) 20
Kinchela, Ronnie 196
King Kong (1933) 108, 202–3
Kingsley, Sidney 285
Kirk, Tommy 334
Kiss the Girls and Make Them Die (1966) 16, 30–33, **31**
Kiss Tomorrow Goodbye (1950) 3
Klondike (TV) 192
Klugman, Jack 152
Kneeter, Herb 259, 260, 265, 266
Kopetzky, Sam 198
Kosleck, Martin 51, 54, 59, 60, 61, 63–64, **64**, 67
Kowalski, Bernard L. 329
Kraft Television Theatre (TV) 49
Kramer, Stanley 321
Krieger, Greg vii
Kronenberg, Mike vii
Kronenberg, Steve vii
Kruger, Otto 75
Kulky, Henry 167
Kuntsler, William 93

Lackteen, Frank 103
Lafayette Escadrille (1958) 347, 348
Laine, Frankie 51
Lambert, Christopher 35
Lampkin, Charles **43**
Lanchester, Elsa **230**
Land of the Giants (TV) 285–86, 293–94, **295**
Land of the Pharaohs (1955) 250
Lang, Otto 285
Langan, Glenn 25
Langdon, Verne 176
Langer, Lawrence 37
Lansbury, Angela 283
Lansing, Joi 101, **102**
Lapenieks, Vilis 203
LaPlanche, Rosemary 141
Laramie (TV) 361
Las Vegas Hillbillys (1966) 214
Lasker, Edward 272
The Last Time I Saw Archie (1961) 193
Last Woman on Earth (1960) 36
Laszlo, Alexander 109
Laughlin, Tom 363
Laughton, Charles **39**, 44
Lawman (TV) 175
Lazenby, George 211
Lee, Bruce 298
Lee, Earl 48
Leewood, Jack 89
Letter to Loretta (TV) 344
Leven, Edward 6
Levey, William A. 154
Leveythes, Peter 286–87
Levin, Henry 32
Levinson, Barry 35
Lewin, Albert 37
Lewis, Ira 64
The Life and Legend of Wyatt Earp (TV) 360
Linaker, Kay 215–33, **216**
Lincoln, Pamela 337
Lippert, Robert L. 88–89, 90, 121–22
Litel, John 101
The Little Prince vii
Littman, Bill vii
Livingstone, Mary 115
Lloyd's of London (1936) 225
Lo Bianco, Tony 25, 34
London After Midnight (1927) 215
The Lone Ranger (TV) 143–45, 155
Long, Richard 117
The Loretta Young Show see *Letter to Loretta*
Loring, Teala 234–42, **236**, **238**, **239**
Lorre, Peter 161, 262–63
Lost Boundaries (1949) 38–39

Index

Lost in Space (TV) 160, 162, 269, 290–91, **292**, 293, 294, 300
The Lost World (novel) 52
The Lost World (1960) 157, 159, 160, 173
Lozowsky, Joe vii
Lubitsch, Ernest 267
Lucas, Tim vii
Lugosi, Bela 98, 234, 238, 239, **239**, 258, 260, 261–62, **262**, 263, **264**, 265, 266–68
Lugosi, Lillian 260, 262, 265
Lukas, Paul 229, 231, 232
Lund, Deanna **295**

Ma and Pa Kettle at Home (1954) 114
MacLane, Barton **23**
MacQueen, Scott vii
Macumba Love (1960) 347, 348–62, **349**, **352**, **359**, 364
Madison, Bob vii
Madison, Guy 86
Madsen, Harry **34**
Maffei, Buck 192, 193
Magers, Boyd vii
The Magnificent Strangers (novel) 136–37
Magnum Force (1973) 258
Mahoney, Jock 332–33
Making It Big in the Movies— The Autobiography of Richard "Jaws" Kiel (book) 194
Malone, Dorothy 7, 8, 15
Man Made Monster (1941) 1
Mank, Greg vii
Manning, Marilyn 192, 198, 199–200, **202**, 203, **204**, **206**
Mannix (TV) 16, 20, 35
Manson, Alan 259
Mantley, John 88
Manulis, Martin 287, 288
Marines, Let's Go (1961) 159
Marshall, Don 293
Marshall, Herbert 122
Marshall, Marion 245
Marsillach, Blanca 129, **130**
Marsters, Ann 210
Martin, Dean 33
Martin, Dewey 243, 249, 250, 269, **273**, 274
Martin, Don 78–79
Martucci, Mark vii
Marx, Groucho 161, 211, 250, 310
M*A*S*H (TV) 269, 289, 300
Master of the World (1961) 97
Matheson, Don **295**
May, Bob 160
Mayer, Louis B. 223–24, 232
McCoy, Tim 99
McCrae, Scooter vii

McDonnell, Dave vii
McDowall, Roddy 308, 309–10
McGee, Vic **183**, 187
McKay, Gardner 158
McKinney, Austin 177, 179, 185
McShane, Ian 25
McVey, Tyler vii, 324
Meisner, Sanford 171
Melton, Sid 102–3
Merck's Manual of Medicine 77
Meredith, Burgess 269, 298
Merrill, Gary 166
Merriwether, Nicholas *see* Hall, Arch, Sr.
Metzger, Radley vii, 69
Middleton, Wallace 101
Midnight Cowboy (1969) 305
Miles, Vera 75
Milland, Ray 250, 273
Millard, Harry 172
Miller, David 20, 21
Mineo, Sal 308
Mr. District Attorney (radio) 325–26
Mitchel, Mary 340
Mitchell, Cameron 84, 86
Mitchum, Robert 193, 269
Monkey Business (1952) 254
The Monolith Monsters (1957) 73, 78, 81–84, **82**, **84**, 93
Monroe, Marilyn 254, 348
The Monroes (TV) 293
The Monte Carlo Story (1957) 302–4
A Month in the Country (stage) 172
Moonraker (1979) 201, 211
Moore, Clayton 143–44, 145
Moore, Roger 157, 158, 192, 211, **212**
Moore, Terry 18, 157
Moorhead, Jean 101
Moran, Frank 237, **238**, **239**
Moreland, Mantan 342
Morey, Edward, Jr. 97
Morgan, John vii
Morley, Rita 51, 54, 61, **62**, 70
Morris, Wayne 7, 15
Morrow, Jeff **255**
Morrow, Vic 205
Moss, Arnold 87
Motorcycle Gang (1957) 101
The Mouse That Roared (1959) 77
Muhl, Edward 81, 82
Mulhall, Jack 102
Munro, Caroline 136
Murders in the Rue Morgue (1932) 284
Murphy, Barry vii
Mustard Seed (magazine) 361
Mystery of the Wax Museum (1933) 219

Mystery Science Theater 3000 (TV) 213, 214

Naish, J. Carrol 143
Napier, Alan 254
The Nasty Rabbit (1964) 203, 208–9, 214
The Nation (magazine) 263
Neal, Tom 4
Nelson, Darby 64
Nelson, Lori **118**
Nelson, Ralph 283
Nelson, Ricky 195–96
Nemeth, Jim vii
The New Loretta Young Show (TV) 344, 345
Newland, John 336
Nichols, Jennifer 250, 254, 255
Nichols, Robert 243–57, **245**, **248**, **252**, **255**, **256**, 269, 272
Nicholson, James H. 24, 27
Nickolaus, John 329
Nielsen, Leslie 304
Nielsen, Ray vii
Night of the Blood Beast (1958) 318, 320–30, **319**, **325**, 331
Ninotchka (1939) 261, 267
Nolan, Jeanette 337
Nolan, Lloyd 143
Nolan, Tommy **338**
Norman, Diane vii
Norris, Ken 34
Novello, Jay **23**
Nyby, Christian 246, 250, 272, **276**, 277

Oakland, Simon 258, 263, 266
Oboler, Arch 36, 39, 40, 41, 42, 43, 44, 45, 46, 47
O'Brien, Edmond 281
O'Carroll, Carroll 35
O'Connell, Brian vii
Of Mice and Men (1939) 1, 14, 147
Off Season (1968) 172
Ohanian *see The Killer Who Wouldn't Die*
O'Hanlon, George 19
O'Hara, Maureen 285, 291
O'Hara, Shirley 263, 266
The Old Dark House (1932) 215, **226**
Old Yeller (1957) 332, 334, 344
On the Beach (1959) 36, 40
One Step Beyond (TV) 336–37
O'Neal, Charles 89–90
O'Neal, Ryan 89–90
Osmun, Jim 64–65
O'Sullivan, Maureen 25
O'Toole, Peter 304
Our Girl Sunday (radio) 48
Our Town (stage) 231

INDEX

Paget, Debra 234, 235, 242
Palance, Jack 20
Paley, William 299
Paluzzi, Luciana 101, 114, 122, 126
Panic in Year Zero! (1962) 36
Paris, Bob 18
Parke-Taylor, Nancy vii
Parker, Fess 24
Parker, Jean 241
Parker, Wes 348
Parnum, John E. vii
Pascaretti, Erin Ray vii
Pascaretti, Nicholas *see* The Little Prince
Pascaretti, Rufus vii
Pascaretti, Tigger vii
Patri, Dan vii
Patton, Bart 339, 340
Paul, Louis vii
Paylow, Clark 97
Payton, Barbara 2–3, 7
Peck, Gregory 309
Peppard, George 362
Pepper, Cynthia 334
Perry Mason (TV) 7, 30, 258
Peters, Susan 259
Petersen, Paul 334
Peyton Place (TV) 269, 293, 296, 300
The Phantom Planet (1961) 203, 213
Phillips, Irna 49
Phillips, Kate *see* Linaker, Kay
Phillips, Mark vii
Phipps, William 36, 39, 42, 43, 44, 48
Picerni, Paul vii, 35
Pidgeon, Walter 290
Pierce, Arthur C. 86
Pit Stop (1969) 343, 344
Planet of the Apes (1968) 302, 304–5, 306, 308
Planet of the Apes (2001) 302, 317
Planet of the Apes (TV) 299
Playboy (magazine) 347
Playhouse 90 (TV) 285
Poor White Trash (1957) 355
The Poseidon Adventure (1972) 169
Post, Ted 258–68, **262**
Prentiss, David *see* Hewitt, David L.
Preston, Robert 143
Price, Mary Grant 122
Price, Vincent 114, 122, 123, 125, 167, 228
The Private Affairs of Bel Ami (1947) 36, 37, **39**
Professor Mamlock (stage) 259
Provine, Dorothy 30–31
Provost, Jeanne vii

Provost, Oconee vii
The Public Enemy (1931) 347
The Puppet Masters (1994) 362

Quincy, M.E. (TV) 152, 315

Rabin, Jack 95, 98, 99, 108, 109, 111
Rachmil, Lewis J. 86, 87
Ragtime (stage) 256, **256**
Rainier III 303
Rains, Claude 157
Randall, Dick 128
Randall, Tony 285
The Range Rider (TV) 332
Rawhide (TV) 262–63, 347
Reader's Digest (magazine) 39
Reagan, Ronald 34, 281
Reason, Rex **255**
The Red Badge of Courage (1951) 246, 251
Red River (1948) 246, 269, 270, 272, 278, 281
Redeker, Quinn 343
Redgrave, Michael 172
Reed, Walter 347, 350, 353, 354–55, 358
Reeves, George 334
Regney, Noël 68
Reif, Harry 97
Renay, Liz 153
Rennie, Michael 157
Return from the Past see Dr. Terror's Gallery of Horrors
Return of the Ape Man (1944) 234, 237–40, **238**, **239**
Return of the Fly (1959) 114, 121–23
Revenge of the Creature (1955) 117–19, **118**
Rhodes, Gary vii
Rice, Bill 196
The Rifleman (TV) 198
Ripps, M.A. 66, 67, 68, 69, 355, 362
The River (1984) 203
Rivkin, Joe 99, 101, 103
Robert Montgomery Presents (TV) 49, 281
Roberts, Ben 20
Robinson, Edward G. 104, 308
Robinson, Hubbell 282
Robotham, George 168
Rodann, Ziva 350, **352**, 354, 358, 360
Rodgers, Richard 56
Rogers, Kenny 213
Rogez, Marcelle 223
Roley, Sutton 168–69
Romain, Yvonne 304
Roman, Lawrence 74
Romero, Cesar 298
Rondeau, Charles 120

Rooney, Mickey 22, 24, 211, 256
Ross, Arthur 79
Roy Colt and Winchester Jack (1970) 129
Rubes, Jan 36, 46, 48–49, **48**, 49–50
Ruggles, Charles 223
Ruggles, Wesley 223
Runaway Daughters (1956) 101, 108
Runser, Mary vii
Russell, Andy 117
Russell, Della 117
Russell, Kurt 271
Russell, William D. 236–37
Ryder, Alfred 170

Sabu 22, 23
The Sadist (1963) 213
The Saint (TV) 157, 158
St. John, Jill 157
Saletri, Frank R. 152–53, 154
Salkow, Lester 7
Salkow, Sidney 125
Sanders, Byron 51, 57, 70
Sanders, George 36, **39**, 167, 225–27, 228
Sands, Tommy 199
Saturday Night Fever (1977) 255
Saxon, John 116
Schiller, Norbert 251
Schlitz Playhouse of Stars (TV) 281–82, 283, 284, 300
Schneider, Jack 290
Schrage, Henry 97, 102, 108–9, 111
Schulberg, Budd 79
Schwalb, Ben 109
Science Fiction Theatre (TV) 73, 74–75, 334, **335**
Scott, Martha 229–31, 232
Screen Thrills Illustrated (magazine) 176
Scrivani, Rich vii
Sea Hunt (TV) 74
Search for Diana (1993) 136
The Searchers (1956) 75
Self, William **245**, 251, 269–301, **273**, **276**, **279**, **300**
Semple, Lorenzo, Jr. 296
Sergeant York (1941) 248
Serling, Carol 283
Serling, Rod 282–83, 284, 304
Seven Swords for the King (1962) 126
77 Sunset Strip (TV) 175
Shane (1953) 334
Shane, Ron *see* Kinchela, Ronnie
Shatner, William 344
Shaw, Peter 283

The She-Creature (1956) **ii**, 94, 101, 111
She Stoops to Conquer (stage) 246
Sheridan, Ann 244, 246
Sheridan, Margaret 251, 272
Sherman, Sam 176
Sherwood, John 82
Sherwood, Lorrie 247
The Shootist (1976) 299, 300
The Show (1927) **218**
The Silence of the Lambs (1991)
The Silencers (1966) 33
Silverheels, Jay 145
Silverman, Fred 299
Sinatra, Frank 55, 56, 101, 282
Siodmak, Curt 1, 3, 6
Sirk, Douglas 74
Skelton, Red 291
Skidoo (1968) 211–12
Skotak, Robert vii
Skouras, Spyros 158
Sky Commando (1953) 29
Small, Edward 103, 109
Smith, Don G. vii
Smith, Harold Jacob 321–22
Smith, Queenie 235
Soma, Ricki 246
The Son of Robin Hood (1959) 158
S O S Coast Guard (1937) 98
The Sound of Music (stage) 56–57
Spencer, Douglas **248**, 249, 250, 273, 277
SPFX (magazine) vii
Spider Baby, or The Maddest Story Ever Told (1964) 332, 338–43, **341**
Spy in Your Eye (1966) 127
The Spy Who Loved Me (1977) 201, 209, 211, **212**
Stack, Robert 173
Stang, Arnold 211
Stanislavsky, Konstantin 259
Stanwyck, Barbara 117
A Star Is Born (1937) 347
Star Trek (TV) 161, 332, 344
Starkweather, Charles 213
Starlog (magazine) vii
Starr, Irving 8
Steckler, Ray Dennis 213
Steele, Bob 101, 105, 125
Steele, Tom 252
Stein, Julian 68
Sterling, Robert 157, 289
Stevens, George 160, 334
Stevens, Robert 283
Stewart, Alexandra 172
Stewart, Larry 293
Stone, Ivory 154
The Story of... (TV) 91
The Story of G.I. Joe (1945) 269

Stopeck, Phil 194
Strasberg, Lee 171–72
Striepeke, Dan 310
Striganza (unmade horror film) 192–93, 195
Stuart, Gloria **226**
Stuart, Randy 245
Studio One (TV) 49
Sturlin, Ross 324
Submarine D-1 (1937) 94
Submarine Seahawk (1958) 94, 95, 101, 104, 123–24
Subotsky, Milton 176
Sudden Fear (1952) 16, 20–21
Superman and the Mole-Men (1951) 332, 334
Sutherland, Donald 362
Sutton, John 122
Swamp Diamonds see *Swamp Women*
Swamp Women (1956) 21–22
Swerdloff, Arthur L. 45

Tabakin, Bernard 280
Tamiroff, Akim 143
Tarantula (1955) 73, 74–81, **76**, **80**, 82, 83, 93
The Tattered Dress (1957) 83
Taylor, Elizabeth 158, 257
Taylor, Samuel 302
Teenage Cave Man (1958) 324
The Ten Commandments (1956) 242
Teresa, Mother 315, **316**
The Terminator (1984) 185
Terr, Mischa 208–9
Terror in the Midnight Sun (1959) 73, 84–86, **85**
Terry-Thomas 30, 33
Theater Guild of the Air (radio) 37, 44
Them! (1954) 80, 95
Thesiger, Ernest **230**
They Dare Not Love (1941) 215, 229–33
The Thing (1982) 254, 271
The Thing from Another World (1951) 243, **245**, 246–54, **248**, **252**, 257, 269, 270–78, **273**, 324
3rd Ave. El (1955) 57
This Island Earth (1955) **255**
Thompson, Marshall 99–100, 101, 285, **286**, **287**
Thriller (TV) 304, 332, 337, **338**
Ticktin, Theodore 97–98
Tierney, Lawrence 7, 15
Tiger Shark (1932) 104
Tigers in the Sky (unfinished movie) 361
Tightrope (TV) 16, 19–20, 21, 29–30

Tilden, Bill 301
Time (magazine) 278
The Time Tunnel (TV) 269, 293, 300
Timpone, Tony vii
Tinnell, Bob vii
Tiomkin, Dimitri 269
'Tis Pity She's a Whore (stage) 54, 55
Tobey, Kenneth 243, **245**, 249, 250, 269, 272–73, 275, **276**
Today It's Me...Tomorrow You! (1968) 136
Today's F.B.I. (TV) 16
Tom Sawyer (1973) 305
Tone, Franchot 4
Too Scared to Scream (1985) 25, 34, **34**
Tootsie (1982) 255
Tors, Ivan 73
Touch of Death (1988) 114, 129–31, **131**, **132**, **133**, 135
Touch of Evil (1958) 80
The Towering Inferno (1974) 169
Tracy, Spencer 270, 301
Transformers (TV) 152
Trial (TV) 91–93
Trundy, Natalie 302–317, **303**, **305**, **306**, **307**, **311**, **313**, **316**
Tsein, Marie 87
Tudor, Ray 51, 54, 66, 70
TV Guide (magazine) 33, 166
The 27th Day (novel) 88
The 27th Day (1957) 73, 86–88, **87**
Twice-Told Tales (1963) 125, 126
Twilight Zone (TV) 204, 258, 282–84, 300, 304
Twilight Zone—The Movie (1983) 205
The Twinkle in God's Eye (1955) 24
Two Dollar Bettor (1951) 7

Ulmer, Arianné vii
Ulmer, Edgar G. 241
Under the Yum Yum Tree (stage) 74
The Underwater City (1962) 109
Unger, Bertil 84–86
Unger, Gustav 84–86
The Untouchables (TV) 35

V (TV) 347
Vacation Days (1947) 141
Valentino, Rudolph 284
Vallin, Rick 143
Van Doren, Mamie 154
Van Enger, Charles 4, 14
van Vogt, A.E. 320
Van Voorhis, Westbrook 284

INDEX

Varconi, Victor 101, 105, 111
Varno, Martin 318–31, **331**
Varno, Roland 318, 319, 323
Verne, Jules 52
Vice Raid (1959) 154
VideoScope (magazine) vii
Vidor, Charles 232
Vogel, Virgil W. 84, 86
Voodoo Woman (1957) 27, **28**, 29, 101, 111
Voskovec, George **87**
Voyage to the Bottom of the Sea (1961) 157, 289, 290
Voyage to the Bottom of the Sea (TV) 156–60, **159**, 161–71, **163, 165, 169, 171**, 172–74, 269, 274, 288–90, 291, 293, 294

Wagon Train (TV) 84, 86, 93, 175, 181, 337, 343
War of the Satellites (1958) 318
Ward, Burt 296, 298, **297**
Warner, Jack L. 2, 3, 270
Warren, James 175, 176, 179–80
Warrenton, Gilbert 97, 104, 108
Washburn, Beverly 332–46, **333, 335, 338, 341, 345**
Washburn, George 343
Wayne, John 299, 300
We Are All Naked (1966) 70
Webb, Jack 193
Weinshienk, Zita 91
Welles, Orson 80, 284
Wellman, Michael 347
Wellman, Tim 347
Wellman, William 17, 18, 269, 270, 347–48, 350, 351, 354, 355
Wellman, William, Jr. 17, 347–64, **351, 352, 359**, 363
Wells, H.G. 52
We're No Angels (1955) 324
West, Adam 296, 298, **297**
Westcott, Helen 10
Whale, James 215, 225–33, **226, 230**
What Makes Sammy Run? (novel) 79
What's Buzzin', Cousin (radio) 193
White Zombie (1932) 238
Who Killed Teddy Bear? (1965) 52
Wild Bill: Hollywood Maverick (1996) 347, 354
Wild Guitar (1962) 208, 209
Wilder, Billy 270
Wilkin, Barbara 51, 54, 55, **58**, 70
Wilkinson, June 347, 348, 350, 351, 354, 358, 359, **359**, 360
Williams, Guy 291
Williams, Wade vii
Willson, Henry 19, 20
Wilson, Anthony 299
Wilson, Barbara 64
Wilson, Carey 299
Windsor, Marie 21
Wings (1927) 347
Winters, Shelley 35
Wise, Robert 121
With These Hands (1950) 75
Withers, Jane 257
Witney, William 97

Wolders, Robert 172
The Wolf Man (1941) 1, 3
Wolff, Ed 123
Wolper, David L. 91
Wood, Wally 175
Woodfield, William Read 160, 162
World in White (unsold TV pilot) 285
World of Giants (TV) 285, **286**, 287, 288, 294
The World, the Flesh, and the Devil (1959) 36
Wrather, Jack 350
Wray, Fay 203
Wright, Frank Lloyd 40
Written on the Wind (1956) 81
Wyatt Earp (TV) see *The Life and Legend of Wyatt Earp*

X Minus One (radio) 320

Yancy Derringer (TV) 332
Yellow Sky (1948) 348
Yesterday's Children (novel) 137
You Bet Your Life (TV) 250
Young, James 243, 249, 251, 253, 269, 274
Young, Loretta 332, 336, 344–45
Young, Ned 321

Zanuck, Darryl F. 289
Zanuck, Richard 298, 306, 308
Zimbalist, Efrem, Jr. 180
Zsigmond, Vilmos 203
Zucco, George 237
Zuckerman, George 74, 81

www.ingramcontent.com/pod-product-compliance
Lightning Source LLC
Chambersburg PA
CBHW081535300426
44116CB00015B/2634